Allegories of Format

signale
modern german letters, cultures, and thought

Series Editor: Paul Fleming, Cornell University
Peter Uwe Hohendahl, Founding Editor

Signale: Modern German Letters, Cultures, and Thought publishes new English-language books in literary studies, criticism, cultural studies, and intellectual history pertaining to the German-speaking world, as well as translations of important German-language works. Signale construes "modern" in the broadest terms: the series covers topics ranging from the early modern period to the present. Signale books are published under a joint imprint of Cornell University Press and Cornell University Library. Please see http://signale.cornell.edu/.

ALLEGORIES OF FORMAT

A Media History of Gottfried Keller's Unlikely Oeuvre

MALIKA MASKARINEC

A Signale Book

CORNELL UNIVERSITY PRESS AND CORNELL UNIVERSITY LIBRARY
ITHACA AND LONDON

Cornell University Press and Cornell University Library gratefully acknowledge the College of Arts & Sciences, Cornell University, for support of the Signale series.

Open access edition funded by the Universität Bern / University of Bern.

Copyright © 2025 by Cornell University

The text of this book is licensed under a Creative Commons Attribution-NonCommercial-NoDerivatives 4.0 International License: https://creativecommons.org/licenses/by-nc-nd/4.0/. To use this book, or parts of this book, in any way not covered by the license, please contact Cornell University Press, Sage House, 512 East State Street, Ithaca, New York 14850.

First published 2025 by Cornell University Press and Cornell University Library

Library of Congress Cataloging-in-Publication Data
Names: Maskarinec, Malika, author.
Title: Allegories of format : a media history of Gottfried Keller's unlikely oeuvre / Malika Maskarinec.
Description: Ithaca [New York] : Cornell University Press, 2025. | Series: Signale: modern German letters, cultures, and thought | Includes bibliographical references and index.
Identifiers: LCCN 2025009484 (print) | LCCN 2025009485 (ebook) | ISBN 9781501784064 (hardcover) | ISBN 9781501784040 (paperback) | ISBN 9781501784057 (epub) | ISBN 9781501784033 (pdf)
Subjects: LCSH: Keller, Gottfried, 1819–1890—Criticism and interpretation. | German literature—19th century—History and criticism—Theory, etc.
Classification: LCC PT2374.Z5 M37 2025 (print) | LCC PT2374.Z5 (ebook) | DDC 833/.7—dc23/eng/20250615
LC record available at https://lccn.loc.gov/2025009484
LC ebook record available at https://lccn.loc.gov/2025009485

Contents

Introduction: Allegories of Format   1

Part I The Format of Life: The Collected-Works Edition

1. Life and Work: *Der grüne Heinrich*   39

2. The Death of the Author: Premature Burial in Keller's Poetry   113

Part II Office Writing: The Document

3. On the Uses and Abuses of Writing: "Die mißbrauchten Liebesbriefe"   153

4. From the Office: Doodling While Documenting   201

Part III Serial Erotics: The Periodical

5. The Male Gaze, Serialized: *Das Sinngedicht*   229

6. Allegorical Closure: Series and Cycle in the *Züricher Novellen*   261

Epilogue: Epigonal Dwarfs   289

Acknowledgments 313
Bibliography 315
Index 335

Introduction

Allegories of Format

The subject of this book is the significance of format—which Jacob Burckhardt calls a "condition for the life" (Lebensbedingung) of the work of art[1]—to the literary oeuvre of the nineteenth-century Swiss author Gottfried Keller (1819–1890). For my purposes, *format* designates the specifications of a medium that govern the presentation, storage, and accessibility of its contents.[2] Format organizes a media

---

1. Jacob Burckhardt, "Format und Bild," in *Werke: Kritische Gesamtausgabe*, ed. Andreas Cesana et al., vol. 13, *Vorträge, 1870–1892*, ed. Maurizio Ghelardi, Susanne Müller, and Reinhard Bernauer (München: C. H. Beck; Basel: Schwabe, 2003), 509. All translations mine unless otherwise noted.

2. My definition of *format* relies on a recent flourishing in the topical literature, which includes Marek Jancovic, Axel Volmar, and Alexandra Schneider, eds., *Format Matters: Standards, Practices, and Politics in Media Cultures* (Lüneburg: Meson, 2020); Bonnie Mak, *How the Page Matters* (Toronto: University of Toronto Press, 2012); Susanne Müller, "Formatieren," in *Historisches Wörterbuch des Mediengebrauchs*, ed. Heiko Christians, Matthias Bickenbach, and Nikolaus Wegmann, vol. 1 (Köln: Böhlau, 2015), 253–67; Michael Niehaus, *Was ist ein Format?* (Hannover:

object's relationship to a world of objects and persons and orders its contents, or in the case of an artwork, what it represents.

A brief analysis of the pencil sketch *Puhlmanns Bücherregal* (1844) by the Berlin painter and draughtsman Adolph von Menzel can help elucidate how format relates to representation and demonstrate why it might be glossed as a "Lebensbedingung" of the work of art, including of literature (see figure 1). By depicting the bookshelf in sumptuous detail, Menzel invites a relationship of intimacy with the viewer, as though one were standing in front of it. The drawing's sense of presence depends on several interlocking ways the depicted bookshelf and paper sheet have been formatted with respect to one other. For one, the sheet is vertically *oriented* for the obvious reason that a portrait format provides a better fit for the shape of the bookcase. Second, the bookshelf has been *scaled* to nearly cover the sheet's surface. As was his habit, Menzel's drawing makes full use of the sheet, so much so that the topmost part of the image (a precarious stack of papers) meets and exceeds the sheet's edge, leaving only a single margin to the left sufficient to accommodate the artist's signature. And third, the bookshelf bears *proportions* similar to those of the sheet (26.9×21 cm, a nonstandard size); by *proportions* I refer to the relation of the height to the width of a quadratic object (e.g., a sheet or a bookshelf)—the very earliest use of the word *format*.[3]

The orientation, scaling, and proportions of the bookshelf depicted in Menzel's drawing establish geometric similarity between the sheet and bookshelf, a similarity that alerts us to further resemblances. For example, the positioning of the bookshelf invites us to compare the lines delineating the shelf and the edges of the sheet, each of which serve to contain their contents and to distinguish them from their surroundings. Sheet and bookshelf represent two archi-

---

Wehrhahn 2018); Jonathan Sterne, *MP3: The Meaning of a Format* (Durham, NC: Duke University Press, 2012); and Axel Volmar, "Das Format als medienindustriell motivierte Form: Überlegungen zu einem medienkulturwissenschaftlichen Formatbegriff," *Zeitschrift für Medienwissenschaft* 22, no. 1 (2020): 19–30.

3. See Niehaus, *Was ist ein Format?*, 7. As Niehaus details, *format* first emerged in seventeenth-century manuals for bookbinders and initially referred to the sizing of a page, though its referents quickly became more varied.

Figure 1. Adolph von Menzel, *Puhlmanns Bücherregal*, 1844. Pencil on paper, 26.9×21 cm. Berlin, Staatliche Museen zu Berlin— Preußischer Kulturbesitz, Kupferstichkabinett.

val technologies that collect, contain, and organize their contents by means of their boundaries. By gathering and ordering a collection, a bookshelf makes its contents visually and manually accessible. After all, the bookshelf is itself an archival technology designed with the management of information in mind, in this case with the organization of a private library. As containers that constrain and order their contents, Menzel's sheet and Puhlmann's bookshelf call attention to format as a set of orders, rules, or norms that facilitate the use, storage, and circulation of media objects.[4] The many multivolume works depicted in *Puhlmanns Bücherregal*—volumes that have been made to conform to one another with a shared format and binding—visualize yet another site, increasingly prominent throughout the nineteenth century, where formatting establishes continuity and contiguity among media objects. In effect, *Puhlmanns Bücherregal*'s subject matter and its manner of representation document the ubiquitous power of format.

The normative function common to sheets and bookshelves is more readily appreciable if we attend to a further affinity between the two. Menzel has organized the picture plane, in the tradition of perspectival drawing since the Renaissance, as a grid made up of vertical and horizontal lines. But because his subject is a bookshelf, which itself consists of an arrangement of vertical and horizontal planes, the grid is not relegated to an organizing background of the image; instead, it is plainly visible as the picture's subject. The bookshelf visibly manifests the normative order of the grid. The sheet, like the bookshelf, constitutes a type of container arranged to impose a strict order on its contents. Format is then, most basically, a matter of fit, of a felicitous correspondence between container and contents, between the normative shape of a medium and its information.

Admittedly, what I have said thus far about the ordering functioning of bookshelves has little to do with the specific character of the bookshelf in Menzel's drawing. While it may be the purported purpose of a bookshelf to arrange books into an easily perceptible order in which individual volumes may be identified and retrieved, *Puhlmanns Bücherregal*, in matter of fact, gives the impression of clutter and chaos. The eight shelves and top overflow with paper objects, primarily books of all different shapes and sizes but also loose sheets, folders, and a box. What stands out most in the drawing are the de-

---

4. On format as a set of rules, see Florian Sprenger, "Standards und Standarten," in *Standardisierung und Naturalisierung*, ed. Martin Müller and Christoph Neubert (Paderborn: Wilhelm Fink, 2019), 21–45.

viations from the rigid grid and from the projected conformity of the book formats. These digressions from the grid materialize as diagonal angles—the many books falling to the side, those standing outside or on top of the proper rows intended by the bookshelf, the haphazard unbound pages nearly sliding off the topmost shelf, and the volume on the top right hanging precipitously over the edge. Individual books likewise defy the bookshelf's grid by exceeding the confines of its space and poking forward to intrude into the space of the viewer. Together, the box jutting out on the bottom and the forward-facing book threatening to fall out of the picture plane on the second shelf from the bottom undermine the hallowed distinction between represented space and the space of the beholder. The cumulative effect of these diagonal digressions and intrusions into the viewer's space—as I have tried to foreground in my choice of verbs, such as *fall, slide, hang*, and *jut*, to describe these paper objects—suggests that the fragile order of the grid is on the verge of collapse. It is an ordering that can barely contain the material plenitude of its contents, calling into question the felicitous fit between container and contents. The rigid format of the bookshelf and its disheveled contents are visibly at odds with one another, a tension that contributes to the sense of presence the image delivers.

Thus, while Menzel's drawing makes us attentive to format as a set of organizing and restrictive norms—whether they be those of a single sheet's cut, a bookshelf, or the uniform binding and size of multiple book volumes—it also foregrounds ways in which the materiality of objects exceeds the containment strategies and normative strictures of a given format. In Menzel's drawing, we perceive the books as material objects with mass and specific surface dimensions, some larger, some smaller. Some conform to the dimensions of their neighboring books in a multivolume set, while others are seemingly unique and unstandardized. Since the books are presented at such a distance and degree of abstraction that we cannot make out the titles on their spines, they primarily come into view as material objects for our hands rather than as bearers of eidetic content that might be read. They have been handled, placed, or misplaced in the positions in which they are depicted. They are objects of human attention and absentmindedness, media that point back to the gestures and bodies of their human users, as we should expect from Menzel's art of embodiment.[5] A focus on format, as elicited by this drawing, thus implies a sensitivity to the materiality of paper and print objects, to the gestures with which they are handled, and to the ways in which their materiality cannot be contained—no matter the normative pressures to which they are subject.[6] The question of fit relates not just to the relationship between medium and information but also to that between a medium and its users, to the ways in which format determines how we engage with a media object. From such an expansive perspective, format necessarily entails an anthropological dimension. Format constitutes a "Lebensbedingung" of the work of art, as Burckhardt so persuasively writes, not only because it exerts regulative pressures on the contents of an artwork, structuring the very task of representation, but also because it regulates the relationship of the artwork to the outside world, shepherding its relationships to other media objects and to human users, beginning with the artist and continuing with whomever might today attend to the object in question. My inquiry establishes the significance of format for Keller's oeuvre by examining these two trajectories: format as guiding the work of representation and as guiding the work's relationship to its environment.

In the first place, *Allegories of Format* aims to situate Keller's literature in the media culture of his time, a line of investigation that has been undertaken regarding some of his closest German contemporaries, most paradigmatically for the work of Theodor Fontane.[7]

---

5. See Michael Fried, *Menzel's Realism: Art and Embodiment in Nineteenth-Century Berlin* (New Haven, CT: Yale University Press, 2002). Fried provides a brief discussion of *Puhlmanns Bücherregal* as well to begin his first chapter.

6. I am thereby drawing on Leah Price's extraordinary point that nineteenth-century users of books (and pictorial media) did not simply view them at a safe distance for the purposes of reading or viewing but rather used and handled these media in myriad ways. They were trampled upon or thrown, for example. See Leah Price, *How to Do Things with Books in Victorian Britain* (Princeton, NJ: Princeton University Press, 2012), 5–7. Menzel's bookshelf is an index of these diverse bodily interactions with paper media.

7. See, for example, Petra S. McGillen, *The Fontane Workshop: Manufacturing Realism in the Industrial Age of Print* (London: Bloomsbury Academic, 2019).

On the basis of such a media-historical investigation, I intend to explore how the demands of nineteenth-century media culture and, more specifically, the norms of specific paper, print, and picture formats represented an irritation to, if not a crisis for, the ideals of the literary work and literary authorship. On account of increasingly industrialized and commercialized means of production and newly emergent print and paper formats, nineteenth-century literary authors felt compelled to reconsider how works of literature could secure their status as singular aesthetic objects and, concomitantly, how they as authors could acquire literary authority. Formatting accrued normative force throughout the nineteenth century in part because of a widespread standardization of media formats. Then as now, standardization was perceived as a threat to artistic creativity and individual expression. It not only normalized media objects but also potentially resulted in a standardization of thought, as Markus Krajewski argues.[8] In the following, I argue that Keller's literature answers the call to resecure the status of literary works as art. His works offer sustained reflection on the relationship between literature as an art form that must exhibit specific aesthetic properties (such as unity, closure, and a harmonious relationship between parts and whole) and the literary work as a material and commercial object subject to the economic realities of an increasingly mechanized and commercialized print market along with the formatting norms it prescribes. If, as Alex Volmar suggests, format is an effect or trace of the surrounding media-industrial environment, then my method can be understood as tracking those traces in Keller's oeuvre.[9]

The most basic purpose of my inquiry is, in other words, to examine how Keller's literature renegotiates specific literary ideals as

---

8. See Markus Krajewski, "DIN A: The Basis of All Thought," trans. Anthony Mahler and Charles Marcrum II, in *Truth in Serial Form: Serial Formats and the Form of the Series, 1850–1930*, ed. Malika Maskarinec (Berlin: Walter de Gruyter, 2023), 253–75. Notably, as Krajewski discusses at length, Wilhelm Ostwald's attempt to establish a world format (*Welt-Format*) for paper was also intended to set norms for the sizing of bookshelves so as to avoid the chaotic impression of Menzel's bookshelf. On the growing measures of standardization in the late nineteenth century, see JoAnne Yates and Craig N. Murphy, *Engineering Rules: Global Standard Setting Since 1880* (Baltimore: Johns Hopkins University Press, 2019).

9. Volmar, "Das Format," 29.

they came under pressure from paper and print formats that were newly dominant in nineteenth-century media culture. In three parts, I examine three formats of growing prominence in Keller's media culture: the collected-works edition, the document, and the periodical. Beyond situating Keller in his contemporaneous media landscape, these formats provide the opportunity to revisit and dismantle false antitheses we have inherited from the nineteenth century: between high and trivial literature, between the singular artwork and mass-media products fabricated by reproductive technologies, and between the creative work of a literary author and the uncreative writing practices of office work.

Within my corpus—and in this respect my object of inquiry and method deviate from previous media-historical investigations on nineteenth-century print culture—the ideals of literature and authorship are renegotiated in the form of allegories. I argue that, on close examination, different fictional worlds, characters, and plots in Keller's literary oeuvre allegorize the problems that specific print and paper formats pose to literary ideals of literature as an art form and to ideals of creative authorship. My definition of allegory is borrowed from Michael Fried's trilogy on real allegory in mid-nineteenth-century realist painting and from Eric Downing's two seminal volumes on German realism—two scholars who have explored in depth what allegory looks like in a realist epoch that resisted, as part of a broader taking leave of rhetoric, describing its own operations as allegorical.[10] Unlike our immediate association of

---

10. For Fried's discussions of allegory in nineteenth-century realist painting, see Fried, *Menzel's Realism*, 185–205; Michael Fried, *Courbet's Realism* (Chicago: University of Chicago Press, 1990), 148–88; and Michael Fried, *Realism, Writing, Disfiguration: On Thomas Eakins and Stephen Crane* (Chicago: University of Chicago Press, 1987), 12–21. In *Menzel's Realism*, Fried suggests that emphasis on allegory is specific to realist artists of the era: "For the moment I want simply to note how each of the nineteenth century's three arch-realists felt compelled on one or more occasion to reflect allegorically on the nature of his art, as if the obsessive particularity of their respective projects demanded to be given explicit expression in this way. That nothing comparable seems to have taken place in the work of their foremost non-realist contemporaries is an equally interesting fact." Fried, *Menzel's Realism*, 117–18. For a discussion of Fried's concept of real allegory, see also my article "Allegory and

allegory with personification, often in the form of mythological beings that would be very much out of place in realism, real allegories depict scenes of everyday life whose prosaic objects and activities supply the very vehicles for allegory. Real allegories, as Fried argues, distinguish themselves through an unwavering commitment to these prosaic objects. Across his three volumes on realist painters, Fried suggests that allegorical reflection constitutes a defining feature of realism—a claim that I adopt as a premise for my interpretation of Keller's realism. In *Courbet's Realism*, for example, Fried undertakes powerful readings of Gustave Courbet's *Stonebreakers* (1849) and *Wheat Sifters* (1854) as portraying scenes of menial labor to allegorize the labor of painting. Real allegories serve as a form for painters to define the media conditions and ambitions of their art. Allegory, in other words, becomes the means for realist art to interpellate its medium—a second claim I extend to Keller's literature.

Closer at hand, Downing's two volumes on German realism, *Double Exposures* and *The Chain of Things*, identify Keller's fiction as inviting a specifically allegorical mode of reading.[11] To take one example, Downing reads Keller's "Eugenia" from the *Sieben Legenden* (1872), a story of Eugenia's conversion to Christianity, as an example of real allegory. Acknowledging that the retelling of legends might appear as an especially inappropriate choice of genre to reflect on realism (in light of realism's professed commitment to the prosaic and its disregard for the fantastical or supernatural), he

---

Analogy in Menzel's *The Iron Rolling Mill*," *Zeitschrift für Kunstgeschichte* 84, no. 1 (2021): 58–77. This is not to say that realism entirely takes leave of earlier forms of allegory such as personification. As I make note of throughout my readings, multiple functions of allegory remain operative in Keller's literature; the thematization of print culture, however, specifically adopts the form of real allegories. For a broader historicization of allegory, see Bettine Menke, "Allegorie: 'Ostentation der Faktur' und 'Theorie'; Einleitung," in *Allegorie*, ed. Ulla Haselstein (Berlin: Walter de Gruyter, 2016), 113–35.

11. See Eric Downing, *Double Exposures: Repetition and Realism in Nineteenth-Century German Fiction* (Stanford, CA: Stanford University Press, 2000); and Eric Downing, *The Chain of Things: Divinatory Magic and the Practice of Reading in German Literature and Thought, 1850–1940* (Ithaca, NY: Cornell University Press, 2018).

writes, "Whereas from one perspective the seven legends that Keller retells can hardly be considered realistic tales in their plots and characters, they can still from another quite clearly be seen as tales of realism, almost as allegories of realism, that translate the terms and operations of their 'realist' representation into those of their characters and plots."[12]

Building on Fried's and Downing's claims that allegory is a defining characteristic of late nineteenth-century realisms, I interpret select narratives from Keller's oeuvre as sustained allegories that "translate," to use Downing's term, profound aesthetic concerns arising from paper and publishing formats and the conditions of the nineteenth-century media market into stories. Storytelling becomes a procedure for negotiating the anxieties of an increasingly commercialized literature. By approaching the topic of format and print history through allegorical representation, I intend to move media-historical scholarship away from agglomerations of empirical facts regarding publishing or, for that matter, inquiries into the social or epistemological affordances of media objects. I instead want to argue that when approached from a perspective informed by the conditions of print history, narratives reveal themselves as important sources of reflection on the nature and perceived obstacles of a media culture—that is, those very social or epistemological affordances of media objects—and that format reveals itself to be significant to the form and content of literary works and not just a matter of paper dimensions. To understand why specific print or paper formats matter to the task of representation, in other words, it does not suffice to attend to paper quality, its bare dimensions or orientation, or circulation patterns. Attention to how formats are imagined and allegorized discloses what is at stake in the specific format of a work of art. Conversely, as in my reading of *Puhlmanns Bücherregal*, the weave of representation can only be fully appreciated when regarded as responding to and taking leave from the specificities of format. For my

---

12. Downing, *Double Exposures*, 97. Downing's reading of Keller's "Eugenia" identifies the story's statues as the most poignant instance of such a translation procedure. "The statue," Downing writes, "is to embody a realist program: it becomes perhaps the clearest instance of Keller's translation of the terms and conditions of his narration into the subject matter of his tale" (113).

methodology, close reading serves as a vital tool for media-historical investigation, and media history informs my close readings.

In the following three sections, I want to outline the directions of scholarship most pertinent to my inquiry, then present select theses that emerge from my findings, and finally gloss individual chapters. To begin, it bears recapitulating some defining characteristics of realism. The epoch of realist literature is conventionally situated between Romanticism and naturalism and dated to the collapse of the revolutions of 1848, which were followed by widespread disenchantment with the revolutions' democratic ideals and a retreat into reactionary politics and the private sphere of bourgeois life. *Puhlmanns Bücherregal* illustrates key features of realist art that are likewise recognizable in German-language literature. Paradigmatic is a turn to the prosaic objects of private, everyday life, a taking leave of the fantastical, heroic subjects of Romanticism for the sake of portraying, for the bourgeois reader, the dilemmas of bourgeois life.[13] As Sabine Schneider points out, realism takes its etymology seriously. It gives priority to the things of the world, its res, which come to dominate, if not clutter, realist fiction.[14] Realist fiction, like the bookshelf in Menzel's drawing, details each and every object to deliver its luxurious "reality effect."[15] As more recent scholarship has emphasized, literature thereby transforms itself into an archival technology for collecting, cataloguing, and containing these things, for managing the newfound clutter of bourgeois life.[16] So focused is a realist text on the fullness of

---

13. See Franco Moretti, *The Way of the World: The Bildungsroman in European Culture*, trans. Albert Sbragia (London: Verso, 1987), 65.
14. See Sabine Schneider, "Einleitung," in *Die Dinge und die Zeichen: Dimensionen des Realistischen in der Erzählliteratur des 19. Jahrhunderts*, ed. Sabine Schneider and Barbara Hunfeld (Würzburg: Königshausen & Neumann, 2008), 14.
15. Roland Barthes, "The Reality Effect," in *The Rustle of Language*, trans. Richard Howard (Berkeley: University of California Press, 1989), 148.
16. On the obsession of German-language realists with collecting and on realist literature as such a technology of collecting, see Samuel Frederick, *The Redemption of Things: Collecting and Dispersal in German Realism and Modernism* (Ithaca, NY: Cornell University Press, 2021); and Daniela Gretz and Nicolas Pethes, eds., *Archiv/Fiktionen: Verfahren des Archivierens in Literatur und Kultur des langen 19. Jahrhunderts* (Freiburg im Breisgau: Rombach, 2016).

things and their description that the very events and eventfulness that we expect from narrative threaten to fall from view.[17] On first sight, realist texts verge—and Keller's texts are no exception—on being long and boring, *langwierig*, and on doing little else than replicating private bourgeois habits and mores.

The prodigious boom in scholarship on German-language realism over the past twenty years exhibits two predominant trends. The first takes as its starting point the epochal title, *realism*, and the programmatic texts that traditionally give the epoch this name, including Adalbert Stifter's preface to *Bunte Steine* (1853), Theodor Fontane's "Unsere lyrische und epische Poesie seit 1848" (1853), and Otto Ludwig's "Der poetischer Realismus" (1858–1860). Central to this scholarship has been excavating the self-undermining ideals of realist programs: on the one hand, to mimetically reproduce the realities of prosaic life; on the other, to simultaneously aestheticize or poeticize those realities as appropriate to the norms of high art in such a way that not mere reality but a more profound or transfigured (*verklärte*) reality—in Stifter's famous formulation, "real reality"[18]—comes into view. German-language realism heeds the imperative to portray an unfiltered, authentic, unmediated picture of reality, but at the same time it knows all too well that the task of representation infallibly relies on the mediating work of sign systems. Christian Begemann's *Die Welt der Zeichen* and Albrecht Koschorke's essay on Stifter's "Granit," each of which adopts a semiotic perspective on these conflicting demands, have deftly shown how realism's compulsion to mimetic reproduction conversely leads

---

17. See Georg Lukács, "Narrate or Describe? A Preliminary Discussion of Naturalism and Formalism," in *Writer and Critic, and Other Essays*, ed. and trans. Arthur Kahn (London: Merlin, 1970), 110–48.

18. Adalbert Stifter, "Nachkommenschaften," in *Werke und Briefe: Historisch-kritische Gesamtausgabe*, ed. Alfred Doppler, Wolfgang Frühwald, and Hartmut Laufhütte, vol. 3.2, *Erzählungen*, ed. Johannes John and Sibylle von Steinsdorf (Stuttgart: W. Kohlhammer, 2003), 65. On the epistemology of Stifter's realism and the affinity of his "real reality" to Lacan's concept of the real, see Elisabeth Strowick, *Gespenster des Realismus: Zur literarischen Wahrnehmung von Wirklichkeit* (Paderborn: Wilhelm Fink, 2019), 11, 109–16.

to a foregrounding of its artifice.[19] As Begemann demonstrates at length, in what has proved to be a most productive examination of realism, Stifter's preoccupation with eclipsing the work of representation has precisely the unwanted consequence of foregrounding the very process of signification. That foregrounding manifests itself, for example, in the rote and nearly meaningless sentences of Stifter's late works. Similarly, the materiality and abundance of things, the many scenes of clutter familiar from Menzel's drawings and Keller's literary works, put that artifice under additional pressure. If Menzel's bookshelf visualizes the normative force of realism's artifice, then the falling book and spilling papers signal the eruptive return of the real into realism, which Erika Weitzman has most recently described as the obscene penetration of the "darkness of matter" into the rhetorical artifice of realism.[20] While Stifter, and not Keller, has emerged as the primary investigative object for this scholarly trend, Downing's analyses of Keller's "Eugenia" and *Der grüne Heinrich* have shown that Keller's allegories reveal similar internal tensions of realism. As Downing argues for "Eugenia," the representation of the real in art outperforms and thus eclipses reality itself.[21]

---

19. See Christian Begemann, *Die Welt der Zeichen: Stifter-Lektüren* (Stuttgart: J. B. Metzler, 1995); Albrecht Koschorke, "Das buchstabierte Panorama: Zu einer Passage in Stifters Erzählung 'Granit,'" *Vierteljahresschrift des Adalbert-Stifter-Instituts des Landes Oberösterreich* 38, no. 1/2 (1989): 3–13.

20. Erica Weitzman, *At the Limit of the Obscene: German Realism and the Disgrace of Matter* (Evanston, IL: Northwestern University Press, 2021), 8. Also representative for such a reading of the relationship between the real and realism, with a similar focus on detritus, are Sabine Schneider, "Vergessene Dinge: Plunder und Trödel in der Erzählliteratur des Realismus," in Schneider and Hunfeld, *Die Dinge und die Zeichen*, 157–74; and Frederick, *Redemption of Things*. Frederick's book is particularly helpful because it relates the question of realist clutter to realism's archival ambitions. If realism seeks to document or archive things, then it must establish forms that can contain and order the ensuing clutter: "In his [Keller's] fiction we see how each impulse informs the other in a dialectical process that also demonstrates their essential interdependence. Whatever aesthetic order his works display can only be maintained by also making room for the clutter that characterizes our world." Frederick, *Redemption of Things*, 216.

21. See Downing, *Double Exposures*, 91–128. For Downing's allegorical reading of *Der grüne Heinrich*, see Downing, *Chain of Things*, 36–120.

While the results of this scholarly trend are not to be disputed, it often leaves the impression of wanting to rescue realism from its own conservative ideologies and tedium by drawing it into the safer sphere of a modernist aesthetic. Realism becomes, on these readings, a form of protomodernism, anticipating the historical moment when preoccupation with the means and media of representation would overwhelm representation itself.[22] What's more, the preoccupation with realism or mimeticism has unintendingly obscured from view the in-matter-of-fact diverse aesthetic concerns of the epoch. Keller's writing addresses a wide array of aesthetic criteria beyond either mimeticism or transfiguration (*Verklärung*). My readings demonstrate the persistent relevance of more classical, formal norms, including closure, unity, and the presentation of an aesthetic form as an organic whole. Indeed, these values gain potency as a corrective to the fragmentation and disunity perceived as arising from modern publishing conditions.

The second and more recent trend in the current scholarship consists in a wave of media-historical investigations. These studies begin with the premise that the focus on realism as an aesthetic has obscured the historically specific conditions of print and publishing in the second half of the nineteenth century. The nineteenth century understood itself as "the paper age,"[23] a moniker that refers to the contemporaneous flood of paper media in Europe and beyond and to the way in which the self-representation of the nineteenth century relied on these paper media: from the paper prints decorating living rooms and transportation schedules for newly established railways to a booming penny press and the flourishing paperwork of bureaucracies. It was the age of the industrialization of the book.[24]

---

22. For an example of scholarship that reads realism as a form of protomodernism, see Ralf Simon, "Gespenster des Realismus: Moderne-Konstellationen der Moderne in den Spätwerken von Raabe, Stifter und C. F. Meyer," in *Konzepte der Moderne*, ed. Gerhart von Graevenitz (Stuttgart: J. B. Metzler, 1999), 202–33.

23. Apianus, "Aus unserem papiernen Zeitalter," *Die Gartenlaube*, 1874, no. 45, 730–34.

24. See Jürgen Osterhammel, *The Transformation of the World: A Global History of the Nineteenth Century*, trans. Patrick Camiller (Princeton, NJ: Princeton University Press, 2014), 29–39; Rob Banham, "The Industrialization of the Book 1800–1970," in *A Companion to the History of the Book*, ed. Jonathan Rose and Simon Eliot (Oxford: Blackwell, 2007), 273–90; and Scott E. Casper et al.,

The technological developments that made a flood in paper media possible—the invention of the rotary printing press and the ability to make paper from wood pulp and thereby to uncouple its production from limited supplies of cloth pulp—have been amply documented, as has the explosive population growth, rising literacy rates, and newly found leisure time that made possible a mass readership in which, for the first time, female readers constituted a substantial contingent if not the majority.[25] While the German-language book market largely remained depressed throughout the period I treat, an expansive market of periodicals bloomed to meet the demands of the reading public, fundamentally transforming how and what readers read and writers wrote.[26] Until they were replaced by newspapers toward the end of the nineteenth century, periodical magazines were the dominant medium of the first mass-media culture in history. They functioned to advance literacy, to popularize knowledge, and to generate and sediment national identities among their geographically dispersed readership.[27] For the emergent nation-states of the nineteenth century, mass media became an indispensable tool of nation building and globalization.

---

eds., *The Industrial Book, 1840–1880*, vol. 3 of *A History of the Book in America* (Chapel Hill: University of North Carolina Press, 2007).

25. On the history of paper and printing, see Lothar Müller, *White Magic: The Age of Paper*, trans. Jessica Spengler (Cambridge: Polity, 2014). On the nineteenth-century invention of modern bureaucracy and its paperwork, see David Graeber, *Utopia of Rules: On Technology, Stupidity, and the Secret Joys of Bureaucracy* (New York: Melville House, 2015), 149–206. For a very helpful overview of the development of a mass readership, see Lynne Tatlock, "Introduction: The Book Trade and the 'Reading Nation' in the Long Nineteenth Century," in *Publishing Culture and the "Reading Nation": German Book History in the Long Nineteenth Century*, ed. Lynne Tatlock (Rochester, NY: Camden House, 2010), 1–21.

26. The number of books printed annually in the German-language market was largely stagnant between 1840 and 1870. See Reinhard Wittmann, *Geschichte des deutschen Buchhandels* (München: C. H. Beck, 2011), 295–328.

27. Benedict Anderson's analysis of the relationship between mass media and the nation-state has been developed more specifically for a German national identity by Kirsten Belgum regarding the most circulated German-language periodical, *Die Gartenlaube*. See Benedict Anderson, *Imagined Communities: Reflections on the Origin and Spread of Nationalism* (London: Verso, 1983); and Kirsten Belgum, *Popularizing the Nation: Audience, Representation, and the Production of Identity in "Die Gartenlaube," 1853–1900* (Lincoln: University of Nebraska Press, 1998).

The influence of periodical publishing on German-language literature has constituted a subject of both early and more recent media-historical investigations. Beginning with groundbreaking scholarship of Gerhart von Graevenitz and Rudolf Helmstetter—who were the first to examine the leading periodicals in which canonical realist literature was published—media-historical investigations of German-language realism have proliferated, following a similar trend regarding Victorian literature.[28] From this media-historical perspective, realist literature emerges as one of many participants in the mediated (because medial) construction of reality and the newly porous boundary between fact and fiction, reality and reality effects: In aspiring to imitate an antecedent reality, realism participates in making that reality. A turning point concerns whether this emergent mass-media environment represented an obstacle to the creativity of the author and the autonomy of literature, possibly to the extent that, as Manuela Günter argues, an autonomous literary system gave way to entertainment if not "infotainment," suspending the difference between high and trivial literature as well as their respective gendering as male and female.[29] More recently, Günter's view has been challenged with the coun-

---

28. See Gerhart von Graevenitz, "Memoria und Realismus: Erzählende Literatur in der deutschen 'Bildungspresse' des 19. Jahrhunderts," in *Memoria: Vergessen und Erinnern*, ed. Anselm Haverkamp and Renate Lachmann (München: Wilhelm Fink, 1993), 283–304; Gerhart von Graevenitz, *Theodor Fontane: Ängstliche Moderne* (Konstanz: Konstanz University Press, 2014); and Rudolf Helmstetter, *Die Geburt des Realismus aus dem Dunst des Familienblattes: Fontane und die öffentlichkeitsgeschichtlichen Rahmenbedingungen des Poetischen Realismus* (München: Wilhelm Fink, 1998). Paradigmatic for the proliferation of research on periodical literature are two volumes dedicated to *Die Gartenlaube*, namely, Belgum, *Popularizing the Nation*; and Claudia Stockinger, *An den Ursprüngen populärer Serialität: Das Familienblatt "Die Gartenlaube"* (Göttingen: Wallstein, 2018).

29. See Manuela Günter, *Im Vorhof der Kunst: Mediengeschichten der Literatur im 19. Jahrhundert* (Bielefeld: Transcript, 2008). In a separate essay, Günter specifically identifies Fontane's "women's fiction" as examples of infotainment specifically adapted to the expectations of their mass readership. See Manuela Günter, "Realismus in Medien: Zu Fontanes Frauenromanen," in *Medialer Realismus*, ed. Daniela Gretz (Freiburg im Breisgau: Rombach, 2011), 167–90. For a second representative of the view that periodical publishing entailed the downfall of creative, autonomous authorship, but to the detriment of literature, see Hans-Jürgen Schrader, "Im Schraubstock moderner Marktmechanismen: Vom Druck Kellers und Meyers in

terargument that while the spread of mass media certainly altered how literature was written and read, it by no means did away with it and instead served as an enabling condition for literary innovation. In this vein, Petra McGillen argues that Fontane's adroit maneuvering within the economic realities of the literary marketplace became the source of his creativity and poetics, while Daniela Gretz claims that periodicals served Keller and Wilhelm Raabe as a field for experimental literary innovation.[30] Norms of format become generative. Most basically, these media-historical investigations have introduced a methodological shift: rather than merely relying on the most readily accessible and supposedly authoritative book editions, literary historians now appreciate the diversity of formats in which nineteenth-century readers encountered texts.[31]

While I engage with the format of the periodical in part 3, I also intend to make the case that despite the growing extent of periodical culture, book formats continued to preoccupy nineteenth-century authors and readers. Moreover, they shared many publishing practices with periodicals. The alleged death of the book that was widely bemoaned in the late nineteenth century was as untrue then as it is today. The fact that Keller, like many of his contemporaries, regarded lending libraries, which were the primary purchasers of fiction (*Belletristik*), and the Christmas book market as the greatest sources of publishing pressure in his writing life bespeaks the continued significance of book formats both as an economic reality and, even

---

Rodenbergs *Deutscher Rundschau*," *Jahresbericht der Gottfried Keller-Gesellschaft* 62 (1993): 3–38.

30. See McGillen, *The Fontane Workshop*, 17; and Daniela Gretz, "Das Wissen der Literatur: Der deutsche literarische Realismus und die Zeitschriftenkultur des 19. Jahrhunderts," in Gretz, *Medialer Realismus*, 99–126.

31. The convention of employing book editions rather than periodical prints can be traced back to Wilhelm Dilthey's 1893 essay "Archive für Literatur," in *Gesammelte Schriften*, ed. Karlfried Gründer, vol. 15, *Zur Geistesgeschichte des 19. Jahrhunderts: Portraits und biographische Skizzen; Quellenstudien und Literaturberichte zur Theologie und Philosophie im 19. Jahrhundert*, ed. Ulrich Herrmann, 3rd ed. (Göttingen: Vandenhoeck & Ruprecht, 1991), 1–16. For a discussion of the implications of Dilthey's argument for the discipline of literary studies in the twentieth century, see Vance Byrd and Sean Franzel, "Introduction: Periodical Literature in the Nineteenth Century," in "Periodical Literature in the Nineteenth Century," ed. Vance Byrd and Sean Franzel, special issue, *Colloquia Germanica* 49, no. 2–3 (2016): 105–18.

more significantly, in literature's symbolic economy. Though they may have paid less well than periodical preprints, books, on account of their durability and continued symbolic capital, continued to constitute the vanishing point of authorial aspirations. A collected-works edition, as I discuss in part 1, represented the essential culmination of literary authority.

The most basic point I adopt from these media-historical investigations for my own project is the insight that the industrialization of literature in the second half of the nineteenth century put the artistic ideals of literature and creative authorship under immense pressure. The recognition that "literature is a medium with a material basis and that *everything* about this medium changes when the basis shifts from limited reproduction to mass reproducibility,"[32] which McGillen attributes, for one, to Wilhelm Hauff's 1827 satire "Die Bücher und die Lesewelt," serves equally well as a premise for these more recent media-theoretical accounts of German realist literature and for my project: The changing conditions for the production and reproduction of literature compelled authors to adapt their texts and their understanding of authorship to these new media. It is on this basis that emergent print and paper formats within this new mass-media culture became a productive irritation for Keller's literature. If, as David Giuriato's poetics of paper proposes, the "format, color, and texture of paper" can become part of a specific literary message insofar as these properties are "discussed, instrumentalized, and problematized" in that message,[33] so too can print and paper formats become a focal point of a text's reflection on its media and conditions of production.

Keller has been a minor subject of interest for both of these primary trends in the scholarship on realism (Stifter, as I have noted, dominates the first; Fontane, on account of his prolific periodical publishing in multiple venues, the second). Keller has likely received less attention from studies on late nineteenth-century media culture because he, unlike Fontane or Raabe, published relatively little, in

---

32. McGillen, *The Fontane Workshop*, 48.
33. Davide Giuriato, "Paper and Poetics," *Configurations* 18, no. 3 (Fall 2010): 213, 214.

a relatively small sphere of venues, and primarily in book formats. Keller might not seem like a particularly informative example for the era's booming periodical culture; true to his geography, having spent most of his life in Zurich, he inhabited the periphery of the publishing centers of Leipzig, Frankfurt, and Berlin. Similarly, when he is treated at all, Keller has served the semiotic approach to realism as a passing example (the leading exception being the work of Downing, for whom Keller is central). Most frequently discussed in this respect is the protagonist of *Der grüne Heinrich*, who aspires to become a landscape painter in a post-Romantic age and fails because his excessively lively imagination makes it impossible for him to abide by the imperatives of realism—he draws and paints absurdly unrealistic scenes and fails to realize his artistic ambitions. His story has thereby provided the scholarship with an elucidating example of the epochal conflicts between Romanticism and realism, as well as of conflicts between realist aesthetic ideals and the material or economic realities of producing art.[34]

The current scholarship on Keller is well outlined by the emphases of the first four volumes in the series *Gottfried Kellers Moderne*, which began on the occasion of the author's two hundredth birthday: narrative, media, worlds, and knowledge.[35] The most productive focus of recent Keller scholarship is on the relationship of his work to inherited genre forms, for example, on *Der grüne Heinrich* as a case of the bildungsroman, the artist novel, or autofiction, but more broadly on Keller's playful recoveries of the fairy tale, the legend, the novella, or the village story (*Dorfgeschichte*). If we take Michael Niehaus's observation that the terms *format* and *genre* have increasingly come to operate as synonyms and that, even when the

---

34. For a recent and helpful contextualization of Keller within a realist poetics, see Frauke Berndt, "Grass: Gottfried Keller's Structural Realism," trans. Alastair Matthews and Anthony Mahler, in "German Realisms around 1850," ed. Frauke Berndt and Dorothea von Mücke, special issue, *Colloquia Germanica* 53, no. 4 (November 2021): 421–48; and Dorothea von Mücke, "'A Village Romeo and Juliet' and Gottfried Keller's Realism," in Berndt and von Mücke, "German Realisms around 1850," 449–72.

35. See Frauke Berndt and Philipp Theisohn, eds., *Gottfried Kellers Moderne*, 4+ vols. (Berlin: Walter de Gruyter, 2022–).

terms are not used interchangeably, an instance of a genre is only recognizable on account of its format, then Keller's reworking of established genres adds urgency to the point of departure I have selected for my inquiry.[36] The three formats I have selected—the collected-works edition, the document, and the serialized periodical—highlight the intimate relationship of genre and format, though I maintain their difference for methodological purposes. My examination of the normative pressures of format and the production history it indexes thus brings an additional perspective to Keller's negotiation of genre rules.

Keller's corpus also continues to be approached by a tradition of biographical scholarship that began, in keeping with the philological proclivities of the period, with the work of his contemporary Jakob Baechtold, who was first tasked with managing Keller's *Nachlass*, and was prominently continued in the Keller monographs by the half brothers Adolf and Walter Muschg. I critically examine this tradition in chapter 3 and the epilogue. In my view, three reasons explain the continuance of this biographical approach to Keller's literature.[37] First, the partially autobiographical nature of his best-known work, *Der grüne Heinrich*, invites comparisons between his life and his fiction. Second, the long-standing influence of Gerhard Kaiser's psychoanalytic study, *Gottfried Keller: Das gedichtete Leben*, from 1981 has perpetuated, by more subtle means, earlier biographical readings. And third, Keller remains essential to the mythos of a Swiss national literature—an appropriation he himself, however, would have fiercely opposed, as he very much wished to be identified with a broader German-language canon—and this mythos insists on biographical readings. The persistence of such a biographical perspective provides my inquiry with a welcome opportunity to question both the model of authorship with which literary studies at times continues to operate, especially on an institutional level, and to historicize that model with an examination of how Keller imaginatively

---

36. See Niehaus, *Was ist ein Format?*, 79.
37. The recent *Gottfried Keller-Handbuch* exemplifies this biographical approach, an approach admittedly typical of the genre and indicative of its limitations. See Ursula Amrein, ed., *Gottfried Keller-Handbuch: Leben—Werk—Wirkung*, 2nd ed. (Stuttgart: J. B. Metzler, 2018).

reconceived authorship. Keller's model of authorship, which I argue envisions a form of artistic subjectivity adapted to the conditions of a heavily commercialized literary market, will therefore be one leading thread of my inquiry.

Before outlining the individual chapters of the book, in which I examine how paper and print formats and the challenges they pose to literary and authorial ideals are negotiated in literary works, I would like to situate Keller's oeuvre in the media culture of his time by way of two overarching theses, the first of which regards the relationship between his oeuvre and format, the second his rethinking of authorship. Situating Keller in his contemporaneous media culture is greatly facilitated by the relatively modest scope of his work and by the fact that Keller's correspondence with his three primary publishers during his lifetime (Eduard Vieweg in Leipzig, Ferdinand Weibert in Stuttgart, and Wilhelm Hertz in Berlin) and with Julius Rodenberg, the editor of the literary periodical *Deutsche Rundschau*, in which Keller published so-called preprints of three of his book-length works and various poems, is well preserved and serves as prodigious documentation of his relationship to the publishing market.

A premise of my argument is that format became a point of irritation, if not a crisis, in the creation of literary works and that this can be traced back, in part, to the contemporaneous commercialization of literature and the power held by market demands and individual publishers.[38] As McGillen writes, "The form had to follow the format, and the format was always on the writer's mind," a state of affairs she summarizes as "the priority of format."[39] As I understand it, "the priority of format" in the late nineteenth century exacerbated a situation Steffen Martus has analyzed extensively with regard to German classicism, namely, the "book shape of the work's

---

38. For a broad history of the commercialization of the book market and its effect on German-language literature, see Martha Woodmansee, "The Genius and the Copyright: Economic and Legal Conditions of the Emergence of the 'Author,'" in "The Printed Word in the Eighteenth Century," ed. Raymond Birn, special issue, *Eighteenth-Century Studies* 17, no. 4 (Summer 1984): 425–48.

39. McGillen, *The Fontane Workshop*, 57.

conception," the way in which a work of literature is conceived and developed with a specific format in mind, typically the format of a book.[40] Works of literature are never conceived independently of their material carriers, as the myths of creative inspiration and of the artistic genius would have us believe. Rather, as a standardized order or norm, format always possesses a "prefigurative or prescriptive character"[41] that anticipates the work to come and thus participates in the process of its crafting; one could say that format *preformats* content even before content begins to take shape. In turn, I will show that the conception of the work as a book is a pervasive and central feature of Keller's oeuvre. *Allegories of Format* thereby also pursues the question posed by Carlos Spoerhase's seminal elaboration of format as a concept in literary studies, namely, the question "how the formats of material texts are tied to literary form."[42] Though we might regard formatting as something that happens to a text at a late stage, once a manuscript has been written and has entered the publishing house to be subject to typesetting, layout, and printing, Martus and Spoerhase persuasively argue that anticipated features of the literary work as a finished material object inform the literary project and its content, genre, and form from the very beginning. While the format of handwritten manuscripts would certainly also lend itself to analysis, my focus, like Martus's and Spoerhase's, concerns this moment of anticipation: the anticipation of the more standardized media object that represents the literary work and from which authors derive their authority.

How the conception of the work as a book, or the priority of format, might make itself known can be gleaned from the most extensive description of formatting a book in Keller's oeuvre. Despite the prodigious historical distance between Keller's time of writing and the fictional medieval setting that this description applies to, the scene is informative for an inquiry into format for two reasons:

---

40. Steffen Martus, *Werkpolitik: Zur Literaturgeschichte kritischer Kommunikation vom 17. bis ins 20. Jahrhundert mit Studien zu Klopstock, Tieck, Goethe und George* (Berlin: Walter de Gruyter, 2007), 462.

41. Volmar, "Das Format," 22.

42. Carlos Spoerhase, *Das Format der Literatur: Praktiken materieller Textualität zwischen 1740 und 1830* (Göttingen: Wallstein, 2018), 45.

first, because it conjures the very setting from which the term *format* derives, namely, the craft of bookbinding; and second, because of the way in which format is shown to establish the "elementary parameters" for the work to come, the way in which representation or content conforms to the norms of the media object.[43] In the story "Hadlaub," contained in the *Züricher Novellen* (1877), the eponymous protagonist, a delicate boy, is raised in a medieval monastery to be a copier and illustrator of manuscripts. Eventually Hadlaub becomes a composer of his own love songs, with which he woos his beloved, marries her, and stops writing: a coincidence of a happy end and an end to writing characteristic of Keller's many narratives featuring authors. But before he can compose his own love songs, he is tasked with compiling a collection of minnesong in danger of becoming lost to history. The project is initiated with the creation of the media object in which the songs will be archived as they are collected. Hadlaub receives the following instructions:

> Just be diligent and begin with the copy soon. Take beautiful large parchment without any blemishes and trimming mistakes, cut a large number of uniform sheets right at the outset, start a sufficiently thick bundle for each singer we already have, and line it neatly; in this way you can begin at all points at the same time and leave the necessary space at every name for future entries! Of course, you have to calculate the space to set aside based on the circumstances. For example, it's hardly likely that we will ever acquire more than the eight songs that are here by Emperor Henry, so you only need to arrange one sheet for him!
>
> Sei nur fleißig und beginne bald mit der Abschrift. Nimm schönes großes Pergament, ohne Makel und Bortfehler; schneide eine große Zahl gleichförmiger Blätter gleich anfangs zu und lege für jeden Singer, den wir bereits haben, ein hinlänglich starkes Konvolut an, liniiere es sauber, so kannst Du auf allen Punkten zugleich beginnen und bei jedem Namen den nötigen Raum leer lassen für die künftigen Einträge! Natürlich mußt Du den vorrätigen Raum nach Umständen bemessen. Von Kaiser Heinrich z. B. werden wir schwerlich jemals mehr als die acht Lieder erhalten, die hier sind; da brauchst Du also nur ein Blatt dafür herzurichten![44]

---

43. Volmar, "Das Format," 24.
44. Gottfried Keller, "Hadlaub," in *Züricher Novellen*, vol. 6 of *Sämtliche Werke: Historisch-Kritische Ausgabe*, ed. Walter Morgenthaler (Basel: Stroemfeld;

The project begins with the formatting of the individual leaves, which are sized, cut, and lined with appropriate margins and titles, then divided into the needed subsections, and finally bound as a single-volume book. Individual pages and the codex as a whole are designed with an eye to their future texts, while, conversely, these contents will have to conform to the existing format—one can only hope that no more than the eight songs already attributed to Kaiser Heinrich will be found. Only once the book has been made can Hadlaub commence his journey in search of the songs needed to fill the prefabricated container. The passage celebrates the medium of the book as an archival technology and aesthetic object (its own beauty will ultimately impress its audience as much as the songs it contains) and lays bare how the very idea of the work begins with the material carrier. Indeed, considering that Hadlaub later becomes an author of minnesong, an ability he acquires by copying and later imitating existing songs, one might take the scene to illustrate how not only the work is conceived in the shape of a book but also how the author originates in the process of formatting. Formats are not an afterthought but an initiator of the work and of authorship. Keller's literature is replete with examples of media objects that have been formatted and await their content, often in vain. To give just one more example, in "Der Schmied seines Glückes" (1865)—a novella in *Die Leute von Seldwyla*—Adam Litumlei long ago designed a family tree of his decedents, even though he still has no progeny whose names he could add to the document. The possibility of filling in the family tree only arises through humorous circumstances in which his wife is impregnated, without his knowing, by a houseguest. The story suggests that not only are texts and authorship derivative of specifically formatted media objects but also life itself.

The priority of format is also an enduring characteristic in the making of Keller's oeuvre, even more so than for Hadlaub. With the exception of only a single work, *Sieben Legenden*, the literary works we now attribute to Keller rarely germinated from an idea for a story; instead they arose from an idea for a publishing project that

---

Zürich: Neue Zürcher Zeitung, 1999), 55. This edition of Keller's collected works is hereafter cited as *HKKA* by volume and page number.

was anticipated to bear specific contours regarding size, length, and genre. This state of affairs has typically been attributed to Keller's early impoverished conditions, which compelled him to agree to contracts with publishers long before beginning to write a text, typically in the hope of receiving an advance payment. While these financial necessities were certainly prodigious, especially during the early decades of Keller's life, I would argue that it was not merely financial necessity but also the priority of format that was responsible for this process. The first edition of *Der grüne Heinrich*, both volumes of *Die Leute von Seldwyla*, the *Züricher Novellen*, *Das Sinngedicht*, and *Martin Salander* each began with a publishing agreement that ensured that format preceded form, which is to say, that form had to adapt to format. In the cases when the form of one of Keller's projects did not or could not adapt to the format—in which the two became incongruous, giving rise to a problem of fit—the author, publisher, and public deemed the project a failure. As I detail in chapter 1, in the case of *Der grüne Heinrich*, Keller famously entered a contractual obligation to deliver a manuscript for a single-volume work of twenty-five full sheets (*Bogen*) in two weeks' time. The novel was finally completed eight years later at more than four times the projected length. Or to take a second example: The first record of Keller's intention to write what would become his second and final novel, *Martin Salander*, was his proposal in April 1881 to write "a rather small one-volume novel" (einen einbändigen kleineren Roman)—a project conceived merely according to its single-volume format, only to be elaborated with content many years later.[45] Keller would have abandoned the project had it not been for a public announcement published repeatedly

---

45. Keller to Julius Rodenberg, April 8, 1881, in *HKKA*, 24:451. In the letter, Keller makes explicit that he has no plans for the novel beyond its single-volume format: "For once I also want to indulge in the vice of carelessness and begin a book whose shape I don't yet know and instead complete the manuscript and then later copy it again myself, nicely and neatly" (Ich will mich auch einmal dem Laster des Leichtsinns überlassen und ein Buch anfangen, dessen Gestalt ich noch nicht kenne, dafür aber die Handschrift durchführen und nachher selbst wieder abschreiben, schön und deutlich). *Martin Salander* would ultimately be published in the pages of the *Deutsche Rundschau* in 1885 and 1886 under constant pressure to supply the pages of the unwritten novel by the publisher's deadlines.

in the *Neue Zürcher Zeitung* in August and September 1884 that Keller's newest novel would be published that fall—again before Keller had put pen to paper. Here, too, the media object is projected before it acquires content. Without spelling out how each of Keller's works were conceived according to their format, these examples should suffice to demonstrate that the genesis of Keller's literature, not unlike Hadlaub's collection of songs, was initiated by projecting a specific publishing medium, setting the stage for form to follow format.

While I am arguing that the priority of format is crucial to understanding the genesis and themes of Keller's literary oeuvre, I want to emphasize that, on my reading, the influence of format is not limited to the visual gestalt of the text, to its word count, title, genre, and orthographic conventions, all of which Gretz has rightly identified as sites where the influence of formats and periodical editors become manifest.[46] My argument, to summarize the point again, is that format penetrates into the diegesis, where the aesthetic problems its norms pose are allegorized, negotiated, and, in the examples I have selected for analysis, most often resolved in some way. Storytelling becomes a medium for reflecting on format understood not as a set of mere empirical properties but as a set of norms that generate aesthetic concerns and shape narrative content. Second, although I appreciate format as a determining or enabling condition of literary form, as the examples of Menzel's bookcase and the scene from "Hadlaub" illustrate, this does not imply, in my view, a simple determinism. Instead, Keller's allegories interact and creatively respond to the norms of format. In other words, I am suggesting that by exploring formats in relation to literary representation, we can recognize how their norms are generative.

Nonetheless, the fact that literary projects are initiated in the form of a projected format comes with multiple repercussions for Keller's writing process, his literary ideals, and his model of authorship.

---

46. See Daniela Gretz, "Ein literarischer 'Versuch' im Experimentierfeld Zeitschrift: Medieneffekte der *Deutschen Rundschau* auf Gottfried Kellers *Sinngedicht*," *Zeitschrift für deutsche Philologie* 134, no. 2 (2015): 191–215.

Taken together, these repercussions highlight the precarity of Keller's authorship and the subsequent unlikelihood of his literary legacy. In the first place, because his publishing agreements significantly preceded writing—because he was writing to fill a projected and promised volume under contract—Keller was perpetually behind, delivering manuscript portions too late to the perpetual ire of publishers and editors. As Walter Benjamin acutely remarks, Keller consistently underestimated himself regarding literary quality yet overestimated himself in terms of quantity.[47] Keller's tardiness with regard to publishing deadlines is doubled, I would argue, with a lateness in a second sense, namely, as being born too late and consequently as understanding oneself as an epigone to the foregone high point of German literature. Keller's oeuvre is thus characterized by constantly playing catch-up to a bygone moment, accentuating the unlikelihood of its making. In addition, because perpetually too late, Keller was consistently under an obligation to send any quantity of manuscript he had to his publishers, although later parts of the text had yet to be written. Often, as I will detail in the following chapters, these early portions of manuscripts had been published, circulated, and read—which is to say, had achieved the format of a finished text—long before the writing process was completed. Keller perceived this state of affairs as a crisis of fragmentation, a profound threat to the ideal of a literary work as a self-identical, unified, and harmonious whole. This fragmented writing process thrusts the question of integrity and coherency into the forefront of Keller's aesthetics. Many of the perceived crises negotiated in Keller's stories, as I will demonstrate, have their origin in the spatial and temporal dispersion of the work across various printed parts.

Finally, the book shape of Keller's oeuvre, in which each work was conceived and developed based on a projected format, entailed that Keller regarded printed texts as possessing a finality and

---

47. See Walter Benjamin, "Gottfried Keller: In Honor of a Critical Edition of His Works," trans. Rodney Livingstone, in *Selected Writings*, vol. 2.1, *1927–1930*, ed. Michael W. Jennings, Howard Eiland, and Gary Smith (Cambridge, MA: Belknap Press of Harvard University Press, 1999), 56.

authority that usurped his own as their author. The work, in other words, was more closely bound to the material object than to the author's person or intentions. Such a view explains, for one, why Keller so rarely made substantial revisions between different editions of his texts (with the exception of the second edition of *Der grüne Heinrich*). When he did make revisions—as for the second edition of *Der grüne Heinrich* or when revising periodical preprints for book editions, as in the case of the *Züricher Novellen*—Keller consistently used his print copy as the template. This meant that revisions were performed not merely with pencil on paper but also with scissors and glue that Keller and his publishers used to enter corrections and compile new editions. While I will return throughout the book to this array of tools and practices—in particular, copying—by which the texts were made (rather than being simply written), I mention the process here to emphasize that Keller regarded published texts as authoritative and as establishing the terms for later projects. The priority of format thus refers not only to the projected format of a work to come but also the normative force that past publications imposed on those yet to be completed.

The authority of the printed text comes to the fore in Keller's exchange with the critic and author Berthold Auerbach concerning the latter's doubts about the conclusion to the novella "Romeo und Julia auf dem Dorfe." In a letter to Auerbach, Keller defends the story (though he did later revise the ending in conformity with Auerbach's narrow-minded suggestion) with the assertion that the novella belongs to the world of paper, a world beyond his own agency.

> Now I would certainly delete the base ending of "Romeo und Julia" and will do so if the small book is ever printed again. But I must somewhat come to the defense of the title of the same story. First, what we ourselves write is also printed on paper and belongs from this perspective to the paper world, and second, Shakespeare is, though printed, still only life itself and not a lifeless reminiscence.

> Den schnöden Schluß von Romeo und Julie würde ich sicherlich jetzt streichen und werde es tun, wenn das Büchlein irgend wieder einmal abgedruckt wird. Dagegen muß ich den Titel der gleichen Erzählung etwas in Schutz nehmen. Erstens ist ja das, was wir selbst schreiben, auch auf

Papier gedruckt und gehört von dieser Seite zur papiernen Welt, und zweitens ist ja Shakespeare, obgleich gedruckt, doch nur das Leben selbst und keine unlebendige Reminiszenz.[48]

While the printed status of the story, its belonging to the "paper world," guards against revisions, it is equally noteworthy that Keller insists that the world of print, at least in the case of so canonical an author as Shakespeare, belongs to the realm of life. As a print object, the work takes on a life of its own. The normative force embodied by previously published works is also appreciable in how Keller's publishing contract does not name a standardized format at any point but instead refers to specific previously published works as precedents, a practice that illustrates the extent to which Keller's media environment was not yet saturated by standardization. For example, both the second edition of *Die Leute von Seldwyla* and the volume *Züricher Novellen* were designed to approximate the format and length of the first *Leute von Seldwyla*. In this way, too, Keller's works in progress were compelled to play catch-up to a bygone moment.

The second thesis I would like to introduce by way of situating Keller in the media culture of his time concerns the reconception of authorship that takes place throughout the works I analyze, specifically with regard to its gendering.[49] As has been well documented, the professionalization of authorship initiated by the new mass-media

---

48. Gottfried Keller to Berthold Auerbach, June 3, 1856, in *Gesammelte Briefe in vier Bänden*, ed. Carl Helbing, 4 vols. (Bern: Benteli, 1951–1954), 3.2:186.

49. Previous scholarship on gender in Keller's works has focused on how his texts reproduce contemporaneous gender norms or has adopted a more psychoanalytic approach that attends to the role of the mother and father. For examples of the first, see Ursula Amrein, *Augenkur und Brautschau: Zur diskursiven Logik der Geschlechterdifferenz in Gottfried Kellers "Sinngedicht"* (Bern: Peter Lang, 1994); and Caroline von Loewenich, *Gottfried Keller: Frauenbild und Frauengestalten im erzählerischen Werk* (Würzburg: Königshausen & Neumann, 2000); for the second, see Gerhard Kaiser, *Gottfried Keller: Das gedichtete Leben* (Frankfurt am Main: Insel, 1981). Eric Downing's *Double Exposures*, in contrast, excavates in what way the *Sieben Legenden* portray gender as a social construction. See Downing, *Double Exposures*, 98–118.

environment set myriad anxieties into motion.[50] To summarize the point here, precisely because paper and paper media were so widely available, the industrialization of literature was perceived as a threat to literature's aesthetic quality and to the autonomy of the author. The newfound influence of editors, the purchasing power of readers, and practices of extensive reading meant that the production and reception of literary texts was an increasingly dispersed and collaborative process that compromised the position of the author as uniquely responsible for the making of literature. While the image of the creative and inspired Romantic artist continued to dominate the literary imagination, such an ideal seemed entirely out of reach in a marketplace ruled by an overabundance of paper media and rapid consumption. At worst, an author like Keller perceived himself as one of many wage laborers in the mechanized process of literary production. In this spirit, Keller accused the publisher of his first novel, Eduard Vieweg, of infringing on his authorial freedom in just this way: "The way you wanted to possibly forbid me from working freely for a purpose other than completing the book owed to you reminds me, quite frankly, of the way factory workers are treated."[51]

In this book, I will examine different ways in which Keller's literature responds to these anxieties concerning the changing nature of authorship in a mass-media marketplace. A central claim is that Keller's literature casts artistic subjectivity as a playful removal from binary sexual differentiation and of the associated division of biological reproductive labor, an aspect that Benjamin first observed as integral to Keller's work.[52] The reoccurring figure of the bache-

---

50. On the professionalization of authorship in the nineteenth-century literary market, see Rolf Parr, *Autorschaft: Eine kurze Sozialgeschichte der literarischen Intelligenz in Deutschland zwischen 1860 und 1930* (Heidelberg: Synchron, 2008); and Robert Patten, *Charles Dickens and "Boz": The Birth of the Industrial-Age Author* (Cambridge: Cambridge University Press, 2012).

51. "Die Art, wie Sie mir eventuell das freie Arbeiten für einen andern Zweck, als den der Vollendung des Ihnen schuldenden Buches verbieten wollten, erinnerte mich, offen gestanden, an die Art, mit der man einen Fabrikarbeiter behandelt." Keller to Eduard Vieweg, February 20, 1861, in *Gesammelte Briefe*, 3.2:145.

52. "While the active and weighty elements of life are seemingly unaffected and are present in their true proportions, the male imperceptibly changes into the female and vice versa." Benjamin, "Gottfried Keller," 57. As Eva Geulen points out, Benja-

lor is the most obvious example of that retreat, but not the only one. The authorial body imaginatively takes the form of an androgynous or hermaphroditic figure, which by "promising wholeness, appears to contest binarism," as Catriona MacLeod has observed for German realism more broadly.[53] Keller's texts specifically develop bodies that incorporate creative, productive powers, gendered as male, and reproductive capacities, gendered as female. As a body that straddles a gender binary—a type of "hermaphroditic ink animal" (zweigeschlechtige[m] Tintentier), as Keller once described the extraordinarily successful writing couple Fanny Lewald and Adolf Stahr[54]—the author becomes able to reconcile the at-first-sight incompatible domains of literary autonomy and the procedures of mechanical reproduction that produce literature as a commercial object. As I later show, artistic subjectivity, as reimagined in Keller's literature, absorbs the procedures of reproduction essential to the proliferation of media objects. The authorial body is endowed with the capacity for autonomous reproduction (having combined male and female parts) and simultaneously redirects this potential away from biological reproduction to the making of art. The author exemplifies the capacity for self-generation and self-perpetuation; authorship is a form of life perpetuated not only by creative inspiration and generation but just as much by "a desire to reproduce," as Keller describes the artist's motivation to restore broken fragments to wholeness in the preface to his *Sieben Legenden*.[55] The likeness-to-life imperative of realist texts was thus

---

min's interest in hermaphroditic figures in Keller's work and elsewhere is tantamount to the feminization of a masculine body. See Eva Geulen, "Toward a Genealogy of Gender in Walter Benjamin's Writing," *German Quarterly* 69, no. 2 (1996): 166–67.

53. Catriona MacLeod, *Embodying Ambiguity: Androgyny and Aesthetics from Winckelmann to Keller* (Detroit, MI: Wayne State University Press, 1998), 11. On the semantics of biological reproduction in descriptions of artistic inspiration, as I claim for Keller, see Christian Begemann and David E. Wellbery, eds., *Kunst— Zeugung—Geburt: Theorien und Metaphern ästhetischer Produktion in der Neuzeit* (Freiburg im Breisgau: Rombach, 2002).

54. Keller to Lina Duncker, March 6, 1856, in *Gesammelte Briefe*, 2:154.

55. "As the painter is incited by a fragmentary patch of cloud, an outline of a mountain, an etched scrap by some forgotten master, to fill a whole canvas, so the author experienced a desire to reproduce those broken, elusive images; although it must be owned that in the process their faces have often been turned to another

not merely a matter of mimeticism but also an imperative to exhibit the property most essential to life-forms, namely, the capacity of self-reproduction.

Keller's models for an authorial body should be understood as a form of intervention in the gender politics of German realism. The model of hermaphroditic authorship I excavate addresses the widespread perception of the epoch's literature on the part of its contemporaries as feminine literature, the view that mass literature is emasculated. One impetus for such a perception was the newfound participation of women, as both readers and writers, in the literary marketplace; another—if Helmstetter and Günter are correct—was the deployment of narrative patterns apposite to a women's literature that would meet the favor of these readers.[56] "Our literature has become, with few exceptions, merely women's, perhaps even girl's literature," quips one commentator of periodical culture, while another glosses the presence of female readers as tantamount to the castration of the poet, arguing that the periodical "makes a craftsman out of the poet and systematically forces him to trivialize himself, knowingly and deliberately, to literarily castrate himself, so to speak."[57] Keller's literary work guards itself against the perceived dangers of (symbolic) castration on account of its service to mass-media literature by imaginatively incorporating the reproductive mechanisms of mass media into the authorial persona. Importantly, that persona does not manifest itself in a single homogenous way. Instead, the ideal of the author, its gendering, and

---

quarter of the heavens than that towards which they looked in their extant forms" (Wie nun der Maler durch ein fragmentarisches Wolkenbild, eine Gebirgslinie, durch das radierte Blättchen eines verschollenen Meisters zur Ausfüllung eines Rahmens gereizt wird, so verspürte der Verfasser die Lust zu einer Reproduktion jener abgebrochen schwebenden Gebilde, wobei ihnen freilich zuweilen das Antlitz nach einer anderen Himmelsgegend hingewendet wurde, als nach welcher sie in der überkommenen Gestalt schauen). Gottfried Keller, "Preface," in *Seven Legends*, trans. Martin Wyness (London: Gowans & Gray, 1911), 3; Keller, "Vorwort," in *Sieben Legenden*, in *HKKA*, 7:333.

56. See Helmstetter, *Die Geburt des Realismus*; Günter, "Realismus in Medien."

57. Heinrich Hart and Julius Hart, "Für und gegen Zola," *Kritische Waffengänge* 2 (1882): 54; Arthur Zapp, "Schriftstellerleiden," *Die Zukunft*, November 12, 1898, 305. See Helmstetter, *Die Geburt des Realismus*, 72, 74.

the very gestalt of the body selected to model authorship vary depending on the print and paper format under consideration. The gendering of the author is thus one way in which Keller's literary texts imaginatively elaborate what is at stake in different formats.

Allegories of Format aims to give a comprehensive overview of Keller's literature not by examining each and every text but by selecting representatives of different genres and formats that constitute the author's oeuvre and, second, by attending to a mix of the best-known (*Der grüne Heinrich*) works and the most neglected ones (the volumes of poetry). Because one of the central questions of the book is how a literary legacy takes shape, in particular, how a relationship between life and work is imagined to be essential to such a legacy, the chapters of this book are arranged to review the ten volumes of Keller's collected works and, in doing so, to follow the different idealized biographical stations of the author's life: the young, impoverished poet; the state bureaucrat; and the seasoned yet disillusioned author of the *Spätwerk*. Accordingly, part 1 examines Keller's earliest undertakings to establish himself as an author, including the first edition of his novel *Der grüne Heinrich* and even earlier publications: two essentially forgotten volumes of poetry. These texts would later comprise the first three and last two volumes, the bookends, of the collected-works edition that appeared with Hertz Verlag at the end of Keller's lifetime. In chapter 1, I argue that the drawn-out publishing history of *Der grüne Heinrich* and its multivolume format precipitate a crisis concerning the protagonist's identity over time. That crisis is negotiated in the life story of the protagonist, which attempts to give, in the tradition of the bildungsroman, his life a form that is at odds with the format of its own media object. Just as the crisis of identity and novelistic form reacts to a multivolume print format, so too does the novel answer that crisis by imagining, in the mode of allegory, the possibility of a unified life as refracted in a second, alternative print format: the collected-works edition. Chapter 2, in turn, explores Keller's overlooked fascination with premature burial, which became, in his earliest volumes of poetry, fertile ground for exploring the nature of authorship and the media conditions of a literary legacy. Scenes of premature burial elaborate the biological death of the author as a condition of authorship, as ensuring the ability to speak to posterity through print media.

Drawing on Keller's occupation as a state bureaucrat and his fictional representations of bureaucratic practices, part 2 explores the relationship between practices of administrative writing and the making of literature. Chapter 3 aims to undermine an entrenched distinction between the creative act of composing original literature and the formulaic, routinized practices of bureaucratic writing. I begin by questioning the persistent exclusion of Keller's occupation as the state chancellor (*Staatsschreiber*) of the canton of Zurich from literary portraits, an exclusion premised on the ground that the occupation represents an aberration from, rather than a deepening of, his activities as a writer. My reading of "Die mißbrauchten Liebesbriefe" from the novella cycle *Die Leute von Seldwyla* (volumes 3 and 4 of the collected works) demonstrates that the well-known novella undermines such a denigration of office work. The novella celebrates bureaucratic writing as a proper purpose and practice of writing, while literature is in danger of becoming a deleterious aberration, indeed, a perversion of a practice whose purpose lies in bookkeeping. In elevating the ideal of bureaucratic writing practices, "Die mißbrauchten Liebesbriefe" reenvisions the author as withdrawing from conventional sexual differentiation and biological reproduction. At the same time, I show how the publication of the novella depended on and cannot be extricated from office management and paperwork—yet another way these two supposedly antithetical forms of writing ultimately dovetailed. In chapter 4, I more closely examine Keller's responsibilities as state chancellor, with a focus on the *Protokolle* ("minutes" or "protocols") of the meetings of the cantonal government council (*Regierungsrat*). The specific example of the protocol, a type of document that is ideally authorless, provides a fruitful opportunity for establishing a more expansive definition of authorship than that of a creative, solitary author. The chapter specifically attends to Keller's habit of doodling on his records of the meetings and argues that, although they might appear as interrupting the process of recordkeeping, such doodles actually participate in the documentation process.

Part 3 examines two novella cycles with readings of *Das Sinngedicht* (volume 7 of the collected works) and "Der Landvogt von Greifensee" from the *Züricher Novellen* (volume 8). Chapters 5 and 6 attend to Keller's experiences with and handling of practices of serialization, the publishing format of the mid- to late nineteenth century that has easily received the most scholarly attention. Because each was preprinted in the *Deutsche Rundschau*, these novella cycles provide opportunities for examining how Keller's storytelling incorporates serialized formats into the narrative design. By relating these texts to a history of novella collections from Boccaccio's *Decameron* onward, my readings demonstrate that each text is structured around an erotic energy that is tasked with extending a serial structure and providing the series with a closure more typically associated with cyclical forms. I show that the story of "Der Landvogt von Greifensee" attempts to reconcile, in allegory, series and cycle, periodical and book publications, while at the same time portraying the author as embodying not only the productive but also the reproductive capacities needed to secure his future legacy.

The epilogue to this book provides a final summary account of Keller's self-positioning in his contemporaneous media landscape, especially with a view to his perceived status as an epigone, born too late to participate in the high point of German literature. Borrowing a term from Friedrich Nietzsche's condemnation of this epigonic generation, I identity Keller's media strategy as one of *Selbstverkleinerung*, of "making oneself small," so as to ensure oneself a place, no matter how marginal, in literary history. Making oneself small is nothing less, I argue, than a comprehensive gesture of Keller's oeuvre: a reformatting of media objects and inherited literary forms to an imagined anthropological reality of diminished men; a rescaling of literary subject matter with a focus on prosaic life apposite to these small formats; and finally, a persistent tone of comic irony that ensures that these miniatures do not attain the aggrandized status of exemplars. An encompassing gesture of self-belittlement adapts to and accommodates the perception of diminished greatness with an embrace of apposite small formats.

Part I

The Format of Life

The Collected-Works Edition

1

Life and Work

Der grüne Heinrich

Gottfried Keller's novel *Der grüne Heinrich* has been described as his *Lebensbuch*, his "life book," and with good reason.[1] To begin with, the novel is partially autobiographical: It loosely recounts the author's childhood, education, and failure as a landscape painter. Second, writing and revising *Der grüne Heinrich* occupied Keller for much of his life. He declared his intention to write the novel as early as 1847 (by some accounts as early as 1843), published the first

---

1. See Rainer Diederichs, "Kellers Lebensbuch: Vorwort," in *"Der grüne Heinrich": Gottfried Kellers Lebensbuch—neu gelesen*, ed. Wolfram Groddeck (Zürich: Chronos, 2009), 7–9. Diederichs applies the term *Lebensbuch* to the novel in the first and second senses I offer here but not in the third. Keller himself used *Lebensbuch* to refer to Heinrich's "Jugendgeschichte," the half of the novel's first edition written in the first person. See Keller to Theodor Storm, June 25, 1878, in *HKKA*, 19:382. Keller strongly identified with the novel as a whole, but particularly with this *Lebensbuch*, which reflected his own time as an aspiring artist in Munich. See, for example, Keller's description of the novel in the proposal to Eduard Vieweg, May 3, 1850, in *HKKA*, 19:170–76, esp. 174.

edition in four volumes in 1853 and 1855, and then spent the remainder of his life until his death revising it for the second, third, and fourth editions.[2] Finally, the term *Lebensbuch* is fitting because *Der grüne Heinrich* participates in the conception of the novel, specifically that of the bildungsroman, as giving form to life, a conception succinctly summarized by Rüdiger Campe: "Uniquely and for the first time among all genres, the form of the novel can only be described as a form of life. With the (modern) novel, literary form becomes a matter no longer of poetical forms but of the form of life."[3]

Though it may be considered his *Lebensbuch*, Keller viewed the first edition of his novel as a flop, as indeed it was on the book market. To his mind, the novel was defined by its "formlessness" (Unförmlichkeit);[4] it possessed, as he later described it, a "knitted-sock form" (Strickstrumpfform),[5] a turn of phrase I will return to later in this chapter. The novel had failed at the very form-giving process with which the genre of the novel is tasked. As historians of the genre of the novel remind us, since this most modern genre falls outside any poetic or rhetorical system and need not (and cannot) adhere to any set of rules, each exemplum must create its form anew, taking as its example not another example but life itself: "Being a

---

2. For a chronology of the novel's production, see Peter Stocker, Walter Morgenthaler, Thomas Binder, Karl Grob, and Dominik Müller, "*Der grüne Heinrich*: Entstehung und Publikation," in *HKKA*, 19:15–27.

3. Rüdiger Campe, "Form and Life in the Theory of the Novel," *Constellations* 18, no. 1 (2011): 54. While Campe's article is the central point of departure for my argument, I more broadly follow Franco Moretti and David Wellbery in understanding the bildungsroman as a narrative of socialization that negotiates the competing claims of an individual's imaginative self-realization and those of a symbolic order. See Franco Moretti, *The Way of the World: The Bildungsroman in European Culture*, trans. Albert Sbragia (London: Verso, 1987), 3–14; and David E. Wellbery, "Die Enden des Menschen: Anthropologie und Einbildungskraft im Bildungsroman (Wieland, Goethe, Novalis)," in *Das Ende: Figuren einer Denkform*, ed. Karlheinz Stierle and Rainer Warning, Poetik und Hermeneutik 16 (München: Wilhelm Fink, 1996), 600–639.

4. Keller, "Vorwort," in *Der grüne Heinrich* (1st ed., 1854–1855), in *HKKA*, 11:14.

5. Keller to Hermann Hettner, June 26, 1854, in *HKKA*, 19:272; Keller repeats the turn of phrase in a letter to Ferdinand Freiligrath when he speaks of "the damned knitted sock" (den verfluchten Strickstrumpf). Keller to Ferdinand Freiligrath, December 1854, in *HKKA*, 19:288.

form of life, the form of the novel has to be established anew each time, and it does not differ in essence from instances of forming life in other fields."[6] A bildungsroman like *Der grüne Heinrich*, typically a story of a male protagonist on his way to becoming a socialized adult and subject, epitomizes this search for a form of life that is at the same time the form of the novel.[7] This entwinement of form and life is confirmed not only by Keller's assessment that he failed to endow his novel with a form but also by the general verdict that the protagonist, Heinrich, fails to give his life a form, a verdict that persists in today's characterization of *Der grüne Heinrich* as the first antibildungsroman, a story about the modern social and economic impediments to creating a form of life for oneself.[8]

Keller's preface to the novel, published in 1853 in the novel's third volume (alongside the first and second volumes), makes no secret of the author's dissatisfaction with the text. There he attributes the novel's formlessness to two factors. First, the presence of two narrative voices begets a "divided form" (getrennte form).[9] In the novel's first edition, the primary object of my analysis, the text begins in the voice of an omniscient third-person narrator, who introduces the protagonist, Heinrich, journeying from his native Zurich to Munich, where he hopes to pursue an education in landscape

---

6. Campe, "Form and Life," 54.

7. As Andreas Gailus explains, the intersection between life as form and the form of the novel is especially urgent for nineteenth-century German aesthetics because of (1) a specific conception of life as the development of form and (2) the recognition that form is both biological and symbolic. The bildungsroman narrativizes the development of an endogenous form as a simultaneously biological and social entity. See Andreas Gailus, *Forms of Life: Aesthetics and Biopolitics in German Culture* (Ithaca, NY: Cornell University Press, 2020), 10–11. In his introduction, Gailus provides a very helpful elaboration of the historical semantics of the term *form of life*.

8. For a recent reading of *Der grüne Heinrich* as defying the tradition of the bildungsroman and failing to establish a form of life, see Elisabeth Strowick, "Gottfried Kellers Szenographie des Wirklichen," *Sprache und Literatur* 49, no. 2 (2020): 215–40. Strowick argues that the novel relates not to the life of an individual but to a depersonalized life that always exceeds itself so as to resemble the undead: "*Der grüne Heinrich* is a *different* sort of bildungsroman: far from being a novel *about* the life of Heinrich Lee, the novel is rather itself *a* life" (237).

9. Keller, "Vorwort," in *Der grüne Heinrich* (1st ed., 1854–1855), in *HKKA*, 11:14.

painting. Upon his arrival, Heinrich reads his childhood memoir, which is itself narrated in the first person; this is the very part of the novel that Keller describes as the protagonist's *Lebensbuch*. Then, at the conclusion of the childhood memoir, the third-person narrator resumes narration and recounts Heinrich's precarious existence in Munich and his long journey back home, at the conclusion of which he returns just in time to see his mother being buried and, in a matter of days, dies himself. Hence, roughly half of the novel is narrated in the first person and half in the third person, resulting, in Keller's estimation, in a divided form.

Second, having admitted that its earliest pages were written six years prior, the preface attributes the lack of form to the protracted time of writing. The prolix length of the manuscript (the preface seemingly anticipates the yet-to-be-published fourth volume, which would become the bulkiest of the novel's four, with a total sum of 1,667 pages) is offered as further evidence of that protraction.[10] In effect, the two reasons Keller gives for the formlessness of his novel interweave the three definitions of *Lebensbuch* in contradictory ways: Because *Der grüne Heinrich* is a *Lebensbuch* in the first sense of being partially autobiographical and in the second sense of occupying so much of its author's life, it is unable to fulfill the aspiration expressed in the third sense of giving form to a life. From Keller's perspective, the very nature of his own writing life prevented him from satisfying the task he knew to be normative for the genre of the novel: the presentation of life as form.

The preface bears citing at length because the frustrations voiced therein evidence Keller's acute sensitivity to the problem of form in the genre of the novel. Over the course of the passage, Keller not only diagnoses the dual cause of the novel's formlessness; he also spells out, *ex negativo*, normative standards for the achievement of form.

> The first sheets of this novel date from the year 1847; the last were recently produced, and the manner in which the whole is composed resembles that of a long and detailed letter one writes about a confidential

---

10. See Keller, "Vorwort," in *Der grüne Heinrich* (1st ed., 1854–1855), in *HKKA*, 11:13–14.

matter, often being interrupted by the changes and pressures of life. One leaves the letter lying around through whole periods of time; in many ways, one becomes another person; but when one takes up what was written again, one continues exactly where one had left off, and even if the changes of life are revealed in what one emphasizes or keeps silent about, one stills finds that one has remained the same in relation to the person the letter is addressed to and with regard to the matter. [. . .] The result is certainly not a rigorously structured work of art, but perhaps it is an all the more faithful expression of what one was and what one wanted with the letter. It is another question, however, whether this comparison manages to excuse or gloss over a certain formlessness in this novel. I am far from wanting to attempt to do so; with the comparison, I would merely like to intimate my hope that the reader will take with them, if not the pleasure of a pure and masterly work of art, then at least the impression of a message that was truly felt and moving in manifold ways.—The aforementioned lack of form is mainly due to how the novel falls apart into two different pieces, namely, an autobiography of the hero after he has been introduced and the proper novel, in which his further fate is narrated and the question posed in the autobiography is resolved to a certain extent. The first of these parts is far too expansive to be considered an episode of the other, and so it only remains to be hoped that the unity of the content may sufficiently join the two and make us forget the divided form.

Die ersten Bogen dieses Romanes datiren noch aus dem Jahr 1847, die letzten entstanden in diesen Tagen, und die Entstehungsweise des Ganzen gleicht derjenigen eines ausführlichen und langen Briefes, welchen man über eine vertrauliche Angelegenheit schreibt, oft unterbrochen durch den Wechsel und Drang des Lebens. Man läßt den Brief ganze Zeiträume hindurch liegen, man wird vielfältig ein Anderer; aber wenn man das Geschriebene wieder zur Hand nimmt, fährt man genau da fort, wo man aufgehört hatte, und wenn sich auch in dem, was man betont oder verschweigt, der Wechsel des Lebens kund thut, findet sich doch, daß man gegen den, an welchen der Brief gerichtet, und in dieser Sache der Alte geblieben ist. [. . .] So entsteht freilich nicht ein streng gegliedertes Kunstwerk, aber vielleicht ein um so treuerer Ausdruck dessen, was man war und wollte mit dem Briefe. Eine andere Frage aber ist es nun, ob das Gleichniß hinreiche, eine gewisse Unförmlichkeit vorliegenden Romanes zu entschuldigen oder zu beschönigen. Ich bin weit entfernt, dies versuchen zu wollen; einzig und allein möchte ich durch das Gleichniß die Hoffnung andeuten, der geneigte Leser werde wenigstens, wenn auch nicht den Genuß eines reinen und meisterhaften Kunstwerkes, so doch den Eindruck einer wahr empfundenen und mannigfach bewegten Mittheilung davon tragen.—Besagte Unförmlichkeit hat ihren Grund hauptsächlich in der Art, wie der Roman in zwei verschiedene

> Bestandtheile auseinander fällt, nämlich in eine Selbstbiographie des Helden, nachdem er eingeführt ist, und in den eigentlichen Roman, worin sein weiteres Schicksal erzählt und die in der Selbstbiographie gestellte Frage gewissermaßen gelöst wird. Der eine dieser Theile ist viel zu breit, um als Episode des anderen zu gelten, und so bleibt nur zu wünschen, daß die Einheit des Inhaltes Beide genugsam möge verbinden und die getrennte Form vergessen lassen.[11]

The normative standards Keller names for the achievement of form are effectively borrowed from the description of a classical artwork. Since his novel is not a "rigorously structured work of art," it cannot provide aesthetic pleasure, "the pleasure of a pure and masterly work of art." It lacks the good proportions and unity of its parts imperative to the achievement of aesthetic form and consequently falls into disparate segments bound only through a common theme. The same criticisms became a mainstay of the novel's reviewers, who were quick to appreciate that the preface preempted their critiques.[12] To give just three examples: Julian Schmidt complains that "the composition of the work as a whole is imperfect," a problem he attributes to "a quite strange conception of life in general"; of the protagonist, Ferdinand Gustav Kühne regrets how the "awakening consciousness splits into two parts"; and even Hermann Hettner, Keller's close friend and confidant throughout the writing process, notes that "the composition does not have any inner unity; it disintegrates into two thoroughly separate parts."[13] Hettner, who confirms the author's claim that he learned to write while writing the novel, concludes with the optimistic prophecy "that in the future he

---

11. Keller, "Vorwort," in *Der grüne Heinrich* (1st ed., 1854–1855), in *HKKA*, 11:13–14.

12. In his review from 1854, Ferdinand Gustav Kühne remarks: "In the preface to the work, in which he apologizes for the formlessness [Unförmlichkeit] of his book, the author [...] provides the best self-criticism." Ferdinand Gustav Kühne, "*Der grüne Heinrich*: Roman von G. Keller," *Europa: Chronik der gebildeten Welt*, April 27, 1854, 286.

13. Julian Schmidt, "*Der grüne Heinrich*, Roman von Gottfried Keller," *Die Grenzboten: Zeitschrift für Politik und Literatur* 13, no. 1 (1854): 401; Kühne, "*Der grüne Heinrich*," 286; Hermann Hettner, "*Der grüne Heinrich*: Roman von Gottfried Keller," *National-Zeitung*, May 5, 1854.

[Keller] will no longer put his hand to working out the particulars before he has rounded out a clear and unified image of the whole." For these earliest critics, as for Keller, the sense that the novel does not cohere as an organic whole and instead disintegrates into at least two, if not numerous, parts is tantamount to a lack of form. Moreover, these reviewers extend this lack of novelistic form to the form of the protagonist's life. The novel's divided form is, as Kühne writes, also the divided consciousness of the protagonist.

While Keller appreciated the key demands of the genre of the novel—to invent the form anew with each instantiation and, in so doing, to give a life a coherent, closed, and unified form—the perception of the novel's formlessness did not merely derive from the protracted time of writing or the presence of two narrative voices but also from the conditions of its production and its media format. On my reading, Keller's frustrations and, more to the point, the novel's plot demonstrate how the achievement of form (or its failure) in the novelistic genre is fundamentally entwined with the specifications of media formats and the conditions of production in which these formats materialize. The primary reason Keller names in the preface for the novel's formlessness—the divided form issuing from two narrative voices—itself points to one site where text and production become entwined. As Russell Berman forcefully argues, the commercialization of literature in the nineteenth century was perceived not only to constrain authorial autonomy and creativity in unprecedented ways but also to destabilize the narrative voice. Because writers under capitalism do not speak as autonomous subjects, the market introduces "a hiatus between writer and text, between speaker and speech, and this distance engenders a desubjectification of the literary product which ceases to be the public expression of a private person."[14] The analogy Keller draws between his novel and the epistolary genre, accompanied by an insistence on the sincerity of its speech in the preface of *Der grüne Heinrich*— "the impression of a message that was truly felt and moving in

---

14. Russell Berman, "Writing for the Book Industry: The Writer Under Organized Capitalism," *New German Critique* 29 (1983): 56.

manifold ways"—unsuccessfully tries to efface this very hiatus and the uncertain status of the two narrators, themselves a symptom of a newly unstable literary culture.[15]

While the tandem narrators of *Der grüne Heinrich* and the two genres they imply (biography and autobiography)—an aspect discussed extensively in the extant scholarship—are the most immediate symptom of a destabilized narrator, they are only one manifestation of how the conditions of production and specifications of format interfere with the novel's form-giving process.[16] In the following, I argue that Keller's perception of his novel as being formless can additionally be traced to its fractured publication in four volumes that were marketed and sold as they were printed (see figure 2).

For Keller, this spatially and temporally fractured book format—a book divided into four, disparate parts—impresses itself on the diegetic material, engendering problems and even crises for the life and identity of the protagonist. The process of the novel's commercial production and its format become points of irresolvable irritation to the novel's form and the form of life it must establish for its protagonist, rendering it impossible to represent Heinrich's life as *a* life.[17] *Der grüne Heinrich* thus exemplifies a crisis of disintegrative form that can be concurrently traced back to the novel's format and to the life story of its protagonist in which that crisis is negotiated. The novel thereby compels us to appreciate how its task of giving

---

15. On the pervasive significance of the epistolary genre to *Der grüne Heinrich*, see Wolfram Groddeck, "'Eine gewisse Unförmlichkeit': Briefeschreiben und Romangeschehen," in Groddeck, *"Der grüne Heinrich,"* 36.

16. See, for example, Sabine Schneider, "'Poesie der Unreife': Autobiographisches Schreiben im Roman," in Groddeck, *"Der grüne Heinrich,"* 55–77. Schneider argues that the novel's difficulties (and originality) lie in the tensions between the novelistic and autobiographical forms. The first-person perspective of the autobiography renders impossible the achievement of objectivity, which the nineteenth-century realist program aspired to and Keller himself avowed.

17. Among the current scholarship, the problem of the form of Heinrich's life is best articulated by Caroline Torra-Mattenklott: "How is it possible to assess life in its temporality, complexity, and openness and translate it into a narrative form that also constitutes a coherent, self-contained aesthetic whole?" Caroline Torra-Mattenklott, *Poetik der Figur: Zwischen Geometrie und Rhetorik; Modelle der Textkomposition von Lessing bis Valéry* (Paderborn: Wilhelm Fink, 2016), 160.

form to life is refracted through the specific contours of its medium, especially in an epoch of increasingly commercialized literature.

After describing the history of this fractured publishing format, I will argue that the novel both stages this crisis of disintegrative form and format and imaginatively answers it by envisioning a second publishing format, the collected-works edition, as providing an alternative model and a better fit for the relationship between book formats and the form of life. I read the novel's plot as negotiating the relationship between print formats and the novel's task to give form to life. In its final redaction, *Der grüne Heinrich* paradoxically suggests that life is only a posthumous achievement, that it achieves form not during the time of its narration but in being cut short—a poetics of the scissors, if you will.

Form and Format

My starting point is the claim that in the age of print capitalism, when book publishing became an affair of mass production and heightened commercialization, the materiality of the book and the specificities of its format came to bear on the form-giving process and the question of how to give life a form. To acknowledge that influence entails calling into question a persistent Platonic view of authorship, according to which an author's idea for a novel precedes its realization as a material text and is compromised in that realization. Such an idealistic view of authorship is palpable, for example, in the oft-repeated claim that Keller possessed a clear and elaborated idea for the plot of his novel before ever setting pen to paper, an idea whose realization was subsequently partially thwarted by his villain-like publisher.[18] In matter of fact, the novel's plot, the

---

18. For example: "To make matters worse for Keller, writing down the works he had thought out in his head was generally extremely difficult for him, and he always had to enlist the help of publishers and magazine editors, who had to wring the manuscripts out of him sheet by sheet." Dominik Müller, "*Der grüne Heinrich* (1879/80): Der späte Abschluß eines Frühwerks," in *Interpretationen: Gottfried Keller; Romane und Erzählungen*, ed. Walter Morgenthaler (Stuttgart: Philipp Reclam, 2007), 38. Müller points to both the book proposal Keller sent his publisher,

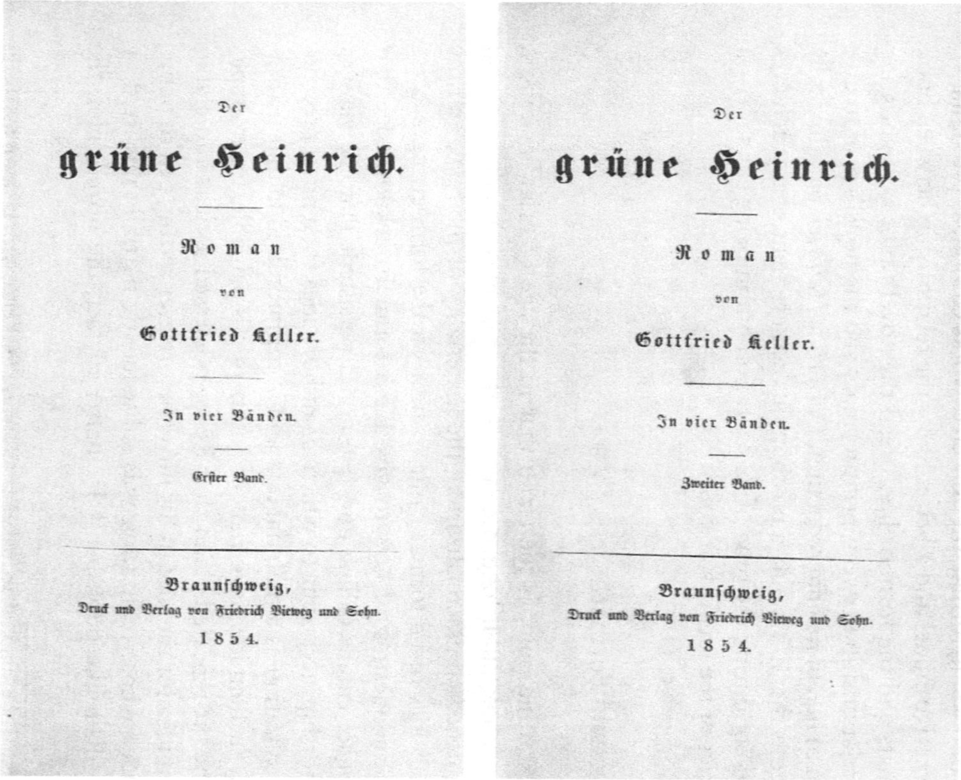

Figure 2. Title pages of Gottfried Keller, *Der grüne Heinrich*, 4 vols. (Braunschweig: Friedrich Vieweg und Sohn, 1854–1855).

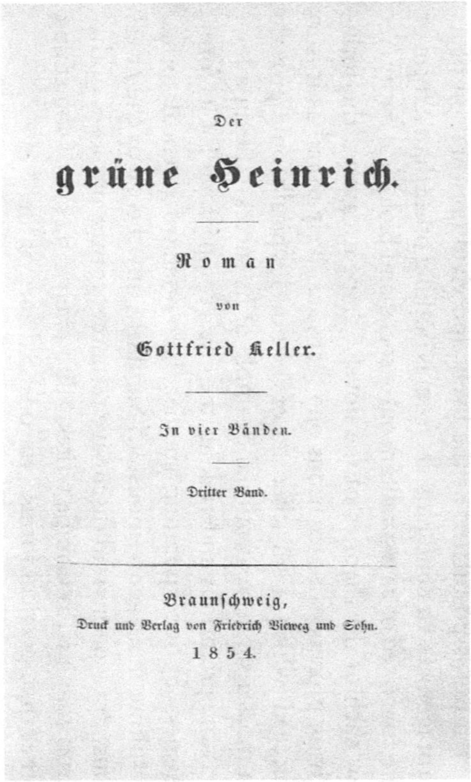

Der
grüne Heinrich.

Roman
von
Gottfried Keller.

In vier Bänden.

Dritter Band.

Braunschweig,
1854.

Druck und Verlag von Friedrich Vieweg und Sohn.

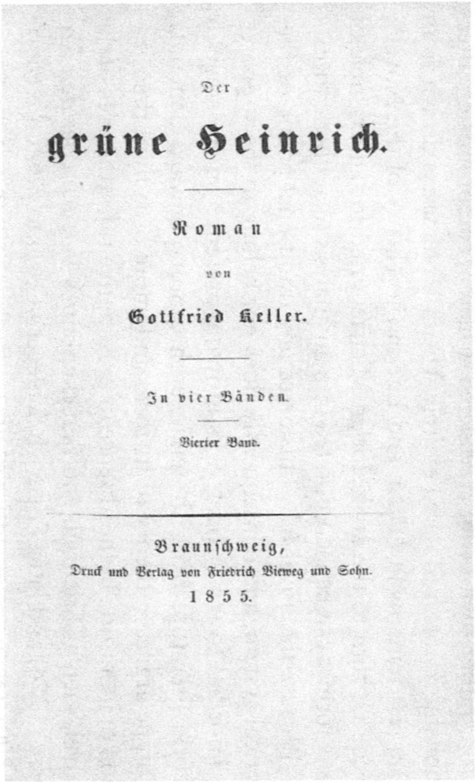

Der
grüne Heinrich.

Roman
von
Gottfried Keller.

In vier Bänden.

Vierter Band.

Braunschweig,
1855.

Druck und Verlag von Friedrich Vieweg und Sohn.

Figure 2. (*continued*)

task of representation, imaginatively responds to the process of production and the specifications of format. Yet before I detail how narrative form responds to format in *Der grüne Heinrich*, I would like to introduce two theoretical premises that explain why format should be incorporated as a generative element into accounts of a novel's form, rather than being considered a merely compromising afterthought, if not overlooked entirely. The first premise is drawn from Campe's remarks in "Form and Life in the Theory of the Novel"; second, I turn to the art historian Michael Fried for an example of how format can be incorporated into an analysis of aesthetic form.

Because the novel falls outside of any traditional poetic or rhetorical system, and consequently does not belong to the supposed primordial forms of poetry, its growing presence on the stage of world literature from the eighteenth century onward demands, Campe argues, a theory of its form and, more broadly, a theorization of literature. In the absence of prescriptive rules, theories of the novel, such as Friedrich von Blanckenburg's *Versuch über den Roman* (1774) and later Friedrich Schlegel's *Gespräch über die Poesie* (1800), rely on a semantics of life to describe the form of the genre. The novel is postulated as the lively and vivid presentation of its protagonist's vita and bios; its form is nothing other than a form of life conceived of as a simultaneously social and biological entity. Yet for each of the theories of the novel Campe excavates, the form-giving process is a precarious one that is as likely to fail as it is to succeed (which is why theories of the novel typically only provide at most a single, exceptional example of its success). Being a lawless and precarious undertaking, the novel compensates for its formlessness by incorporating smaller, better-defined poetical forms, resulting in a "genre-monster." Similarly, any theory of the novel must draw on myriad discursive resources for the purposes of theorization; it is, as Campe writes, "ultimately a theory of something other than poetical forms," for one, a theory of life.[19]

Eduard Vieweg, on May 3, 1850, and the way in which the novel's beginning and end mirror one another as evidence for the well-defined contours of Keller's early idea of the novel.

19. Campe, "Form and Life," 55.

In this vein Campe makes a note in passing that deserves sustained reflection, namely, that a theory of the novel as a form of life is always also a theory of its medium: "Thus the novel exists only through and as theory; and this theory then is a theory of something other than poetical forms. It is a theory of literature, culture, and media, or, as Schlegel himself claims, the novel's theory is the art of life."[20] Taking Campe's aside seriously means adopting a media-theoretical perspective when exploring the novel's form-giving process. It alerts us to the potential significance of format as the specific configuration of a medium in accounting for how a novel gives form to life. For one, that perspective compels us to appreciate, as Carlos Spoerhase's *Das Format der Literatur* has recently done at great length, how the medium of the novel is not an invariable constant, not merely "a book"; rather, the medium of the "book" encompasses a wide variety of formats with potential consequences for the way in which a novel gives form to life.[21]

It is perhaps unsurprising that the discipline of art history, for which the question of picture format has always been central, provides an example of how the specific configurations of media can and should be incorporated into a description of a form-giving process. Fried elaborates such an account when interpreting works from the 1960s by the American painters Kenneth Noland and Frank Stella. For the first time in the history of painting, Noland and Stella made shape a central concern in the project of painting. In Noland's and Stella's painting, shape becomes a medium in which painting demands and holds our attention; it becomes "capable of [. . .] compelling conviction."[22] For the purposes of his analysis, Fried differentiates between "literal shape," the shape or format of the canvas, and "depicted shape," the shape painted and pictured on the canvas. The form of a painting, as Fried argues in his powerful reading of Stella's *Moultonboro III* (1966), emerges from the relationship of the literal

---

20. Campe, "Form and Life," 55.
21. See Carlos Spoerhase, *Das Format der Literatur: Praktiken materieller Textualität zwischen 1740 und 1830* (Göttingen: Wallstein, 2018), 9.
22. Michael Fried, "Shape as Form: Frank Stella's Irregular Polygons," in *Art and Objecthood: Essays and Reviews* (Chicago: University of Chicago Press, 1998), 78.

shape to the depicted shape, between the shape of the canvas and the image, whose interplay in this specific painting gives rise to what Fried calls the Z form, a form identical with neither the picture format nor the image but emergent from the interplay between the two.[23]

Fried's claim that the material format, the "literal shape," is operative in how the painting *Moultonboro III* establishes its form provides an example of what it might mean to consider a media format, in this case the specific shape and dimensions of the canvas onto which the paint is applied, as a motivating force of the form-giving process, that is, as activating aesthetic representation. Fried's proposal effectively elaborates the very etymology of the term *format*, derived from the Latin *formare* and its participle, *formatum*; *format* is a forming of something or something that has been formed, making it only natural to consider format as an aspect of a novel's way of giving form to life.[24] In this spirit, my reading of *Der grüne Heinrich* aims to show that format becomes a point of irritation, occasioning the formlessness or "knitted-sock form" that bedeviled Keller for years to come and eliciting a narrative negotiation of the relationship between form and format. It is not my intention to obscure the important differences between the media of painting and those of literature since, as we know at least since Gotthold Ephraim Lessing, poetry and literature rely on a different semiotic system than pictorial media, one in which it would be difficult to identify equivalent aspects to literal and depicted shapes. Nor do I wish to obscure the excellent scholarship that has given attention to the question of format and book media. As Ernst Robert Curtius's *European Literature and the Latin Middle Ages* reminds us, Western literature is inseparable from perceptions of the material book as a deeply symbolic, if not sacred, object.[25] Or, as innumerable histori-

---

23. See Fried, "Shape as Form," 94.
24. See Michael Niehaus, *Was ist ein Format?* (Hannover: Wehrhahn, 2018), 9.
25. See Ernst Robert Curtius, *European Literature and the Latin Middle Ages*, trans. Willard R. Trask (Princeton, NJ: Princeton University Press, 2013), 302–47. Curtius's survey of book metaphors from antiquity to German Romanticism emphasizes that these metaphors, such as the book of nature or the book of life, reflect the cultural value and sacredness of the book. He concludes by citing Keller's poem "Aus dem Leben" (1849) as evidence of the enduring currency of

ans of print have elucidated over the past years, the dominance of the novel in the past two centuries of Western literature lies not simply in the emergence of a bourgeois class that sees its way of life and values, foremost its concern with the conflict between individualization and socialization, reflected in novelistic plots but also in the evolution of print technologies that made this genre so widely accessible as a book object. The novel's claim to give form to life has always depended both on the symbolic value of the material book and on its accessibility as an increasingly affordable media object.

My reading of *Der grüne Heinrich* argues that just as the ability of the novel to give form to life typically relies on the symbolic value of the medium of the book as embodying an autonomous entity, so too does the perceived failure of *Der grüne Heinrich* to achieve a form reside, for one, in its fractured format. If, as Andrew Piper writes, "the printed book's physical boundedness and typographical regularity became perfect embodiments of temporal continuity and spatial autonomy on which both the modern subject (as an individual) and the political form of the nation were to be founded,"[26] then the fractured four-part format of *Der grüne Heinrich* becomes a point of crisis for the form of the novel and the form of an individual's life it must establish. This fracture of format, in the encompassing sense in which I employ the term, penetrates and threatens the integrity of Heinrich's form of life and the novel's form as well. In response, the plot negotiates the relationship between print formats and the representation of a unified life within the protagonist's life story and its rich allegorical imagery.

Form and Format: *Der grüne Heinrich*

The crisis of disintegrative form that plagued the making and history of *Der grüne Henrich* and penetrated its plot has its origin in

---

these metaphors. Keller's characterization of Heinrich's bound *Jugendgeschichte* as Heinrich's *Lebensbuch* is yet a further example.

26. Andrew Piper, *Dreaming in Books: The Making of the Bibliographic Imagination in the Romantic Age* (Chicago: Chicago University Press, 2009), 13–14.

the specific production history of the novel and in the very medium of the book as well. Constitutive of the medium of the book—and very much at odds with the "singularity and indivisibility" it is meant to embody—is its easy reproducibility and ensuing plurality, which allows it to be dispersed across space and time;[27] the fact, in other words, that the literary work, as Raimar Zons writes, "does not have a material original but is rather reproduction through and through."[28] While the bound body of a book has the potential to embody or stand in for a modern subject, as Piper argues, the same object is always characterized by an inherent instability deriving from its mass reproduction. That plurality compels the question of wherein its self-sameness or identity might be rooted, whether it be the author, the text, the sameness of format, or a more difficult to define notion of the work.[29] What guarantees the identity of different copies or different editions of the "same" book? In *The Archaeology of Knowledge*, Michel Foucault compellingly articulates this problem, which might be summarized as the metaphysical identity of the book (although Foucault's immediate concern is less with the identity of the book than with the identity of a statement). Beginning with the observation that a statement must be manifested in a material form, Foucault writes:

---

27. Piper, *Dreaming in Books*, 14.

28. Raimar Stefan Zons, "Über den Ursprung des literarischen Werks aus dem Geist der Autorschaft," in *Kolloquium Kunst und Philosophie*, ed. Willi Oelmüller, vol. 3 (Paderborn: Ferdinand Schöningh, 1983), 116.

29. For a recent account of the ontology of the literary work, see Amie L. Thomasson, "Die Ontologie literarischer Werke," in *Das Werk: Zum Verschwinden und Fortwirken eines Grundbegriffs*, ed. Lutz Danneberg, Annette Gilbert, and Carlos Spoerhase (Berlin: Walter de Gruyter, 2019), 29–46, esp. 37. Thomasson adopts the thesis from Roman Ingarden's *Das literarische Kunstwerk* (1931) that the work is neither a physical nor an ideal object but instead an intentional object. As such, the work is something that persists through time and depends on but is not identical to a material object (e.g., the bound book). It is created by an artist (or author) under specific historical conditions, which also stipulate the terms of its identity. Michael Cahn calls attention to the same problem with regard to collected-works editions: If the texts in such an edition are the same as in earlier publications, why attribute exceptional philological or symbolic value to these editions? See Michael Cahn, "*Opera omnia*: The Production of Cultural Authority," in *History of Science, History of Text*, ed. Karine Chemla (Dordrecht: Springer, 2004), 81–94, esp. 85.

A text reproduced several times, the successive editions of a book, or, better still, the different copies of the same printing, do not give rise to the same number of distinct statements: in all the editions of *Les Fleurs du mal* (variants and rejected versions apart), we find the same set of statements; yet neither the characters, nor the ink, nor the paper, nor even the placing of the text and the positions of the signs, are the same: the whole texture of materiality has changed. But in this case these "small" differences are not important enough to alter the identity of the statement and to bring about another: they are all neutralized in the general element—material, of course, but also institutional and economic—of the "book": a book, however many copies or editions are made of it, however many different substances it may use, is a locus of exact equivalence for the statements—for them it is an authority that permits repetition without any change of identity.[30]

Foucault's analysis seemingly displaces (rather than resolves) the problem of the identity of a book onto the identity of the statement that we identify as being the same, allowing for what we deem insignificant differences including glitches in printing, the variations that arise from use, and, more fundamentally, the multiplicity of individual copies. But in doing so, he calls attention to the fundamental instability of a book's identity, the many dimensions of difference that are inscribed into its avowed sameness.

---

30. Michel Foucault, *The Archaeology of Knowledge and the Discourse on Language*, trans. A. M. Sheridan Smith (New York: Pantheon Books, 1972), 102. In an earlier chapter, Foucault raises the question of the identity of a book and of an oeuvre more generally, arguing that neither can be identified with the material object because the text is embedded within and references plural discourses:
> The material unity of the book? [...] The frontiers of a book are never clear-cut: beyond the title, the first lines, and the last full stop, beyond its internal configuration and its autonomous form, it is caught up in a system of references to other books, other texts, other sentences: it is a node within a network. [...] The book is not simply the object that one holds in one's hands; and it cannot remain within the little parallelepiped that contains it: its unity is variable and relative. As soon as one questions that unity, it loses its self-evidence; it indicates itself, constructs itself, only on the basis of a complex field of discourse. (23)

Instead of problematizing the identity of a work or oeuvre with reference to a "complex field of discourse"—a problem that has been the subject of the vast work on intertextuality—I want to address how the book itself as a material, plural object insufficiently stabilizes the metaphysical identity of a work or oeuvre.

While the problem of the identity of a book across multiple nonidentical objects is constitutive of the medium and thus typically ignored, the drawn-out publishing history and particular publishing formats of *Der grüne Heinrich* exacerbate the potential sense of dispersal and disunity, forcing this problem to the fore. *Der grüne Heinrich*, a title I understand as referring to a work whose identity is up for debate, experiences fracture at numerous sites. While those sites of fracture are not untypical for the media culture of the mid-nineteenth century—indeed, *Der grüne Heinrich* is perhaps of particular interest because it reflects conventional publishing practices—their profusion and the way in which they plagued Keller to the point of crisis are unique to the novel. Among these dissimilar sites of fracture are (a) the "divided form" issuing from the tandem narrative voices; (b) the publication of the first edition of the novel in four separate volumes, the first three volumes being printed and sold by the Leipzig publisher Vieweg and Söhne starting in 1853 and the fourth, lengthiest volume beginning in 1855. The breaks between these volumes are discontinuous with the breaks between the frame story and the childhood memoir (between, in other words, the parts written in the third and first person) such that the childhood memoir begins partway through the first volume and concludes partway through the third. The sense of fracture to the point of crisis might well have been eased had the breaks in diegesis and the divisions between volumes coincided.

To these two sites are added (c) the three further editions of the novel published during Keller's lifetime. First, Keller rewrote the entire novel from the first-person perspective for publication twenty-five years after the first edition, a process intended to heal the initial edition's divided form. Faced with the proliferations of nonidentical texts bearing the title *Der grüne Heinrich*, Keller designated the revised novel not as a second edition but as a "new edition" so as to insist that it replaced and effaced, rather than followed, the first. This "new edition" appeared between 1879 and 1880 with Weibert Verlag in Stuttgart (this time in three volumes); a third edition (based on the second and consisting primarily of orthographic revisions) appeared in 1884. Its name retrospectively casts the "new" edition as merely the second edition. And finally, a fourth edition appeared as part of Keller's collected works in 1889 with Hertz Verlag in Berlin. While republishing texts in multiple editions belongs to the standard marketing strategies of the nineteenth century, the multiplicity and divergence of the editions and volumes published under the same title engendered headaches for Keller and his readers alike. For one, the multiplicity of editions overtly undermined the selfsameness of the text and the work, raising for perpetuity the question of the definitive authoritative version of the novel.[31]

While today's Keller scholarship remains divided on this question, Keller's commitment to the second edition was unequivocal. The specific measures he took to resolve the matter definitively on the occasion of the publication of the "Neue Ausgabe" point to the destabilized relationship between the identity of the work and the materiality of the plural book object. Since the terms (stated in his correspondence, which took the place of a never-drafted book contract) with Vieweg, the publisher of the first edition, stipulated that all the copies of the first edition had to be sold before a second edition could be issued, Keller was compelled to purchase the hundred remaining unsold and incomplete copies of the first edition of his novel at the cost of 625 German marks (the copies were incomplete because, returning to the first site of fracture issuing from the publishing formats, it was largely the fourth volume of the novel that had remained unsold). To make way for the second edition and to resolve the question of the authoritative version, Keller proceeded to systematically destroy those copies of the first edition he had purchased in an act of auto-da-fé, as he had previously imagined, one should note, in at least two scenes of *Der grüne Heinrich* and in his earliest volumes of poetry as well.[32] Keller gave the purchased

---

31. Two divergent answers to the question of how to resolve the relation of the first and second editions demonstrate that the problem still persists. One paradigmatic answer is to deem each edition a separate work, as Müller does when he calls the first and second editions "two works, each in their own right." Müller, "*Der grüne Heinrich*," 40. Taking a rather different approach to the identity of the work, Walter Morgenthaler argues "that it's a matter of two different articulations of *one* work." Walter Morgenthaler, "Die *Grünen Heinriche*: Zur Text- und Überlieferungsgeschichte eines Romans," in Groddeck, "*Der grüne Heinrich*," 11.

32. See Jan Behrs, "Manuskripte brennen (nicht): Nachlassbewusstsein bei Gottfried Keller," in *Nachlassbewusstsein: Literatur, Archiv, Philologie, 1750–2000*, ed. Kai Sina and Carlos Spoerhase (Göttingen: Wallstein, 2017), 294–312.

remaining volumes of *Der grüne Heinrich* to his sister, Regula Keller, with the instruction to use them as fuel in the family stove. This is a dramatic scene of what in German is termed *Nachlassverwaltung*, "literary-estate management," the ways in which authors vie to dictate which texts will be attributed to them posthumously. In Keller's case, the destructive handling of these remaining print copies discloses the degree of irritation the material books posed to Keller's vision of a selfsame *Grüner Heinrich*. Keller perceived their obliteration in this incendiary act to be a necessary condition for establishing the definitive authority of the second edition. He hoped that even after his death, only the latter editions of *Der grüne Heinrich* would be reprinted, a desire that was in fact respected until the 1985 edition of Keller's oeuvre, so for nearly a hundred years.

Yet in defiance of these efforts, Keller's friends and critics began to undertake, much to his distress, careful comparisons between the first and second editions upon the publication of the second edition in 1879 and 1880—a practice that is still at the core of today's scholarship on *Der grüne Heinrich*.[33] Despite his best efforts, Keller was forced to confront the inefficacy of his maneuvers to resolve the question of the authoritative text for the remainder of his life: First two, and ultimately four editions remained in circulation and competed for readership. As he complained, the first edition was regularly excavated in a macabre show, often for the purpose of illustrating how not to write a novel. In a letter to Marie von Frisch-Exner, Keller complains:

> Now come the so-called critics, and instead of judging the current book on its own merits, they compare it philologically with the old one to exhibit their methods and thus drag around the dead and do not touch the living, for they never understand it. It is rather like burying an old pug in the garden, and the neighbors come at night, dig it out again, and lay the poor monster at one's door, and so on.
>
> Nun kommen die sog. Kritiker und anstatt das jetzige Buch aus sich heraus zu beurtheilen, vergleichen sie es in philologischer Weise mit dem

---

33. For example, current online editions are explicitly formatted for the purpose of comparing the texts from 1853–1855 and 1879–1880. See "*Der grüne Heinrich* (beide Fassungen parallel)," Gottfried Keller, Universität Zürich, accessed July 26, 2023, https://www.gottfriedkeller.ch/GH/GH_Parallel.htm.

alten, um ihre Methode zu zeigen, und zerren so das Abgestorbene herum und lassen das Lebendige liegen, denn das verstehen sie ja niemals. Er ist ungefähr die Situation, wie wenn man im Garten einen alten Mops begräbt, und es kommen nächtlicher Weise die Nachbaren, graben ihn wieder heraus und legen das arme Scheusal Einem vor die Hausthür u. s. w.[34]

By burning the first edition to make way for the second, Keller had, so to speak, declared the dog dead and obsolete and wished to expunge it from public memory. Yet by comparing the two editions of the novel, Keller's critics exhumed it through philological practice and permitted it to retain some degree of poetic authority. As will become evident in chapter 2, the morbid imagery of the excavated canine corpse is in no way arbitrary and reflects Keller's conception of authorship and a literary work as a posthumous achievement. For the moment, my point is that Keller could not effectively efface the first edition from the history of *Der grüne Heinrich*, for which reason it continued to pose an uncanny threat to the desired self-identity of the work.

However, the achievement of a self-identical work was not merely imperiled in the transition from the first to the second edition. The crisis of disintegration initiated at a historically earlier point of fracture, during the publishing process of the very first edition. The relevant facts are well recorded in the correspondence between Keller and his Leipzig publisher and, if nothing else, help situate Keller in the media culture of his time. On December 10, 1849, Vieweg and Söhne agreed to publish the novel after Keller confidently assured Eduard Vieweg that the manuscript was nearing completion and could be submitted in two weeks' time. In matter of fact, although Keller had intended to write a loosely autobiographical novel at least since 1847, precious little text had been drafted when he entered into the agreement with Vieweg. As a result, Keller was continually unable to deliver the manuscript sheets promised, a situation greatly exacerbated by Keller's lifelong procrastination habits and unrealistic if not duplicitous promises to send them soon. To make matters worse, his concurrent escalating debts compelled him to turn his attention to

---

34. Keller to Marie von Frisch-Exner, November 21, 1880, in *HKKA*, 19:442.

additional projects, including republishing his earliest volume of poetry and outlining the novella cycle that would be published as *Die Leute von Seldwyla*. Years later Keller would claim that if only he had had the financial means to support himself while writing and to cover the costs of printing himself, he could have composed a coherent whole.[35] Instead, starting in May 1850, Keller received advanced payments for the manuscript he had promised and could not deliver. It is worth noting that the payments, as typical of contemporaneous publishing arrangements, were calculated per *Bogen* (per full sheet of paper, which would be folded and cut into sixteen pages of text in an octavo), providing Keller with a financial incentive to write a longer book than he originally intended—as indeed he did.[36] For the next

---

35. For example, Keller writes to his publisher Vieweg:
If I had had the means during the whole undertaking of this book, I would have had it reprinted before the first three volumes were published; for that is the reason for the whole misfortune that I had to write the first work of this kind in advance, and since everything was immediately printed, due to my clumsy and inexperienced arrangement, I could not change a single line. Had I been able to assess the whole at the end and delete at will, the cost of a new printing would have very probably been worthwhile.

Hätte ich während des ganzen Verlaufes dieses Buches die Mittel gehabt, so würde ich dasselbe schon vor Erscheinen der 3 ersten Bände haben umdrucken lassen; denn hierin liegt das ganze Mißgeschick, daß ich die erste Arbeit dieser Art vorweg schreiben mußte und, da Alles gleich gedruckt wurde, in Folge meiner ungeschickten und unerfahrnen Anordnung, nicht eine Zeile mehr abändern konnte. Hätte ich das Ganze am Schluss übersehen und beliebig streichen können, so hätten sich die Kosten eines neuen Druckes sehr wahrscheinlich rentirt.

Keller to Eduard Vieweg, May 3, 1856, in *HKKA*, 19:311. While most Keller scholars express sympathy for Keller's seeming enslavement to rigid publishing conditions, I am more inclined to regard Vieweg's demands as having enabled the composition of the novel at all.

36. Keller envisioned a novel of twenty-five full sheets in length, less than a fourth of the final 107 full sheets: "I am currently working on drafting a small novel that will be about twenty-five sheets long, so I am already in the process of looking for a publisher" (Gegenwärtig beschäftige ich mich mit der Ausarbeitung eines kleinen Romanes, der etwa 25 Bogen stark werden wird, und bin also im Falle mich bereits nach einem Herren Verleger umzusehen). Keller to F. A. Brockhaus [Heinrich Brockhaus], January 4, 1849, in *HKKA*, 19:158. To Vieweg he first proposed a novel of 430 to 440 octavo pages that would be complete in two weeks. See Keller to Eduard Vieweg, December 10, 1849, and February 28, 1850, in *HKKA*, 19:166, 167–68.

six years until 1855, Vieweg waited for the repeatedly promised manuscript pages and hounded Keller in an increasingly acrimonious exchange of letters, in which the publisher appealed to the original agreement, to Keller's honor, to the capital and interest that he was losing on account of being unable to sell the novel in its entirety, and, finally, to the aesthetic argument that artworks cannot tolerate interruptions. In Vieweg's words: "The impression of the artwork must not be torn apart by long interruptions."[37] The dispute intensified at two points in the eight-year ordeal when Vieweg threatened to sue Keller for financial damages as a result of his inability to complete the novel and to hold hostage manuscript pages of Die Leute von Seldwyla that Keller had submitted for Vieweg's review in the hopes of coming to a further publishing agreement.[38]

To compound Keller's problems, as he completed pages of the manuscript, he mailed them to Leipzig, where they were immediately typeset and returned to him for corrections. The periodic deliveries of pages to Vieweg are well documented.[39] Because Keller hoped to complete the novel quickly, he permitted Vieweg to print

---

On the *Bogen* as the primary unit for measuring literary manuscripts and mediating publishing processes, see Carlos Spoerhase, "Poetic Creativity from Material Constraints: On Goethe's West-Eastern Divan," in *Goethes Spätwerk/On Late Goethe*, ed. David E. Wellbery and Kai Sina (Berlin: Walter de Gruyter, 2020), 141–56.

37. Eduard Vieweg to Keller, June 13, 1853, in *HKKA*, 19:244. Throughout his exchange with Vieweg, as throughout his publishing life, the fact that Keller considered writing too laborious to make copies of texts and did not possess the means to pay a scribe to complete such copies for him meant that he relied on the goodwill of his epistolary contacts (and the postal service) to return to him the single extant copies of his manuscripts.

38. Keller accuses Vieweg of holding the novellas hostage in Keller to Eduard Vieweg, July 31, 1854, in *HKKA*, 19:274–76. Vieweg threatens to sue Keller in Eduard Vieweg to Keller, June 12, 1852, in *HKKA*, 19:223–24, and again in Eduard Vieweg to Keller, October 23, 1854, in *HKKA*, 19:281–83.

39. On the dates of Keller's deliveries of manuscript pages to Vieweg, see the detailed chart in Stocker, Morgenthaler, Binder, Grob, and Müller, "*Der grüne Heinrich*: Entstehung und Publikation," in *HKKA*, 19:36. For a more extended account of Keller's frustrations with the publishing process on account of being unable to make changes to earlier portions of the text, see Morgenthaler, "Die *Grünen Heinriche*." Morgenthaler, who generally portrays Vieweg as the antagonist in the novel's publishing history, claims that these earlier portions of the manuscript were printed without Keller's explicit consent.

the manuscript incrementally—a procedure that generally expedited typesetting and printing, while also reducing the quantity of type needed—and to sell the first three volumes in 1853, even though he had yet to begin drafting the fourth. This publishing process bore two significant consequences for Keller's composition of the novel. First, immediately mailing pages to Vieweg for typesetting meant that Keller at no point possessed a complete manuscript of even a single volume, let alone of the novel as a whole, for which reason he had to write subsequent sections of the novel without having the earlier portions available to refer to. Years later, when completing the first volume of *Die Leute von Seldwyla*, Keller bemoans having never possessed a complete manuscript of his novel, having always been compelled to submit texts piece by piece: "I wish to keep them in my hands until the end so as to be able to go through the finished manuscript at the end for once, which I have never had the possibility of doing because of my own stupidity and which gave me some grief in the case of the novel."[40] Second, since the pages were set and printed as soon as they were received, and, beginning in 1853, also sold, Keller could not make revisions to earlier portions of the manuscript in light of later developments. So even before the novel was printed, bound, and distributed in book form, it had disintegrated into both geographically and temporally distant parts, a state of fracture greatly exacerbated once the first three volumes were on the market. For Vieweg, in contrast, both printing incrementally and in the popular multivolume format were distinctly profitable. The multivolume format, for one, promised higher profits both because it allowed him to start selling the novel before it was completed and because smaller volumes sold more easily to lending libraries (which, in turn, preferred multiple smaller volumes that could be circulated individually), his primary customers for fiction.

For Keller, conversely, the temporally and spatially dispersed status of the manuscript while writing and then across the four vol-

---

40. "Ich wünsche sie bis zum Schluß in der Hand behalten zu können, um ein Mal ein ganz fertiges Manuskript am Ende nochmals durchgehen zu können, was mir bis jetzt wegen meiner eigenen Dummheit noch nie vergönnt war und namentlich bei dem Romane manche Uebelstände herbeiführte." Keller to Eduard Vieweg, November 9, 1858, in *HKKA*, 23.1:333.

umes of the first edition engendered a profound crisis concerning the identity of the work, a crisis that he would continually return to—for example, when burning the copies of the first edition in his possession so as to establish the primacy of the second edition—but could not definitely resolve. Petra McGillen's observation regarding nineteenth-century periodical publishing that "for authors, this scattered mode of publication made it harder to be perceived as autonomous entities" holds true for Keller's book publishing as well.[41] From his perspective, there was no perspicacious standpoint from which he could perceive the materially divided parts of the novel as belonging to the same whole, as constituting a single work by a single author. For example, while attempting to complete the long overdue fourth volume of the novel in 1854, Keller describes the fragmented state of the text, each part having originated at different points in time and much of it now inaccessible to him on account of his handwriting being illegible even to himself. In this vein, he laments to Vieweg: "The manuscript of my novel consists of notebooks, sheets, and fragments of the most various kinds. Much of it was already written four years ago, some one year ago, and I myself have difficulty reading some of it."[42]

Retrospectively, Keller holds the physical dispersal of the manuscript and the incremental publishing process accountable not only for his difficulties completing the novel but also for the diegetic events that his moralizing commentators would later fault him for, including Heinrich's erotic encounters with Judith and his failure to return home prior to his mother's death. In a letter to Emil Kuh, one of these sympathetic though narrow-minded commentators, Keller revisits the fracture of the novel across chapters and pages, printed and

---

41. Petra S. McGillen, *The Fontane Workshop: Manufacturing Realism in the Industrial Age of Print* (London: Bloomsbury Academic, 2019), 56. In this context McGillen cites Jean Paul's lament that he had splintered himself across his magazine publications, a sentiment at the core of Keller's perception of the authorship of his first novel as well.

42. "Das Manuskript meines Romanes besteht aus Heften, Bogen und Fragmenten der verschiedensten Art. Vieles ist schon vor vier Jahren geschrieben, Anderes vor Einem und ich habe selbst Mühe, Manches zu lesen." Keller to Eduard Vieweg, January 24, 1851, in *HKKA*, 19:195.

unprinted, and compares the work to an unfinished drawing that displays the many smudges of the drawing process. To Kuh he summarizes the frustrations of the writing process:

> The book's misfortune lies in the way it was produced. The publisher began to print as soon as he had some of the manuscript; I nevertheless continued slowly but had to send off everything I had written immediately and so was literally almost never able to look over the finished chapters and pages a second time; that is why there remain a lot of tasteless and tactless things that one usually discovers and removes on a second or rather first rereading. The opus thus resembles a drawing in which in addition to the last pen strokes, all the initial charcoal and pencil strokes can still be seen side by side, and even the working hand's spoiling and dirtying of the paper remains visible.
>
> Das Unglück des Buches liegt in seiner Entstehungsweise. Der Verleger fing gleich an zu drucken, als er etwas Manuskript hatte; ich fuhr dennoch langsam fort, mußte aber dafür alles Geschriebene sofort absenden u konnte so buchstäblich die fertigen Kapitel u Seiten fast nie zum zweiten Mal übersehen; so blieben eine Menge Geschmack- u Taktlosigkeiten stehen, die man schon bei einer zweiten oder vielmehr ersten Wiederlesung zu entdecken u beseitigen pflegt. So gleicht das Opus einer Zeichnung, auf welcher neben den letzten Federstrichen noch alle anfänglichen Kohlen- u Bleistiftstriche nebeneinander zu sehen sind, ja sogar noch der Verderb u Schmutz des Papieres durch die arbeitende Hand haftet.[43]

To Keller's mind, the developments of the plot that met with the disfavor of even his most sympathetic critics were tantamount to residue arising from the stress of the writing process. The writing process had smudged and tainted the moral and didactic clarity and objectivity to which the story had aspired. In my view, Keller is correct in his assessment that the publishing process left its mark on the novel's plot, yet incorrect as to how. The crisis of fracture experienced in the novel's publishing history and visible in its format is in fact negotiated as a problem of the protagonist's identity as a cohering subject.

---

43. Keller to Emil Kuh, April 3, 1871, in *HKKA*, 19:330.

The Fracture of the Self

Throughout the history of modern European publishing, the question of a work's identity has been most immediately addressed in discourses of copyright law. The emergence of copyright law in the eighteenth century turned—as Heinrich Bosse, Martha Woodmansee, and others have articulated—on the question of wherein or whereby the identity of a text is to be situated and whose property it constitutes.[44] When transitioning from an age in which the writer was, at best, an inspired craftsman who benefited from a system of patronage to a modern age of copyright (*Urheberrecht*), eighteenth-century Prussia came to the consensus that the identity of a book resides in the "spirit of the author."[45] Bosse summarizes the transition from an earlier model he glosses as the metaphysical identity of the book to a more modern emphasis on the spirit of the author, who is represented in the work and whose presence conjoins its material and immaterial properties (as book and form, as text and idea) as follows: "In place of the metaphysical identity, the personal spirit of the author now provides the handwritten-spiritual, material-immaterial identity of his work, in which he is depicted and which can represent him."[46] Packed into that transition, of course, are claims that relate to the emergent notion of authorship, the contours of which Keller was still negotiating decades later.[47]

---

44. See Heinrich Bosse, *Autorschaft ist Werkherrschaft: Über die Entstehung des Urheberrechts aus dem Geist der Goethezeit* (Paderborn: Wilhelm Fink, 2014); and Martha Woodmansee, *The Author, Art, and the Market: Rereading the History of Aesthetics* (New York: Columbia University Press, 1994). In his history of authorship, Mark Rose makes the question of property rights central, arguing that discourses of originality only developed in conjunction with the emergence of the theorization of property and ownership. According to Rose, notions of singularity and originality motivate authors' claims as the proprietors of their texts. Mark Rose, "The Author as Proprietor: *Donaldson v. Becket* and the Genealogy of Modern Authorship," *Representations* 23 (Summer 1988): 54.

45. Bosse, *Autorschaft ist Werkherrschaft*, 24.

46. Bosse, *Autorschaft ist Werkherrschaft*, 106. Bosse additionally formulates the central argument as follows: "The author is present in all the print formats of his book, endowing them with unity" (55).

47. I would argue, for example, that Keller relates to the publisher Vieweg as a potential patron, one who would pay him lump sums in advance for unwritten

They include the idea of an author as a uniquely creative individual (or genius), whose person is represented in what he or she writes; in Johann Gottlieb Fichte's poignant formulation, the book constitutes an "imprint" of the author.[48]

The proposal that the spirit of the author underwrites the identity of the textual work is premised on the exclusion of diverse other participants in production and distribution as well as participants in the communicative relay the work is meant to establish. Excluded from laying claim to works as their property are publishers and printers, both those of original editions and those who may wish to print copies (*Nachdrucke*), including pirated ones, as well as the public. If texts, or at least the ideas they contain, were considered the property of a public domain, then authors would be in no position to exert any specific privilege (financial or otherwise) on the texts they had written. Hence, with the emergence of the modern author as "peculiarly responsible for the finished product (the book)," publishers and the public surrendered their rights to the text.[49] In effect, Keller operates in a discourse of authorship in which he supposedly bears sole responsibility for the generation of a text and in which his spirit (*Geist*) underwrites the identity of a work in its materially dispersed state (rather than, for example, the identity of the statement to which Foucault points us). This vision of the author as underwriting the identity of the work—a work that can be materialized in plural media objects—is central to Keller's perception of the formlessness of his novel and how it might, in an alternative publishing format, be overcome.

---

texts, rather than as a modern-day publisher, who pays for the rights to print an already drafted manuscript. At the onset of writing *Der grüne Heinrich*, Keller also benefited from a modern-day patronage system, namely, state support in the form of a grant from the canton of Zurich. Keller's authorship is thus an example of the long transition, indeed coexistence, of patronage and copyright models.

48. See Martha Woodmansee, "The Genius and the Copyright: Economic and Legal Conditions of the Emergence of the 'Author,'" in "The Printed Word in the Eighteenth Century," ed. Raymond Birn, special issue, *Eighteenth-Century Studies* 17, no. 4 (Summer 1984): 447.

49. Woodmansee, "The Genius and the Copyright," 442.

Why then could Keller not assuage his worries about the identity of *Der grüne Heinrich*, fractured over the time of its making and in its four-volume print format, with the assurance provided by authorship discourses and contemporaneous copyright law that its identity resided in his own person? In the case of *Der grüne Heinrich*, the spirit of the author should have sufficed to underwrite the selfsameness of the text despite the dispersal effected by its format and the temporally distanced editions (and reprints) as well; in other words, it should have sufficed to compensate for the dispersal of the book as a plural object over time and space. To summarize the answer: For Keller, the identity of the author could not compensate for the state of fracture because he perceived the author and the protagonist, and consequently the novel, to have failed to maintain their identity over time. The fractured format undermined Keller's very sense of himself as a self-identical author who could stabilize the identity of the multiple volumes and editions in a single work. As early as 1851, at which point the manuscript had hardly taken shape, yet the first volume had already begun to be printed, Keller writes, "My old undying novel, *Der grüne Heinrich*, has finally progressed to the point where the first volume is printed. [...] I have only rarely been working on writing the book, which has in the meantime become a quite different one from what was originally planned."[50] Just as the work (Keller speaks of the "book") had become something else during the time of writing, so

---

50. "Mein alter unsterblicher Roman, der grüne Heinrich, ist endlich soweit gediehen, daß der erste Band gedruckt ist. [...] Ich habe nur selten an dem Buche, welches indessen ein ganz Anderes, als das ursprünglich angelegte, geworden ist, geschrieben." Keller to Wilhelm Baumgartner, March 27–September 1851, in *HKKA*, 19:203. The very duration of this letter's drafting is itself sufficient to introduce the question of identity over time. In a very similar vein, three years prior, Keller had already lamented to Heinrich Brockhaus, the head of F. A. Brockhaus Verlag, that the interruptions in writing had caused the little book (note the diminutive) to become something different than it initially was: "My novel has experienced a long holdup, for in addition to the fact that I anyways write slowly and with frequent interruptions, I have experienced so much inside of me that the attitude of the little book has become totally different" (Mein Roman hat eine lange Stockung erfahren, denn außer dem, daß ich sonst langsam und mit öftern Unterbrechungen schreibe, habe ich hier innerlich so viel erlebt, daß die Haltung des Büchleins eine ganz andere

too had, from his perspective, the identity of the author changed over time. These concerns are voiced throughout Keller's correspondence with Vieweg, where he repeatedly worries whether he, the person writing the later parts of the novel, is the same person who had written the portions of the manuscript already published. From Keller's perspective, the protracted time of writing undermined the identity of the author and the identity of the protagonist as well.

The question whether the protagonist of the novel retains his identity over time is thematized throughout the diegesis. Both the first and the later editions of *Der grüne Heinrich* reflect at length on the identity of a work of literature in relation to its material status as a book and in relation to the answer given by Prussian copyright law that the selfsame identity of the "spirit of the author" guarantees the identity of the work among its print copies. The problem is initially posed in the already cited preface to the novel, where the author admits that the continuity of the linear script belies the changing nature of the author—a hazard the preface once again seeks to efface from view by means of drawing an analogy between the novel and the epistolary genre:

> One leaves the letter lying around through whole periods of time; in many ways, one becomes another person; but when one takes up what was written again, one continues exactly where one had left off, and even if the changes of life are revealed in what one emphasizes or keeps silent about, one still finds that one has remained the same in relation to the person the letter is addressed to and with regard to the matter.[51]

Such a problem of continuity is usually eclipsed from view since we typically posit, as Daniel Müller Nielaba rightly points out in his discussion of the novel, the narrator as a unified entity that precedes the narration rather than acknowledge the narrator as a precarious

---

geworden ist). Keller to F. A. Brockhaus [Heinrich Brockhaus], May 28, 1849, in *HKKA*, 19:164.

51. Keller, "Vorwort," in *Der grüne Heinrich* (1st ed., 1854–1855), in *HKKA*, 11:13.

construction that must arise from the process of narrating.[52] The peculiar description of Heinrich writing his autobiography in the final sentence of the childhood memoir in the first edition emphasizes that task of subject construction: "But from then on, my sole ambition was to cross the Rhine as soon as possible, and I wrote this for myself [mir diese Schrift geschrieben] to make the time pass more quickly until then."[53] The circuitous phrasing "mir diese Schrift geschrieben" announces an attempt to bind the writing self to the written text and anticipates the problem of identity construction between temporally distinct writing and reading selves.

The worry as to what acts as the stabilizing element within the nexus of author, work, and book also becomes a central crux of the protagonist's experience. For one, the differing narrative perspectives of the childhood memoir and frame narrative, which Keller faulted as the cause of the novel's formlessness, force the question of identity to the fore. In each edition, the protagonist reads the story of his youth, which is to say that he encounters his self in the format of a book. What bridges the reading self and the autobiographical self recorded in the book of the childhood memoir? What ensures that these two are one and the same person? The problem of bridging these two selves becomes particularly apparent in the novel's second edition at the same crucial juncture when the first-person narrator has just finished reading his autobiographical childhood memoir, which he intends to resume writing within the frame narrative. Heinrich muses: "What a long time it is since I wrote what is set down above. I am hardly the same person, my handwriting changed long ago, and yet it seems to me as if I were continuing to write now from

---

52. On the generation of the narrator through narration, Müller Nielaba writes, "This 'narrator' is obviously first generated by the narra*tion*, and by no means vice versa, as one would realistically otherwise like to believe." Daniel Müller Nielaba, "'Besser schreiben' gelernt—Heinrich Lees Erzähler," in Groddeck, *"Der grüne Heinrich,"* 83.

53. "Mein einziges Trachten ging aber von nun an dahin, so bald als möglich über den Rhein zu gelangen, und um mir bis dahin die Stunden zu verkürzen, habe ich mir diese Schrift geschrieben." Keller, *Der grüne Heinrich* (1st ed., 1854–1855), in *HKKA*, 12:105.

where I left off yesterday."[54] The passing of time during the author's life calls into question whether he possesses the authority to extend his text and whether he has the ability to do so as well, that is, whether the text of the childhood memoir belongs to a different self than he is now (i.e., Heinrich at age twenty-eight). The very duration of writing and the ongoing life of the fictional author threaten to undermine the selfsameness of the autobiographical author and text. While writing one's autobiography should serve as a performative act of establishing the unity and continuity of the self over time, in *Der grüne Heinrich* the practice instead reveals a destabilized self.[55]

It is worth noting that the scene of reading also records another drama of the novel's publishing history I mentioned earlier, namely, the fact that Keller was forced to discard early parts of his manuscript because he was unable to decipher his own handwriting. Here the difference in handwriting constitutes material evidence of the prodigious distance between a younger and an older self. At the same time, the format of the book offers the possibility of transcending these instabilities. The scene of writing is not only a reflection on past and present moments; it also anticipates a future in which the differences in handwriting and selves will be effaced through the medium of print. The more rigidly standardized medium of print, in other words, possesses the capacity to cast retrospectively the author and hence the work as self-identical over time. A standardized typography stabilizes the identity of the self.

---

54. "Wie lange ist es her, seit ich das Vorstehende geschrieben habe. Ich bin kaum derselbe Mensch, meine Handschrift hat sich längst verändert, und doch ist mir zu Mut, als führe ich jetzt fort zu schreiben, wo ich gestern stehen blieb." Gottfried Keller, *Green Henry*, trans. A. M. Holt, rev. ed. (London: Alma Classics, 2023), 301; Keller, *Der grüne Heinrich* (2nd ed., 1889), in *HKKA*, 2:93.

55. Contrary to my claims, Groddeck argues that the continuity of writing within the novel makes up for the interruptions in the time of writing: "Apparently, there is—that is how I understand this coincidence—a time of writing that has a different logic than the time of narration or even the narrated time of the novel itself. The gaps in time that open in every narrative are closed in the experience of writing." Groddeck, "Eine gewisse Unförmlichkeit," 36–37. I would argue that the scenes of writing in the novel also reveal breaks in the time of the protagonist's life and his sense of self, as marked, for example, in the difference in his handwriting.

While not printed, the bound manuscript of Heinrich's childhood memoir, which is described at length within the novel, becomes a totem-like object for stabilizing the identity of the protagonist. In both editions, Heinrich concludes his stay in Munich starving and destitute, having sold all his possessions, including his oeuvre of paintings. His only remaining possession, in whose company he makes the arduous and interrupted journey back home, is the book in which his childhood memoir is recorded, and for whose binding he spends his very last pennies: "The numerous sheets which I had written I took forthwith to a bookbinder to have them clothed in my personal colour, in the shape of green linen binding [. . .]. Instead of linen, he had used silk, he had gilded the edges and supplied metal clasps to close the book."[56] In the fourth volume of the novel recording Heinrich's perilous journey, the survival of the author becomes tied to the survival of that very book. Clothed in an expensive green silk dress, it serves as a metonymical substitute for its author and is repeatedly imperiled on the journey, being more sensitive to the elements than its author. In the episode preceding his arrival at the sanctuary of the Graf's home, for example, the book becomes soggy and threatens to disintegrate from the rain. Having been rescued by the Graf, Heinrich awakes to the scene of Dortchen drying its pages by the fire. She restores the autobiography and so equally restores its author. Indeed, in the fourth volume, the material book nearly replaces its author as the primary protagonist, a trajectory that is unsurprising when one considers that in the first edition, Heinrich is outlived by his book. Throughout the fourth volume (in the first and second editions), as in the scenes of reading and writing, it is the material existence of the book object, endowed with its totemic function, that is intended to guarantee the continuity of Heinrich's self—reversing and destabilizing a relationship whereby the identity of the author's self guarantees the identity of the work among plural media objects.

---

56. "Die vielen beschriebenen Blätter brachte ich unverweilt zu einem Buchbinder, um sie mittelst grüner Leinwand in meine Leibfarbe kleiden zu lassen [. . .]. Statt Leinwand hatte er Seidenstoff genommen, den Schnitt vergoldet und metallene Spangen zum Verschließen angebracht." Keller, *Green Henry*, 446; Keller, *Der grüne Heinrich* (2nd ed., 1889), in *HKKA*, 3:59–60.

Keller's initial yet unrealized plans to revise the novel would have further intensified this inverted relationship between self and book. As he proposes in a letter to Theodor Storm, the young Heinrich was to gift his childhood memoir to Judith, his second youthful infatuation, upon the occasion of her emigration to America. When she returns a decade later, she would then recognize him on account of the earlier autobiography, return the book, and so make way for Heinrich's happy reunion with her and his former self qua book.[57] The book would thus function as the operative element in a scene of anagnorisis. Though this scene never materialized, in the second edition Heinrich does recover his autobiography at the novel's end from Judith's *Nachlass* after her death, at which point he writes the remaining part of his life story. The restoration of the book (as a reunion of Heinrich's two selves, past and present) stands in for a more conventional happy ending in which Heinrich and Judith would marry. The return of the book thus serves as the condition for establishing the continuity of the self and so reifies the imagined relationship between book and self that seemed so cruelly absent in writing the first edition of *Der grüne Heinrich*.

Before turning to the ways in which the novel attempts to answer these crises of fracture in the format and the problem of identity, I

---

57. "She [Judith] recognizes the old Heinrich through the life book he had written" (Sie erkennt den alten Heinrich an dem Lebensbuch das er geschrieben). Keller to Theodor Storm, June 25, 1878, in *HKKA*, 19:382. Keller fails to explain what it means that Judith would recognize Heinrich by his book, a realization that only seems possible on the grounds of the totemic identification of book and self. Ultimately, the ending omits the moment of anagnorisis in which Judith recognizes Heinrich on account of the book, yet it retains the happy ending in which the book is restored to him, allowing him to continue writing and ensuring the continuity of his self. "I had one day, to her great delight, presented her with the manuscript book of my youthful days. According to her wish, I have received it back from her belongings, and have added the second part in order once again to walk the old green path of remembrance" (Ich hatte ihr einst zu ihrem großen Vergnügen das geschriebene Buch meiner Jugend geschenkt. Ihrem Willen gemäß habe ich es aus dem Nachlaß wieder erhalten und den andern Teil dazu gefügt, um noch einmal die alten grünen Pfade der Erinnerung zu wandeln). Keller, *Green Henry*, 581; Keller, *Der grüne Heinrich* (2nd ed., 1889), in *HKKA*, 3:281. This ending introduces a formidable discrepancy in the plot, as Heinrich had previously left the book in Dortchen's and not in Judith's hands.

would like to suggest that the "divided form" Keller named in the initial preface and the multiplicity of selves (what Müller Nielaba identifies as the "doppelgänger configuration"[58]) that haunt Heinrich's character are exemplary of a more pervasive constructive principle of the novel. The character constellations repeatedly consist of contrasting opposites that could be understood as reflecting the split self of the protagonist (and of the author as well), who is unable to ensure his identity over time.[59] The most obvious instance of such contrasting figures are the two objects of Heinrich's infatuation, Anna and Judith, whose very difference precipitates a crisis of self for Heinrich. On the final page of the second volume, that is, immediately before a break in the medium, he states: "I felt like my being was split into two parts and would have liked to hide from Anna when I was with Judith and from Judith when I was with Anna."[60] Because, as Sabine Schneider has so convincingly argued, both women are tantamount to narcissistic projections of the male protagonist, they are tasked with reassuring him of his selfsameness, as they repeatedly do.[61] Judith, for example, assures Heinrich, "You are still the same!"[62] Yet the very doubleness of these narcissistic projections means that they become a source of destabilization of his self rather than the reassurance he seeks in them, the same reassurance he sought in writing a childhood memoir and binding it in his own green image.

---

58. Müller Nielaba, "'Besser schreiben' gelernt," 82.

59. Michael Lipkin has most recently identified such a principle of construction, focusing on the contrasting atheists that regularly visit Frau Margarethe. See Michael Lipkin, "'To Make an Example of Myself': The Problems of an Instructive Realism in Gottfried Keller's *Der grüne Heinrich*," *German Studies Review* 44, no. 2 (2021): 255–73.

60. "Ich fühlte mein Wesen in zwei Theile gespalten und hätte mich vor Anna bei der Judith und vor Judith bei der Anna verbergen mögen." Keller, *Der grüne Heinrich* (1st ed., 1854–1855), in *HKKA*, 11:470. In the same chapter, Heinrich repeats the worry that he might be another when visiting Anna: "There I seemed to be someone else and here someone else and yet still the same person" (Ich schien mir dort ein Anderer und hier ein Anderer und doch immer der Gleiche zu sein). Keller, *Der grüne Heinrich* (1st ed., 1854–1855), in *HKKA*, 11:460.

61. See Schneider, "'Poesie der Unreife,'" 75.

62. "Du bist immer noch der Gleiche!" Keller, *Der grüne Heinrich* (1st ed., 1854–1855), in *HKKA*, 11:463.

The Barren Moment

What is the alternative to a format that fragments in temporally and spatially distinct parts, whose identity cannot hold? What are for Keller the media conditions of a self-identical totality free of fracture? In 1853, two years before the first edition of the novel was completed, Keller expressed his anxieties concerning the duration of writing and the subsequent formlessness of the text to his friend Hermann Hettner. In this letter, he envisions an alternative medium of creation, an escape from the prolonged time of production:

> If I could rewrite the book again, I would now want to make something lasting and thoroughly sound out of it. There are a slew of unbearable affected and shallow points in it, as well as major formal mistakes; to see all this before the publication, to have to continue to write it with this mixed consciousness, while printed volumes had long been available, was a purgatory that nowadays might not benefit everyone. [. . .] I keep thinking that one day I will make something that is absolutely necessary, justified, and from a single casting, and I'll calmly let this moment approach; for it will then contain a whole life within itself.

> Könnte ich das Buch noch einmal umschreiben, so wollte ich jetzt etwas Dauerhaftes und durchaus Tüchtiges daraus machen. Es sind eine Menge unerträglicher Geziert- und Flachheiten, auch große Formfehler darin; dies Alles schon vor dem Erscheinen einzusehen, mit diesem gemischten Bewußtsein noch daran schreiben zu müssen, während gedruckte Bände lange vorlagen, war ein Fegefeuer, welches nicht Jedem zu gute kommen dürfte heutzutage. [. . .] Es geht mir etwas im Kopfe herum, daß ich einmal irgend etwas machen werde, welches durchaus nothwendig, berechtigt und aus Einem Gusse ist, und ich lasse diesen Augenblick ruhig heran kommen; denn er wird alsdann ein ganzes Leben in sich tragen.[63]

---

63. Keller to Hermann Hettner, August 3, 1853, in *HKKA*, 19:247. Keller repeatedly employs metaphors of the forge, specifically of melting, to describe his revisions for the second edition. He writes, for example, that he must first melt down two-thirds of the text before shaping it anew: "On the side [. . .] I am working on my ill-fated novel, which I must first melt down by two-thirds because I have acquired a completely different point of view and ending to my life up to now" (Nebenbei [. . .] arbeite [ich] an meinem unglückseligen Roman, welchen ich, da ich einen ganz andern Standpunkt u Abschluß meines bisherigen Lebens gewonnen habe, erst wieder zu 2/3tel umschmelzen muß). Keller to Eduard Dößekel, February 8, 1849, in *HKKA*, 19:160. In addition, in *Der grüne Heinrich*, the narrator expresses admira-

If the writing process of *Der grüne Heinrich* was too protracted and too delayed to produce a self-cohering whole, then its counterpart is the *Guss*, the simple pouring of molten material into a ready-made mold, whose strict and set form has the strength to contain the whole of life.[64] The totality of life is emphatically tied to the sameness of the form (note how the article in "Einem Gusse" is capitalized and thereby emphasized). Both the established form of a mold, unlike the form of the novel that must be repeatedly invented anew, and the concentration of the artist's efforts in a single moment, rather than across a prolonged process, would ensure that this casting contains the entirety of a life within it and not the bits and pieces of a life that make up the first edition of *Der grüne Heinrich*. To return to my initial point of departure: A *Lebensbuch* only succeeds in the third sense of the term, as giving form to life, if it transcends the second sense of the term, as being composed over the course of the whole life of the author. Keller here pointedly subscribes to the promise of the instantaneous moment (*Augenblick*) as transcending the duration of time and therefore capable of containing life as a complete and selfsame whole, which would provide

---

tion for the craftsmanship of metal casting and even attributes the origin of poetry to it: "The cradle of a hero, statesman, or poet should once stand in such a workshop where bronze figures and a world of proportionate ornamentation are formed out of passionate labor from one core and the long-lasting creation resembles a living epic" (Die Wiege eines Helden, Staatsmannes oder Dichters müßte einmal in solcher Werkstatt stehen, wo unter leidenschaftlich bewegter Arbeit die ehernen Gestalten und eine Welt ebenmäßiger Zierrathen aus Einem Kerne sich bilden und das lang ausdauernde Schaffen einem lebendigen Epos gleicht). Keller, *Der grüne Heinrich* (1st ed., 1854–1855), in *HKKA*, 12:147. Cornelia Zumbusch's brilliant analysis of the novel's color theory attributes the admiration for metalwork to a poetics of radiance that is seen to break through the drab gray-green, because modern, world Heinrich inhabits. See Cornelia Zumbusch, "Grauer Grund: Keller, Goethe und der Glanz der Prosa," in *Die Farben der Prosa*, ed. Eva Eßlinger, Heide Volkening, and Cornelia Zumbusch (Freiburg im Breisgau: Rombach, 2016), 98.

64. I am arguing, in other words, that the form of the *Guss* has an established shape, a criterion similar to the one that Schneider identifies as central to Goethe's aesthetics. Because the pregnant moment must contain the infinite—the totality of past, present, and future—in a finite form, Goethe insists on the necessity of a strict contour to contain the threat of formless diffusion. See Sabine Schneider, "'Ein strenger Umriß'—Prägnanz als Leitidee von Goethes Formdenken im Kontext der Weimarer Kunsttheorie," *Goethe-Jahrbuch* 128 (2011): 98–106.

the continuity and identity of the self that eluded the author and protagonist of his novel. The imaginary *Augenblick* is removed from ongoing time, which was perceived as a threat to the continuity of the self and to the aesthetic ideal of the self-identical work—in a word, to the form of the novel as a form of life.

While the moment, as envisioned in Lessing's and later Goethe's poetics, is pregnant because it renders past and future present in a single moment, Keller's *Augenblick* so suppresses the dimension of time that it could well be described as barren. Barrenness is a motif throughout *Der grüne Heinrich*: The many female figures, despite the maternal roles they play for Heinrich, are largely preserved in their youthful virginity, while the one birth in the novel, in the house where Heinrich resides in Munich, ends in the death of the mother and child. It is an enigma of *Der grüne Heinrich* that despite its fixation on the symbolic roles of the mother, it evades any scene or suggestion of biological reproduction. The motif of biological barrenness and the poetics of the barren *Augenblick* come together in an episode in which Heinrich, who suffers many unhappy und unfulfilled love affairs, experiences fleeting happiness with Anna, a character who is characterized throughout by timelessness and death. The narrative sediments these associations by refraining from developing her character (for example, she rarely speaks). Instead, Heinrich relates to her as an image object, repeatedly painting her or putting her behind glass, thereby rendering her a static, shallow, and immortal image removed from all forms of growth and development.[65] In painting Anna, Heinrich celebrates the frigid stasis of

---

65. Eric Downing contextualizes Heinrich's practice of painting Anna in a broader aesthetics of realism in which the artwork constitutes life's other. For Downing, to paint Anna is the exercise of a magical and deadly force: "Painting—and the same holds for writing and art in general—is recognized as a sphere intrinsically opposed to the life it is meant to re-present, and the portrait of a dead subject self-consciously includes painting as a potentially, even intrinsically deadly force in the realist world—or rather, behind the world, in a suggestively allegorical (and metatextual) space." Eric Downing, *The Chain of Things: Divinatory Magic and the Practice of Reading in German Literature and Thought, 1850–1940* (Ithaca, NY: Cornell University Press, 2018), 49. On the way in which Heinrich's objects of desire are premised on the logic of the narcissistic image, see Sabine Schneider, "Ikonen der Liebe: Heinrichs Frauenbilder," in Groddeck, *"Der grüne Heinrich,"* 201–19.

their relationship of distance: "because our relationship always remained the same."⁶⁶ His relationship to her as an image attempts to recuperate the sameness absent from his sense of self and life story. As in Keller's letter to Hettner and in Hettner's own suggestion that Keller should only begin to write once the whole is present to him as a clear and unified image, the medium of the image consistently represents an immediate totality that contrasts with the durative and thus destabilizing experience of reading and writing.

Although the distance to Anna is rarely overcome, they do experience occasional brief moments of happy intimacy. One such moment takes place one evening following a community reenactment of Friedrich Schiller's *Wilhelm Tell* as they ride through the forest together toward Anna's home. Ernst Osterkamp, who has analyzed the scene at length, identifies the landscape, carefully composed by means of detailed visual elements, as presenting the totality of a life within a single moment of time.⁶⁷ The passage is remarkable for the contrast between the accelerating movements (the horse's gallop, Anna's hair in the wind) and the slowing narrative rhythm to the point that time is arrested in a single moment. The passage reads:

> Then Anna gave the white horse a smart stroke with the whip and set it into a gallop; I did the same; a mild breeze was blowing against us, and when I suddenly saw that she—all flushed, breathing in the balmy air, and while her hair was floating horizontally like a shining streak, fluttering out long—that she was smiling to herself gleefully, her head held high with the sparkling little crown, then I drew close to her side, and so we chased along for five minutes across the lonely hill. But these five minutes, short as a moment, seemed to be an eternity of happiness; it was a bit of existence in which time lost its measure; it perfectly resembled a flower, a flower from which one doesn't need to expect any fruit because the mere memory of its blossoming is a full satisfaction and an insurance for all the future.

---

66. "Denn unser Verhältniß blieb sich immer Gleich." Keller, *Der grüne Heinrich* (1st ed., 1854–1855), in *HKKA*, 11:370.
67. "As a fixed image, it [the landscape] becomes the epitome of the eternal moment in which they imagine themselves. While they ride through the endless space and so through endless time, the landscape presents itself to them as an endless moment." Ernst Osterkamp, "Erzählte Landschaften," in Groddeck, *"Der grüne Heinrich,"* 153.

> Da gab Anna dem Schimmel einen kecken Schlag mit der Gerte und setzte ihn in Galop, ich that das Gleiche; ein lauer Wind wehte uns entgegen, und als ich auf einmal sah, daß sie, ganz geröthet die balsamische Luft einathmend und während ihr Haar wie ein leuchtender Streif wagrecht schwebte, langhin flatternd: daß sie so ganz vergnügt vor sich hin lächelte, den Kopf hoch aufgehalten mit dem funkelnden Krönchen, da schloß ich mich dicht an ihre Seite, und so jagten wir wohl fünf Minuten lang über die einsame Höhe dahin. Aber diese fünf Minuten, kurz wie ein Augenblick, schienen doch eine Ewigkeit von Glück zu sein, es war ein Stück Dasein, an welchem die Zeit ihr Maß verlor, welches einer Blume vollkommen glich, einer Blume, von der man keine Frucht zu verlangen braucht, weil die bloße Erinnerung ihrer Blüthezeit ein volles Genügen und ein Schutzbrief ist für alle Zukunft.[68]

The passage is revealing not only because it exemplifies, as Osterkamp argues, the image character of Keller's poetics of the *Augenblick* but also for the way in which it thoroughly casts this fleeting moment of happiness as being overshadowed by death. Riding home through the forest after the performance, Heinrich and Anna kiss three times, a number that recalls Peter's betrayal of Jesus and thereby anticipates Anna's impending death rather than an evolving romance (so much so that Heinrich subsequently feels as if he had kissed a lifeless being).[69]

Following the third kiss, their happiness suddenly and seemingly permanently dissipates, and the two are as alienated from one another as ever. In the final image of the episode, both sit next to each other and gaze not at each other but into their reflections in the lake. The scene reenacts the story of Narcissus, except the narcissistic self

---

68. Keller, *Der grüne Heinrich* (1st ed., 1854–1855), in *HKKA*, 11:443–44.

69. Anna's likeness to Christ, inaugurated in the oft-emphasized purity of her being and her premature death, is solidified in this forest scene. After kissing her three times and leaving her at her father's house, Heinrich betrays her by subsequently visiting Judith. At Judith's, he twice denies his love for Anna—"I denied the matter most determinedly" (läugnete ich die Sache auf das Bestimmteste); "and I denied it a second time out of willfulness" (und ich läugnete es aus Muthwillen zum zweiten Male)—thereby adopting the role of Judas. Keller, *Der grüne Heinrich* (1st ed., 1854–1855), in *HKKA*, 11:462, 465. At the conclusion of the scene, when Heinrich feels that he has been cast from a beautiful garden, we are reminded of both the childhood paradise that Heinrich has now exited and the olive garden in which Jesus (that is, Anna) was betrayed the night before his crucifixion.

is not simply split into two, self and image, but into four: Heinrich, his reflection, Heinrich's beloved, and her reflection, a doubling already anticipated in the palindrome of her name. The scene is a fitting summary of Heinrich's love for Anna, in which his fixation on himself, his fixation on Anna as a projection of his desires, and Anna as a character in her own right are impossible to disentangle, effecting the fracture of the self. Gazing into their reflections with, again like Narcissus, nothing more to their futures than death, Anna and Heinrich are only joined by the memory of their kiss. Anna recalls the moment in the past tense: "Oh, it was so beautiful!"[70] This is the *Augenblick* as reimagined by *Der grüne Heinrich*: In bringing time to a halt, it contains the fullness of happiness and of life, but only retrospectively and with no future, pregnant only, so to speak, with the immediacy of death. This is not Lessing's pregnant moment (*fruchtbarer Augenblick*) or Goethe's poetics of repletion (*Prägnanz*), in which the moment bears the singular potential to express the fullness of a life. In *Der grüne Heinrich*, the moment is programmatically fruitless ("a flower from which one doesn't need to expect any fruit"), a moment containing merely its own barrenness. As envisioned in the pouring of the mold in the letter to Hettner and in the forest scene between Heinrich and Anna, Keller's *Augenblick* is thus only fully present not in virtue of its potentiality but in its having been and now standing outside of time as a totalizing, selfsame, and permanent moment. The relationship to Anna unfolds in a manner true to that ideal. Anna's health soon deteriorates to the point of death, at which moment she most fully becomes image. With her death, her family lineage dies out, as does Heinrich's family upon his death at the end of the novel. Two family lineages are cut short.

In the following section, I turn to another scene of the novel in which Heinrich again experiences a happiness so intense that time comes to a halt, though it is similarly colored by the presence of death. The scene answers to the fracture of format and the crisis of form that Keller experienced in writing *Der grüne Heinrich* and that

---

70. "O es war so schön!" Keller, *Der grüne Heinrich* (1st ed., 1854–1855), in *HKKA*, 11:447.

is thematized in its plot. In the scene, Keller portrays a second publishing format as achieving the unity of life and work that evaded him when writing *Der grüne Heinrich*, namely, a book format that would give form to life. Insofar as it offers an allegorical elaboration of what the achievement of authorship and a literary corpus might look like, the scene constitutes the most significant episode of the novel, if not of Keller's oeuvre in general, regarding the question of format.

Reading Goethe's *Ausgabe letzter Hand*

In *Der grüne Heinrich*, the ideal of a cast (*Guss*) that gives form to life and makes life visible as a selfsame totality is represented in a second model of life (as opposed to that of a novel) and in a second print format: the collected-works edition. Just as the crisis of the genre of the novel, and more particularly of the bildungsroman, is refracted through the print format of *Der grüne Heinrich*, so too is its counterimage equally informed by the material objects of contemporaneous print culture. In the novel, Heinrich encounters life as form as embodied by Johann Wolfgang Goethe's collected works. The scene of reading Goethe's collected works, positioned prominently at the beginning of the third volume of the novel, introduces the possibility that the narration of life can overcome temporal and spatial fracture and present life as a self-identical totality. In Goethe's collected works, Heinrich experiences the presence of "a whole life."[71]

The remarkable scene of reading and rereading Goethe's works begins when Heinrich returns from visiting his uncle's family to his mother's home to find books left behind on a small daybed by a peddler who both knows that they represent an unaffordable luxury item for Heinrich and is equally aware of Heinrich's loose and ultimately destructive spending habits. Although the novel does not inform us what specific edition of Goethe's works lands in Heinrich's living room, he probably reads the "Taschenausgabe" of

---

71. Keller to Hermann Hettner, August 3, 1853, in *HKKA*, 19:247.

Goethe's Werke: Vollständige Ausgabe letzter Hand, which was published incrementally in forty volumes by the J. G. Cotta'sche Buchhandlung between 1827 and 1830 and then extended between 1832 and 1842 with an additional twenty volumes issued as *Goethes nachgelassene Werke.*[72] The scene begins as follows:

> I immediately noticed that a small change had taken place in our living room. Against the wall there was a little daybed, which my mother had bought as a favor from an acquaintance who could no longer find space for it; it was very simple, light, and delicately built, and instead of upholstery it was only covered with woven white and green straw, and yet it was a very lovely piece of furniture. But on it lay a handsome pile of books, about fifty small volumes, all bound in the same way, with red labels and gold titles on the spines, and held together by a strong multistrand cord, as only a woman or a secondhand dealer can bind something together. It was Goethe's complete works, which one of my tormentors had brought here for me to look at and buy. [...] From that same moment on, I did not leave the daybed and read for thirty days straight, during which it turned once again to harsh winter and then again to spring; but the white snow passed me by like a dream I saw glistening obscurely from the side.

> Ich bemerkte sogleich, daß in unserer Stube eine kleine Veränderung vorgegangen war. Ein artiges Lotterbettchen stand an der Wand, welches die Mutter aus Gefälligkeit von einem Bekannten gekauft, der dasselbe nicht mehr unterzubringen wußte; es war von der größten Einfachheit, leicht und zierlich gebaut und statt des Polsters nur mit weiß und grünem Stroh überflochten und doch ein allerliebstes Möbel. Aber auf demselben lag ein ansehnlicher Stoß Bücher, an die fünfzig Bändchen, alle gleich gebunden, mit rothen Schildchen und goldenen Titeln auf dem Rücken versehen und durch eine starke vielfache Schnur zusammengehalten, wie nur eine Frau oder ein Trödler etwas zusammenbinden kann. Es waren Göthe's sämmtliche Werke, welche einer meiner Plagegeister hergebracht hatte, um sie mir zur Ansicht und zum Verkauf anzubieten.

---

72. Morgenthaler suggests that Heinrich reads this edition, which would also become formative for Keller's thinking about his own *Nachlass*. Walter Morgenthaler, "Die Gesammelten und die Sämtlichen Werke," *Text: Kritische Beiträge* 10 (2005): 14. Morgenthaler's essay provides an overview of different editions of Goethe's collected works and their influence on Keller. For a more detailed overview of the editions of Goethe's collected works authorized during his lifetime, see Waltraud Hagen, "Werkausgaben," in *Goethe Handbuch*, ed. Bernd Witte et al., vol. 4.2, *Personen, Sachen, Begriffe L–Z*, ed. Hans-Dietrich Dahnke and Regine Otto (Stuttgart: J. B. Metzler, 1998), 1137–47.

> [. . .] Ich entfernte mich von selber Stunde an nicht mehr vom Lotterbettchen und las dreißig Tage lang, indessen es noch ein Mal strenger Winter und wieder Frühling wurde; aber der weiße Schnee ging mir wie ein Traum vorüber, den ich unbeachtet von der Seite glänzen sah.[73]

Upon finding these volumes, Heinrich reads uninterrupted for thirty days.[74] So absorbed is he that the duration of time, represented by the alternating seasons outside his window, becomes suspended in a moment of profound interiority in which time comes to a halt. The complete attention he gives to the books is only interrupted when the peddler returns and takes the books with him because Heinrich does not have the money needed to purchase them.[75] Here, as throughout the novel, the poetic ideality of the moment gives way, in the end, to economic realities.

Standard interpretations of this scene of reading in the extant Keller scholarship characterize Heinrich's absorption as a case of *Lesesucht*, "reading addiction," in which immersive reading and fanciful imagining become so intense that they were believed to threaten an industrious, goal-driven life.[76] On this account, reading

---

73. Keller, *Der grüne Heinrich* (1st ed., 1854–1855), in *HKKA*, 12:14–15.

74. Thirty days of reading might be understood to encapsulate the thirty years of Jesus's lifetime, thus underlining that the scene of reading represents the totality of life in a timeless moment. In the third and fourth editions, Keller extends the time of reading to forty days, thus inviting an alternative association with Jesus's and Moses's forty days of fasting. See Keller, *Green Henry*, 245; Keller, *Der grüne Heinrich* (2nd ed., 1889), in *HKKA*, 2:11. The fact that Keller made this change to the third edition (not in the first publication of the second edition in 1879–1880), an edition that consisted primarily in orthographic revisions, also suggests the significance this scene bore for the novel's author.

75. I emphasize attention in view of Steffen Martus's argument that the very idea of a literary work was conditioned by a regime of attention defined by disinterested observation, a scrutiny of detail and of the seemingly mundane, and a near-myopic gaze. Heinrich is exemplary for how, as Martus describes, "the work ensures that one's attention is sequestered." Steffen Martus, *Werkpolitik: Zur Literaturgeschichte kritischer Kommunikation vom 17. bis ins 20. Jahrhundert mit Studien zu Klopstock, Tieck, Goethe und George* (Berlin: Walter de Gruyter, 2007), 15.

76. For an example of such an interpretation of scenes of reading from *Der grüne Heinrich*, see Anne Brenner, *Leseräume: Untersuchungen zu Lektüreverfahren und -funktionen in Gottfried Kellers Roman "Der grüne Heinrich"* (Würzburg: Königshausen & Neumann, 2000), esp. 69–78, which contextualizes Heinrich's reading practices in the eighteenth- and nineteenth-century debates on

Goethe is yet another digression on the meandering and incomplete path of Heinrich's *Bildung*, another instance in which he succumbs to his imagination instead of confronting prosaic reality. To be sure, the scene of reading Goethe belongs to a string of reading experiences that repeatedly warn of the didactic and moral pitfalls of reading. The series includes an anecdote about neighborhood children who are enthralled by trashy novels; in an overt example of *Lesesucht*, the neighborhood girls are seduced by romances, while the boys read chivalric tales they then playfully reenact.[77] Later in the novel, Heinrich is absorbed in reading an unnamed novel by Jean Paul that he finds in the local lending library. Here, too, reading is stylized as a scene of dangerous, disoriented fantasy untethered from all healthy realism.[78] Without dwelling on these earlier scenes of

---

Lesesucht. Brenner regards Heinrich as working his way through a standardized literary canon.

77. "The girls were very interested in the first kind and let their participating lovers kiss and caress them ad nauseam; for us boys, however, these prosaic and nonsensical depictions of a reprehensible sensuality were fortunately still off-putting" (Die Mädchen hielten sich mit großem Interesse an die erste Art und ließen sich dazu von ihren theilnehmenden Liebhabern sattsam küssen und liebkosen; uns Knaben waren aber diese prosaischen und unsinnlichen Schilderungen einer verwerflichen Sinnlichkeit glücklicher Weise noch ungenießbar). Keller, *Der grüne Heinrich* (1st ed., 1854–1855), in *HKKA*, 11:165.

78. Keller, *Der grüne Heinrich* (1st ed., 1854–1855), in *HKKA*, 11:320–21. The passage reads:

> This splendor stunned me; this seemed to me the true and just! And in the midst of the sunsets and rainbows, the lily forests and star seedlings, the pouring and pattering storms that washed the childlike face of the rising sun such that it disappeared in tears and dimmed for a moment, only to shine all the more purely and joyfully, in the middle of all the fireworks, high and low, wrapped in this seamless, shimmering cloak of the world—the Infinite, great but full of love, holy but a god of smiles and jests, terrifying in its power yet nestling and hiding itself in a child's breast, peeking out of a child's eye, like an Easter bunny made of flowers!

> Diese Herrlichkeit machte mich stutzen, dies schien mir das Wahre und Rechte! Und inmitten der Abendröthen und Regenbogen, der Lilienwälder und Sternensaaten, der rauschenden und plätschernden Gewitter, die der aufgehenden Sonne das Kinderantlitz wuschen, daß es einen Augenblick sich weinend verzog und verdunkelte, um dann um so reiner und vergnügter zu strahlen, inmitten all' des Feuerwerkes der Höhe und Tiefe, in diesen saumlosen schillernden

reading, I would like to note features of Heinrich's early reading habits that help specify how he then reads Goethe. First, insofar as he is shown to be susceptible to immersive reading habits at an early age, we are forewarned of Heinrich's proclivity to being seduced by reading, which is to say, his proclivity to becoming effeminate when reading. As a likely case of *Lesesucht*, Heinrich's reading habits serve as a marker of his compromised masculinity.[79] Second, in these earlier scenes, reading is a prelude to social acts of community building: With the neighborhood children, he imaginatively reenacts chivalric tales, and he first encounters Schiller in the form of community performances of *Wilhelm Tell*. Reading Goethe, in contrast, takes place in the secluded interior of his mother's living room, a space whose seclusion stands for the intense interiority of this specific reading experience. Third, while in these earlier scenes of reading, Heinrich becomes immersed in the plots and diegetic worlds they represent, when he reads Goethe, his attention is directed toward the author rather than the plot. That reorientation of his attention away from the contents and toward the author is tethered to the book format. The scene of reading Goethe unfolds the novel's profound examination of the format and purpose of a collected-works edition.

It is significant that Keller's earliest work of fiction includes a reflection on the book format that conventionally constitutes the culminating achievement of authorship. As I will elaborate in the following chapter, such a precocious reflection on the culminating achievements of an author's life is by no means unusual for the

---

Weltmantel gehüllt der Unendliche, groß, aber voll Liebe, heilig, aber ein Gott des Lächelns und des Scherzes, furchtbar von Gewalt, doch sich schmiegend und bergend in eine Kinderbrust, hervorguckend aus einem Kindesauge, wie das Osterhäschen aus Blumen!

79. On the gender coding of *Lesesucht*, see Luisa Banki and Kathrin Wittler, "Historische Praktiken der Lektüre in geschlechtertheoretischer Perspektive: Zur Einführung," in *Lektüre und Geschlecht im 18. Jahrhundert: Zur Situativität des Lesens zwischen Einsamkeit und Gesellligkeit*, ed. Luisa Banki and Kathrin Wittler (Göttingen: Wallstein, 2020), 7–28; and Dominik von König, "Lesesucht und Lesewut," in *Buch und Leser: Vorträge des ersten Jahrestreffens des Wolfenbütteler Arbeitskreises für Geschichte des Buchwesens 13. und 14. Mai 1976*, ed. Herbert G. Göpfert (Hamburg: E. Hauswedell, 1977), 89–113.

young Keller, who was concerned from the very beginning of his publishing career with the future form and format of his legacy. The scene of Heinrich reading Goethe serves as an opportunity for Keller to consider his own future standing in the literary canon, including how his works will fit as material objects in a collection of similar objects. Heinrich's absorption in Goethe's collected works and his reading experience reflect on the potential of such editions and their specific properties to present the unity of the life and work of an author and to give form to the author's life.[80]

Given both Goethe's enduring status as the apotheosis of German literature and culture and the flurry of ever-larger editions of Goethe throughout the nineteenth century, it is unsurprising that Keller's idealization of this publishing format concerns this author. Goethe's collected works exemplified a stabilized nexus of author, work, and book format at the heart of the idea of authorship Keller shared with his contemporaries and to some extent even still shares with us today. While the first German-language collected-works edition marketed as such was the 1794 publication of Christoph Wieland's works by Göschen Verlag, Goethe was famously the first author to extensively concern himself with the shape of his collected works while still alive.[81] Goethe understood that his oeuvre would only cohere within the material contours of a specific edition; to use Steffen Martus's apt formulation, Goethe was attentive to the "book shape before any work-likeness of his texts," so much so that "the shape of the book" itself became "the driving force in the production

---

80. For an account of a second genre that models the unity of life and work, see Gabriele Guercio's history of the genre of the artist's monograph, entitled *Art as Existence: The Artist's Monograph and Its Project* (Cambridge: MIT Press, 2006). To the artist's monograph we owe the idea, Guercio writes, of "the artist both as an individual empirically linked to a body of work through historical facts and as a personality created solely by that body of work" (6). That idea is equally constitutive of the historically later emergence of the collected-works edition.

81. On Goethe's extensive and well-documented efforts regarding his *Nachlassverwaltung*, see Cornelia Vismann, *Files: Law and Media Technology*, trans. Geoffrey Winthrop-Young (Stanford, CA: Stanford University Press, 2008), 114–17; and Dirk Werle, "Nachlass, Nachwelt und Nachruhm um 1800: Am Beispiel Johann Wolfgang Goethes," in Sina and Spoerhase, *Nachlassbewusstsein*, 115–31.

of the work."[82] The title of the Cotta edition of Goethe's collected works from the years 1827–1830 marks this authorial participation by means of its reference to the *Vollständige Ausgabe letzter Hand*, the hand standing metonymically for the author's body and intentions. The title thereby incorporates the function of the book as a medium facilitating contact between the body of the reader and the body of the author; as Leah Price aptly formulates the point, "The contact between hand and page stands in for the contact between one body and another."[83] As the last authorized edition, the title additionally marks its proximity to the author's death and so underwrites the claim to completeness, though of course later editions would become larger in terms of both the number of volumes and the scope of texts included.

Throughout the nineteenth century, collected-works editions became increasingly widespread and also increasingly important to the recognition, legacy, and canonicity of authors. As Piper notes in his brilliant study on nineteenth-century book history and literature, collected-works editions acquired prominence from the end of the eighteenth century onward as a "category for stabilizing the very definition of literature in the age of too much literature."[84] In managing this alleged excess, collected-works editions anointed specific authors as possessing outstanding cultural significance and

---

82. Martus, *Werkpolitik*, 462–64. Martus very helpfully recounts Goethe's sensitivity to the book market and book culture of his time, which made it possible for him to exploit that market not only to his financial advantage but also in terms of his cultural capital. For example, Martus elaborates both the timing and expanding girth of the five different collected-works editions Goethe published during his lifetime and his writing of *Dichtung und Wahrheit* with an eye to such an edition as two moments in which the collected-works edition became formative for Goethe's conception of a work. See Martus, *Werkpolitik*, 462–63.

83. Leah Price, *How to Do Things with Books in Victorian Britain* (Princeton, NJ: Princeton University Press, 2012), 197.

84. Piper, *Dreaming in Books*, 54. On the history and cultural significance of the collected-works edition, see also Michael Anesko, "Collected Editions and the Consolidation of Cultural Authority: The Case of Henry James," *Book History* 12 (2009): 186–208; and Andrew Nash, ed., *The Culture of Collected Editions* (Basingstoke: Palgrave Macmillan, 2003). On the collected-works edition as a form of cultural distinction that "counteracts the egalitarian implication of print," see Cahn, "Opera omnia," 85.

promised an exhaustive and definitive version of an author's oeuvre, rendering further purchases of the author's works redundant. They were typically published in anticipation of an author's death or shortly thereafter and marked the summation and culmination of their literary output (and although I say "their," in matter of fact, collected-works editions were a highly gendered institution: Even though female German-language authors acquired a considerable market presence through periodical circulation in the late nineteenth century, they were largely denied this monumental form until the end of the century).[85] Over the course of the century, the market for collected-works editions expanded to encompass everything from limited luxury editions with watermarked sheets and bindings sewn by hand to mass-produced and mass-marketed bargain editions purporting to make an author's work available to audiences of little means. Collected-works editions thereby respond to the problem of too much literature through practices of distinction and discrimination: Select authors are endowed with authority by means of their collected editions and specific readers acquire social distinction by means of the authoritative copies they possess. Heinrich experiences this form of distinction only in passing, since, as noted, he cannot afford to acquire the books.

However, those who either purchased or read these editions were offered much more than simply the "most authoritative" version of specific works of literature and much more than a luxury good to adorn their bookshelf. For what guarantees the coherence of a set of texts radically dissimilar in terms of genre or time and place of first publication is nothing other than the life and the person of the author. Their value lies, for one, in the representation of the life of

---

85. For an informative history of collected-works editions for female authors (albeit in the context of American literature), see Amanda Gailey, *Proofs of Genius: Collected Editions from the American Revolution to the Digital Age* (Ann Arbor: University of Michigan Press, 2015), 33–54. For an account of late nineteenth-century collected-works editions for female authors in Germany, with special attention to the significance of binding, see Lynne Tatlock, "Afterlife of Nineteenth-Century Popular Fiction and the German Imaginary: The Illustrated Collected Novels of E. Marlitt, W. Heimburg, and E. Werner," in *Publishing Culture and the "Reading Nation": German Book History in the Long Nineteenth Century*, ed. Lynne Tatlock (Rochester, NY: Camden House, 2010), 122–31.

the author as an exemplary individual in a book format. The unity of the author's life underwrites the unity of the volumes compiled in a collected-works edition while, conversely, the books are cast as an index or imprint of that person. What a collected-works edition achieves, in other words, is nothing less than the creation of a corpus that stands in for the author's body and life and is contained in an artifact that could be endlessly reproduced and circulated and still stay the same. Collected-works editions posit the very idea of an identical self (the person of the author) in perfect sympathy with industrial-scale reproduction, commercialization, and circulation. To repeat the point: The collected-works edition promises a stabilized because self-identical concept of the author and the work (and, moreover, their relationship to one another), a notion that Keller perceived as unavailable to his fractured novel. Goethe's collected works thus provide the imaginative alternative to the crisis of formlessness experienced in the publishing history of *Der grüne Heinrich* and in the identity of its protagonist.

The idea that a collected-works edition stands in for the unity of the life and person of the author relies heavily on the visual cues of book design. The collected-works edition is, as Cahn writes, a "typographical device" that relies on the power of standardization as a "magic wand which can turn books into works."[86] For one, the individual volumes are ideally provided with uniform covers, titled identically (as *Sämtliche Werke*, for example), and numbered consecutively. Goethe himself well understood the significance of a unified format. At the beginning of *Dichtung und Wahrheit*, he writes of his first collected-works edition with Cotta: "One cannot refrain from viewing the twelve volumes as a whole, since they stand before us in identical format, and from them one would like to sketch a portrait of the author and his talents."[87] Unlike individually published volumes, in

---

86. Cahn, "Opera omnia," 83, 87.
87. "Man kann sich nicht enthalten, diese zwölf Bände, welche in Einem Format vor uns stehen, als ein Ganzes zu betrachten, und man möchte sich daraus gern ein Bild des Autors und seines Talents entwerfen." Johann Wolfgang Goethe, *From My Life: Poetry and Truth*, trans. Robert R. Heitner, ed. Thomas P. Saine and Jeffrey L. Sammons, vol. 4 of *The Collected Works* (New York: Suhrkamp, 1994), 15; Johann Wolfgang Goethe, *Aus meinem Leben: Dichtung und Wahrheit*, ed. Klaus-

which the title of the work is typically most prominent, the covers and title pages in a collected-works edition are designed to foreground the name of the author. In the edition of Goethe that Heinrich probably reads, for example, the leading title page entirely forgoes the title of a work, reserving the space for the name of the author, staging the encounter with him front and center. Equally important is a portrait of the author, most often preceding the first volume of poetry, the ostensibly most personal or emotive of genres. When one handles these volumes, it is of course eminently clear that despite the best efforts of publishers, the volumes are by no means identical. They differ in coloration, cut, texture, and binding—the many differences that Foucault's critique of the ontology of the book alerts us to. But the projection of unity, by means of the visual elements of the book, is essential to the promise of establishing a unified corpus, a fitting receptacle for the life of the author. When the books are purchased and placed in a bourgeois living room, they do not simply provide access to texts, they promise an intimate bond to the person of the author within the intimate, domestic space of reading. His mother's living room is thus a befitting setting for Heinrich's reading.

Most often a collected-works edition simulates the continuity of the author's life by organizing the volumes not by genre but by chronology.[88] However, Heinrich does not read Goethe's books in chronological order, or in the order that the *Vollständige Ausgabe letzter Hand* is numbered. Instead, sensitive as he is to dimensions of print, he reads according to typography:

Detlef Müller, vol. 14 of *Sämtliche Werke: Briefe, Tagebücher und Gespräche*, ed. Dieter Borchmeyer et al. (Frankfurt am Main: Deutscher Klassiker Verlag, 1986), 11.

88. The initial twenty volumes of the *Vollständige Ausgabe letzter Hand* retained the order of the third collected-works edition (published between 1815 and 1819) and supplemented it with largely autobiographical texts. For a history of how collected-works editions were increasingly organized chronologically rather than according to genre in order to better represent the biography and personal development of the author, see Philip Ajouri, "Chronologische Werkausgaben im 19. Jahrhundert," in *Archiv/Fiktionen: Verfahren des Archivierens in Literatur und Kultur des langen 19. Jahrhunderts*, ed. Daniela Gretz and Nicolas Pethes (Freiburg im Breisgau: Rombach, 2016), 85–105. As Ajouri explains, Goethe's works, as Goethe first conceived them and as they were issued through the nineteenth century, are a notable exception to this gradual shift to chronological principles of organization.

First, I reached for everything that looked like drama based on the print, then I read everything that rhymed, then the novels, then *Italienische Reise*, then some monographs on art, and when the stream ran up into the prosaic fields of everyday work, of solitary toil, then I put the rest aside and started over again and this time discovered how the individual constellations were beautifully positioned with regard to one another and among them the individual strangely shining stars, such as *Reineke Fuchs* or *Benvenuto Cellini*. So I wandered through this sky once more and read many things twice and finally discovered a totally new bright star: *Dichtung und Wahrheit*.

Ich griff zuerst nach Allem, was sich durch den Druck als Dramatisch zeigte, dann las ich alles Gereimte, dann die Romane, dann die italienische Reise, dann einige künstlerische Monographien, und als sich der Strom hinauf in die prosaischen Gefilde des täglichen Fleißes, der Einzelmühe verlief, ließ ich das Weitere liegen und fing von vorn an und entdeckte diesmal die einzelnen Sternbilder in ihren schönen Stellungen zu einander und dazwischen einzelne seltsam glänzende Sterne, wie den Reineke Fuchs oder den Benvenuto Cellini. So hatte ich noch ein Mal diesen Himmel durchschweift und Vieles wieder doppelt gelesen und entdeckte zuletzt noch einen ganz neuen hellen Stern: Dichtung und Wahrheit.[89]

If one assumes that Heinrich does read the *Vollständige Ausgabe letzter Hand*, then he begins with volumes 8–12, then reads volumes 16–23, 40, and 35, and finally volumes 24–26. While the order may at first seem impulsive, on second light, the sequence brilliantly encapsulates a minibiography of Keller's own earliest literary ambitions. He was first an aspiring dramatist, then published a book of poetry, then *Der grüne Heinrich*, and finally intended to write an autobiography near the end of his life. In the act of reading against the grain of the chronological order, Heinrich appropriates Goethe's collected works to project a narrative of Keller's life and work. Through Goethe's collected works, Keller imagines the contours of his own legacy.

Heinrich's grasp of Goethe's edition is particularly evident in his reading of *Dichtung und Wahrheit*, Goethe's autobiography, which Goethe had written while preparing the third authorized edition of his collected works from 1815 to 1819, and which was itself an important model for *Der grüne Heinrich* in how to weave together

---

89. Keller, *Der grüne Heinrich* (1st ed., 1854–1855), in *HKKA*, 12:15–16.

autobiographical fact and fiction.[90] Goethe claims to have conceived *Dichtung und Wahrheit* as providing the lens, key, or code for understanding the rest of his collected works.[91] The announcement for the later *Vollständige Ausgabe letzter Hand* in the *Morgenblatt für gebildete Stände*, drafted by Goethe himself, explicitly refers to how the collected works can bring form to the author's life and work:

> German culture is already at a very high point where one seems almost more eager to learn how a work was produced and the actual events from which it was developed than to enjoy the work itself, so this purpose was particularly taken into consideration, and the designation *vollständig* means that both in the selection of the unknown works and in the positioning and arrangement in general, special care was taken to bring clearly into view the author's disposition, education, development, and manifold experiments in all directions, since the viewer would otherwise only end up uncomfortably confused.
>
> Die deutsche Cultur steht bereits auf einem sehr hohen Punkte, wo man fast mehr als auf den Genuß eines Werkes, auf die Art, wie es entstanden, begierig scheint und die eigentlichen Anlässe, woraus sich jenes entwickelt, zu erfahren wünscht; so ward dieser Zweck besonders in's Auge gefaßt, und die Bezeichnung *vollständig* will sagen, daß theils in der Auswahl der noch unbekannten Arbeiten, theils in Stellung und Anordnung überhaupt vorzüglich darauf gesehen worden, des Verfassers Naturell, Bildung, Fortschreiten und vielfaches Versuchen nach allen Seiten hin klar vor's Auge zu bringen, weil außerdem der Betrachter nur in unbequeme Verwirrung gerathen würde.[92]

Because the edition included *Dichtung und Wahrheit*, it could claim to present not just the individual works of literature but also an account, grounded in the story of the author's *Bildung*, of how these

---

90. See Johann Wolfgang Goethe, *Goethe's Werke*, 20 vols. (Stuttgart: J. G. Cotta'sche Buchhandlung, 1815–19). *Dichtung und Wahrheit* was reprinted as volumes 17–19 of this edition. On the relation of *Dichtung und Wahrheit* to this edition of Goethe's collected works, see Hagen, "Werkausgaben," 1142.

91. Martus is again helpful on this point: "Autobiography was supposed to compensate for the chronological order of the works that was denied to readers, [...] and it took on the task of simulating the work-political ideal of the completeness of the work." Martus, *Werkpolitik*, 466.

92. Johann Wolfgang Goethe, "Anzeige von Goethe's sämmtlichen Werken," *Intelligenz-Blatt*, no. 25, 98, supplement to *Morgenblatt für gebildete Stände*, no. 171, July 19, 1826.

works originated, even though, as I have noted, the editions were not organized chronologically. As Philip Ajouri explains, Goethe's collected works established, "like no other, the paradigm in which an author's writings refer directly back to the author such that biography and work are closely related, indeed, are two sides of the same coin."[93] The attentive reader that he is, Heinrich recognizes *Dichtung und Wahrheit* as "a totally new bright star" from which the constellation of the collected works can be charted: the lens, in other words, though which the unity of the many volumes is understood to refract the unity and singularity of the authorial person.[94]

Heinrich proves to be so adept at understanding how one is supposed to read a collected-works edition that, although he abandons the well-ordered sequence, he fully grasps that the books render Goethe's life and person present to him—a binding of life and work that would later become enshrined as a presupposition of modern philology in Wilhelm Scherer's *Geschichte der deutschen Literatur* (1883) and then Wilhelm Dilthey's *Das Erlebnis und die Dichtung* (1906). When the *Vollständige Ausgabe letzter Hand* enters Heinrich's house, it is not just the works of literature but the essence, the personality of the man himself, he encounters: "I felt as if the great shadow himself had crossed my threshold."[95] The literary corpus in the alleged completeness and wholeness of a collected-works edition stands in for the now immaterial body of the author. So in contrast to other renowned fictional readers in nineteenth-century novels—one might think of Catherine Morland from Jane Austen's *Northanger Abbey* (1817) or Gustave Flaubert's title character from *Madame Bovary* (1856)—whose all-consuming reading habits lead them to dangerously project themselves into the dramatic life of novelistic heroines, Heinrich loses himself to the felt presence of an

---

93. Ajouri, "Chronologische Werkausgaben," 95.

94. Heinrich's reading of *Dichtung und Wahrheit* provides an excellent example of what Martus describes as the necessarily reciprocal definitions of *Einzelwerk* and *Gesamtwerk*; not only do the complete works contain the sum of the individual works, the individual work must also contain, as an autonomous form, the totality of the complete works in itself. See Martus, *Werkpolitik*, 461.

95. "Es war mir zu Muthe, als ob der große Schatten selbst über meine Schwelle getreten wäre." Keller, *Der grüne Heinrich* (1st ed., 1854–1855), in *HKKA*, 12:15.

author, as the book format of Goethe's collected works invites him to do.

But that difference does not mean that Heinrich's projection lacks the erotic investment of these female heroines in their reading. A long line of convincing scholars, from Gerhard Kaiser to Eric Downing, have interpreted Goethe's presence as a phantasmagoric substitute for Heinrich's own deceased father, who is purposed with shepherding the boy's entrance into the social symbolic order, but they have thereby missed the scene's erotic dimensions.[96] On account of these erotics, the imagined Goethe occupies the symbolic position of Heinrich's deceased father and shares strong affinities with Heinrich's female objects of desire. In other words, Goethe straddles the promise of *Bildung* associated with his other father figures (his uncle, Römer, the Graf) and the erotic force of at least Judith. The erotic overtones of the scene of reading are introduced most poignantly in the guise of the *Lotterbettchen*—a bed for loitering or leisure, or also for "a pair of lovers or for prostitution"[97]— whose arrival in Heinrich's mother's house coincides with the arrival of Goethe's works. The bed is described as "delicately built," woven of fine straw in green and white, a color coding that establishes the furnishing as a metonymical substitute for Heinrich himself (with the implication that Goethe qua books and Heinrich qua bed have entered this space of interiority together). Heinrich spends thirty days on the bed reading Goethe's corpus, subsumed in an ecstatic if not orgiastic fantasized union with the man himself. Goethe's shadow, as the text informs, has seemingly penetrated him; it is "as if the great shadow himself had crossed my threshold." Spread on the bed in his collected works, the male author has successfully made himself present to his infatuated and feminized reader.[98] Later in the novel, Heinrich will find Anna's black

---

96. See Gerhard Kaiser, *Gottfried Keller: Das gedichtete Leben* (Frankfurt am Main: Insel, 1981), 120; and Downing, *Chain of Things*, 60.

97. *Duden*, "Lotterbett," online edition, accessed August 16, 2024, https://www.duden.de/node/91138/revision/1269046.

98. The possibility that Goethe's sensual work might lead unsuspecting youth astray was, of course, not unique to Keller's novel. For an account of Goethe as both an idealized father figure and a potential erotic temptation for the nineteenth

coat lying on the same *Lotterbettchen* when she arrives in town to be treated by a doctor. The coat, like Goethe's books on the bed, signifies Anna's simultaneous presence and absence (Anna is momentarily in Heinrich's mother's home but will soon die) and reinforces her status as Heinrich's object of desire. Together, the two mentions of the *Lotterbettchen* establish the bed as a site of Heinrich's erotic fantasies.

In anticipation of his encounter with Goethe on the *Lotterbettchen*, the chapter's opening assigns Heinrich to a feminized position. The chapter begins the morning after the community performance of *Wilhelm Tell*. Heinrich wakes late and discovers that the night's heavy rains (in which he recovered his sobriety) have caused the local stream to swell and threaten neighboring fields. When he awakes at a leisurely hour, all the village's men are working to stem the flood. Heinrich eats breakfast among the women who have stayed behind—his three female cousins, his grandmother, and Judith and Anna as well—a situation typical of the novel's village scenes in which Heinrich is almost continually and exclusively surrounded by women. After realizing that he will be of no use to the toiling men, he returns to his mother's house where he finds the books. The scene of reading Goethe is thus preceded by a contrast between the industrious, laboring men and the feminine spaces of interiority (his aunt's table, his mother's house) in which Heinrich invariably lingers. Heinrich's leisurely loitering in bed with Goethe's corpus reifies his position as submissive, feminized, and infantilized.

---

century, see Claudia Stockinger, "Paradigma Goethe? Die Lyrik des 19. Jahrhunderts und Goethe," in *Lyrik im 19. Jahrhundert: Gattungspoetik als Reflexionsmedium der Kultur*, ed. Steffen Martus, Stefan Scherer, and Claudia Stockinger (Bern: Peter Lang, 2005), 93–125. Alexander Baumgartner, for one, warns of the sensual dangers Goethe poses for young readers—a warning that echoes Heinrich's experience and his feminization: "For women and girls in particular, Goethe is the most harmful and fatal writer. [...] Just as he entices and flatters the girl's imagination with many beautiful, magnificent figures, like a shining will-o'-the-wisp, into the swamp of the most vulgar sensuality, so too does he enervate and soften the boy's mind, blurs his clear sense of all that is great, true, and ideal and inevitably leads him to the disastrous conclusion that eroticism is the source, the goal, and the blossom of all poetry." Alexander Baumgartner, SJ, *Göthe's Lehr- und Wanderjahre in Weimar und Italien* (Freiburg im Breisgau: Herder'sche Verlagshandlung, 1882), 369. On Baumgartner, see Stockinger, "Paradigma Goethe," 104.

The scene of reading Goethe furthermore adheres to the strongly formalized pattern of Heinrich's erotic fantasies throughout the novel. As Winfried Menninghaus details in depth, the event of Heinrich's first childhood crush establishes a libidinal template that later resurfaces in the relationships to Anna and Judith, a pattern of repetition that cements the frustration of Heinrich's desire.[99] In the early childhood scene, Heinrich substitutes an image of distant white clouds hovering over mountain peaks, made red and golden by the sun, for a girl from the neighborhood.[100] Menninghaus's analysis shows that the different women who subsequently become Heinrich's objects of desire consistently manifest these same cloudlike properties: They are white (chaste), formless or undefined (that is, beyond the determinations of language and consequently only describable through substitution), and distant (i.e., unavailable). These properties and their color coding (white, red, and gold) reemerge in Heinrich's affairs with Anna and Judith, *and* in the encounter with Goethe. The scene of reading Goethe is particularly strongly stylized to echo the formative moment from Heinrich's childhood. Like the initial scene in which Heinrich views the clouds outside the window of his mother's house and substitutes them for the absent girl, the scene of reading is another moment of intensified interiority that

---

99. See Winfried Menninghaus, *Artistische Schrift: Studien zur Kompositionskunst Gottfried Kellers* (Frankfurt am Main: Suhrkamp, 1982), 14–60.
100. The passage reads:
Since the distant snowcaps were sometimes veiled, sometimes lighter or darker, white or red, I thought they were something alive, marvelous, and powerful, like the clouds, and I had the habit of also calling other things clouds or mountains [...]. That is why I named [...] the first female figure that I liked, a girl from our neighborhood, the white cloud, based on the first impression she made on me in a white dress.

Da die fernen Schneekuppen bald verhüllt, bald heller oder dunkler, weiß oder rot sichtbar waren, so hielt ich sie wohl für etwas Lebendiges, Wunderbares und Mächtiges wie die Wolken und pflegte auch andere Dinge mit dem Name Wolke oder Berg zu belegen [...]. So nannte ich [...] die erste weibliche Gestalt, welche mir wohlgefiel und ein Mädchen aus der Nachbarschaft war, die weiße Wolke, von dem ersten Eindrucke, den sie in einem weißen Kleide auf mich gemacht hatte.
Keller, *Der grüne Heinrich* (1st ed., 1854–1855), in *HKKA*, 11:85.

contrasts with a formless white beyond the window, a harbinger of his failed socialization in the outside world. However, when he is reading Goethe, it is not the clouds that shine through the window but similarly formless snow, whose glow penetrates through the glass pane ("but the white snow passed me by like a dream I saw glistening obscurely from the side") and contrasts with the bright red of the bound books that stand in for the distant body of the author accessible only in Heinrich's fantasy. Even the color gold, despite being less integral in the formalized pattern of Heinrich's desire, resurfaces in this scene as the gold lettering on the bound volumes.[101] The fact that red and gold are supplied in the scene by means of the books' binding is a further indication of the extent to which the material objects and their format are central to the scene of reading. While Heinrich never experiences erotic fulfillment vis-à-vis the novel's women, reading Goethe is a fleeting and ultimately interrupted fantasy of erotic satisfaction that ends when the books, like Heinrich's earliest object of desire, leave the room after having, so he imagines, embraced him.

In this eroticized scene of reading, the young and effeminate Heinrich is made to contrast with the older Goethe, who is primarily defined by the quality of "greatness," a term intended to designate both his perceived size and his singularity. Goethe's greatness is underscored four times in the scene of reading: first, in the childhood memory that "the great Goethe has died"; second, in the equally "great shadow" the great man casts; third, in the "handsome pile of books, about fifty small volumes," of his collected works; and fourth in "the golden fruits of his eighty-year life" represented in those books.[102]

---

101. Heinrich's visit to the cemetery with Anna operates with a similar color palette of red, white, and golden lettering: "Here and there a dull golden inscription gleamed in the darkness, or a bush of white roses glowed like snow; Anna broke off [. . .] enough white and red roses to fill her gathered-up black dress" (Da und dort blinkte eine matte goldene Schrift aus dem Dunkel oder leuchtete ein Busch weißer Rosen wie Schnee hervor, Anna brach [. . .] ihr aufgeschürztes schwarzes Kleid ganz voll weißer und rother Rosen). Keller, *Der grüne Heinrich* (1st ed., 1854–1855), in *HKKA*, 11:304.

102. "Der große Göthe ist gestorben"; "die goldenen Früchte des achtzigjährigen Lebens." Keller, *Der grüne Heinrich* (1st ed., 1854–1855), in *HKKA*, 12:15.

Heinrich's encounter with Goethe is, of course, not simply erotic; or to put it more aptly, the erotic is only one constitutive dimension of the specific kind of relationship imagined as conjoining author and reader. Staged as the erotic encounter between the accomplished elder and the inexperienced, subordinate, and passive youth, the relationship acquires the contours of a pederastic one. Heinrich, the eromenos, is the natural opposite of this great, older, and even aristocratic man: young, of slender if not short stature, and without any financial means or future. Central to a classical poetics of pederasty, as most recently elaborated by W. Daniel Wilson, is that the relationship is specifically envisioned as a didactic arrangement.[103] In exchange for the attention and admiration of a youth, the elder partner offers the younger an education. The consummation of the relationship does not take place in biological reproduction, which would run counter to the novel's insistence on barrenness I identified earlier, but instead aims at education. In his fantasized encounter, Heinrich, like his eromenos prototype Ganymede, becomes Goethe's subordinate and, in exchange, enjoys his bodily proximity, affection, and an education to which he would have otherwise never had access. Heinrich specifically adopts the guise of the cupbearer Ganymede in the moment in which he has his hands full attempting to contain the brimming cornucopia of books that threaten, in their plentitude, to spill from the bed: "Then the golden fruits of his eighty-year life fell apart in the most beautiful way, spread out over the daybed [Lotterbettchen], and spilled over the edge onto the floor such that I had my hands full keeping the abundance together."[104] In being tasked with containing the plentitude of Goethe's corpus, Heinrich (for the fleeting moment that this fantasy persists) becomes the receptacle of

---

103. See W. Daniel Wilson, "But Is It Gay? Kissing, Friendship, and 'Prehomosexual' Discourses in Eighteenth-Century Germany," *Modern Language Review* 103, no. 3 (July 2008): 767–83; W. Daniel Wilson, *Goethe, Männer, Knaben: Ansichten zur "Homosexualität,"* trans. Angela Steidele (Berlin: Insel, 2012); and more generally on pederasty, Ian Fleischmann, "Pederasty and/as Narrative Form: André Gide's Queer Coinages," *French Forum* 45, no. 2 (2020): 155–69.

104. "Da fielen die goldenen Früchte des achtzigjährigen Lebens auf das Schönste auseinander, verbreiteten sich über das Ruhbett und fielen über dessen Rand auf den Boden, daß ich alle Hände voll zu thun hatte, den Reichtum zusammen zu halten." Keller, *Der grüne Heinrich* (1st ed., 1854–1855), in *HKKA*, 12:15.

Goethe's aesthetic education. As a result, the moment he finishes reading the collected works, he exits his mother's house and senses a capacity for art that he never before possessed.[105] The cornerstone of that aesthetic perception is the feeling of love, reflecting the entwinement of erotic and didactic aspects of the relationship established during the experience of reading. The experience on the *Lotterbettchen* thus gives way to a more expansive feeling of ecstasy whose object is the natural world: "As my gaze embraced everything, I felt a pure and lasting pleasure that I had never known before. It was a devotional love for everything in existence, a love that honors the right and significance of each thing and that feels the coherence and depth of the world."[106] The lingering erotics of the encounter with Goethe have thus been effectively sublimated and transferred onto the natural world: The love for Goethe has become, as commensurate with the aims of an aesthetic education, a pantheistic love of nature; the sense of wholeness that Heinrich perceived in the fifty bound volumes is revealed to him as the wholeness of nature, bound together through his love. At first the scene of reading seemingly provides Heinrich with the education and disposition to become the landscape painter he aspires to be. Like the relationship to Anna, it removes him from the sphere of sexual bifurcation and biological reproduction and endows him with an effeminate if not androgynous body. Endowed with that body, he aspires to perpetuate not his family lineage but the creation of his own artworks following the example of Goethe's greatness.

---

105. Downing, too, dwells on the significance of this passage, noting that it stands out within the entirety of the novel because of a shift in tense from a retrospective imperfect to the present. Downing explains the shift as representing a "Goethean Weltbild": "The implication of this is that, for Heinrich as narrator (as himself behind the text world), Goethe is 'the great shade' behind the natural world, the laity principle, as it were, that animates the novel and that Heinrich as character is set amidst." Downing, *Chain of Things*, 284n74. Downing more generally argues that Heinrich, in reading Goethe, encounters the nondiscursive principle of *Stimmung*.

106. "Indem meine Blicke Alles umfaßten, empfand ich ein reines und nachhaltiges Vergnügen, das ich früher nicht gekannt. Es war die hingebende Liebe an alles Gewordene und Bestehende, welche das Recht und die Bedeutung jeglichen Dinges ehrt und den Zusammenhang und die Tiefe der Welt empfindet." Keller, *Der grüne Heinrich* (1st ed., 1854–1855), in *HKKA*, 12:16.

Loose and Woven Thread

Heinrich's encounter with Goethe is stylized in yet another tradition of reading, namely, as a scene of conversion that stands in the long tradition of conversions catalyzed through reading, such as those of Augustine or Petrarch.[107] Reading Goethe is a transformative moment that ideally overcomes all of Heinrich's preceding life. Inspired by his reading, under the impression of the whole, his *Gesamteindruck,* Heinrich leaves the house and intends to return to nature to begin what he anticipates will be a "a splendid collection" (vortreffliche[] Sammlung) of drawings in which each part contributes to a meaningful whole: "In my mind I already saw a rich treasure trove of works before me, which all looked pretty, valuable, and substantial, filled with delicate and strong strokes, none of which were without meaning."[108] But the conversion falls spectacularly flat. When drawing, he discovers that he still lacks artistic ability, a state of affairs that reading Goethe could not rectify. The absorptive moment of reading Goethe is as barren as the moment of happiness with Anna; it yields no fruit for Heinrich's life. Looking at his typically poor drawing, which he had hoped would be the beginning of an incredible collection (inspired, quite obviously, by the collected works he has just completed reading, yet another instance in which format precedes content), he comes to the unhappy realization that he is still stuck with his preconversion self: "I sat down outside to begin the first sheet of this splendid collection; but it then turned out that I had to continue just where I had last left off and that I was not at all capable of suddenly creating

---

107. On the Christian tradition of conversion through reading, with analyses of the scenes in Augustine and Petrarch, see Christopher Wild, "*Apertio Libri*: Codex and Conversion," in *Literary Studies and the Pursuits of Reading,* ed. Eric Downing, Jonathan M. Hess, and Richard V. Benson (Rochester, NY: Camden House, 2012), 17–39.

108. "Im Geiste sah ich schon einen reichen Schatz von Arbeiten vor mir, welche alle hübsch, werth- und gehaltvoll aussahen, angefüllt mit zarten und starken Strichen, von denen keiner ohne Bedeutung war." Keller, *Der grüne Heinrich* (1st ed., 1854–1855), in *HKKA,* 12:19.

something new."[109] If he wants to draw, this abject experience suggests, Heinrich should have read outside in the garden instead of in the dark and dusty interior of his mother's house, or better yet, he should have forgone reading books altogether and read from the book of nature instead. Reading Goethe could not compensate for a lack of artistic ability and practice, for an education that takes place not in one's fantasy but within the natural and social fabric of the world.

But the shortcomings of this transformative moment are not simply a matter of where or what Heinrich reads. His misfortune and the cause for his renewed failure as an artist is that *his* life, unlike Goethe's, is still being formed. He must begin, as the text tells us, where he left off. There is no form of paper artifact, neither a single bound book nor a multivolume collection, that could capture his life as a form. Put differently, the transformative moment of conversion fails because it was not fully sufficient to interrupt the continuity of his life and education, to cut it off and begin it anew. Heinrich and the novel's readers are powerfully reminded of this fact in the moment when Goethe's collected works leave his mother's house. At that moment, Heinrich feels "as if a host of glowing and singing spirits had left the living room, making it suddenly seem silent and empty; I jumped up, looked around, and thought myself as in a grave if my mother's knitting needles had not made a friendly noise."[110] Here, as throughout the novel, Heinrich's mother is depicted as spinning thread and knitting Heinrich's shirts and socks. Regarded allegorically, however, Heinrich's mother is knitting the fabric of Heinrich's life such that only the sound of her needles can relieve Heinrich of the momentary impression that he is dead ("as

---

109. "Ich setzte mich in's Freie, um das erste Blatt dieser vortrefflichen Sammlung zu beginnen; aber nun ergab es sich, daß ich eben da fortfahren mußte, wo ich zuletzt aufgehört hatte, und daß ich durchaus nicht im Stande war, plötzlich etwas Neues zu schaffen." Keller, *Der grüne Heinrich* (1st ed., 1854–1855), in *HKKA*, 12:19.

110. "Als ob eine Schaar glänzender und singender Geister die Stube verließen, so daß diese auf einmal still und leer schien; ich sprang auf, sah mich um und würde mich wie in einem Grabe gedünkt haben, wenn nicht die Stricknadeln meiner Mutter ein freundliches Geräusch verursacht hätten." Keller, *Der grüne Heinrich* (1st ed., 1854–1855), in *HKKA*, 12:16.

in a grave"). The clicking needles remind him that his life is still in the making and that it thus cannot assume the form of completeness and integrity represented by the collected-works edition.

Both the thread of life and the thread Heinrich's mother spins belong to the novel's leitmotifs, and they are worth dwelling upon because they constitute an image repertoire closely bound, as I will show, to the ideal of the collected-works edition, with which the novel imagines an ideal form of life as continuous, self-identical, and with beginning and end. But before deepening my analysis of the novel's specific use of this imagery in relation to print formats, let me briefly draw attention to the very rich iconography of the Fates that informs *Der grüne Heinrich*. This iconography, in conjunction with the metaphors of thread and cloth, lends the scene of reading its more explicit allegorical dimension: Elaborated in the depiction of Goethe's collected works is not merely the literal ideal of a collected-works edition but the allegorical depiction of life as form. The thread of life, an established mythological metaphor for someone's lifespan, rests in the hands of the three Fates or Moirai.[111] Johann Gottfried Schadow's grave relief for Alexander von der Mark from 1790 in the Dorotheenstädtische Kirche in Berlin (now at the Alte Nationalgalerie in Berlin) is an apposite illustration, particularly for a novel composed in the same city (see figure 3). To the Moirai belong Clotho, who is depicted with a spindle and who spins the thread of life; Lachesis, who measures the thread (specifically, a linen thread), which is the fullness of life; and Atropos, who cuts it and thereby brings about the moment of death.[112] To appreciate just one example of how this iconography informs *Der grüne Heinrich*, consider the scene of Anna's death. As Anna lies dying,

---

111. In the story about Regine from *Das Sinngedicht*, the three Moirai are invoked by name, a further indication that their iconography informs Keller's oeuvre. See Keller, *Das Sinngedicht*, in *HKKA*, 7:88. On depictions of the Moirai in art and literature, see Gernot Michael Müller, "Moiren," in *Mythenrezeption: Die antike Mythologie in Literatur, Musik und Kunst von den Anfängen bis zur Gegenwart*, ed. Maria Moog-Grünewald, vol. 5 of *Der Neue Pauly Supplemente*, ed. Hubert Cancik, Manfed Landfester, and Helmuth Schnieder (Stuttgart: J. B. Metzler, 2008), 436–40.

112. On this conventional depiction of the Moirai, see Robert Graves, *The Greek Myths* (London: Penguin Books, 1992), 204.

Figure 3. The three Moirai on Johann Gottfried Schadow, *Grabmal des Grafen Alexander von der Mark*, 1788–1790. Marble, 623×370 cm. Berlin, Staatliche Museen zu Berlin—Preußischer Kulturbesitz, Nationalgalerie.

Heinrich remains outside her room, absentmindedly playing with a pair of scissors, an object that associates him with Atropos and thereby suggests he bears responsibility for her approaching death.[113]

---

113. The passage reads:
A few moments later, when she [Katherine] had left, the schoolmaster came in, and I saw that he took a beautifully bound devotional book with him when he went away again to go to Anna's room. I, on the other hand, was looking at all the little things lying on the table, playing with her [Katherine's] scissors, and could not seriously think that Anna should be in any danger.

Einige Augenblicke nachher, als sie gegangen, kam der Schulmeister herein und ich sah, daß er ein schön eingebundenes Andachtsbuch mitnahm, als er sich wieder entfernte, um in Anna's Zimmer zu gehen. Ich hingegen beschaute alle Sächelchen, welche auf dem Tische lagen, spielte mit ihrer Scheere und konnte mir gar nicht ernstlich denken, daß irgend eine Gefahr für Anna sein sollte.

Keller, *Der grüne Heinrich* (1st ed., 1854–1855), in *HKKA*, 12:41. It is notable that the scene of Anna's death concludes the same chapter (book 3, chapter 1) that begins with the scene of reading Goethe. This makes evident that an iconography of the

However, Atropos is also sometimes depicted not as handling a pair of scissors but rather—as on Schadow's relief (see figure 3)—as reading from a book, the book of fate, from which she determines a person's time of death. Similarly, Lachesis is alternatively shown not measuring thread but bearing an overflowing cornucopia from which she measures the fullness of life. Since antiquity and into the nineteenth century (at least among the era's wealthy, as is the case for Schadow's grave relief), these three figures have often been used to adorn tombs. The three are also regularly depicted, as exemplified by the third-century Roman sarcophagus depicted in figure 4, in conjunction with the mythological figure Endymion, who also informs *Der grüne Heinrich*. Having fallen in love with the beautiful youth Endymion, the moon goddess Selene petitioned for his immortality from Zeus in order to preserve his beauty. Zeus granted Endymion immortal sleep in a cave in which he by some accounts fathered fifty of Selene's daughters.[114] Endymion is thus a figure of fecundity and a mythological case of immortality achieved through premature interment. The third-century Roman sarcophagus visualizes the iconographic proximity of these two mythologies as two ways of allegorizing death: The three Moirai are depicted in the upper left; Endymion in the bottom right.

When Heinrich hears his mother's knitting needles clicking, he is reminded that he is still alive (and not, as he first perceived, prematurely buried in his own tomb), that his life's thread is still being spun. Here, as throughout the novel, Heinrich's mother is associated with Clotho, an association reinforced by her making of and concern for cloth. Contrary to that association, the narrative structure of the

---

thread of life is particularly salient to this chapter. The thread of life is also named in conjunction with the spiral lines Heinrich paints in Munich, which the secondhand dealer describes as Heinrich's "true lifeline" (wahre Lebenslinie). Keller, *Der grüne Heinrich* (1st ed., 1854–1855), in *HKKA*, 12:311. For a discussion of this scene, see Torra-Mattenklott, *Poetik der Figur*, 205–7.

114. *Der grüne Heinrich* is replete with references to the mythological Selene to describe Judith, who is herself moonlike. White-skinned and most alluring in the moonlight in which she regularly meets Heinrich, Judith casts herself, like Selene, as the seductress of a male youth. See Keller, *Der grüne Heinrich* (1st ed., 1854–1855), in *HKKA*, 11:457, 461.

Figure 4. Sarcophagus with a scene related to the myth of Endymion and Selene and the three Moirai in the upper left, late second to early third century AD. Marble, 66 × 240 × 80 cm. Rome, Musei Capitolini, Palazzo Nuovo. Photograph by Egisto Sani.

childhood memoir at first sight attributes the origin of Heinrich's thread of life to his father, whose own thread is prematurely and tragically cut short. It famously begins with a well-rounded biography, a bildungsroman in miniature, of Heinrich's father, who is described as handing Heinrich a golden string,[115] a thread that Heinrich himself spins further when writing the childhood memoir and that he hopes to perpetuate in living a well-ordered life. Throughout the novel, writing is thus conceived as a practice akin to spinning for giving one's life the continuous, linear form of a thread or string, a durative form that contrasts with the immediacy of an image or a cast-

---

115. The passage reads:
Before the midday height of his life, he stepped back into the inscrutable universe and left behind the traditional golden string of life, whose beginning no one knows, in my weak hands, and all that remains for me to do is to tie it to the obscure future with honor or perhaps to tear it forever, when I too will die.

Er ist vor der Mittagshöhe seines Lebens zurückgetreten in das unerforschliche All und hat die überkommene goldene Lebensschnur, deren Anfang Niemand kennt, in meinen schwachen Händen zurück gelassen und es bleibt mir nur übrig, sie mit Ehren an die dunkle Zukunft zu knüpfen oder vielleicht für immer zu zerreißen, wenn auch ich sterben werde.

Keller, *Der grüne Heinrich* (1st ed., 1854–1855), in *HKKA*, 11:81.

ing.[116] In light of the significance the novel assigns to knitting and spinning, consider again Keller's description of his failed novel as having a "knitted-sock form." It is a characterization that aligns the tasks of giving form to the novel and the protagonist with the feminized semantic reservoir of thread, knitting, and weaving. Keller conceives of himself, in contrast to Heinrich's mother, as having merely woven a shapeless sock when writing his novel.

In attributing the golden string of Heinrich's life to his father, yet persistently associating Heinrich's mother with thread and cloth, the novel stages a contest as to which parent represents the primordial source of that thread. In an early scene in the novel, as Heinrich packs his trunk to leave for Munich, the text tries to resolve this contest as to the origin of Heinrich's life thread by instituting a gender dichotomy in which cloth belongs to the domain of the mother and paper to that of the father, a division that suggests that women have no feeling for the significance of paper formats. When packing, Heinrich must rearrange the folders, papers, and books that his mother has stuffed into his trunk, for only he appreciates that format is a matter of fit between the format of the trunk and the format of its content, its paper objects.

> Heinrich looked into the trunk; with the right idea, the good woman had spread folders and books on the bottom; only she had, with less neatness, not sufficiently stacked various sheets and papers together, so some of them were bent against the walls of the trunk, which the son eagerly

---

116. Heinrich reads his childhood memoir in search of a thread to guide him. Writing, in turn, is a practice of seeking continuity, a thread, between the past of the childhood memoir and the present, beginning at the point he reads that autobiographical text. "He was holding a bound manuscript in his hands and leafing through it as if he wanted to find a *guiding principle* or at least the starting points for one. It was the story of his youth up to now, which he had written down in youthful subjectivity and writing bliss during the time right before his departure to develop a kind of conclusion and overview" (In der Hand hielt er ein eingebundenes Manuscript und blätterte darin umher, als ob er eine *Richtschnur* oder wenigstens die Anknüpfungspunkte für eine solche herausfinden wollte. Es war die Geschichte seiner bisherigen Jugend, welche er in jugendlicher Subjektivität und Schreibseligkeit während der letzten Zeit vor seiner Abreise niedergeschrieben hatte, um sich eine Art Abschluß und Uebersicht zu bilden). Keller, *Der grüne Heinrich* (1st ed., 1854–1855), in HKKA, 11:62; emphasis mine.

fixed. Most housewives do not have much of a feeling for paper because it does not belong to their domain. Their paper is white cloth, which must be available in large, well-ordered stacks, since they write their whole philosophy of life, their sorrows, and their joys on it.

> Heinrich guckte in den Koffer; mit richtigem Sinn hatte die gute Frau Mappen und Bücher auf den Boden gebreitet; nur hatte sie mit weniger Zartheit verschiedene Bogen und Papiere nicht genugsam zusammengeschichtet, so daß einige derselben an den Wänden des Koffers gekrümmt wurden, was der Sohn eifrig verbesserte. Für Papier haben die meisten Hausfrauen überhaupt nicht viel Gefühl, weil es nicht in ihren Bereich gehört. Die weiße Leinwand ist ihr Papier, die muß in großen, wohl geordneten Schichten vorhanden sein, da schreiben sie ihre ganze Lebensphilosophie, ihre Leiden und ihre Freuden darauf.[117]

However, while the passage introduces a dichotomy whereby men are associated with paper and women with cloth, that dichotomy is also immediately undercut in a number of ways: first, by the fact that paper was still produced in the mid-nineteenth century from cloth scraps, meaning that these two materials are not so very different, and second, by the very facts of Heinrich's life. After all, his mother's spinning produces canvas (*Leinwand*), a term that encompasses both the cloth Heinrich wears and the cloth he uses as canvas for painting. In line with the material realism of the novel, his mother spins to cover his basic necessities (his shirts) and the material basis of his artistic production (the canvas).[118] Similarly, at a key point in the novel, his mother is described as dedicating herself in Heinrich's absence in a decidedly spiderlike manner to spinning and weaving an incredible quantity of cloth in the hope that his happiness will be written upon it:

> It seems that by weaving this supply of white cloth each year, she believes to be luring in your happiness, as if in an outstretched net that may be filled with a virtuous household, or as scholars and writers are stimu-

---

117. Keller, *Der grüne Heinrich* (1st ed., 1854–1855), in HKKA, 11:22–23. The scene is also notable as an example of the problem of format as fit.

118. On the symbolism of cloth in the novel, which he identifies as belonging to a set of metaphors encompassing letters, paper, canvas, and the breast, see Groddeck, "Eine gewisse Unförmlichkeit," 38–39.

lated and induced to write a good work by a book of white paper, or as painters to paint a beautiful piece of life by a stretched canvas.

> Wie es scheint, glaubt sie durch diesen Vorrath weißen Tuches, das sie jedes Jahr weben läßt, Ihr Glück herbeizulocken, gleichsam wie in ein aufgespanntes Netz, damit es durch einen tüchtigen Hausstand ausgefüllt werde, oder gleichsam wie die Gelehrten und Schriftsteller durch ein Buch weißes Papier gereizt und veranlaßt werden sollen, ein gutes Werk darauf zu schreiben, oder die Maler durch eine ausgespannte Leinwand, ein schönes Stück Leben darauf zu malen.[119]

She regards the cloth, analogously to a white sheet of paper or a blank canvas, as a prefabricated media object awaiting its content. Her cloth thus becomes the material condition for the very possibility of composing not only Heinrich's but also her own life story. Insofar as the passage explicitly compares the cloth to both the canvas and paper on which a work might materialize, it reminds us of the preformatted, material basis of any work and undermines the very binary of paper–cloth that Heinrich attempted to pin on the binary father–mother.

In spinning the canvas or paper on which a work might materialize and providing the very basic material means for his pursuit, Heinrich's mother constitutes the material origin of his existence and of his potential artistic subjectivity as well. In beginning with the biography of his father and attributing to him a golden thread, Heinrich's childhood memoir once again misses the mark and fails to recognize who is spinning his life's thread. Because Heinrich fails to incorporate this maternal origin into the narrative of his self, both insofar as he fails to narrate the story of his mother as he has done for his father and insofar as he cannot provide the material means for his existence and instead remains parasitically dependent on her, he cannot spin the thread of his own life. Heinrich, in other words, fails at the task of giving his life a form because he fails to incorporate the maternal, material origins of artistic production into his artistic subjectivity. The original outline of the novel that Keller sent Vieweg in 1850 appropriately already employs the imagery of the

---

119. Keller, *Der grüne Heinrich* (1st ed., 1854–1855), in *HKKA*, 12:324.

thread as originating from Heinrich's mother to paint a violent picture of the novel's conclusion: "The ribbon that binds him backward to humanity seems to him [after his mother's death] to have been cut off bloodily and violently, and for that reason he also cannot grasp the loose half end of it that leads forward, and this also brings about his death."[120] The image of violent rupture anticipates Heinrich's failure at the task of giving his life a form such that he too must die following the death of his mother. His mother's death represents not only the depletion of his economic resources but more fundamentally the termination of the source of his life's thread. To employ the metaphor of the thread of life: Because Heinrich has yet to acquire the ability to spin his own thread of life, he cannot give his life a form, and his death invariably follows upon that of his mother's. A poetics of the scissors thereby again manifests itself as a cutting of genealogical threads. The condition for the achievement of artistic subjectivity, elaborated *ex negativo* in Heinrich's example, is to incorporate the maternal source of one's material existence and artistic subjectivity into one's own being.

Goethe's Thread

The thread of Goethe's life is the clear counterimage to Heinrich's formless life still being spun. In the scene of reading, Goethe's thread of life, which has already been spun, apportioned, and cut, returns as the piece of string that ties together the fifty volumes of the collected works. In the very moment that Heinrich unties the string that binds the books together, it is as if he holds Goethe's thread of life in his hands.

> The unknown dead man went through almost all occupations and interests, and everywhere he pulled the tied threads to himself, whose ends only disappeared in his invisible hand. As if I now had all these threads

---

120. "Das Band, welches ihn nach rückwärts an die Menschheit knüpft, scheint ihm blutig und gewaltsam abgeschnitten und er kann deswegen auch das lose halbe Ende desselben, das nach vorwärts führt, nicht in die Hände fassen und dies führt auch seinen Tod herbei." Keller to Eduard Vieweg, May 3, 1850, in *HKKA*, 19:172–74.

in the hulking knot of the string that went around the books, I fell upon it and hurriedly began to untie it, and when it finally came undone, the golden fruits of his eighty-year life fell apart in the most beautiful way, spread out over the daybed, and spilled over the edge onto the floor such that I had my hands full keeping the abundance together.

Der unbekannte Todte schritt fast durch alle Beschäftigungen und Anregungen und überall zog er angeknüpfte Fäden an sich, deren Enden nur in seiner unsichtbaren Hand verschwanden. Als ob ich jetzt alle diese Fäden in dem ungeschlachten Knoten der Schnur, welche die Bücher umwand, beisammen hätte, fiel ich über denselben her und begann hastig ihn aufzulösen, und als er endlich aufging, da fielen die goldenen Früchte des achtzigjährigen Lebens auf das Schönste auseinander, verbreiteten sich über das Ruhbett und fielen über dessen Rand auf den Boden, daß ich alle Hände voll zu thun hatte, den Reichthum zusammen zu halten.[121]

Goethe's thread of life ties together the fifty volumes—potentially fractured across time and space, like the four volumes of *Der grüne Heinrich*—into a unified corpus, one body from the manifold volumes, the cornucopia of Goethe's life and work. In the apportioned form of the string, Goethe's life also becomes part of the work's format tasked with ensuring that unity arises from the disparate volumes. Secured in a knot, the thread of life loses beginning, end, and duration, and instead gives form to the books (the corpus).[122] Put differently, Goethe's life assumes a form that also itself contains Goethe's life again twice over: once in the form of the autobiography *Dichtung und Wahrheit* and once in the sum of Goethe's life work.

Because the string that binds Goethe's books together constitutes a more easily recognizable allegorical image with a sustained iconographic tradition, namely, the thread of life, it alerts us to the specific tenor of Keller's real allegory. Read allegorically, as I have emphasized, the passage stylizes the collected-works edition as a complete and unified corpus that substitutes for the body of the author and makes him present in the confines of Heinrich's childhood home. However, the allegorical functions of the string and books as

---

121. Keller, *Der grüne Heinrich* (1st ed., 1854–1855), in *HKKA*, 12:15.
122. For a contrasting use of the metaphor of the knot as representing entanglement rather than organic unity, see Sean Franzel, *Writing Time: Studies in Serial Literature, 1780–1850* (Ithaca, NY: Cornell University Press, 2023), 18–19.

representing Goethe's life exemplify a realist poetics that directs our attention to prosaic and seemingly insignificant objects. Keller's real allegory selects quotidian, or "real," objects to bear allegorical significance. For one, the knot that embodies the moment Goethe's life comes together as a form is pejoratively described as a "hulking" knot as might be tied by a woman or a secondhand dealer, descriptions that embed these objects within the world Heinrich inhabits. Similarly, the scene of reading Goethe strongly emphasizes that the collected-works edition is not only a carrier of Goethe's life and a substitute for his person but also a commercial, mass-produced object that Heinrich cannot afford. The strength of Keller's real allegory lies in maintaining these two elements in view: books and string as everyday material objects and, at the same time, as the vehicles of realist allegory.

In anticipation of the following chapter, one final aspect of this allegory demands elaboration. Goethe's advantage as an artist and author is to have his work of eighty years bound together with his life thread into a single whole. Heinrich's curse, as a painter and author, is to have to pick up where he left off, to be unable to escape the progression of the time of his life (for which reason he still cannot draw after reading Goethe's collected works and must instead continue to endure the sound of his mother's needles knitting his life's fabric). The ideal of authorship elaborated in this brilliant scene of reading thus insists that alongside the work of Clotho, the spinning and weaving traditionally associated with storytelling, Atropos and the instrument of the scissors, which bring the thread to an end and render it final and complete, are fundamental to the form of life. Because the novel remains committed to a poetics of barrenness in which the fullness of life is present only in a moment removed from the duration of time, its protagonist cannot achieve a form of life from within that life itself.

To say that the work of Atropos and her scissors is portrayed as central to the making of a form of life is to say that the form of life is contingent on its pastness, on the finality of the protagonist's life.[123]

---

123. On the difficulties of narrating a life that has yet to be completed, see Gerhart von Graevenitz's two illuminating essays, "Geschichte aus dem Geist des Nekrologs: Zur Begründung der Biographie im 19. Jahrhundert," *Deutsche Vier-*

True to this logic, and to the logic of the collected-works edition as representing the unity of an author's life and work, the scene of reading Goethe begins with Heinrich's memory from his early childhood in which a carpenter working in the house announces, "The great Goethe has died." The logic of the collected-works edition—a logic that Keller's narrative faithfully reproduces—stipulates that only after this pronouncement, after the death of the author, can these books enter Heinrich's home. It is this deceased person who returns to life in an eroticized shadow form as Heinrich reads. The unity of life and work is necessarily a posthumous achievement.

Goethe's advantage, to make the point again, is to have his work of eighty years bound together with his life thread as a single whole. Life achieves a form not in the story of its formation as we expect from the genre of the novel but in its posthumous containment in the format of the collected works, in the cutting and tying of the life thread into a formed knot. Goethe's *Vollständige Ausgabe letzter Hand* is then a sarcophagus—a container for a corpse, or in this case a corpus—from which the immortal poet continues to speak. So closely bound to the hand and body of the author, so near to his intentions, and so complete and exhaustive in their representation of his life, these volumes reproduce the author himself in the confines of the living room—if only Heinrich had the financial means to purchase them. Heinrich's curse, as a painter and author, is to have to pick up where he left off, to be unable to escape the plodding progression of time, which prevents him from seeing his own life as cut off and tied into a unified knot. The idea of the collected works answers, in other words, the crisis of the fracture of form and the diagnosis of the novel's formlessness; it also underlines the importance not of the Moira Clotho, who is embodied in Heinrich's mother, but of Atropos, who cuts life's thread.

The unique temporality of this moment, the moment of reading Goethe that contains the entirety of a life but is itself barren or

---

teljahrsschrift für Literaturwissenschaft und Geistesgeschichte 54, no. 1 (1980): 105–70; and "Das Ich am Ende: Strukturen der Ich-Erzählung in Apuleius' *Goldenem Esel* und Grimmelshausens *Simplicissimus Teutsch*," in Stierle and Warning, *Das Ende*, 123–54.

fruitless for the reader, makes it apparent that Keller's difficulties completing the novel are of a different order than simply the struggles of perpetual procrastinator or the fate of an author hounded by his publisher. By strongly associating the achievement of authorship with the format of a posthumous collected-works edition, Keller renders each text unfinished and wanting in authority simply because the author remains alive, leaving the texts and the spirit of the author potentially subject to changes and revisions. Publishing a second, third, and fourth edition of his novel and attempting to eradicate the first are symptomatic of that bind. They are an attempt to keep pace with an alternating and necessarily incomplete sense of self. In Keller's case, each edition of the "same" novel invents its form anew because the definitive edition is postponed to the finality of a collected-works edition and the author's death. A collected-works edition can fulfill the aspiration to archive and reproduce the whole of an author's oeuvre not only on account of its completeness and because it indexes the person of the author but also because it ideally appears at the point of no return at which the corpus can no longer be revised or augmented (an ideal that naturally overlooks the plurality of collected works often issued by authors during their lifetimes and the many that follow thereafter). A collected-works edition published during an author's lifetime is thus constitutively incomplete and lacking in authority, a point that was, for example, gleefully exploited in advertisements for newer editions of Goethe's collected works. In contrast, Keller's ambition when writing *Der grüne Heinrich* was not simply to fashion and establish himself as an author after a failed bout of painting. His ambition was to write a work that would act as a placeholder for his collected works yet to be written; to write an autobiographical novel that could serve his later readers and interpreters as the key or code to deciphering his literary work, allowing them to see the unity of life and work as a single form. The scale of that ambition possibly warrants, or at least explains, the copious time Keller spent writing and rewriting his first novel.

2

The Death of the Author

Premature Burial in Keller's Poetry

In my interpretation of Heinrich's reading of Goethe, I argued that the form of life is imagined in the terms of a collected-works edition as the retrospective presence of a life in its totality and furthermore, that the possibility of that form is contingent on the pastness of that life. The achievement of the collect-works edition depends on the work of the scissors, that is, on the thread of life having been cut. The scene of reading Goethe in *Der grüne Heinrich* introduces this condition of authorship insofar as the entry of the books into Heinrich's mother's home is preceded and prepared by the childhood memory of Goethe's death: "The great Goethe has died."[1] The collected-works edition can represent a form of life because, for one, it is a posthumous achievement. The scene of reading Goethe thereby elaborates Walter Benjamin's claim that the storyteller "has borrowed his au-

---

1. "Der große Göthe ist gestorben." Keller, *Der grüne Heinrich* (1st ed., 1854–1855), in *HKKA*, 12:15.

thority from death," but it specifies that authority with reference to a single publishing format.² If, as Benjamin writes, a person possesses at the moment of death a unique ability to see a "sequence of images [...] unfolding the views of himself in which he has encountered himself without being aware of it," then the collected-works edition is imagined to be a cultural artifact that records that privileged view upon one's life and makes it available to those that outlive the author.³

Authorship is thereby strongly aligned with the question of a posthumous legacy and cultural prestige. The collected-works edition is conceptualized as a medium through which the bygone author speaks and retains a lifelike presence among the living, while practices of reading enact the revival of that voice. As Leah Price notes with reference to the metonymical invocations of the author's body in the titles of such editions—for example, with reference to the hand of the author (*Vollständige Ausgabe letzter Hand*)—collected-works editions are thereby imagined to function similarly to relics in which the presence and power of the deceased are preserved: "It is a peculiarity of bookplates that they bring 'the dead hand' always before the imagination. Borrowing from the logic of the saint's relic, association copies invest the object with value borrowed from the identities of its human users. And like the saint, the previous owner must be dead."⁴ At issue here is thus neither the death of the author in the sense of Roland Barthes, who declared the author dead so that we might turn our attention to the agency of the structure of language, nor is it the death of the author in the sense of Michel Foucault, who too declared the author's death to emphasize that texts are not determined by the choices of their author's but by historical discourses, one of those discourses being

---

2. Walter Benjamin, "The Storyteller: Observations on the Works of Nikolai Leskov," trans. Harry Zohn, in *Selected Writings*, vol. 3, *1935–1938*, ed. Howard Eiland and Michael W. Jennings (Cambridge, MA: Belknap Press of Harvard University Press, 2002), 151.

3. Benjamin, "The Storyteller," 151. For a discussion of Jean Paul Friedrich Richter's grappling with the same nexus of concerns, but with a very different response than the one I attribute to Keller, see Sean Franzel, *Writing Time: Studies in Serial Literature, 1780–1850* (Ithaca, NY: Cornell University Press, 2023), 238–61.

4. Leah Price, *How to Do Things with Books in Victorian Britain* (Princeton, NJ: Princeton University Press, 2012), 257.

the concept of authorship itself.[5] The death I am excavating does not refer to a metaphorical end to the author function but to the constitutive role of the individual author's literal death in the historical and structural discourse of authorship. Keller's texts suggest that for the specter of the author to arise in modern discourse as a key to understanding and interpreting a text—and thus as a specter that Barthes and Foucault point to as structural or historical in nature—the author must either die or their death must be imagined. From the perspective of Keller's earliest poetry and prose, the poet must be biologically deceased for the unity and identity of life and work to come into view.

The folio editions of Shakespeare's works, which served (alongside Goethe) as a further crucial example for the unity of life and work for the nineteenth century and for Keller, provide a powerful historical precedent for the view that the death of the author constitutes a condition of authorship as exemplified in a collected-works edition. The First Folio of Shakespeare was famously adorned with an epigraph (or epitaph) by Ben Jonson, whose own works were formative for the history of the collected-works edition. The epigraph reads:

[. . .] Soule of the Age!
The applause! delight! the wonder of our Stage!
My *Shakespeare*, rise; I will not lodge thee by
Chaucer, or *Spenser*, or bid *Beaumont* lye
A little further, to make thee a roome:
Thou art a Moniment, without a tombe,
And art aliue still while thy Booke doth liue,
And we have wits to read, and praise to giue.[6]

---

5. See Roland Barthes, "The Death of the Author," in *Image, Music, Text*, trans. Stephen Heath (Glasgow: Fontana Paperbacks, 1977), 142–48; and Michel Foucault, "What Is an Author?," in *Aesthetics, Method, and Epistemology*, ed. James D. Faubion, vol. 2 of *Essential Works of Foucault, 1954–1984*, ed. Paul Rabinow (New York: New Press, 1998), 205–22.

6. Ben Jonson, "To the Memory of My Beloued, The Avthor Mr. William Shakespeare: And What He Hath Left Vs," in *Mr. William Shakespeares Comedies, Histories, & Tragedies* (London: Isaac Jaggard & Edward Blount, 1623), n.p.

Here the book substitutes for the tomb, and the corpus for the corpse. Like the saint's relic, which promises direct access to the saint's miracles to the faithful through touch,[7] the collected-works edition commemorates and provides physical and thaumaturgical access to the author. It thereby restores the vitality of a past completed life for posterity. So too does the Cotta edition of Goethe's collected works for Heinrich in Keller's novel, where the corpus stands in for Goethe's body and realizes his presence on the daybed. Authorship, as imagined in Keller's early work, is thus achieved and guaranteed for posterity by means of a very specific kind of material artifact: the definitive and all-encompassing publication of an author's *Werkausgabe*, the complete or collected works in which an author's life is preserved posthumously.

Der grüne Heinrich further elaborates an ideal of authorship that depends on the author's biological death with regard to the second apotheosis of German literature, Friedrich Schiller. While Schiller's dramas make numerous appearances throughout the novel in the form of community reenactments (always with the narrator's caveat that it is not Schiller's texts themselves that are faithfully reenacted but bastardized versions in plentiful circulation), Heinrich later reflects on Schiller's life and work when struggling in Munich.[8] In fact, Keller's novel was written during the very years in which Schiller's descendants sued the state in the hopes of extending his expiring copyright, a privilege they were denied, thereby permitting Schiller's works to enter the public domain.[9] Keller's passage por-

---

7. See Philippe Ariès, *The Hour of Our Death: The Classic History of Western Attitudes Toward Death over the Last One Thousand Years*, trans. Helen Weaver (New York: Vintage Books, 1981), 202–96.

8. The narrator explains: "The performance was based on Schiller's *Tell*, which was widely available in an edition for public schools and only lacked the love episode between Bertha von Brunneck and Ulrich von Rudenz" (Man legte der Aufführung Schiller's Tell zu Grunde, welcher in einer Volksschulausgabe vielfach vorhanden war und welchem nur die Liebesepisode zwischen Bertha von Brunneck und Ulrich von Rudenz fehlte). Keller, *Der grüne Heinrich* (1st ed., 1854–1855), in *HKKA*, 11:410. On the significance of these scenes of community reenactment in relation to Keller's politics and the idea of the nation, see Michael Lipkin, "'A Public Spectacle': Keller, Schiller, and the Civic Festival," in *Kellers Medien: Formen—Genres—Institutionen*, ed. Frauke Berndt (Berlin: Walter de Gruyter, 2022), 289–312.

9. For a summary of the nineteenth-century lawsuits concerning the copyright of Schiller's works, see Ulrike Vedder, *Das Testament als literarisches Dispositiv:*

trays Schiller's oeuvre as an index of a completed life that I recounted in my analysis of Heinrich reading Goethe. While the passage is not free from an irony with which the narrator views his naive protagonist, the description nonetheless brims with admiration for Schiller as a publishing ideal. Schiller clearly represents the opposite to Heinrich's formless and unproductive life.

> If, however, one wants to consider an example of influential work from the great public world that is at the same time a true and decent life, then one must look at Schiller's life and work. [...] But one can say, it was only after his death that his honest, clear, and true working life began to show its impact and earning capacity, and even if one totally disregards the intellectual legacy he left the world, one must still be amazed by the material movement, by the mere physical benefit, he left behind him through the mere, faithful emphasis of his intellectual ideal. As far as the German language reaches, there is in the cities hardly a house and in the villages at least one or two houses in which one or more copies of his works do not stand on the shelf or in the bookcases. And the further the education of the nation spreads, the greater will be the already immense multiplication of these works, penetrating in the end into the humblest hut. A hundred profit-hungry opportunists are only waiting for the printing privilege to expire to spread Schiller's noble life work as widely and cheaply as the Bible, and the extensive life earnings that occurred during the first half of the century will double during the second half and perhaps double again in the coming century. What a throng of papermakers, paper merchants, book printers, salesmen, errand boys, commentators of the works, leather merchants, bookbinders have earned and will continue to earn their bread, what an enduring deed, what a lasting source of earnings in the most material sense were thus Schiller's short years of work and life. In contrast to the Revalenta Arabica of much activity, this is also an extensive movement but with a sweet and substantial core, and only the outer coarse shell of an even greater and more important intellectual happiness, of the purest national joy.

> Will man hingegen aus der großen öffentlichen Welt ein Beispiel wirkungsreicher Arbeit, die zugleich ein wahres und vernünftiges Leben ist, betrachten, so muß man das Leben und Wirken Schiller's ansehen. [...] Aber nach seinem Tode erst, kann man sagen, begann sein ehrliches, klares und wahres Arbeitsleben seine Wirkung und seine Erwerbsfähigkeit zu zeigen, und wenn man ganz absieht von seiner geistigen Erbschaft,

Kulturelle Praktiken des Erbes in der Literatur des 19. Jahrhunderts (München: Wilhelm Fink, 2011), 162–64.

welche er der Welt hinterlassen, so muß man erstaunen über die materielle Bewegung, über den bloß leiblichen Nutzen, den er durch das bloße treue Hervorkehren seines geistigen Ideales hinterließ. So weit die deutsche Sprache reicht, ist in den Städten kaum ein Haus, in welchem nicht seine Werke ein- oder mehrfach auf Gesims und Schränken stehen, und in Dörfern wenigstens in einem oder zwei Häusern. Je weiter aber die Bildung der Nation sich verbreitet, desto größer wird die jetzt schon ungeheure Vervielfältigung dieser Werke werden und zuletzt in die niederste Hütte dringen. Hundert Geschäftshungrige lauern nur auf das Erlöschen des Privilegiums, um die edle Lebensarbeit Schiller's so massenhaft und wohlfeil zu verbreiten, wie die Bibel, und der umfangreiche leibliche Erwerb, der während der ersten Hälfte eines Jahrhunderts stattgefunden, wird während der zweiten Hälfte desselben um das Doppelte wachsen und vielleicht im kommenden Jahrhundert noch einmal um das Doppelte. Welch' eine Menge von Papiermachern, Papierhändlern, Buchdruckersleuten, Verkäufern, Laufburschen, Commentatoren der Werke, Lederhändlern, Buchbindern verdienten und werden ihr Brot noch verdienen, welch' eine fortwährende That, welch' nachhaltiger Erwerb im materiellsten Sinne waren also die kurzen Schiller'schen Arbeits- und Lebensjahre. Dies ist, im Gegensatz zu der Revalenta arabica manches Treibens, auch eine umfangreiche Bewegung, aber mit einem süßen und gehaltreichen Kern, und nur die äußere derbe Schale eines noch größeren und wichtigeren geistigen Glückes, der reinsten nationalen Freude.[10]

Schiller's legacy manifests itself as the coincidence of monetary value stemming from the extraordinary sales of his collected works that now adorn nearly every German household—a demand sufficient, as the passage notes, to support an entire bookmaking industry and to make Schiller's collected works rival the Bible as the book of all books—and from his equally widely distributed cultural prestige. In this respect Schiller provides an excellent example for the difference and potential overlap between competing currencies, in this case, monetary and cultural, that Fritz Breithaupt has argued are essential to the realism of *Der grüne Heinrich*.[11] Monetary profit and cultural prestige represent the dividends earned from an "honest, clear, and true working life," which pays precisely in the years after one's life

---

10. Keller, *Der grüne Heinrich* (1st ed., 1854–1855), in *HKKA*, 12:272–73.
11. See Fritz Breithaupt, "Homo Oeconomicus," in *1848 oder das Versprechen der Moderne*, ed. Jürgen Fohrmann and Helmut J. Schneider (Würzburg: Königshausen & Neumann, 2003), 85–112.

has been completed, indeed, whose earnings are predicted to grow the more the author's life fades into the past. While in the scene of reading Goethe, the overflowing corpus of volumes is proportional to the bountiful eighty years of Goethe's life, Schiller's posthumous impact is in no way compromised by his comparatively short life span. Not only does the clause "it was only after his death that his honest, clear, and true working life began to show its impact" delineate his death as a condition of his authorial success, his early passing also initiates the education of the nation through his literary estate: Schiller's passing makes way for his work to execute a broad aesthetic education. It is worth noting that Schiller's work, here as elsewhere in the novel, is also attributed with the potential to create and strengthen a community, in this case, to create a German nation whose cohesion is grounded in the individual ownership of Schiller's volumes, much like his dramas allegedly did for the Swiss communities in which they were reenacted. Goethe's literature, in contrast, is destined for the solitary reader whose reading practice is characterized by interiority and intimacy. While Benedict Anderson attributes the formation of the imagined community of the modern nation-state to mass-circulated periodicals,[12] *Der grüne Heinrich* attributes, 130 years earlier, the mass distribution of Schiller's collected works with a similar formative power.

Yet to make the achievement of authorship contingent on having completed one's life and issuing a collected-works edition places the living author, especially one at the beginning rather than at the conclusion of his literary career, in an unmistakable bind. In this chapter, I intend to elaborate Keller's early response to the predicament of being a nascent author starting his publishing career, an author whose collected-works edition and death were far from immanent. Remarkably, Keller's earliest poetry collection—that is, a relatively youthful Keller's debut as an author a decade before publishing *Der grüne Heinrich*—already insists on the biological death of the author as a necessary source of authority and a condition of authorship. These early efforts make evident that Keller wrote, from the early 1840s

---

12. See Benedict Anderson, *Imagined Communities: Reflections on the Origin and Spread of Nationalism* (London: Verso, 1983), 35–36.

onward, not only with an eye toward either a collection or a novella cycle, as Walter Morgenthaler has noted, but also with the culminating format of authorship, the collected-works edition, in mind.[13]

That response, in a nutshell, imagines the premature burial of the living author as a possibility for achieving the status of authorship and the creation of a *Nachlass* that can only operate posthumously. Having one's life cut prematurely short and so being permitted to speak from the standpoint of a completed life recovers the possibility, in other words, of being an author of literature at all. It is against this background that we can, for one, make sense of Heinrich's somewhat peculiar feeling that the moment Goethe's collected works leave the house at the conclusion of the scene of reading was as if he were in a grave: "It was as if a host of glowing and singing spirits had left the living room, making it suddenly seem silent and empty; I jumped up, looked around, and thought myself as in a grave if my mother's knitting needles had not made a friendly noise."[14] Absorbed in the deep interiority of reading and embraced by Goethe's shadowy specter, Heinrich momentarily imagines himself to inhabit, alongside Goethe and Schiller, the ghostly world of the dead, thereby seemingly literalizing Ralf Simon's observation that "the canon is, in a certain sense, a gathering of ghosts."[15] Only Heinrich's mother's needles remind him that his life thread is still being spun, that he has not been buried alive, making it impossible to perceive his life as a form.

As the two leading examples of collected-works editions from *Der grüne Heinrich* suggest, this ideal of authorship is inseparable

---

13. "The *Gesammelte Werke* forms the logical conclusion to a literary oeuvre whose works were conceived as cycles and collections from the very beginning." Walter Morgenthaler, "Grattier, Gratthier oder Steinbock? Zur Textkonstitution bei Conrad Ferdinand Meyer und Gottfried Keller," *MLN* 117, no. 3 (April 2002): 540–41.

14. "Es war, als ob eine Schaar glänzender und singender Geister die Stube verließen, so daß diese auf einmal still und leer schien; ich sprang auf, sah mich um und würde mich wie in einem Grabe gedünkt haben, wenn nicht die Stricknadeln meiner Mutter ein freundliches Geräusch verursacht hätten." Keller, *Der grüne Heinrich* (1st ed., 1854–1855), in *HKKA*, 12:16.

15. Ralf Simon, "Gespenster des Realismus: Moderne-Konstellationen in den Spätwerken von Raabe, Stifter und C. F. Meyer," in *Konzepte der Moderne*, ed. Gerhart von Graevenitz (Stuttgart: J. B. Metzler, 1999), 232.

from a perceived condition of epigonality. "The great Goethe has died" marks not just the end of an eighty-year life but also the end of the possibility of German literature at all. To have not yet completed one's life, in turn, becomes a marker of having been born too late to participate in this bygone golden era of literature. The imperative that the author be deceased is one way Keller responds to his status as epigone, as being born too late to participate in the culminating high point of German literature that Schiller and Goethe inhabited. To imagine oneself as prematurely buried, to speak from the grave, is to place oneself in the prestigious company of a past cultural elite.

Premature Burial in Keller's Oeuvre

My claim that Keller answers the bind of being a living author who cannot achieve the posthumous monetary value and cultural authority of Goethe or Schiller through the motif of premature burial acquires plausibility if one appreciates the astonishing pervasiveness of this topic across his work, so pervasive that it ultimately rivals his contemporary Edgar Allan Poe's better-known fascination with the danger of being buried alive.[16] Keller clearly participates in a transatlantic fascination with the phenomenon of premature burial due to suspended animation (*Scheintod*) that swept through the eighteenth and nineteenth centuries, riding on changing perceptions of death.[17] The subject appears in many of his early poems, including "Winternacht" from the collection *Neuere Gedichte* (1851) and the cycle "Gedanken eines Lebendig-Begrabenen" (1846), which my analysis will primarily focus on because it most explicitly imagines

---

16. On Poe's fascination with premature burial, see J. Gerald Kennedy, "Poe and Magazine Writing on Premature Burial," *Studies in the American Renaissance* (1977): 165–78; and Carl H. Sederholm, "Bodies out of Place: Poe, Premature Burial, and the Uncanny," *Forum: University of Edinburgh Postgraduate Journal of Culture and the Arts* 24 (Spring 2017): https://doi.org/10.2218/forum.24.1877.

17. On the preoccupation of the eighteenth and nineteenth centuries with the phenomena of premature burial and *Scheintod*, see Jan Bondeson, *Buried Alive: The Terrifying Story of Our Most Primitive Fear* (New York: W. W. Norton, 2001); and Ariès, *The Hour of Our Death*, 396–408.

the poet as someone who speaks from a premature grave. *Der grüne Heinrich* abounds with examples, including the Meretlein or the living animals Heinrich grotesquely entombs from his menagerie. And the subject more famously drives the plot of the novella "Dietegen," which was published in 1874 as part of the second volume of *Die Leute von Seldwyla* but was conceived much earlier under a title that very explicitly foregrounded the subject of reanimation: "Leben aus dem Tod."[18] Keller's best-known novella from *Die Leute von Seldwyla*, "Romeo und Julia auf dem Dorfe," also begins with a scene of a playful live burial in which the two children bury their doll and a hapless fly while their fathers plough the field. And the concluding scene in which the two lovers float down the stream to their deaths might be considered to mirror the premature burial at the beginning. The barge in which they float serves as their shared coffin.

Not only does premature burial serve Keller as a staple in his literary oeuvre, it also exhibits surprisingly coherent contours. In comparison to the grisly scene in which Montresor entombs his companion in the wine cellar in Poe's "The Cask of Amontillado," to take a contemporaneous point of comparison, Keller's scenes of premature burial are quite heavily sanitized and moralized. For one, Keller's victims are buried not on account of malice but because of accidents, in particular on account of a presiding doctor's neglect or oversight (the exception being when children playfully bury their lifelike toys and living playthings, as is the case with Heinrich's menagerie).[19] More significantly, on those occasions when the prematurely buried are discovered and exhumed, they entirely lack the gothic, ghoulish appearances characteristic of Poe's resurrected; none of Keller's characters,

---

18. Keller first titled his novella "Leben aus dem Tode" and later revised it to "Leben aus Tod," and Ferdinand Weibert, Keller's editor, changed it to "Dietegen." For a facsimile and description of the manuscript's first page that records these changes, see Peter Villwock, Walter Morgenthaler, Peter Stocker, Thomas Binder, and Dominik Müller, "Druckmanuskript für LW4 'Dietegen,'" in *HKKA*, 21:106–7.

19. Though the Meretlein and Dietegen are the victims of murderous disciplinary practices of their medieval societies, the failure to kill them as intended, which results in their premature burials, is directly attributed to the negligence of the presiding doctors—a ubiquitous worry in nineteenth-century accounts of *Scheintod*. See Bondeson, *Buried Alive*, 281.

to draw the comparison to Poe once again, bear the traces of Madeline from "The Fall of the House of Usher," who claws her way out of her tomb, wounded, disfigured, and enraged. Instead, and this is of significance for my later argument concerning the cycle "Gedanken eines Lebendig-Begrabenen," Keller's victims of premature burial are unanimously children or adolescents at the threshold of sexual maturity. Their brief lives and juvenile bodies have been truly cut short; they constitute one subset of the many youths in *Der grüne Heinrich*, including Meierlein, the Snow White–like Anna, and Heinrich himself, who die prematurely.

Even in the cases in which Keller's characters are truly dead rather than merely catatonic, their bodies are not merely free of the signs of decomposition that the nineteenth century took to be the most certain confirmation of death, they also have yet to display any symptoms of natural aging. Premature death arrests their bodies at the height of their vitality. The image of the green grass growing on Henrich's grave—the concluding image of *Der grüne Heinrich*—is precisely one such manifestation of the remaining vitality that has its source in the youthful body buried below.[20] Consequently, in "Das Meretlein" and "Dietegen"—as in "Gedanken eines Lebendig-Begrabenen," in which the speaker is a male youth—the topic of *Scheintod* serves to aestheticize if not eroticize the apparently deceased body. For example, the Meretlein is tormented throughout her life and ultimately killed by the disciplinary measures of *Bildung* imposed on her body and person, measures that culminate in her physical confinement in a coffin; she becomes the object of such efforts not least because her body is also an object of desire for the men around her (including the doctor, the preacher, and her father). Her rising from the grave as a virgin is then presented as an aesthetic moment of luminous radiance: "And since at that very moment the rays of Phoebus, strangely penetrating, pierced the clouds, she looked, in her yellow brocade and with her shining coronet, like a faery or goblin

---

20. "He was buried with astonishment and sympathy on a beautiful, pleasant summer evening, and truly fresh and green grass has grown on his grave" (Es war ein schöner freundlicher Sommerabend, als man ihn mit Verwunderung und Theilnahme begrub, und es ist auf seinem Grabe ein recht frisches und grünes Gras gewachsen). Keller, *Der grüne Heinrich* (1st ed., 1854–1855), in *HKKA*, 12:470.

child."[21] Her *Scheintod* is thus staged as a play on the very word: Her death gives way to a scene of *Schein*, of luminescent beauty. That bewitching beauty is then preserved in the chronicle Heinrich reads, as though her vitality were transferred to the pages and binding of the book, an object with which she was already strongly associated in her lifetime.[22] Analogously, in the poem "Winternacht," when a mermaid who is trapped under a lake's frozen surface pleads with the lyric voice above to rescue her from her live burial, her body is also subject to his lofty, erotic gaze: "Just right under my feet I then saw/Her white beauty, each limb after limb" (Dicht ich unter meinen Füßen sah/Ihre weiße Schönheit Glied für Glied).[23] For readers of *Der grüne Heinrich*, the mermaid's situation is strongly reminiscent of Anna's burial, where Heinrich gazes at her body through a pane of

---

21. "Und wie im selbigen Moment die Strahlen Phöbi seltsam und stechend durch die Wolken gedrungen, so hat es in seinem gelblichen Brokat und mit dem glitzrigen Krönlein ausgesehen, wie ein Feyen- oder Koboltskind." Gottfried Keller *Green Henry*, trans. A. M. Holt, rev. ed. (London: Alma Classics, 2023), 31; Keller, *Der grüne Heinrich* (2nd ed., 1889), in *HKKA*, 1:55. Having identified the iconography of the Meretlein's resurrection as drawn from that of Maria Immaculata, Frauke Berndt points out that the doctor recognizes her not only as a magical creature (as a fairy or imp) but also as an embodiment of the Holy Virgin. See Frauke Berndt, "'Das Meretlein': Zur Ikonographie der Novelle in Gottfried Kellers *Der grüne Heinrich*," in *Historismus und Moderne*, ed. Harald Tausch (Würzburg: Ergon, 1996), 172. It is not least because of her radiance at her moment of death and resurrection that the Meretlein has been read as a recasting of Goethe's Mignon, whose death epitomizes the arrestation of the youthful body as an art object for the male gaze. On the disciplinary and narrative attempts to bind the erotic force that the Meretlein exerts, see Eric Downing, *The Chain of Things: Divinatory Magic and the Practice of Reading in German Literature and Thought, 1850–1940* (Ithaca, NY: Cornell University Press, 2018), 50–52.

22. The Meretlein is repeatedly, albeit subtly, associated with the object of the book, beginning with the book in which Heinrich reads her story. Additionally, when her portrait is painted, she wears a crown of "gold and silver leaves" (Gold- und Silberblättchen) from "beech leaves" (Buchenlaub), invoking not only the "beech tree" (Buchbaum) Heinrich first tries (and fails) to sketch but also a book (*Buch*) and its pages (*Blätter*). Keller, *Der grüne Heinrich* (1st ed., 1854–1855), in *HKKA*, 11:97, 102. While the crown of pages, like a crown of thorns, could be considered a disciplinary tool meant to torment her, the painted crown and the book in which her story is recorded instead borrow on her vital force and carry it into the present. The aesthetic force of her posthumous representations thrives on the vitality she embodied at the time of her death.

23. Keller, "Winternacht," in *Neuere Gedichte* (1851), in *HKKA*, 13:179.

glass and arrests her, once again, as an image. An early death, as in Anna's case, or a premature burial, as with the Meretlein and the mermaid, preserves a young woman's body in the erotic gaze of a first-person narrator. Both Anna and the Meretlein exemplify German realism's preoccupation with the artwork, though tasked with imitating life, as a form of deathly arrestation fundamentally opposed to life. Through its association with arrestation, the artwork becomes life's other, rather than its realistic mirror, a transition also essential to how, I argue, the work acquires authority.

The eroticizing and nonetheless moralizing potential of premature burial is most explicit in "Dietegen," in which a mistreated orphan is reborn to a second life through the electrifying power of the girl Küngolt's love. After being prematurely taken down from the gallows where he was hanged by the sadistic community of Ruechenstein, Dietegen is revived when Küngolt removes the lid of his coffin. When he comes to, it is "as if he had awakened in paradise" (wie wenn er im Paradies erwacht wäre).[24] His resurrection effectively relieves him of the burden of the original sin of his birth, which had condemned him to a desultory life as an orphan, since Küngolt's father then adopts him. That he has awakened in paradise is underlined when, immediately following his rescue, he is taken by the women of Seldwyla to a forest clearing where he is bedecked in flower garlands and caressed. While Dietegen's revival first reminds the reader of the raising of the son of the widow from Nain in the midst of his funeral procession, as reported in the Gospel of Luke, the second scene in the forest clearing is more symptomatic of Seldwyla's proclivity to Dionysian excess that occasions the moral downfall of Küngolt's mother and subsequently herself. Dietegen's paradise becomes the setting for sin, from which Küngolt too will have to be redeemed. The full reversal of Dietegen's and Küngolt's fortunes again relies on an invocation of premature burial. The nadir of Küngolt's downward trajectory is staged as her interment by the local gravedigger in a mausoleum-like chamber

---

24. Gottfried Keller, "Dietegen," in *Seldwyla Folks: Three Singular Tales*, trans. Wolf von Schierbrand (New York: Brentano's, 1919), 104; and Keller, "Dietegen," in *Die Leute von Seldwyla*, in HKKA, 5:194.

bordering the graveyard.²⁵ Just as she once revived Dietegen from his coffin, only Dietegen's nightly visits to her tomb lift her spirits and maintain her bond to the world of the living.

Gedichte and the *Gesammelte Werke*

The most explicit thematization of premature burial is Keller's early cycle of poems with the unambiguous title "Gedanken eines Lebendig-Begrabenen," a poem so strange and so seemingly difficult to situate in Keller's work that it is typically politely overlooked. For the most part, the cycle—the subject matter of which seems most appropriate for the format of a broadsheet, though it first appeared in the pocketbook volume *Gedichte*, published by C. F. Winter of Heidelberg in 1846—has been ignored by nearly two centuries of scholarship; the subject of premature burial is perhaps too tasteless to reconcile with either Keller's earlier image as an edifying national poet or with more recent accounts of his reflective realism.²⁶ Jakob Baechtold's biography of Keller, citing an interview

---

25. "Dietegen went along in order to see how she would be housed. It turned out that her quarters would be an open, small antechamber of the house itself, immediately adjoining the graveyard and only separated from it by an iron fence" (Dietegen ging mit, um zu sehen, wo sie untergebracht würde. Das war in einer offenen kleinen Vorhalle des Hauses, welche unmittelbar an den Totengarten grenzte und von demselben durch ein eisernes Gitter abgeschlossen war). Keller, "Dietegen," trans. Schierbrand, 161; Keller, "Dietegen," in *HKKA*, 5:230.

26. Vedder's discussion of the poem in the context of changing views on death during the nineteenth century is a notable exception. She attributes the poem's dubious quality to the fact that it takes the subject of premature burial all too seriously as it tries to represent a situation that cannot in matter of fact be represented. See Ulrike Vedder, "Scheintod, Koma, Testament: Wissenschaftliche und literarische Fiktionen an der Grenze des Todes," in *Engineering Life: Narrationen von Menschen in Biomedizin, Kultur und Literatur*, ed. Claudia Breger, Irmela Marei Krüger-Fürhoff, and Tanja Nusser (Berlin: Kulturverlag Kadmos, 2008), 53–69, esp. 59–60. Keller's treatment of premature burial is a good example of German realism's fascination with the uncanny, ghoulish, and macabre, which has become a focal point of recent research, as exemplified by Strowick's *Gespenster des Realismus* and Christian Begemann's "Realismus und Phantastik," in *Die Wirklichkeit des Realismus*, ed. Veronika Thanner, Joseph Vogl, and Dorothea Walzer (München: Wilhelm Fink, 2018), 97–113. However, as both exclude Keller from their analyses, they invertedly reify the

with the author, attributes the patronage of the poem to Zurich's taphephobic Leonhard Ziegler; in exchange for a generous quantity of wine, Keller supposedly agreed to write the cycle as a public warning concerning the risk of incorrect determinations of death.[27] If this account is accurate, "Gedanken eines Lebendig-Begrabenen" belonged to a growing corpus of popular texts intended to educate the public on the dangers of premature burial and to convince them of the necessity of instituting mortuaries in which a corpse would be housed and observed for a number of days to allow for death to be established with greater certainty. The precautionary genre was made most (in)famous by Keller's Berlin contemporary Friederike Kempner, promoter of the Deutsche Anti-Scheintod-Liga. Kempner's "Das scheintote Kind" adopts the same narrative situation as Keller's cycle.[28] Yet unlike the pathetic cries of Kempner's buried child pleading to escape, the prematurely buried first-person speaker of Keller's cycle praises his situation as "quiet and cozy" (still und behaglich) and seems to assuage, rather than confirm, the terror presumably induced by premature burial.[29] As Baechtold acknowledges, if Ziegler did indeed commission the poem, he must have been severely disappointed by the outcome (and based on the publishing format, it was also unlikely to reach a large audience). More

---

dominant view of Keller as the poet of green idylls. If nothing else, "Gedanken eines Lebendig-Begrabenen" confirms that Keller shares his contemporaries' preoccupation with that which unsettles the real. Downing's account of Keller's magical realism comes closest to acknowledging the uncanny dimension of Keller's realism. See Downing, *Chain of Things*, 36–120.

27. "About the other cycle, 'Gedanken eines Lebendig-Begrabenen,' Keller gave me the following information. Leonhard Ziegler zum 'Egli' (1782–1854), a well-known figure in Zurich and the cantonal authority responsible for maintaining the hospital, possessed not only a good Tokay but also an insurmountable fear of being buried alive. One day he offered the poet a hundred bottles of his fine wine if he would write for him a poem on the subject that would be beneficial for all. Keller set to work, though the result was, of course, something quite different from what the customer had wanted." Jakob Baechtold, *Gottfried Kellers Leben: Seine Briefe und Tagebücher*, 3 vols. (Berlin: Wilhelm Hertz, 1894–1897), 1:224.

28. Friederike Kempner, "Das Scheintote Kind," in *Die sämtlichen Gedichte der Friederike Kempner*, ed. Eiger Blühm and Lutz Mackensen (Bremen: Carl Schünemann, 1964), 44–45.

29. Keller, "Gedanken eines Lebendig-Begrabenen," in *HKKA*, 13:93.

likely is that Baechtold's biography takes certain liberties with relevant biographical facts in an attempt to dissociate this strange poem from Keller's person and poetic intentions.[30]

Although "Gedanken eines Lebendig-Begrabenen" has been largely overlooked in the scholarship on Keller, reviewers of the poetry volume in which it first appeared felt compelled to respond to the cycle. Their sole point of consensus was that the difficult, which is to say tasteless, subject of premature burial provides a true testing ground for poetic ability. The reviews, both public and private, are notable for their parasitic use of the metaphors of growth, flight, and burial that are central to the poem. For example, Karl August Varnhagen von Ense wrestles with his obvious distaste for the subject and concludes that it is only admissible when it buries the genre of poetry as well—"unless it [the subject matter] also buries it [poetry]"—which is to say, it is not admissible at all.[31] More favorable responses, such as from the sympathetic Wilhelm Schulz writing in the *Blätter für literarische Unterhaltung* and from Keller's friend Eduard Dößekel, more generously interpret the thematization of live burial as evidence of poetic license, of the poet's "carte blanche" regarding his choice of subject;[32] they claim that the

---

30. The fact that there are no extant handwritten manuscripts or notes for "Gedanken eines Lebendig-Begrabenen" makes it more difficult to identify Keller's motivation. Its publication in Keller's first volume of collected poems, *Gedichte*, rather than in a more publicly available periodical or as a broadsheet—which would have been more apposite to the purposes of public edification on the dangers of live burial—also speaks against Baechtold's account of the poem's origins. Treatises and popular poetry on the pervasive dangers of misjudging death constituted a staple of nineteenth-century mass media. See Gerlind Rüve, *Scheintod: Zur kulturellen Bedeutung der Schwelle zwischen Leben und Tod um 1800* (Bielefeld: Transcript, 2008), 99–154.

31. Varnhagen praises Keller for having made the most of the moralizing potential of the subject (its "moral, religious power") but finds it insufficient to justify making it the poem's topic, writing "that I consider the songs of this buried-alive person an error of judgment in terms of their content; the gruesome subject matter can barely dress itself in poetry for a moment, and it cannot hold on to poetry, unless it also buries it." Karl August Varnhagen von Ense to Keller, August 19, 1846, in *HKKA*, 27:401.

32. Wilhelm Schulz, "Der Schweizer Dichter Gottfried Keller," *Blätter für literarische Unterhaltung*, November 1–2, 1846, 1220; repr. in *HKKA*, 27:484. For his review, Schulz borrows the same metaphor of fantasy taking flight with which

theme shows that Keller has passed the ultimate litmus test of the true poet. As Dößekel writes, "Only now when rereading did it dawn on me. Precisely such subject matter is the true touchstone for poetic creativity." He lauds Keller as having withstood this test, using the same range of arboreal and aerial metaphors that pervade Keller's entire volume of poems: "From an unremarkable seed, you have grown a tree in whose strange tops hang the most beautiful diamonds of feeling and fantasy."[33]

The most devastating yet fitting criticism of "Gedanken eines Lebendig-Begrabenen"—fitting insofar as it immediately addresses the obvious subject of live burial around which most critics, then and now, attempt to skirt—stems from Arnold Ruge. He mocks Keller, likely also on account of political motivations, writing, "He wants to redeem the world poetically, and he gives it an endless funeral dirge, a whimper of death, a hope of resurrection; he takes it to the churchyard, indeed, he puts it in a coffin with 'the buried alive.'"[34] The criticism does not seem entirely unwarranted for a text that makes use of such plump rhymes as "der Jammer/[. . .] meine

---

Keller's cycle begins: "The poet as such has a carte blanche, which gives him the right to take on the wings of his imagination any phenomenon that is not outside the realms of aesthetics and psychological possibility, including if it is a depiction of states of the soul, and to remove it from the bounds of the merely ordinary."

33. Eduard Dößekel to Keller, March 20, 1848, in *HKKA*, 27:412.

34. Arnold Ruge, "Aus dem literarischen Zürich," *Literatur- und Kunstbericht*, no. 34 (1846): 131–35; no. 35 (1846): 138; repr. in *HKKA*, 27:482. Ursula Amrein attributes Ruge's odious attack to the lines of division in the so-called *Ichel-Streit* between Ruge, Zurich's leading atheist, and his opponent, the German emigrant August Adolf Ludwig Follen, who supported Keller in publishing his *Gedichte*. Amrein locates Keller's cycle in a lineage with the literature of the *Vormärz* and specifically with Georg Herwegh's *Gedichte eines Lebendigen* (1841). As she explains, "Keller, who greatly owed his career to his contact with the German émigré scene in Zurich, was inspired by Herwegh's political poetry as well as by poems by other authors, including Anastasius Grün and Ludwig Uhland, both of whom take up the motif of mistaken death to interpret the contemporary political situation." Ursula Amrein, "Todesfiguren: Zur Begründung des Realismus bei Gottfried Keller," in *Gottfried Keller und Theodor Fontane: Vom Realismus zur Moderne*, ed. Ursula Amrein and Regina Dieterle (Berlin: Walter de Gruyter, 2008), 72. Beyond the thematic similarities, it's worth nothing that Herwegh's volume *Gedichte eines Lebendigen* served as the model for the format, layout, and typography of Keller's *Gedichte*, although Keller's volume was, in effect, slightly smaller in format and of greater girth. See Keller's publishing proposal to Anton Winter, January 5, 1846, in *HKKA*, 27:386–87.

Todtenkammer" and "diese Bretterstücke/[...] mich zurücke."[35] The fact that Keller later crossed out this cycle in his personal copy of *Gedichte* suggests that he had taken the sentiments of the more critical reviews to heart.[36] Throughout the following decades, he withheld the poem from republication, complaining that his younger self had been too quick to publish. In 1859, for example, in response to Heinrich Kurz's request either to include a selection of poems in an anthology of multiple poets or to publish a new edition of Keller's work alone (the scope of that project was still up for discussion), Keller requested that both "Gedanken eines Lebendig-Begrabenen" and the cycle "Siebenundzwanzig Liebeslieder," which immediately precedes it in the volume *Gedichte*, be excluded from consideration. He writes:

> In the future, I myself will suppress, with few exceptions, all the love songs like a finished chapter in my life that is partly downright silly. Likewise the "Gedanken eines Lebendig-Begrabenen" (numbers 15 and 16 from it could be saved). I therefore ask you, in the interest of my and your aesthetic conscience, also to leave these two cycles out.

> Die sämmtlichen Liebeslieder werde ich in Zukunft mit wenig Ausnahmen, selbst unterdrücken, als eine gemachte Geschichte, die theilweise geradezu albern ist. ebenso die Gedanken eines Lebendig Begrabenen (die Nummern 15 u 16 dieser Letztern könnten gerettet werden). Ich bitte Sie also, im Interesse meines und Ihres ästhetischen Gewissens diese beiden Cyklen ebenfalls laufen zu lassen.[37]

---

35. Keller, "Gedanken eines Lebendig-Begrabenen," in *Gedichte*, in *HKKA*, 13:94, 100. The editors of volume 27 of the *HKKA* point out that August Adolf Ludwig Follen's influence, who was eager to support a young local poet and who brokered the first publication of Keller's poems in the annual volume *Deutsches Taschenbuch*, was of such an extent that he should be considered a coauthor of the texts that appeared in its pages. See Walter Morgenthaler, Peter Stocker, Thomas Binder, Karl Grob, and Dominik Müller, "Zur Entstehung der frühen Gedichtsammlung," in *HKKA*, 27:59–60. There is, however, no record of edits, typically communicated by letter, relating to the "Gedanken eines Lebendig-Begrabenen," making it difficult to assess the extent of Follen's authorship.

36. See Walter Morgenthaler, Peter Stocker, Thomas Binder, Karl Grob, and Dominik Müller, "Detailkommentar und Varianten: *Gedichte* 1846," in *HKKA*, 27:190.

37. Keller to Heinrich Kurz, November 18, 1859, in *HKKA*, 26:227.

These omissions make it all the more remarkable that Keller then included an edited version of "Gedanken eines Lebendig-Begrabenen" under an abbreviated title in his *Gesammelte Gedichte*, published with Wilhelm Hertz in 1883, and then again in the two tomes of poetry published, again with Hertz, as volumes 9 and 10 of his *Gesammelte Werke* in 1889. The fact that Keller republished the poem in his collected works exemplifies what Steffen Martus describes as the principle of "nonselective attention," which guided the placement of poetry within editions of collected works in the late eighteenth and early nineteenth centuries.[38] The ideal of the collected works as representing the totality of not simply an author's work but more centrally of his life—and, moreover, the unity of the two—gave preference to completeness over and against the question of poetic quality. As Martus argues, from the perspective of a collected-works edition, it is the poet and not the poem that counts.[39] Or, to cast the same point differently, the ideal of the *Gesamtwerk* as a *Gesamtbild* of the author selects for quantity over quality. Precisely such a concern for quantity motivated Keller's vision of his poetry collections, which he conceived of throughout his lifetime in terms of their literal mass. Keller favorably anticipated the volume *Gedichte* as a "heavy quantity" (schwere Menge).[40] Later preparations for the volume *Gesammelte Gedichte*—which, as Morgenthaler points out, was intended to serve as "a kind of lyric summation and can also be seen as a sublation (negation and synthesis) of the earlier collections of poetry"[41]—give even greater consideration to girth: "Some ballast seems to benefit rather than harm lyrical vehicles on our shallow seas. I will therefore make my collection as fat as possible," Keller writes to Jakob Baechtold in

---

38. "Time replaces poetic quality as the primary principle of selection, and it serves to increase the complexity through sequential order, that is, through reducing the need for selection." Steffen Martus, "Zwischen Dichtung und Wahrheit: Zur Werkfunktion von Lyrik im 19. Jahrhundert," in *Lyrik im 19. Jahrhundert: Gattungspoetik als Reflexionsmedium der Kultur*, ed. Steffen Martus, Stefan Scherer, and Claudia Stockinger (Bern: Peter Lang, 2005), 66.
39. Martus, "Zwischen Dichtung und Wahrheit," 65.
40. Keller to Julius Rudolf Leemann, September 16, 1845, in *HKKA*, 27:383.
41. Morgenthaler, "Grattier, Gratthier oder Steinbock?," 539.

1879.[42] True to his word and to the principle of nonselective attention, *Gesammelte Gedichte* encompasses five hundred pages—double the size, as Morgenthaler and the other editors of volume 25 of the *Historisch-Kritische Gottfried Keller-Ausgabe* point out, of Theodor Storm's comparable collection and no less than five times that of Keller's friend and colleague Paul Heyse.[43]

Admittedly, not only considerations of the volume's girth motivated Keller to include these early poems in the later volumes but also considerations of how they would contribute to providing a full account of his life and work as an author, particularly as a record of the emergence of his youthful poetic voice. As part of the *Gesammelte Gedichte* and later of the *Gesammelte Werke*, they become a second bookend to the cumulative portrait of the life and work of the author, a "complement and counterpoint to the prose," as Morgenthaler writes.[44] While the order of the individual volumes of Keller's *Gesammelte Werke* breaks with the historical chronology of his publications, such that the pride of place of the initiatory two volumes is reserved for the revised edition of *Der grüne Heinrich* and the collections of poetry conclude the ten volumes, the early poems are no less essential to the dream of completeness and unity to which the edition aspires.[45] Their contribu-

---

42. "Etwas Ballast scheint lyrischen Fahrzeugen auf unseren seichten Seeen eher gut zu thun, als zu schaden; ich werde darum meine Sammlung auch so dick als möglich machen." Keller to Jakob Baechtold, November 21, 1879, in *HKKA*, 26:289.

43. See Walter Morgenthaler, Thomas Binder, Peter Stocker, Karl Grob, and Dominik Müller, "Zur Entstehung und Rezeption der *Gesammelten Werke*," in *HKKA*, 25:32.

44. Morgenthaler, "Grattier, Gratthier oder Steinbock?," 540.

45. Morgenthaler provides a highly compelling analysis of the structure of the ten volumes of Keller's *Gesammelte Werke*. The decision to publish his works in a well-rounded ten volumes, the structure of the ten volumes around symmetrical relationships, and the decision to exclude what could not be integrated into that structure reflect, in Morgenthaler's words, how "the author wanted to hand down [his literary legacy]" in a "clear architectonic arrangement." Morgenthaler, "Grattier, Gratthier oder Steinbock?," 540. In a further publication, Morgenthaler outlines this symmetrical ordering of the ten volumes. Volumes 1, 2, and 3 contain *Der grüne Heinrich* and thereby mirror his other novel, *Martin Salander*, as volume 8 and the poetry collections in volumes 9 and 10. These frame the cyclical works: *Die Leute von Seldwyla* in volumes 4 and 5, the *Züricher Novellen* in volume 6, and *Das Sinngedicht* and the *Sieben Legenden* together in volume 7. Morgenthaler con-

tion to the *Gesamtbild* is further exemplified by the fact that volume 9 bears Keller's portrait on the page facing the title page, suggesting that it is in poetry that the entwinement of author and work is most intimate. As the poetry in volume 9 largely stems from Keller's early publications, it stands in for the work of the youthful poet in the making and fleshing out of the author's portrait, or effigy. In view of this purpose, "Gedanken eines Lebendig-Begrabenen" comes into view as having a shared purpose with the poems in "Sonnetten," "Siebenundzwanzig Liebeslieder," and select items from the rubric "Vermischte Gedichte," such as "Poetentod" and the satirical "Aus ihrem Leben: Dichtung und Wahrheit"; together, they provide an account of becoming a poet. The cycle "Gedanken eines Lebendig-Begrabenen" is the work of a highly precocious young poet, who upon the occasion of his first book publication imaginatively conceives the conditions of his own legacy—an undertaking later further elaborated in the scene of reading Goethe in *Der grüne Heinrich*.[46] In republishing "Gedanken eines Lebendig-Begrabenen," in spite of the strange subject matter and dubious poetic quality, Keller recovers the cycle's original poetological purpose within the frame of the *Gesammelte Gedichte*.

The reception of the *Gesammelte Gedichte* acknowledged both the symbolic and biographical purpose of the early poems. For example, Ferdinand Avenarius, the editor of *Der Kunstwart*, reads these poems as charting the writer's education from feeling to reason: "The

---

cludes that in this collected-works edition, "The oeuvre acquires a defining character as opposed to the single text." Walter Morgenthaler, "Überlieferung und Textkonstitution bei Gottfried Keller," *Schweizer Monatshefte* 73 (1993): 509.

46. I am thereby dating Keller's preoccupation with his legacy to his earliest published volume. However, Morgenthaler convincingly argues that even Keller's earliest, unpublished attempts at poetic composition, recorded in Keller's *Studienbücher*, manifest a concern for the future reception of his works. This is further convincing evidence of what I have described as Keller's precocious (if not premature) preoccupation with his legacy. Morgenthaler describes Keller's signature performed on a sheet below what are thought to be Keller's two earliest poems as ensuring the citability and correct attribution of the texts. Walter Morgenthaler, "Gottfried Kellers Studienbücher," in *Bilder der Handschrift: Die graphische Dimension der Literatur*, ed. Davide Giuriato and Stephan Kammer (Frankfurt am Main: Stroemfeld, 2006), 112. The page of the *Studienbuch* in question is reproduced and transcribed in Keller, "Studienbuch Ms. GK 1," in *HKKA*, 16.1:128–29.

arrangement of the *Gesammelte Gedichte* exhibits, to a degree, a progression from purely lyrical creations to ones in which the life of the will and reason increasingly play a part."[47] Similarly, Luzius Gessler's 1964 dissertation—to the best of my knowledge, the most recent discussion of "Gedanken eines Lebendig-Begrabenen"—effusively identifies the three "Tannen-Gedichte" (poem numbers 14–16 in the cycle) as doing nothing less than establishing the idyllic, contemplative tone characteristic of *Der grüne Heinrich* and *Die Leute von Seldwyla*: "The essence of Keller's grand style is revealed here more clearly. It is the style of someone buried alive."[48] The degree of significance that Gessler ascribes to these three poems as establishing Keller's style, the style of someone prematurely buried, evidences how well "Gedanken eines Lebendig-Begrabenen" ultimately fulfilled its purpose within the *Gesammelte Werke* as exemplifying the youthful poet and his voice, a voice that would, according to the narrative of the collected edition's format, mature throughout his later works.

To put the argument differently, "Gedanken eines Lebendig-Begrabenen" and the volume *Gedichte* perform the task of recasting and embellishing an earlier autobiographical fiction concerning the discovery of Keller's poetic voice. That autobiographical moment is famously captured in a letter to his friend the painter Rudolf Lee-

---

47. Ferdinand Avenarius, "Gottfried Keller als Lyriker," *Tägliche Rundschau: Feuilletonistische Beilage*, June 14, 1884, 546–47; June 15, 1884, 550–51; quoted in *HKKA*, 25:58. Avenarius thereby endows the volume with the same broad biographical function that Goethe advertised for his standard-bearing *Vollständige Ausgabe letzter Hand* upon its publication.

48. Luzius Gessler, *Lebendig begraben: Studien zur Lyrik des jungen Gottfried Keller* (Bern: A. Francke, 1964), 92. Gessler is specifically referring to the stanza beginning with "The roofs are now for certain warmly lit/By sunny spring, by the young ether blue" (Gewiß sind jetzt die Dächer warm beschienen/Vom sonn'gen Lenz, vom jungen Aetherblau). Keller, "Gedanken eines Lebendig-Begrabenen," in *HKKA*, 13:98. The degree of significance Gessler attributes to "Gedanken eines Lebendig-Begrabenen" is evident from the title of his Basel dissertation, which adopts the name of the poem for his entire study of Keller's poetry, yet he omits any discussion of premature burial as such, instead focusing on the natural imagery in the poem. So fully does Gessler elide the poem's topic that it remains unclear to what degree he senses the perverse irony of claiming that the "purest poetry arises out of the deepest *Versenkung*" (meaning "absorption" but also, more literally, "sinking") in response to an account of being buried alive. Gessler, *Lebendig begraben*, 89.

mann from September 1845, where Keller writes of the reawakening and redirection of his creative drives. Because it describes a media switch from painting to poetry that will be negotiated throughout Keller's oeuvre, this turning point has become a favorite of Keller's biographers. Less flattering is how Keller attributes this transition, which he pointedly describes as one of decline (*Verfall*), to financial motives, as he hopes to partially pay for future travels abroad through what he imagines as a poetry collection that will propel him to financial security and to an improved social position as well.

> My creative instinct awoke again in the spring of 1843; but as I found no consolation or success in painting, I involuntarily and unconsciously resorted to verse making and discovered, to my great surprise, that I could *rhyme*! I made a heavy quantity of poems and decided to publish them, at that time only to procure a sum of money to return to Munich, where all my thoughts were directed. [...] It [the collection of poems] was passed back and forth and looked at; at last it was said that I was a "poet," and from then on I came into distinguished, honorable company and started studies in literature.
>
> Im Frühling 1843 wachte mein Schöpfungstrieb wieder auf; da ich aber im Malen keinen Trost und Erfolg empfand, verfiel ich unwillkürlich und unbewußt aufs Versmachen und entdeckte höchst verwundert, daß ich *reimen* könne! Ich machte Gedichte die schwere Menge und faßte den Entschluß, sie herauszugeben, damals nur, um eine Summe zu erschwingen, um nach München zu kehren, wohin alle meine Gedanken noch gerichtet waren. [...] Sie wurde hin und her beguckt und geworfen; endlich hieß es, ich sei ein "Dichter," und von *da* an kam ich in ausgezeichnete ehrenvolle Gesellschaft und begann literarische Studien.[49]

The volume *Gedichte*, in turn, bears the burden of providing an alternative narrative to the financial motivations to which Keller here attributes his turn to poetry. In this vein, I read "Gedanken eines Lebendig-Begrabenen" as an account of the death of the author that relates the media conditions of authorship; this constellation of conditions is varied throughout the volume *Gedichte*. When regarded as providing such a founding myth, the cycle appears as a natural fit both for the volume and for the *Gesammelte Werke*.

---

49. Keller to Rudolf Leemann, September 1845, in *HKKA*, 27:14–15.

My intention is in no way to detract from the peculiarly dark preoccupation with premature burial. Instead, what makes this poem of interest despite the rather worn and dated nature of its tropes is that it chooses a subject matter more appropriate to the genre of the *Schauerballade* or to a broadside publication to contrive its account of authorship (its morbid character being on par with, yet lacking the obvious humor of, Keller's cannibalistic "Ballade vom dürren König"). The poem's subject of live burial makes an integral contribution to the imagined biographical totality and synchronization of life and work that Keller attributed to a collected-works edition. Premature burial is thematized in the cycle to envision the premature arrestation of a young, vivacious life to produce an artful body that will, on account of its youth and mistaken burial, bear an unmistakable resemblance (*Schein*) to life. In clear contrast to the Pygmalion myth that Keller later repeatedly invokes in his later publications, "Gedanken eines Lebendig-Begrabenen" proposes the death of the artist as a precondition for his artwork to come to life as the eternal corpus of the *Gesammelte Werke*.[50]

Poetic Awakening, Seven Feet Deep

In its initially published version, "Gedanken eines Lebendig-Begrabenen" consists of a numerated cycle of nineteen poems. Each poem has a varying number of stanzas, and each stanza four lines with varied rhyme schemes. Keller included two of the poems, the so-called "Tannen-Gedichte," in his second volume of poetry, *Neuere Gedichte*, published in 1851 (and republished in 1854). Abbreviated

---

50. For a comparable scenario intended to contrast with how Pygmalion brings his artwork to life, see Mathias Mayer's analysis of the nineteenth century's invocation of King Midas to describe an artist who arrests his artwork in death. This "countermyth" subjects the artist to the paradox "of only being able to endow life with duration in art and beyond death by depriving life of its natural vitality and relinquishing it to the eternity of art and death. [...] Only at the price of life can meaning and sense be obtained as the origin of art." Mathias Mayer, "Midas statt Pygmalion: Die Tödlichkeit der Kunst bei Goethe, Schnitzler, Hofmannsthal und Georg Kaiser," *Deutsche Vierteljahrsschrift für Literaturwissenschaft und Geistesgeschichte* 64, no. 2 (1990): 291.

to fourteen poems, heavily edited, and also scrambled, the cycle was then largely incorporated in the *Gesammelte Gedichte* and in the collected-works edition published soon thereafter under the more succinct title "Lebendig begraben." Yet the term "Gedanken" in the original title charts the poem's primary narrative, as it prophesizes the growth of the buried material body into a spiritual one. The trajectory advanced in the title is thus much like Paul's prophecy of the resurrection: "It is sown a physical body, it is raised a spiritual body."[51] To begin, the prophecy seems likely to go into effect as the lyric voice claims to have dissociated himself from his material body: "I do not feel my limbs, they have grown stiff;/Yet bright and cheerful glows my soul in me" (Ich fühle nicht die Glieder, die erstarrten;/ Doch hell und heiter glimmt die Seele mir).[52] At least the original version of the poem delivers on this promise with the suggestion that the poem's speaker has been redeemed. Accordingly, the penultimate poem begins "I'm liberated, all my sorrow gone" (Ich bin befreit, mein Weh hat sich gewendet),[53] thereby fulfilling the moral-didactic mandate that nineteenth-century readers might well have regarded as the only justification for such gothic subject matter.[54] The inability of the speaker to turn his body within the small space of his interment becomes sublimated in the greater turning (*gewendet*) toward his second life. The poem then concludes, following a grim account of suffocation given as his final cause of death, with the clearly anticipatory "My heart beats faintly—breaks in expectation—" (Matt schlägt das Herz,—bald bricht's—erwartungsvoll—).[55] The poem thereby attempts to counteract the impossibility of recording one's death in the first person by writing up until the very moment of death, the nearest possible approximation.

---

51. 1 Cor. 15:44 (New Revised Standard Version).
52. Keller, "Gedanken eines Lebendig-Begrabenen," in *HKKA*, 13:93.
53. Keller, "Gedanken eines Lebendig-Begrabenen," in *HKKA*, 13:104.
54. The later version from 1883, entitled "Lebendig begraben," replaces this pious outlook on the afterlife with a more melancholic reflection on transience: "Pass away, oh self! transient idol,/Whoever you are, good-bye, you, farewell!" (Fahr' hin, o Selbst! vergängliches Idol,/Wer du auch bist, leb' wohl du, fahre wohl!). Keller, "Lebendig begraben," in *Gesammelte Gedichte*, in *HKKA*, 9:147.
55. Keller, "Gedanken eines Lebendig-Begrabenen," in *HKKA*, 13:104.

The narrated time of the cycle, the period between the time of burial and his redemptive death as a spiritual being, is protracted by means of relaying the many ways the buried speaker is continuously disturbed by the relentless materiality of his surroundings. These disruptions and the way in which they compel him to overcome or repress the associated bodily sensations are described in minute, realistic detail. Hunger, the water seeping in from the wet ground that leaves him damp, the sawdust from the freshly cut wood chafing under his neck—"The shavings grate against the back of my neck" (Die Späne knirschen unter dem Genick)[56]—and the sounds of the outside world continually interrupt his thoughts and redirect his hopes away from spiritual redemption and toward being literally resurrected and excavated in this lifetime.

The sounds from outside the tomb initiate the cycle's individually numerated poems, as they awaken the boy from sleep and prompt his song: first the sound of the grave diggers, later the drunken sexton, and then the bells of the nearby church. The anticipation of his resurrection as a spiritual being consumed in fiery thought—he imagines himself as an erupting volcano whose force will expel him from the ground—at the poem's onset is thus repeatedly delayed and gives cause for the intermittent stanzas. Within that arrangement, the composition of the cycle serves as a tool of affect management, a means of maintaining consciousness against the threat of terror, despair, and insanity: "Stop now, oh madness! For I *still* am master/And will remain so until my last breath!" (Halt' an, o Wahnsinn! denn *noch* bin ich Meister / Und bleib' es bis zum letzten Odemzug!).[57] Extrapolating from this poem cycle, the volume *Gedichte* thus offers a conventional portrayal of poetic speech as the overcoming of youthful effusions of feeling.

The thinking, spiritual entity whose alternately literal or spiritual awakening the cycle envisions is none other than the poet himself. The poem begins when the catatonic speaker buried seven feet deep is awakened by the terrible sounds of the gravedigger and, rather than giving way to panic, recognizes his interment as an opportunity

---

56. Keller, "Gedanken eines Lebendig-Begrabenen," in *HKKA*, 13:94.
57. Keller, "Gedanken eines Lebendig-Begrabenen," in *HKKA*, 13:94.

for Romantic flights of poetic fancy unavailable to him in his previous, prosaic life.

> Ah, what a noise!—The awful thunder
> Of rubble and earth, bones crashing from high!
> I cannot laugh and also cannot cry—
> How is this going to end, I wonder!
>
> Now it's becoming still. They're shuffling home
> And leaving me seven feet deep to lie;
> Now fantasy! let all your eagles fly,
> They will never pull me out of this tomb!
>
> Ei wie das kracht!—Abscheuliches Geroll
> Von Schutt und Erde, polternden Gebeinen!
> Ich kann nicht lachen und kann auch nicht weinen—
> Es nimmt mich Wunder, wie das enden soll!
>
> Nun wird es still.—Sie trollen sich nach Haus
> Und lassen mich hier sieben Fuß tief liegen;
> Nun, Phantasie! laß' deine Adler fliegen,
> Hier schwingen sie wol nimmer mich heraus![58]

Given that the speaker of the poem lived, as is later explained, a largely agrarian life in cohabitation with his mother, premature burial—that is, his life's thread being cut short—emerges as the enabling condition for the possibility of becoming a poet. To underline the point, the virgin poet, reminiscent of a sleeping Amor or Endymion, explains that he was previously unable to voice his affections to his beloved; only when sequestered away from the world and from this beloved does he recuperate the gift of speech. "Gedanken eines Lebendig-Begrabenen" thereby varies the situation of the cycle of poems that immediately precedes it within the volume *Gedichte*. The song cycle "Siebenundzwanzig Liebeslieder" is attributed to the loss and burial of the beloved, by whose graveside the lyric voice now sits:

> Rest in peace, my angel, dear!
> Become light and lighter!

---

58. Keller, "Gedanken eines Lebendig-Begrabenen," in *HKKA*, 13:93.

> In the meantime your boy here
> Has become—a writer!
>
> Wohl ergeh' es, Engel, Dir!
> Werde licht und lichter!
> Ach! Dein Knabe wurde hier
> Unterdeß—ein Dichter![59]

In "Gedanken eines Lebendig-Begrabenen," it is conversely the speaker's own entombment that serves as the enabling condition of poetic becoming.

As an account of the incipient poet, "Gedanken eines Lebendig-Begrabenen" illustrates a (for Keller) surprisingly ascetic set of conditions. The coffin secures a monastic situation that removes the speaker from the petty sinfulness of common society—at one point he is awoken, as I mentioned, by the drunk sexton returning home to the angry complaints of his wife—and makes it possible for him to direct his efforts against forms of bodily desire. Cut off from society in a quiet, cold, damp, and, most significantly, dark environment, he becomes a blind poet. In the dark, the poet can no longer distinguish the visual properties of the objects he otherwise perceives. When he first hears the church bells chime twelve, he imagines the shining sun but then realizes that it might equally well signal midnight, prompting the hope, a common topos of premature burial, that grave robbers might soon appear to dig him out:

> Now twelve o'clock has struck—why then midday?
> Perhaps t'was midnight the stroke meant to say,
> Above the silent stars are passing by;
> I do not know, I cannot see the sky!
>
> Zwölf hat's geschlagen—warum denn Mittag?
> Vielleicht der Mitternacht ja galt der Schlag,
> Daß oben nun die stillen Sterne gehn;
> Ich weiß es nicht, ich kann es ja nicht sehn![60]

---

59. Keller, "Siebenundzwanzig Liebeslieder," in *Gedichte*, in *HKKA*, 13:87.
60. Keller, "Gedanken eines Lebendig-Begrabenen," in *HKKA*, 13:98.

Analogously, in what have become perhaps the two best-known stanzas of the poem, memorialized by Othmar Schoeck's music and James Joyce's translation, the poet momentarily stills his hunger by eating the rose that has been placed in his hands.[61] Despite having consumed the flower, he is frustrated by his inability to know—to "read"—its color:

> If a red one or a white one, simply,
> The color of the rose I'd like to know?
> On the last leaf I'm tearing nimbly,
> Maybe my fingers reading it can show.
>
> Ich möcht' nur wissen, ob es eine weiße,
> Ob eine rothe Rose das gewesen?
> Am letzten Blatt, das spielend ich zerreiße,
> Möcht ich es fühlend mit den Fingern lesen.[62]

It is the impossibility of ascertaining whether the rose is white or red, or whether the twelve chimes indicate midday or midnight, that figures as the central condition for poetic fantasy. Poetry begins in a moment of imposed asceticism and epistemological uncertainty when fantasy can substitute for the indistinguishable properties of the real. Putting aside the open question of whether the consumed rose was red or white, the poet instead insistently imagines *green* pastures and

---

61. In January 1935, Joyce attended a concert in Zurich that included Keller's cycle "Lebendig begraben" set to piano by the local composer Othmar Schoeck. Joyce, who had previously dismissed Keller's writing as "technically conventional," was apparently so taken by the musical performance that he purchased both a volume of Keller's poetry and Cassell's German–English dictionary, with which he then translated and adapted the two stanzas beginning with "Da hab' ich gar die Rose aufgegessen" into English: "Now have I fed and eaten up the rose." James Joyce, "Buried Alive," in *Poems and Shorter Writings* (London: Farber & Faber, 1991), 138. Following his encounter with "Lebendig begraben," Joyce then writes of Keller, "I did not know Keller wrote this kind of gruesome-satiric semi-pious verse but the effect of it on any audience is tremendous." James Joyce to Giorgio Joyce and Helen Joyce, January 15, 1935, in *Letters of James Joyce*, ed. Stuart Gilbert (London: Faber & Faber, 1957), 1:356. On Joyce's engagement with "Lebendig begraben," see Jean L. Kreiling, "A Note on James Joyce, Gottfried Keller, and Music," *James Joyce Quarterly* 25, no. 3 (Spring 1988): 351–52.
62. Keller, "Gedanken eines Lebendig-Begrabenen," in *HKKA*, 13:99.

forests (an adjective repeated sixfold), thereby introducing the coupling of the color green to poetic production, as will inform Keller's yet-to-be-written prose. And unable to distinguish midday from midnight, he instead enters a fantastic, arrested time: "Now this is quite a bizarre, wondrous time" (Das ist jetzt eine wunderliche Zeit!).[63]

It is not merely the situation of being sequestered from a world of visual properties but also the life he will not live that feeds the poet's fantasy. Repeatedly, the speaker interrupts his highly realistic description of the material conditions of his coffin to describe what could have been had he not been prematurely buried. The most extensive of these imaginings takes the tree from which his coffin has been constructed as its protagonist. In the absence of his mother or his beloved at his graveside, not to speak of any other family lineage he could not possibly have at his young age, combined with the failure of his repeated attempts to rouse his buried neighbors, the wood his coffin is made of becomes both his interlocutor and the hero of his verse. In poems 14–16, the speaker mourns the premature interruption of the pine tree's young life and imagines alternative adventurous and glory-filled life stories for it as a ship's mast—"Much better it would be, you cut-up fir,/If you could tower as a slender mast" (Viel besser wär's, zerschnittner Tannenbaum,/Du ragtest als ein schlanker Mast empor)[64]—as a perch for forest birds, as a Christmas tree, and as a patriotic liberty pole (Freiheitsbaum), the latter two of which draw on the speaker's childhood memories and so further interweave his own life with that of the felled tree. The lives not lived become the diegetic substance of more fantastic and heroic lives worthy of lyric storytelling, in contrast to the speaker's previously mundane existence.

A Buried Scene of Writing

As I have noted, the wooden planks that contain the poet must serve in the absence of family and beloved as his initial interlocutor and

---

63. Keller, "Gedanken eines Lebendig-Begrabenen," in *HKKA*, 13:93.
64. Keller, "Gedanken eines Lebendig-Begrabenen," in *HKKA*, 13:100.

as the hero of his poems. The wood also, the poem suggests in passing, must serve as the writing surface for the very composition of the cycle. In one of the poem's stranger stanzas, the poet finds a toothpick and pencil in his pockets:

> It seems that when they were lied to by death,
> They dressed me in my Sunday vest:
> Inside its pockets, I discovered stowed
> A pencil as well as a toothpick old.
>
> Sie haben mir, als sie der Tod belogen,
> Wie's scheint, die Sonntagsweste angezogen:
> In ihren Taschen fand ich einen alten
> Zahnstocher und ein Bleistift aufbehalten.[65]

While the silly and obviously phallic toothpick and pencil are stylized to contrast pathetically with the sword accompanying the burials of past heroes, the pencil invites reading the stanza as envisioning the poem's scene of writing, thereby buttressing the reflection on the media conditions for becoming a poet, who earns his fame through writing rather than through heroic deeds. While the cycle repeatedly simulates orality such that the poet's voice joins the cacophony of surrounding sounds and, at the end, fades into an em dash, the pencil and the planks of wood available as the poet's only writing surface recast this origin as taking place in writing rather than in speech. The confining surface of the coffin becomes the medium for recording and preserving the poet's message. In doing so, "Gedanken eines Lebendig-Begrabenen" aspires to provide the nineteenth century, in which poetry quite obviously circulated largely by means of print media rather than solely or even primarily by speech, with a new genealogy. Poetry need not emerge from the blind bard addressing a community gathered around him but instead has its origin in the durable medium of writing with the potential to form that very same community after the poet's death, the same capacity *Der grüne Heinrich* attributes to Schiller's collected

---

65. Keller, "Gedanken eines Lebendig-Begrabenen," in *HKKA*, 13:95.

works.[66] The scene of writing also provides the poem with its own realistic justification for how a soon-to-be-dead poet might leave behind a record of his death. The durability of the material writing surface ensures that the "life" of the poem surpasses that of its dead and solitary author, relieving him of the immediate need for an audience composed either of his beloved, his family, or his community, all of which he does not possess. The reception of his poetry that has been recorded alongside his ideally mummified body can be postponed until the time of exhumation. The "bizarre, wondrous time" in which the poet finds himself is the time of deferment to a posthumous eternity. Just as Ishmael's coffin at the end of *Moby-Dick* represents, as Kerstin Roose argues, the possibility of the text's own survival,[67] so too does Keller's coffin serve as a promise of textual resurrection. Ultimately, the cycle advocates neither for the possibility of being rescued in this life nor for the possibility of a theological afterlife; instead, the poet will truly be recovered in the memory of those reading or reciting his written word. The text anticipates a future orality premised on the more originary written word, an orality realized at the time of reading.[68]

---

66. On the community-building function of the ballad as circulated in print media and performed with music in nineteenth-century Germany, see Adrian Daub, *What the Ballad Knows: The Ballad Genre, Memory Culture, and German Nationalism* (Oxford: Oxford University Press, 2022), 211–33.

67. Kerstin Roose, "'Letztes Bett' und 'schwarzer Kasten': Der Sarg als Objekt zwischen Ausstellen und Verbergen in Texten des Realismus," *Zeitschrift für Germanistik* 31, no. 3 (2021): 439. Roose's article also provides an extensive discussion of the object of the coffin in *Der grüne Heinrich*, which she convincingly reads as an allegory for narration in "death's imminence," though her analysis of *Moby-Dick* is closer to my own line of argument.

68. For comparison, Maximilian Bergengruen charts the same figure of thought in Jean Paul's *Siebenkäs*, in which "the reader is informed that his soul prefers its own literary texts 'instead of his soon-to-be-vanishing body' as its new home, that is, that it will from now on live 'in the paper.'" "The literary texts he composed" thus become a "new heavenly body and a replacement for the earthly body." Maximilian Bergengruen, "Vita longa: Transformationen einer theosophischen Denkfigur; Jean Pauls *Siebenkäs* und Novalis' *Europa*-Rede," in *Romantische Religiosität*, ed. Alexander von Bormann (Würzburg: Königshausen & Neumann, 2005), 133–34. "Gedanken eines Lebendig-Begrabenen" performs this same sublimation into text with the added condition of premature burial.

The poet's vision that his words will later be resurrected and that they (like a collected-works edition) will then provide a portrait of the deceased artist, preserved in his youthful vitality, is confirmed by an earlier stanza in which the lyric voice envisions precisely just such an image. Instead of dreaming of the many inventive nineteenth-century mechanisms built into coffins to allow, in case of premature burial, the interred to communicate with the exterior world, the poem imagines a coffin outfitted with a mirror that would preserve the grimacing portrait of the living corpse.[69]

> Inside each coffin there should be installed
> A mirror bright and made out of metal,
> Which, as they say, in the deepest darkness
> Would faithfully depict the corpse's likeness.

> In's Innre jedes Sarges sollte man
> Hell von Metall 'nen Spiegel schlagen an,
> Der, wie man sagt, in tiefster Dunkelheit
> Getreu die Leichenzüge konterfeit.

When exhumed, the mirror, "lightly covered by rust" (vom Rost leicht überwebt), will be rejuvenated by sunshine and reveal itself, the speaker suggests, not without a satirical bent, as an "artistic treasure" (Kunstschatz) or one of many "pearls in a gallery of the dead" (Perlen einer Todtengallerie), which will confront their duplicitous owner with "Light and life and youth" (Licht und Leben und die Jugend).[70] The medium of the image absorbs and then indexes the vitality of the interred youth.

Two further poems from the same volume corroborate the claim that "Gedanken eines Lebendig-Begrabenen" proposes premature burial as a means of arresting the poet and deferring his speech for later audiences rather than immediate generations. For one, "Gedanken eines Lebendig-Begrabenen" comes into view as a contrast to

---

69. On mechanisms intended to enable the prematurely buried to communicate with the exterior world, see Ariès, *The Hour of Our Death*, 399–401.
70. Keller, "Gedanken eines Lebendig-Begrabenen," in *HKKA*, 13:95.

"Poetentod" from the rubric "Vermischte Gedichte" later in the same volume. The diegesis of "Poetentod" can be summarized as a scene of "écriture testamentaire," in which the poet announces his final will so as to extend his voice and agency.[71] Because the speaker is a poet, it is also a scene of literary-estate management or *Nachlassverwaltung*, a further confirmation that Keller composed and collected the volume *Gedichte* not simply with regard to his immediate financial worries but also, as I have emphasized, in anticipation of a collected-works edition to be published at the conclusion of his lifetime as a poet. The famed poet of "Poetentod," in immediate contrast to the speaker of "Gedanken eines Lebendig-Begrabenen," passes at the conclusion of a long life whose prolific activity (and reproductivity) is manifest, first, in the wife and children who surround his deathbed and who must execute his final will and, second, in the bountiful papers whose future must now be determined. But unlike the hopeful conclusion to "Gedanken eines Lebendig-Begrabenen," which looks forward to the poet's rebirth, "Poetentod" is decisively melancholic and envisions the poet's work, life, and fame extinguishing in a plethora of images of expiring light. He orders his family to destroy the *Nachlass*—"That book of faded writing give the flames,/It is a garish mirror of my youth" (Gebt jenen Band verblichner Schrift den Flammen,/s'Ist meiner Jugend greller Widerschein)[72]—his rose garden, and his household belongings, and he commands his son to take up the practical life of a craftsman.[73] "Out fame struts with the funeral cortège" (Der Ruhm wallt

---

71. On the will as the only genre in which a person continues to exercise agency beyond the point of their death, see Vedder, *Das Testament*, esp. 105–6.

72. Keller, "Poetentod," in *Gedichte*, in *HKKA*, 13:147.

73. For the 1883 publication of the poem in the volume *Gesammelte Gedichte*, Keller notably strengthens the command, clearly distinguishing between the "Werk" and the "Wust" of the poet's papers: "Throw all that faded writing in the fire,/And let the dust from the workshop decay!/In art, where space and light are so required,/Do not let rubble stand in the work's way" (Werft jenen Wust verblichner Schrift ins Feuer,/Der Staub der Werkstatt mag zu Grunde geh'n!/Im Reich der Kunst, wo Raum und Licht so teuer,/Soll nicht der Schutt dem Werk im Wege steh'n!). Keller, "Poetentod," in *Gesammelte Gedichte*, in *HKKA*, 10:127. For a discussion of these two editions of "Poetentod" in the context of Keller's broader thematization of *Nachlassverwaltung*, see Jan Behrs, *Der Dichter und sein Denker: Wechselwirkungen zwischen Literatur und Literaturwissenschaft in Realismus und Expressionismus* (Stuttgart: S. Hirzel, 2013), 80–108.

mit dem Leichenzug hinaus), he waxes.[74] Because this poet has achieved fame and renown within his life, his death marks the fading of each, a fading that is to be materialized in the destruction of his *Nachlass*. In contrast, because the young poet of "Gedanken eines Lebendig-Begrabenen" only first discovers his ability as a poet through premature burial, his fame is yet to come. His voice will be heard for the first time in the posthumous reading of his coffin-shaped *Nachlass*. The *Gedichte* thus establishes a typology of poets that contrasts those who achieve fame in life, only to see it depleted posthumously, and those, including the speaker of "Gedanken eines Lebendig-Begrabenen," whose cultural capital, like Schiller's, proliferates after a period of latency.

A second set of images closely related to "Gedanken eines Lebendig-Begrabenen" comes from the unlikely source of the anti-Catholic sonnet "Reformation," in which the dead hand of a mummy clutches the grains of a future blossoming.

> Inside the pyramid's bowels, buried deep,
> Within a mummy's black dead hand around
> It was that ancient grains of wheat were found,
> Which had been for millennia asleep.
>
> And these rare gifts were taken to test
> And then thrown into living farmland field;
> Lo and behold: crops golden did they yield,
> On which heart and eye could feast!
>
> For late descendants does the fruit now bloom
> That with the forebear in the grave's womb dozed;—
> To die's an endless rising from the dead.
>
> Who hinders now that we *again* exhume
> From church's mummy hand, what it enclosed:
> *The word of life*, again to spread?
>
> Im Bauch der Pyramide tief begraben,
> In einer Mumie schwarzer Todtenhand

---

74. Keller, "Poetentod," in *Gedichte*, in *HKKA*, 13:146.

> War's, daß man alte Waizenkörner fand,
> Die dort Jahrtausende geschlummert haben.
>
> Und prüfend nahm man diese seltnen Gaben
> Und warf sie in lebendig Ackerland;
> Und siehe da: die gold'ne Saat erstand,
> An der sich Herz und Auge konnt' erlaben!
>
> So blüht die Frucht dem späten Enkelkinde,
> Die mit dem Ahnen schlief in Grabesschooß;—
> Das Sterben ist ein endlos Auferstehen.
>
> Wer hindert nun, daß *wieder* man entwinde
> Der Kirche Mumienhand, was sie verschloß:
> *Das Wort des Lebens*, wieder es zu säen?[75]

While the final stanza makes obvious that the mummy stands in for the reformed church and the grain for God's word, the image of mummification recalls the poet of "Gedanken eines Lebendig-Begrabenen," whose entombment similarly preserves his word for a future time. In the case of "Gedanken eines Lebendig-Begrabenen," in which the word obviously lacks a divine guarantee as God's word, the poet's writing instead derives its backing from the youthful vitality of the poet who bequeaths his vigor to his artwork. Because he is prematurely buried at the height of life in his youth rather than at its conclusion, his language embodies a vital force that will preserve it for the distant future of exhumation. Keller thus includes the grotesque effusions of this victim of living inhumation that has met with two centuries of scholarly near silence in his two large-scale collections of poems so that it would one day, within the context of the *Gesammelte Werke*, be excavated as completing the portrait of the young and vigorous poet in the making.

To conclude, Keller's earliest poetry and prose imagine the author as defined through posthumous prestige, that is, as defined by the ability to speak, through the written word, to subsequent generations. Both the account of Schiller's posthumous works as educating the nation and the scene of reading Goethe demonstrate that cultural

---

75. Keller, "Reformation," in *Gedichte*, in *HKKA*, 13:57.

prestige is made manifest in a collected-works edition, a corpus that stands in for the body of the author and makes him present to future readers, just as Goethe becomes present to the young Heinrich in the fifty volumes of his collected works. Keller's frustrations with writing *Der grüne Heinrich*—the sense that the identity of the work could not be maintained across its fractured publishing history, in part because the very identity of the author had evolved over the duration of writing—give way in the plot of the novel to a vision of an alternative publishing format that unifies a life: the collected-works edition. Read against the background of Keller's fascination with *Scheintod* as preserving the vitality of a youthful body, that is, as lending the deceased body aesthetic, if not erotic, radiance (*Schein*), the collected-works edition comes into view as an imagined sarcophagus that makes present the dead and yet fully vivacious author to its readers: a container for the author's life and work. While Goethe's ghostly copresence with Heinrich on the daybed represents Keller's most elaborate representation of this ideal of authorship, that ideal informs Keller's publishing projects from his earliest poetry volumes to the making of his own collected works.

Part II

Office Writing

The Document

3

ON THE USES AND ABUSES OF WRITING

"Die mißbrauchten Liebesbriefe"

The ten volumes of Keller's *Gesammelte Werke* from 1889 are modest in number not only when measured against the brimming cornucopia, both real and imagined, of Goethe's *Vollständige Ausgabe letzter Hand*; they are also comparatively slim when stacked against the collected works of many of Keller's realist contemporaries, including those of Wilhelm Raabe or Theodor Fontane, and even more so when measured in relation to the output of truly prolific epochal authors such as Paul Lindau or George Hesekiel, each of whom Keller would have certainly dismissed as a "penny-a-word writer" (Geldvielschreiber).[1] While Keller's interminable procrastination and practices of rewriting and republishing certainly contributed to the modest size of his complete works, Keller and his faithful biographers are more likely to point to his fifteen-year service as the state chancellor (*Staatsschreiber*) of the canton of

---

1. Keller to Ferdinand Weibert, May 20, 1875, in *HKKA*, 21:565.

Zurich as an unfortunate interruption in and deterrent to his literary productivity. Much like Franz Kafka a few decades later, Keller perceived his long days at the office as a terrible impediment to writing literature, an activity postponed, as also for Kafka, to the late hours of the evening and night, those periods of the day reserved for private rather than public life. In a letter written near the end of his official appointment, Keller spells out an antithesis between administrative and literary writing practices, a contrast that endures and that is, I would argue, central to our conception of literary authorship: on the one hand, the routine, impersonal, and tedious administrative writing tasks of a bureaucratic office subject to its rules and hierarchies, and on the other hand the autonomous, creative ambitions of the literary author.[2] However, in the same letter, Keller also suggestively points to the literal overlap of these two allegedly antithetical modes of writing in the form of papers cluttering his desk. He writes to his friend the Austrian critic Emil Kuh, "As of July 1, I will be free of my office; I couldn't take it any longer; official business all day long, and in the evenings, I have to write literature, read, keep up with my correspondence, and so on; that doesn't work, and usually everything doesn't get done."[3] Because both practices operate with the same medium of paper, sometimes even making use of identical paper products—as is the case for Keller's introduction to *Die Leute von Seldwyla*, which was

---

2. That antithesis is poignant in Gerhard Kaiser's portrayal of Keller as a mere cog in a great administrative machine. In Kaiser's words, which remain the authoritative account of Keller's literary oeuvre: "The chancellor has become foreign to himself: he feels the clock of his poetic creativity whirring away; he sits amid the gears of an accelerating administrative machine taking on a life of its own; he feels the abstractness, the routinization of an activity that as writing does not have an effect." Gerhard Kaiser, *Gottfried Keller: Das gedichtete Leben* (Frankfurt am Main: Insel, 1981), 384. Kaiser overlooks that it is precisely in the making of literature that Keller most strongly felt himself to be such a cog or "factory worker" (Fabrikarbeiter). See Keller to Eduard Vieweg, February 20, 1861, in *HKKA*, 21:499–500.

3. "Auf 1. Juli bin ich nun von meinem Amte frei; ich habe es nicht länger ausgehalten; den Tag durch Amtsgeschäfte, des Abends soll man schriftstellern, lesen, Korrespondenz führen etc., das geht nicht und bleibt dann meistens alles zusammen liegen." Keller to Emil Kuh, May 15, 1876, in Gottfried Keller, *Gesammelte Briefe in vier Bänden*, ed. Carl Helbling, 4 vols. (Bern: Benteli, 1951–1954), 3.1:203.

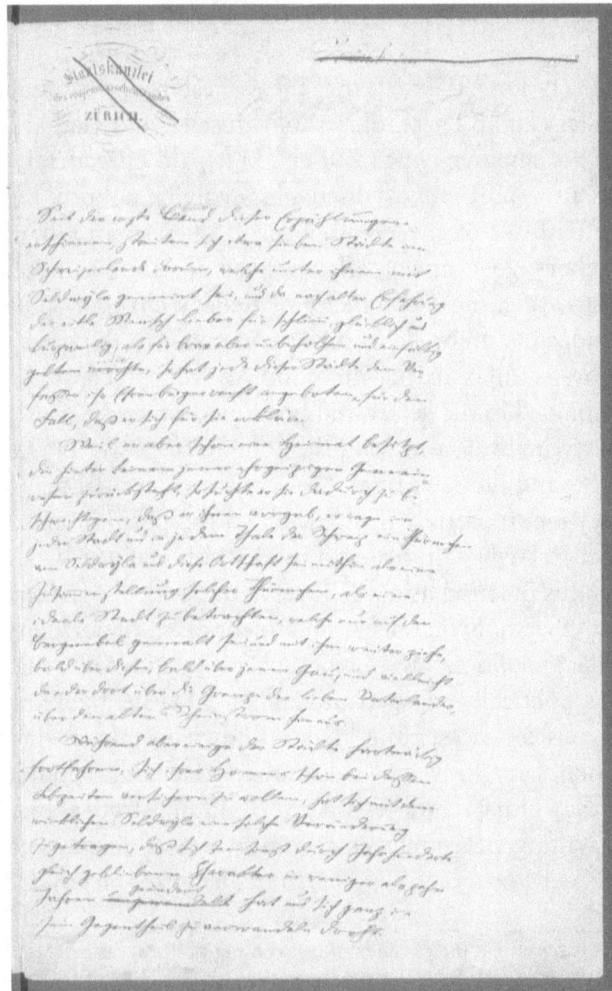

Figure 5. Gottfried Keller, manuscript for the Vorwort to *Die Leute von Seldwyla*, 1869–1873. Zurich, Zentralbibliothek Zürich, Ms. GK 10.

drafted on the letterhead of the state chancery (*Staatskanzlei*; see figure 5)—they easily merge in the same clutter. If one imagines Keller's administrative tasks and literary manuscripts competing not just for time and attention but also for the same instruments of writing (desk, paper, and pens), it is not difficult to reconstruct why the literary introduction was drafted on official governmental letterhead.

To the very limited extent that the earliest, tone-setting interpreters of Keller (Jakob Baechtold, Adolf Muschg, and Gerhard Kaiser) attend to his employment as Zurich's best-paid bureaucrat, they exploit it as an opportunity to discuss his evolving political affiliations from sympathizer of the revolutions of 1848 to an ally of Alfred Escher's liberal government, effectively an about-face in political affinities. However, these chronicles of Keller's changing politics discussed under the umbrella of his appointment to the office of state chancellor—similar to the unanimously rehearsed surprise that Keller remained in the secretarial position despite the change in the ruling party in 1869 following the coming to power of the Democratic Party and the rewriting of the constitution to allow for direct democracy—purposefully misunderstand the position and ethos of the bureaucrat whose office and service was defined by having to eschew, in his function as a public servant, political opinions and allegiances.[4] By employing his appointment as an opportunity to discuss Keller's politics, these biographers intend to "rehabilitate" Keller as a politically engaged and influential father figure of a Swiss national consciousness, rather than acknowledge him as the bureaucratic functionary he was, an acknowledgment that could, on the basis of the cultural antithesis between administrative and literary forms of writing, potentially compromise his standing as a canonical author.[5] Playing on a central theme from *Der grüne Heinrich*, Muschg

---

4. It is precisely on the grounds of his seeming political disinterestedness that the local newspaper *Zürcherische Freitagszeitung* objected to Keller's appointment to the position of state chancellor: "We said his election must have been deeply discouraging for many. This is *the* opinion. It is generally known that until recently Mr. Keller had not familiarized himself with politics in general and even less with the details of administration, and no one had even remotely suspected that he was capable of it." *Zürcherische Freitagszeitung*, September 20, 1861; quoted in Hans Wysling, *Gottfried Keller, 1819–1890* (Zürich: Artemis, 1990), 233.

5. Adolf Muschg refers to the return to Zurich as an "an adventure of rehabilitation." Adolf Muschg, *Gottfried Keller* (München: Kindler, 1977), 274. To be fair, Keller initiated this narrative of rehabilitation when he portrayed his return to Zurich as reestablishing his good name:

I now prefer to live first in Zurich for a time, to establish my unfairly judged personality there and then gradually to see whether I can test and train my

and Kaiser go so far as to cast Keller's years in office as a matter of repaying his debts (*Schuld* and *Schulden*) to his family and fatherland that he accumulated during his years abroad in Heidelberg, Munich, and Berlin. Muschg, for example, writes of this debt: "He perceived the office as working on his *Schuld*—in both senses of the word, as 'guilt' and 'debt'—as repaying his civic deficits. In this office, he had made a pact with his self-respect. It was a matter of conscience, and it did not let him forget that it was also a substitute: a stopgap for forfeited happiness, the ersatz productivity of someone who had socially fallen short."[6] Office work that would otherwise be at odds with the image of the creative author is reincorporated into that persona through a narrative of redemptive patriotic sacrifice.

Unlike these misrepresentations of a bureaucratic office as a political one, Keller himself possessed no illusions about the distinc-

---

usefulness in teaching, for example, through free useful lectures in some form or another, or alternatively, if it should be necessary, to take up a modest position in the state administration; in actual fact, I am not at all as impractical as one might think, once I have some peace and quiet.

Ich ziehe es nun vor, erst einige Zeit in Zürich zu leben, meine ungerecht beurteilte Persönlichkeit dort herzustellen und dann nach und nach zu sehen, etwa durch freie zweckdienliche Vorträge unter irgend einer Form meine Nutzbarkeit zum Lehrfach zu prüfen und auszubilden, oder aber dann, wenn es nötig sein sollte, vielleicht eine bescheidene Stelle in der Staatsverwaltung zu versehen; ich bin im Grunde gar nicht so unpraktisch, als man glaubt, wenn ich nur erst einmal Ruhe habe.

Keller to Jakob Dubs, March 1854, in *Gesammelte Briefe*, 4:46–47.

6. Muschg, *Gottfried Keller*, 271. Kaiser echoes the topos ten years later: "Did Keller, who turned down an appointment as a professor, impose the prosaic office on himself as a penitential exercise to pay off his debts to his fatherland and to mother earth, from which he had sucked his sustenance as an ornamental plant for so long, for too long?" Kaiser, *Gottfried Keller*, 383. For a very insightful summary of Keller's "depoliticization" on the part of literary biographers, see Dominik Müller, "Schriftsteller als Staats-Schreiber? Politische Interventionsformen der Literatur in der Schweiz—von Gottfried Keller zu Guy Krneta," in *Die Wiederkehr der* res publica*: Zu literarischer Repräsentation einer politischen Idee im globalen Zeitalter*, ed. Dariusz Komorowski (Göttingen: Vandenhoeck & Ruprecht, 2021), esp. 110–13. Müller points out that invocations of Keller's name in Swiss political discourses throughout the twentieth century were less likely to repress Keller's politics and often heralded him as an example of an author (and a counterexample to Max Frisch) who faithfully served the state.

tion.⁷ An appreciation for the ideal bureaucrat who publicly abstains from political opinion is conspicuous in Keller's most elaborate fictional characterization of such a salaried official, a *Statthalter*, or district prefect, who was (and sometimes still is) typically appointed by the cantonal government council (*Regierungsrat*) and was responsible for executing the law, maintaining order, taking care of cantonal infrastructure, and resolving disputes. In volume 2 of *Der grüne Heinrich* (in both the first and later editions), the prefect must mediate in the village's contentious debate about whether a new road should be built through the valley or over the mountain pass, and Heinrich asks Anna's father, a schoolteacher, why a man of such good character as their prefect would choose "this disreputable way of life" (diese[] verrufene[] Lebensart) and not pursue the greater life of private enterprise.⁸ The schoolteacher explains to him that the prefect, faced with the collapse of his family's finances, chose the reliable lifelong income of a public servant at the cost of the right to express political opinions rather than live as free as a lily in the field, the very form of life Heinrich seems at risk to conduct: "But he [the prefect] doesn't have the courage to become penniless from one day to the next: he has absolutely no idea how the birds and the lilies of the field nourish and clothe themselves without a fixed income, and so he has sacrificed asserting his own opinions."⁹ Anna's father's characterization of the prefect seemingly makes a lasting impression on the young Heinrich Lee of the second edition, who at the end of the novel occupies a similar position in charge of "the chancery office of a small district" (die

---

7. Mistaking Keller's tenure in the office of a bureaucrat as a political office is additionally sustained, beyond the attempt to rehabilitate him, by the fact that he was also elected to political office during his time as state chancellor and, furthermore, by how earlier occupants of that office, including Adolf Exner and Ferdinand Meyer (Conrad Ferdinand Meyer's father), employed the position as a springboard for political aspirations to become members of the government council.

8. Keller, *Der grüne Heinrich* (1st ed., 1854–1855), in *HKKA*, 11:434.

9. "Allein er hat nicht den Muth, auf einen Tag brotlos zu werden, er hat gar keine Ahnung davon, wie sich die Vögel und die Lilien des Feldes ohne ein fixes Einkommen nähren und kleiden, und daher hat er sich der Geltendmachung seiner eigenen Meinungen begeben." Keller, *Der grüne Heinrich* (1st ed., 1854–1855), in *HKKA*, 11:438.

Kanzlei eines kleinen Oberamtes)[10]—an occupation so unsatisfying that he suffers near-suicidal despair while enjoying a reliable income and performing, the novel's conclusion suggests, an act of personal sacrifice for the sake of the greater community. Upon returning to Zurich after his years of compounding debts in Heidelberg, Munich, and Berlin while writing *Der grüne Heinrich*, Keller had eyed an administrative position in the cantonal government for much the same reason: a position in which he would be free from the financial uncertainty and debts that overshadowed his years abroad, and moreover one that would relieve him from the onus of performing challenging cognitive labor—thinking. Writing in anticipation of his return to Zurich from Berlin, he thus assured his mother: "So I would rather have a different, simple post that doesn't give much to think about."[11] These expectations seem very much fulfilled when he writes years later, from the office, of the "vegetative life" he leads there.[12]

Taking my cue from the portrayal of the idealized district prefect, this chapter seeks to offer an alternative perspective on Keller's occupation as a bureaucrat and its relationship to his literary authorship. I examine Keller's fictional portrayals of a bureaucratic office along with his own office writings as state chancellor not for clues of his political sympathies, nor for evidence of patriotic feeling, but with regard to how one might challenge a culturally entrenched view of administrative writing procedures as a mere interruption in or hindrance to literary authorship, namely, as literature's

---

10. Gottfried Keller, *Green Henry*, trans. A. M. Holt, rev. ed. (London: Alma Classics, 2023), 572; Keller, *Der grüne Heinrich* (2nd ed., 1889), in *HKKA*, 3:266.

11. "So will ich lieber einen sonstigen einfachen Posten, der nicht viel zu denken gibt." Gottfried Keller to Elisabeth Keller-Scheuchzer and Regula Keller, April 10, 1854, in *Gesammelte Briefe*, 1:121. Similarly, Keller anticipates an appointment in Zurich in his correspondence with Vieweg: "I have long been promised an easy position in the state administration that does not take up too much time" (eine leichte Stelle in der Staatsverwaltung, die nicht viel Zeit wegnimmt, ist mir längst zugesagt). Keller to Eduard Vieweg, November 10, 1855, in *HKKA*, 21:474.

12. "I lead, to be sure, a somewhat vegetative life, which consists in eating and sleeping with the insertion of 8–10 hours of office work every day" (Ich führe allerdings ein etwas vegetatives Leben, das aus Essen und Schlafen besteht, mit Einschaltung von 8–10stündiger Amtsarbeit täglich). Keller to Johann Salomon Hegi, May 12, 1869, in *Gesammelte Briefe*, 1:219.

other. I thereby borrow a line of inquiry that Stanley Corngold has developed to bridge the gap between literary and administrative writing practices with respect to the better-known example of Kafka's life and literature: "We are concerned with the way in which Kafka's sense of his fate as a writer is implicated in his work life—the way in which his *Beamtensein*, his 'official' being, is involved in his *Schrifstellersein*, his writerly being."[13] Corngold too begins by acknowledging why one might resist such an inquiry, rehearsing the contrast between these two modes of writing (and, for that matter, modes of being) before attempting their "reconciliation": "At first glance, this association could seem a poor idea—as an adversary relation, yes, but scarcely a fraternal one or one based on resemblance. The comparison suggests a demeaning of writing by its likeness to work that is merely rulebound, calling for ordinary skills of application when not inspired by a philistine detestation of intelligence."[14] These same doubts surely account for why Keller's tasks as a bureaucratic functionary have yet to receive more than merely biographical consideration.

If nothing else, such a reconciliation would provide ample material for endowing Keller's collected works with additional heft: Keller's office writings are estimated to encompass around 200,000 files and an additional 200,000 signatures on official documents—and this despite the fact that Keller is best remembered for his laconic office style and conservative ethos of office management expressed as a preference for sparing paper use and a minimalist production of documents. As Hans Max Kriesi observes in *Gottfried Keller als Politiker* (1918), there is hardly any other author who signed his own name as often as Keller did; hence, there is hardly any other author whose own name makes up such a significant portion of his written corpus, if these documents were included: "There has probably never been an author who signed their name as often as Keller: he must have done so nearly two hundred thousand times;

---

13. Stanley Corngold, "Kafka and the Ministry of Writing," in Franz Kafka, *The Office Writings*, ed. Stanley Corngold, Jack Greenberg, and Benno Wagner (Princeton, NJ: Princeton University Press, 2009), 3.

14. Corngold, "Kafka and the Ministry of Writing," 3.

and likely no other author has ever produced so many manuscripts: at least two hundred volumes, estimated based on the format of his collected works, are still in the archives."[15] In the office of the state chancellor, the repetition compulsion that famously manifested itself in Keller's obsessive scribbling of the name "Betty" on the *Berliner Schreibunterlage* from 1855 is displaced onto the signing of his own name on documents such as *Heimatscheine* or passports, two staple documents issued by the cantonal chancery.[16] The structural homology between these two vastly dissimilar sets of documents points back to an author whose written corpus consists in large part of his own name, itself a challenge to the portrait of a creative author.

Yet along with the letters to his betrothed, Luise Scheidegger, during his tenure as state chancellor—letters that Baechtold, the first manager of Keller's papers (*Nachlass*), destroyed because he deemed them too intimate and a possible detriment to Keller's reputation in light of Scheidegger's decision to commit suicide rather than marry—Keller's office writings have been systematically excised from editions of his work to this day despite the fact that they remain accessible in Zurich's archives.[17] In diametric opposition to the too personal courtship letters, these files are regarded as too impersonal, reflecting only office rules and regulations and too little of Keller's personality and style—in other words, of his aura as an author. As Kaiser writes, driving the antithesis between administrative and literary writing home: "As responsible as the work [as state chancellor] may have been, it is not productive in a deeper sense, neither politically formative nor an expression of one's person. [...] Poetry and capitalism might have points of contact, but poetry and bureaucracy do not."[18] Such a view that Keller's administrative writings do not belong to his oeuvre confirms his continuing epigonal status and perhaps also the epigonal

---

15. Hans Max Kriesi, *Gottfried Keller als Politiker* (Leipzig: Huber, 1918), 15.

16. For a detailed analysis of the *Schreibunterlage*, see Peter Villwock, "Betty und Gottfried: Eine Geschichte in Bildern," in "Der Gottfried-Keller-Rabe," ed. Joachim Kersten, special issue, *Der Rabe* 61 (2000): 150–62.

17. The only exceptions to this practice of exclusion are the five brief *Bettagsmandate* included in the collected essays of the edition of the Deutscher Klassiker Verlag and the *HKKA*.

18. Kaiser, *Gottfried Keller*, 383.

status of the epoch of realism at large. After all, Keller continues to be sandwiched between two authors, Goethe and Kafka, whose occupations as bureaucrats have been well incorporated into their authorial personas and whose office writings concomitantly belong to the editions of their collected works.

Part 2 of this book is tasked with making a first attempt at incorporating administrative writing practices into Keller's authorial persona, namely, by identifying points of contact between poetry and bureaucracy that Kaiser categorically denies. In the first place, once again taking my cue from Corngold's analysis of Kafka, I argue that Keller's administrative activity provided "theme and substance" for his fiction, the figure of the district prefect from *Der grüne Heinrich* being an initial example.[19] While scholarship on Keller typically relates his time as state chancellor to the final novella of *Die Leute von Seldwyla*, "Das verlorene Lachen," or to the *Züricher Novellen* on the grounds that these texts reflect his deepening interest in local history and his perceived responsibility as moralizing educator and critic of a nation he increasingly regarded as taking a turn for the worse,[20] I propose to read a text typically not discussed in conjunction with his tenure as state chancellor, namely, "Die mißbrauchten Liebesbriefe," as a fictional representation of office work, bureaucratic conduct, and the formatting of documents. The text combines a satire of contemporaneous literature with a valuation of these bureaucratic practices. On this basis, the novella can be read as an allegorical interrogation into the uses and abuses of writing, a weighing of its seemingly divided administrative and literary functions. Finally, in chapter 4, I loosen the wedge between practices of administrative and literary writing by examining one type of document produced during Keller's occupation as state chancellor, the protocol (*Protokoll*) in the sense of meeting minutes, and demonstrate how these official transcripts of meetings can become objects not only of biographic but also of critical inquiry.

---

19. Corngold, "Kafka and the Ministry of Writing," 16.
20. Of "Das verlorene Lachen," Kaiser, for example, writes: "In the end, the state chancellor also became a stranger to a political and social system that developed contrary to his wishes and hopes. [. . .] These depressing experiences and expectations are reflected in 'Das verlorene Lachen.'" Kaiser, *Gottfried Keller*, 384.

Destabilizing a strict distinction between administrative and literary writing practices should ultimately challenge our continued commitment to literature as an index of biography or personality and bring it more strongly into view as a product of procedures of paperwork. While Keller's rehabilitation to national poet may have relied on the exclusion of his letters of amorous courtship and his office files, as alternatively representing too much or too little of his person, consideration for Keller's office work and writings provides an opportunity to appreciate texts as products of writing procedures rather than as imprints of an authorial persona. The methodological endeavor promises to strengthen our awareness of how practices with paper media are significant to literary authorship, advancing, to polemicize the point, the recognition that the making of authorship and the shaping of a literary oeuvre comprise forms of paperwork. As Leah Price and Pamela Thurschwell argue, since "ideas of the literary are formed not just by analogy with more mundane kinds of writing, but in opposition to them,"[21] exploring supposedly mundane, routine modes of writing—including their procedures of production, circulation, and storage, and the concepts of originality tied to them—can help us recognize the centrality of similar procedures to the making of literature. The history and narrative of Keller's novella "Die mißbrauchten Liebesbriefe" bring two such shared practices into view: copying and archiving as practices that format documents. The format of the document has the potential to forcefully challenge the antithesis between office work and literature, since, as Lisa Gitelman's recent history of the document emphasizes, its format directly questions entrenched concepts of literary authorship. In Gitelman's words, "Documents are properly a vernacular form for which Foucault's author function in general does not apply."[22] In what way then can we

---

21. Leah Price and Pamela Thurschwell, *Literary Secretaries/Secretarial Culture* (Aldershot: Ashgate, 2005), 2. They continue, "The office doesn't just provide a safely distant dumping-ground for all those aspects of writing and reading which aesthetic experience filters out; it also provides literature with a safely distant space in which to explore (or onto which to refract) questions internal to its own theory and practice."
22. Lisa Gitelman, *Paper Knowledge: Toward a Media History of Documents* (Durham, NC: Duke University Press, 2014), 19.

relate the procedures for making documents to the making of literature? Keller's novella "Die mißbrauchten Liebesbriefe" provides one answer.

Managing the Manuscript of "Die mißbrauchten Liebesbriefe"

One reason that "Die mißbrauchten Liebesbriefe" has yet to have been read against the backdrop of Keller's occupation as state chancellor, namely, as an account of office work, lies in its disputed dating. Keller's first complete draft of the novella is conventionally dated to February 1860, when Keller is known to have sent a manuscript intended as part of the second volume of *Die Leute von Seldwyla* to his publisher Vieweg. In an interview more than a decade later, in 1873, Keller recalled having written "Die mißbrauchten Liebesbriefe" in 1855, leading biographers to conclude that the manuscript sent in February 1855 was the same.[23] However, Walter Morgenthaler, the lead editor of the most recent edition of Keller's works, has made a very compelling argument for dating the completion of the novella significantly later, to the year 1865 (i.e., during Keller's tenure as state chancellor).[24] For one, the novella includes corrections recommended to Keller in 1864. Second, the handwriting exhibits stylistic traits adopted between 1855 and 1865; and third, the novella was published between September 28 and October 16, 1865, in nineteen installments in the *Deutsche Reichs-Zeitung*. The periodical is unlikely to have shelved the manuscript for nearly a decade before printing it. If Keller indeed sent Vieweg the manuscript for "Die mißbrauchten Liebesbriefe" on June 19, 1865, as Morgen-

---

23. Jakob Baechtold's biography of Keller, which served as the primary source for future biographers as well, claims that Vieweg had had the manuscript in his possession since 1855, which implies that Keller would have written the novella in parallel to *Der grüne Heinrich*. Jakob Baechtold, *Gottfried Kellers Leben: Seine Briefe und Tagebücher*, 3 vols. (Berlin: Wilhelm Hertz, 1894–1897), 3:32.

24. See Walter Morgenthaler, "Wann sind Gottfried Kellers *Leute von Seldwyla* entstanden? Zu einigen Datierungsfragen der 'zweiten vermehrten Auflage,'" *Text: Kritische Beiträge* 6 (2000): 99–110.

thaler hypothesizes, then the preprint in the *Deutsche Reichs-Zeitung* would have followed three months later, a brief turnover period much more typical of such preprints. Morgenthaler nonetheless concludes that pending further evidence, the conventional dating of the novella to 1860 on the basis of Keller's recollections must take precedence over the philological evidence to the contrary. To my mind, it seems mistaken simply to give the author the final word on this matter, especially considering all-too-human lapses of memory. More to the point, reading "Die mißbrauchten Liebesbriefe" as an account of administrative writing and bureaucratic discipline—as a novella in which Keller's office work becomes the "theme and substance" of his fiction—strengthens the case for dating the completion of the novella to 1864–1865.

"Die mißbrauchten Liebesbriefe" has been recurrently criticized as being excessively long and as falling into two unrelated parts.[25] The criticism seems merited considering that Keller was, both in 1855 and in 1865, under enormous pressure to produce the contractual number of sheets (*Bogen*) for the second volume of *Die Leute von Seldwyla*, in which the novella would appear.[26] The pressure Keller felt to produce a sufficient number of sheets for the second volume and the degree to which the calculation of this number was key to the basic conception of the volume is evidenced by a well-preserved and much-discussed loose page from Keller's notes titled "Seldwyla II."[27]

---

25. Helmut Pfotenhauer, for example, writes that the second half of the novella is of "minimal interest." Helmut Pfotenhauer, "Einspruch: 'Keine Romane mehr'; Gottfried Kellers vertrackte Absage an eine Literatur, die sich an die Stelle des Lebens drängt," in *"Das wahre Leben ist die Literatur": Konzepte radikaler Autorschaft von Jean Paul bis Robert Walser* (Würzburg: Königshausen & Neumann, 2020), 88.

26. As a result of the prodigious delays in publishing *Der grüne Heinrich*, Vieweg's publishing contract with Keller for the "collection of stories" that would become *Die Leute von Seldwyla* stipulates that failures to deliver the manuscript would be punished monetarily. Paragraph four of the contract dictates: "If, contrary to expectations, this deadline is not met, Mr. Gottfried Keller promises to pay Mr. Eduard Vieweg a standard penalty of 25 thalers, that is, twenty-five thalers, for each month that the delay lasts." Eduard Vieweg, "Vertrag *Die Leute von Seldwyla*," in *HKKA*, 21:456–59. Luckily for Keller, Vieweg generously renounced his right to compensation for the delays.

27. See Gottfried Keller, "Seldwyla II," 1856?–1874?, Gottfried Keller Nachlass, Ms. GK 23, Nr. 59, Zentralbibliothek Zürich. For a discussion of the

The recto of this manuscript page shows an early list of possible themes and motifs for the novellas that he presumably composed after signing the contract with Vieweg for the volume. The verso, on the other hand, shows Keller's notes calculating whether he could match the 500 pages of the first volume of *Die Leute von Seldwyla*.[28] The calculation is additionally significant insofar as it demonstrates that the second volume of *Seldwyla* stories is modeled on the format of the first: another example of the determining influence of the priority of format for the initial conception of a work.

Although there might be good reason to assess the novella as excessively long and discontinuous, close attention reveals a narrative arc to which the first and second parts are equally integral. The plot initially tracks the ambitions of the Seldwyla resident Viktor Störtler (Viggi) to become an original author. In this pursuit, he participates in the activities of different literary societies composed of kindred aspiring authors, all of whom are heavily satirized in the novella's first half. That satire makes Keller's novella valuable to an account of the changing form and format of literature because it delivers an incisive critique of publishing culture.[29] In pursuit of literary fame, Viggi

---

dating of this document as well as a facsimile and transcription, see Peter Villwock, Walter Morgenthaler, Peter Stocker, Thomas Binder, and Dominik Müller, "*Die Leute von Seldwyla*: Paralipomena Nr. 8," in *HKKA*, 21:417–23.

28. For a detailed discussion of Keller's notes on these two pages and a facsimile reproduction, see Peter Stocker, "Gottfried Kellers Arbeitsplan 'Seldwyla II': Zur genetischen Eigendynamik entstehungsgeschichtlicher Dokumente," *Text: Kritische Beiträge* 5 (1999): 63–81.

29. Keller is understood to be criticizing, in the first place, literary societies such as those responsible for initiating a new "Sturm und Drang period," among them the recently established "Young Germanic Society," which he complains about in a letter to Hettner. Keller writes,

> I was recently made to laugh in annoyance by a few issues of the magazine *Teut*, in which a pack of imbeciles proclaim the foundation of a new "Sturm und Drang period" that should ferment the future potent Goethe and Schiller. In the past hundred years, not much progress has been made on the whole in moral attitudes and common sense, otherwise such childishness would not be possible.

> Ein ärgerliches Gelächter haben mir dieser Tage einige Hefte der Zeitschrift "Teut" erregt, worin ein Rudel Schwachköpfe die Stiftung einer neuen "Sturm und Drangperiode" verkünden, aus deren Gährung sich die potenzirten künf-

instrumentalizes his wife, Gritli, in the composition of an epistolary novel; he departs on an extended journey and expects her to participate in an exchange of letters that will become the novel's manuscript. Gritli, refusing to participate in her husband's theatrical staging of effusive sentiment on which the genre is premised, cunningly engages the neighboring schoolteacher to compose her letters. In the second half of the novella, Viggi uncovers his wife's deceit and divorces her, allowing each to be happily remarried to a temperamentally more suitable partner: Viggi is punished for the abuse of his first wife with Kätter Ambach, who is defined by her voracious appetite and corresponding bodily stature, while the sober and sincere Gritli, the embodiment of an ethos of moderation, marries the schoolteacher Wilhelm and is rewarded with a prodigious family lineage. Both the satirical critique of the novella's first half and the matchmaking undertaken in the second operate on an equivalence between the love to eat and the love to write, which are presented as two analogous forms of consumption. Viggi and Kätter are defined by their appetites, as are the aspiring authors introduced at the novella's beginning who meet regularly at local inns and alternatively engage in the indulgent consumption of food and drink or in elaborating their literary ideals, each of which is equally characterized by excess. This entwinement of an immoderate appetite and a will to make literature among the novella's characters encapsulates its satirical critique of literary endeavors. Literature is presented as a perversion, an abuse (*Mißbrauch*) of writing that cannot satisfy one's appetite or desire.[30] In the novella's

---

tigen Göthe und Schiller hervorgehen sollen. An sittlicher Haltung und an allgemeinem Verstand ist man seit hundert Jahren im Ganzen nicht viel vorwärts gekommen, sonst wären dergleichen Kindereien nicht möglich.

Keller to Hermann Hettner, January 31, 1860, in *HKKA*, 21:497. The thematic connection to the satire of "Die mißbrauchten Liebesbriefe" supports the hypothesis that Keller was working on the novella in 1860 and not five years later.

30. On this point I am indebted to Ben Kafka's observation that the stories we tell ourselves about bureaucratic procedures foreground the insatiability of desire, often in the form of voracious appetites. In Kafka's analysis, insatiability marks the absence of acknowledgment that individuals expect and desire from the modern state as represented through the bureaucratic office. In Keller's novella, it is conversely storytelling and not the bureau that excavates and intensifies desire. Ben Kafka, *The Demon of Writing: Powers and Failures of Paperwork* (New York: Zone Books, 2012), 79–86.

dramatic turning point, the moment in which Viggi discovers that the schoolteacher has been writing amorous letters to his wife that she has then been forwarding to him as if they were her own, he collects all the letters on the family table, only to realize that he is hungry and cannot eat them.[31] Literature, so the novella's critique aims to teach us, leaves us hungry. In Keller's moralistic tale, only Gritli, the embodiment of moderation—who, unlike her first husband, understands the proper administrative purposes of writing and embodies, as I show, a bureaucratic ethos—can experience a happy end. The end of the story thus praises Gritli's new family as people "who, without renouncing the enjoyment of life, nevertheless practiced moderation and therefore prospered."[32]

On the Abuses of Writing

While the lampooning of different authors and their "devices of composition" (Kompositionsgeheimnisse) at the beginning of "Die mißbrauchten Liebesbriefe" has been much appreciated among readers,[33] the fact that the satire directs its critique at practices of production rather than at literary content has escaped scholarly attention. Like the account of the "love letters" between Viggi and Gritli later in the novella, the texts produced by these ridiculous and ridiculed authors are never mentioned. Instead, the description of their efforts focuses on the materiality of paper products (as books of different genres, periodicals, loose sheets, and as refuse) and different procedures for making texts, in particular copying and mixing (sampling). Attention to the role that the practice of copying, more apposite to a monastery or a chancery, plays in the novella

---

31. See Gottfried Keller, "The Misused Love Letters," trans. Michael Bullock, in *Two Novellas: The Misused Love Letters; Regula Amrain and Her Youngest Son* (New York: Frederick Ungar, 1974),48; and Keller, "Die mißbrauchten Liebesbriefe," in *Die Leute von Seldwyla*, in *HKKA*, 5:133.

32. "Eine kleine Kolonie von Gutbestehenden anwuchs, welche, ohne einem heitern Lebensgenusse zu entsagen, dennoch Maß hielten und gediehen." Keller, "Love Letters," 94; Keller, "Liebesbriefe," in *HKKA*, 5:179.

33. Keller, "Love Letters," 15; Keller, "Liebesbriefe," in *HKKA*, 5:99.

reveals how the practice undercuts an imaginary of genius poetic composition and exhibits the use of bureaucratic writing procedures in the crafting of literature.

"Die mißbrauchten Liebesbriefe" portrays the task of copying most centrally in the figure of Gritli. Yet the practice is first relayed in the novella through the embedded narrative of the waiter, who encounters copying in the literary circle when he is waiting on them and then, in an act of exquisite mimicry, himself perfects the procedure so as to become "a writer among writers" (ein Schriftsteller unter Schriftstellern).[34] After recognizing the depravity of these literary circles and their ambitions, he returns to the more honorable life of a waiter, from which vantage point he can recount the procedures of textual production with reflective distance. The waiter is originally inspired by Dr. Mewes, who made his name delivering lectures on German literature copied from a book likely stolen from a local library. The soiled condition of the book serves as the sole, albeit suggestive, indication of the quality of its content and the lectures copied from its pages; the stained condition of the book and its having been stolen simultaneously index the moral depravity of Dr. Mewes himself: "He [Dr. Mewes] gave lectures on German literature in the ballroom of the Blue Pike, where I was working at the time, and he copied them word for word out of a book. To judge by the binding, the book must have been stolen from some library; it was dog-eared and covered in spots of ink and grease."[35] As if the book's condition were not sufficient evidence of Dr. Mewes's vice, he copies in bed (rather than at a bureau, or desk), which he likewise soils with ink. That the filthy book is accompanied by a primer on French conversation and a set of pornographic cards suggests that the bed is being soiled during the process of copying by more than ink alone: "Apart from this book he owned a tattered manual of conversational French and a deck of

---

34. Keller, "Love Letters," 17; Keller, "Liebesbriefe," in *HKKA*, 5:101.
35. "Er gab im Tanzsaal beim Blauen Hecht, wo ich damals war, Vorlesungen über deutsche Litteratur, welche er wörtlich abschrieb aus einem Buche. Dasselbe mußte aus irgend einer Bibliothek gestohlen worden sein, dem Einbande nach zu urteilen, und war ganz voll Eselsohren, Tinten- und Oelflecke." Keller, "Love Letters," 17–18; Keller, "Liebesbriefe," in *HKKA*, 5:101–2.

cards with obscene pictures that showed when you held them up to the light. He used to copy out the book in bed to save heating. In the end he upset the inkwell over the eiderdown and the sheet."[36] As in the characterization of Kätter Ambach, the activity of writing is merely one expression of an immoderate, if not perverted, appetite suggestively associated with sexual perversion as well. When asked to pay for the dirty bed linens, Dr. Mewes threatens to defile the good name of the hotel, the Blue Pike, in "his writings and articles" (seinen Schriften und "Feuilletons").[37] While it is left open whether Dr. Mewes makes good on his threat, the bed linens and the pages of his publications are stylized here as interchangeable materials made to absorb and be permanently tainted by Dr. Mewes's secretions.

To reproduce Dr. Mewes's success, the waiter gives himself the nom de plume "George d'Esan"[38] (a mirror copy of his original name, Nase, so an inversion, if not perversion, of his name) and adopts and perfects the practices of copying and sampling that are at the core of Dr. Mewes's writing practice. The waiter's comical description of his activity adds complexity to the act of copying (*abschreiben*), associating it with practices of translation and mixing, that is, a practice more varied than the word-by-word transcription we may first associate with the activity. This by no means adulterates the task of copying. Indeed, copying, as it is cast throughout the novella and beyond in Keller's work, should not be imagined from the perspective of the age of the photocopier as mirrorlike reproduction but instead in the spirit of the medieval copyist, for whom copying entailed improving upon the original when needed and, importantly, contributing to an archive. As Oliver Kohns and Martin Roussel helpfully summarize the point, "Copying thus means summarizing, improving, and—only in the third place—

---

36. "Außer diesem Buche besaß er noch einen zerzaus'ten Leitfaden zur französischen Konversation und ein Kartenspiel mit obscönen Bildern darin, wenn man es gegen das Licht hielt. Er pflegte jenes Buch im Bett auszuschreiben, um die Heizung zu sparen; da verschüttete er schließlich das Tintenfaß über Steppdecke und Leintuch." Keller, "Love Letters," 18; Keller, "Liebesbriefe," in *HKKA*, 5:102.
37. Keller, "Love Letters," 18; Keller, "Liebesbriefe," in *HKKA*, 5:102.
38. Keller, "Love Letters," 19; Keller, "Liebesbriefe," in *HKKA*, 5:103.

preserving."[39] All three of these procedures are integral to Keller's fictional portrayals of copying as well. Such an ideal of copying is already familiar to us from the story "Hadlaub" in the *Züricher Novellen*, where the protagonist of the same name makes an edition of minnesong. Here, too, his copies are of such quality that they, and not the originals, become the authoritative edition of the texts. The hero of the story, after a bout of creative writing in which he crafts his own minnesong, ultimately becomes an honorable chancellor (*Kanzler*)—yet another example, along with the district prefect from *Der grüne Heinrich* and Gritli from "Die mißbrauchten Liebesbriefe," of a bureaucratic hero and a valuation of a bureaucratic ethos over and against that of a literary author.

In the case of the waiter's production scheme, the copy too is a reproduction (*Abschrift*) of the original, but it is by no means identical. The waiter first translates his material from a "pile of old French newspapers" he had collected with the intention of instructing himself in the French language.[40] Instead, they become the raw material of his successful recycling program for the purpose of original literary production. The fact that the waiter makes use of discarded newspapers as his source material evidences a nineteenth-century

---

39. Oliver Kohns and Martin Roussel, "Kopieren," in *Historisches Wörterbuch des Mediengebrauchs*, ed. Heiko Christians, Matthias Bickenbach, and Nikolaus Wegmann, vol. 1 (Köln: Böhlau, 2015), 376. Kohns and Roussel continue: "The copyists of the Middle Ages were—in opposition to today's media practice of copying and the opposition of values between original and copy—'improvers' of the 'truth' of the written tradition." On an idealized image of copying, see also Ernst Robert Curtius's account of the "dignified gravity" of the scribe. "This is demanded by the holiness of the books he is to copy, as well as by accurate reproduction of the text in word and punctuation." Ernst Robert Curtius, *European Literature and the Latin Middle Ages*, trans. Willard R. Trask (Princeton, NJ: Princeton University Press, 2013), 314. More immediately on the significance of copying in Keller's novella, see Irmela Marei Krüger-Fürhoff, "Ab/Schreiben: Handschrift zwischen Liebesdienst und Dienstbarkeit in Goethes *Wahlverwandtschaften*, Eliots *Middlemarch* und Kellers 'Die mißbrauchten Liebesbriefe,'" in *Schreiben als Ereignis: Künste und Kulturen der Schrift*, ed. Jutta Müller-Tamm, Caroline Schubert, and Klaus Ulrich Werner (München: Wilhelm Fink, 2018), 219–39, especially 236. Krüger-Fürhoff argues that each of the main characters can be understood as embodying different practices of copying.

40. "Pack zerlesene Nummern von französischen Zeitungen." Keller, "Love Letters," 18; Keller, "Liebesbriefe," in *HKKA*, 5:102.

transition from practices of rereading to reading and discarding, a practice succinctly described by Keller's publisher Ferdinand Weibert in the context of assuring Keller that a periodical preprint would in no way threaten the symbolic standing of a later book publication. He writes: "A magazine is read many times in the company of others or in journal circles, is torn up, is discarded, in short disappears piece by piece."[41] In Keller's novella, that practice is modified such that these newspapers are neither discarded nor reread but instead become the source material for creative copying. In this (re-)production process, the waiter's deficient grasp of the German language (the target language for his translations) becomes an exceptional stylistic boon.

> From these old newspapers I translated a jumble of stories and gossip of all kinds, including stuff about people I had never even heard of. Because of my imperfect command of German I often retained not only the French order of words and phrases, but also all sorts of Gallicisms, and the twaddle I added out of my own head was written in the same kind of gibberish, which I thought real literary language. When I had scribbled a whole book like this I showed it to my gentlemen and friends as an original work, and would you believe it, they received it with great enthusiasm and were able to get it printed right away. There is something odd about hack writers.

> Aus diesen verschollenen Blättern übersetzte ich einen Mischmasch von Geschichtchen und Geschwätz aller Art, auch über Persönlichkeiten, die ich nicht im mindesten kannte. Aus Unkenntnis der deutschen Sprache behielt ich nicht nur öfter die französische Wort- und Satzstellung, sondern auch alle möglichen Gallicismen bei, und die Salbadereien, welche ich aus meinem eigenen Gehirne hinzufügte, schrieb ich dann ebenfalls in diesem Kauderwelsch, welches ich für echt schriftstellerisch hielt. Als ich ein Buch Papier auf solche Weise überschmiert hatte, anvertraute ich es als ein Originalwerk meinen Herren und Freunden, und siehe, sie nahmen es mit aller Aufmunterung entgegen und wußten es sogleich zum Druck zu befördern. Es ist etwas Eigentümliches um die schlechten Scribenten.[42]

---

41. Ferdinand Weibert to Keller, August 2, 1877, in *HKKA*, 21:581. For a discussion of the shift from practices of rereading to reading and discarding, see Leah Price, *How to Do Things with Books in Victorian Britain* (Princeton, NJ: Princeton University Press, 2012), 252.

42. Keller, "Love Letters," 18–19; Keller, "Liebesbriefe," in *HKKA*, 5:103.

Like Keller's secularizing retelling of legends in the *Sieben Legenden*—in which, as Eric Downing shows, retellings are cast as more original than their sources[43]—the waiter's reproduction and mixing of texts produces a literary work of greatest originality. In fact, the originality of the waiter's texts is humorously affirmed three times: to Nase, they have "real literary language"; to his fellow authors they are an "original work"; and the public hails it as "the very important first work of a brilliant young author."[44] Originality thus becomes dissociated from anteriority.

Because the waiter Nase can narrate how literature is produced by means of copying from a reflective distance unavailable to Dr. Mewes or Viggi, his account of his life as an author does more than lampoon the literary aspirations of these comical dilettantes. In contrast to the unredeemable Dr. Mewes, the ironic distance of the waiter's own description of his mixture of "Gallicisms," "twaddle," and "gibberish" rescues him from the charge of moral depravity (though he too writes in bed). His authorship represents the mere perfection of a popular production process and offers key insights into the media and practices of literary production anchored in a culture of excess consumption. When asked by his disbelieving interlocutor where he could possibly source the "material" (Schreibestoff) for uninterrupted production, the waiter replies that he writes about writing. In effect, the endlessly generative potential of literature is attributed to a self-reflexive turn that makes the instruments and procedures of writing its subject. Relieved of

---

43. Copying invites being understood as one further operation of reproduction or doubling in Keller's work that calls into question the relationship between realism and representation. Downing has elaborated this problem at length with regard to Keller's *Sieben Legenden*, which are introduced as retellings of historical legends, of which he concludes: "The realism requires the repetition that mimetically equates the new representation with the earlier 'reality.' On the other hand, such an original reality is understood to be not 'really' there, but to be itself a fiction reproduced out of a fiction as a fiction." Eric Downing, *Double Exposures: Repetition and Realism in Nineteenth-Century German Fiction* (Stanford, CA: Stanford University Press, 2000), 96–97.

44. "Mein Büchlein wurde sofort als das sehr zu beachtende Erstlingswerk eines geistreichen jungen Autors verkundet." Keller, "Love Letters," 19; Keller, "Liebesbriefe," in *HKKA*, 5:103.

the onus of inspiration, creativity, and composition, the waiter gives an account of writing that enshrines the instruments and procedures of writing and the very discourse of authorship as its contents, a characterization that applies to the contents of "Die mißbrauchten Liebesbriefe" itself. The waiter explains, "I had nothing to write about except writing itself, so to speak. When I dipped the pen in the ink I wrote about this ink. No sooner did I find myself being called a writer than I started writing about the dignity, the duties, rights and needs of writers."[45]

Seen in the broader context of the historical conditions for producing realist literature, the waiter and, later in the novella, Gritli vividly illustrate a practice of mixing dependent on a thriving periodical culture that has been described by Petra McGillen and also often attributed to Keller.[46] McGillen, who describes Fontane as the first realist remix artist, explains that the practice relies on an environment saturated with accessible, low-cost media objects, such as soundtracks or periodicals, whose format makes it possible to subject them to "rebalancing, filtering, or otherwise modifying" so as to produce a new pleasurable object: "As a cultural practice, remixing is significant because it provides a new way of engaging creatively with massive amounts of pre-mediated ('second-hand') materials that are in cultural circulation."[47] Dr. Mewes's and the waiter's industrious copying is contingent on the availability of print products: easily stolen library books, discarded periodicals, and low-cost editions of Goethe's idylls. They belong to a media culture defined by a loop between continuous consumption and consumption-driven production. The specificity of Keller's satire resides in foregrounding the labor of copying that must precede

---

45. "Ich hatte eben keinen Stoff als so zu sagen das Schreiben selbst. Indem ich Tinte in die Feder nahm, schrieb ich über diese Tinte. Ich schrieb, kaum daß ich mich zum Schriftsteller ernannt sah, über die Würde, die Pflichten, Rechte und Bedürfnisse des Schriftstellerstandes." Keller, "Love Letters," 20; Keller, "Liebesbriefe," in *HKKA*, 5:104.

46. On Keller's mixing of different styles, see Alexander Honold, *Die Tugenden und die Laster: Gottfried Kellers "Die Leute von Seldwyla"* (Berlin: Schwabe, 2018), 12.

47. Petra S. McGillen, *The Fontane Workshop: Manufacturing Realism in the Industrial Age of Print* (New York: Bloomsbury Academic, 2019), 16.

the act of compiling and mixing if the materiality of the to-be-mixed media objects—such as library books that may not be cut—does not permit them to be directly pasted together.

The waiter is described as adeptly transferring his expertise as a waiter and the mixing skills that go with that occupation to authorship, that is, as a man who knows how to satisfy appetites by assembling and combining different dishes.[48] He too knows how to mix the sources of his copies, including from the genre of miscellany, itself a combination of morsels of seemingly unrelated content. In the following, the choice of the adjective *rührig* signals both the procedure of mixing and the waiter's industriousness:

> In addition, I carried on an active trade in so-called "inside stories," spreading all sorts of gossip and hearsay in all directions. If there was nothing happening in the present I translated Goethe's *Sesenheimer Idylle* for about the twentieth time from his splendid language into my wretched gibberish and sent it to some provincial rag as the latest research. [...] Or I copied a letter or a poem out of some volume that had just been published and sent it around as a handwritten communication, and I always had the satisfaction of seeing the thing cheerfully circulating through the whole press.

> Ueberdies betrieb ich eine rührige Industrie mit sogenannten "Mitgeteilts" nach allen Ecken und Enden hin, indem ich allerlei Neuigkeitskram und Klatsch verbreitete. Wenn gerade nichts aus der Gegenwart vorhanden war, so übersetzte ich die Sesenheimer Idylle wohl zum zwanzigsten Male aus Goethes schöner Sprache in meinen gemeinen Jargon und sandte sie als neue Forschung in irgend ein Winkelblättchen. [...] Oder ich schrieb wohl aus einem eben herausgekommenen Bande einen Brief, ein Gedicht aus und setzte es als handschriftliche Mitteilung in Umlauf, und ich hatte immer die Genugthuung, das Ding munter durch die ganze Presse zirkulieren zu sehen.[49]

---

48. Nase states, "I was [...] a poor wretch who transferred the habits of a waiter to an activity and conditions of which he had [...] simply no idea at all" (Ich war [...] ein armer Tropf, welcher seine Kellnergewohnheiten in eine Thätigkeit übertrug und in Verhältnisse, von denen er [...] gar keinen Begriff hatte). Keller, "Love Letters," 21; Keller, "Liebesbriefe," in *HKKA*, 5:105. Pfotenhauer reads Nase's occupation as a *Kellner* (i.e., *Keller* plus an *n*) and the later reference to Viggi's cellar (*Keller*) as Keller's self-inscriptions—effectively making the tale a satirical commentary on his own authorship. See Pfotenhauer, "Einspruch: 'Keine Romane mehr,'" 89–90. Pfotenhauer does not, however, spell out the significance of the cellar or waiter as sites of self-inscription.

49. Keller, "Love Letters," 20–21; Keller, "Liebesbriefe," in *HKKA*, 5:105.

Keller's description of this production process identifies mixing not only as a practice of the aspiring author but also as reliant on and contributing to a culture of media circulation.

Further scenes of culinary and textual mixing pervade "Die mißbrauchten Liebesbriefe" in a range of different media; in each case, mixing is described as a process of modification intended to intensify the pleasure of consumption. For example, when Viggi first leaves on his journey, Gritli prepares for him a feast to make the otherwise painful railroad journey more pleasurable. She, like the waiter, is in the position of serving and satisfying appetites. As the centerpiece to many side dishes, she prepares chicken that is described as "skillfully carved up and artistically fitted together again,"[50] which is to say, it is spliced and recompiled. Similarly, toward the story's end, Kätter assumes Gritli's place as mistress of Viggi's household and redecorates it in a manner reminiscent of the chicken's preparation: She "turned everything in Viggi's house upside down by shifting all the furniture around, putting trailers of ivy in all the corners, cutting up the beautiful curtains and making extraordinary serrated banners of them."[51] When Viggi speaks in his self-defense at his divorce proceedings, his speech climaxes in the description of his wife as a "goose armed with vulture's claws" (mit Geierkrallen bewaffnete[] Gans),[52] a monstrous amalgam that disgusts his audience and the reader not only because it so misrepresents his wife but also because it is an inappropriate mixing of metaphors (vulture and goose). The chicken, curtains, and avian metaphors have been cut and superficially reassembled in such a way that the traces of these procedures are left visible. The satire of "Die mißbrauchten Liebesbriefe" ultimately casts the relationship of contemporaneous literature to the past along similar lines: The waiter Nase's literary career begins in an act of imitating his customers, who

---

50. "Das Huhn war vortrefflich zerschnitten und kunstreich wieder zusammengefügt." Keller, "Love Letters," 28; Keller, "Liebesbriefe," in *HKKA*, 5:113.

51. "Sie [. . .] kehrte auch richtig in Viggis Hause das Unterste zu oberst, indem sie alle Möbeln anders stellte, in alle Ecken Epheuranken anbrachte, die schönen Vorhänge zerschnitt und wunderliche gezackte Fähnchen daraus machte." Keller, "Love Letters," 53; Keller, "Liebesbriefe," in *HKKA*, 5:138.

52. Keller, "Love Letters," 54; Keller, "Liebesbriefe," in *HKKA*, 5:140.

themselves are resolved to imitate a past "Storm and Stress Period."[53] Viggi leaves the gathering as its designated Swiss delegate, planning "for the time being to combine in himself both Bodmer and Lavater in order to receive and encourage the new Klopstocks, Wieland, and Goethe on their travels."[54] Contemporary literature, as portrayed in these first few pages of the novella, relates to the past though mimicry and mixing that continually produces the newest originals. A tradition of literature is, in effect, a self-perpetuating act of mimicry—a critique that destabilizes the very notion of an original literary masterpiece and instead places the centrality of copying, in the broad sense, front and center.

Office Management

When reading "Die mißbrauchten Liebesbriefe" as an account of how copying is a practice shared by administrative and literary production, one should keep in mind that we have copying to thank for the very existence of this text, which was nearly lost due to sloppy paper management. Each step of the repeatedly delayed printing history of the second volume of *Die Leute von Seldwyla* points toward the material conditions of making literature: from a strike among typesetters in 1873 to a paper shortage in the same year and an insufficient supply of type for specific letters in setting the sheets—a problem that the publisher unabashedly attributed to

---

53. "That night [. . .], it was formally and solemnly resolved [. . .] to inaugurate a new 'Storm and Stress Period,' and to do so systematically and in accordance with a plan so as to produce artificially that ferment from which alone could spring the classics of the new era" (In dieser Nacht [. . .] ward [. . .] die förmliche und feierliche Stiftung einer "neuen Sturm- und Drangperiode" beschlossen, und zwar mit planvoller Absicht und Ausführung, um diejenige Gährung künstlich zu erzeugen, aus welcher allein die Klassiker der neuen Zeit hervorgehen würden). Keller, "Love Letters," 17; Keller, "Liebesbriefe," in *HKKA*, 5:101.

54. "Er übernahm es, einstweilen Bodmer und Lavater zusammen darzustellen, um die reisenden neuen Klopstocks, Wieland und Goethe zu empfangen und aufzumuntern." Keller, "Love Letters," 22; Keller, "Liebesbriefe," in *HKKA*, 5:106.

Keller's repetitive use of particular words and phrases.[55] The history of the text is, in the end, an account of the exigencies of good office management, in particular of archival skills, in making a literary text. Keller had completed a manuscript of "Die mißbrauchten Liebesbriefe" in either 1861 or 1864, yet when it finally came time to collect the manuscripts and begin typesetting the second volume of *Die Leute von Seldwyla* a decade later, neither Keller nor the original publisher Vieweg could locate the manuscript of the novella. Keller, who considered copying to be of equal labor to crafting an original text,[56] rarely made a copy of his texts for himself when submitting manuscripts to his publishers and was thus dependent on Vieweg for the manuscript. Fortuitously for Keller (and for us as well), Keller had heard rumors that Vieweg had issued a preprint of the novella in the *Deutsche Reichs-Zeitung* (a serialized preprint that Keller later claimed not to have authorized, though the letter exchange with Vieweg suggests otherwise).[57] Writing to Vieweg in search of the periodical print edition, Keller claims that the handwritten manuscript has been effaced by the mechanically printed edition, which now represents the authoritative edition of the text.[58] It is a claim reminiscent of Keller's

---

55. On the delay in paper shipments, see Ferdinand Weibert to Keller, May 9, 1873, in *HKKA*, 21:537. On the limited available type, see Ferdinand Weibert to Keller, August 28, 1874, in *HKKA*, 21:557.

56. When Vieweg complains upon receiving the manuscript for "Pankraz, der Schmoller" that the handwriting is illegible (but nonetheless agrees to the proposed terms of the contract despite not being able to read the text), Keller responds that making a legible copy would cost as much time as writing the text in the first place: "But circumstances make it impossible for me to have it copied right now or to make a fair copy myself that would be more readable, since such a copy takes almost as much time as *making* the book itself" (Die Umstände erlauben mir indessen jetzt nicht, dasselbe kopiren zu lassen, noch selbst eine Reinschrift anzufertigen, welche lesbarer wäre, da eine solche beinahe so viel Zeit erfordert, als das *Machen* des Buches selbst). Keller to Eduard Vieweg, July 15, 1855, in *HKKA*, 21:454.

57. Keller had agreed to preprints of the manuscripts of the second volume. See Keller to Eduard Vieweg, February 13, 1860, in *HKKA*, 21:498.

58. "At the time Mr. Vieweg printed 'Die mißbrauchten Liebesbriefe' in the feuilleton of his former *Deutsche Reichs-Zeitung*; in the process, the manuscript was also destroyed. For that reason, he has sent me that feuilleton, which I ask you to consider as the manuscript" (Die mißbrauchten Liebesbriefe hat Hr Vieweg s. Z. im Feuilleton seiner ehemaligen deutschen Reichszeitung abdrucken lassen, wobei

answer to Berthold Auerbach's criticism of "Romeo und Julia auf dem Dorfe"—which I discussed in the introduction—that the novella, upon being published, had entered the world of print and thereby acquired a life of its own. Along the same lines, Keller wrote to Vieweg in 1871 emphasizing that he would prefer to be sent a copy of the preprint of "Die mißbrauchten Liebesbriefe" rather than the handwritten manuscript (should it have been found in the meantime), not least because the character of print, Keller claims, alters the perception of the text:

> If for some reason the manuscript cannot be sent here, I would appreciate it if you would lend me a copy of the relevant newspaper issues for the above purpose; indeed, the printed copy would serve me even better than the manuscript, as it is easier to see how something looks when it is printed. But I can also use the manuscript if there are no expendable copies left.
>
> Wenn nun etwa das Manuskript nicht hergesandt werden kann, so würden Sie mich verbinden, wenn Sie mir ein Exemplar der betreffenden Zeitungsnummern zu obigem Zwecke leihen wollten, ja es würde mir der Abdruck sogar besser dienen, als die Handschrift, da man besser sieht, wie sich ein Ding ausnimmt, wenn's gedruckt ist. Doch kann ich auch das Manuskript brauchen, wenn kein entbehrliches Exemplar mehr vorhanden ist.[59]

The extant copy of the periodical edition of "Die mißbrauchten Liebesbriefe" in Keller's literary estate suggests that upon receiving the nineteen issues of the *Deutsche Reichs-Zeitung* in which the novella had been serialized beginning in October 1865 on the recto and verso of the first page *unter dem Strich* (on the ground floor), Keller cut and collated his text from its pages so as to compile a new typescript (see figure 6). Weibert, who became Keller's publisher for *Die Leute von Seldwyla*, recommended that Keller glue paper around the edges of the preprint edition to enter his corrections on (and even offered that

---

das Manuskript ebenfalls zu Grunde ging. Er hat mir deshalb besagtes Feuilleton geschickt, welches ich als Manuskript zu betrachten bitte). Keller to Ferdinand Weibert, May 5, 1873, in *HKKA*, 21:537.

59. Keller to Firma Vieweg, July 25, 1871, in *HKKA*, 21:515.

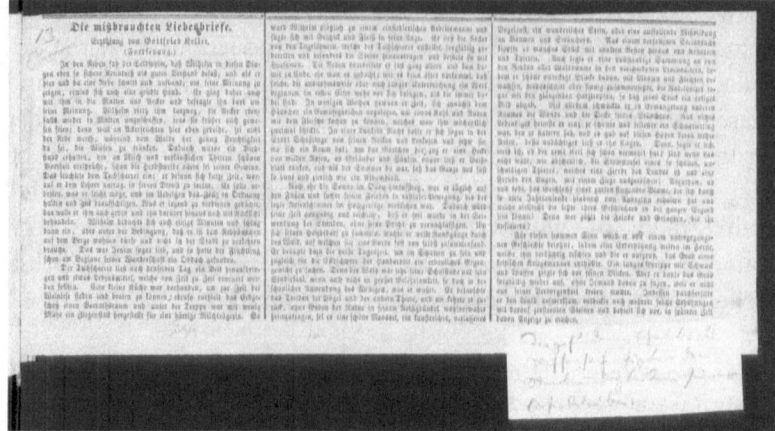

Figure 6. Keller's cut-and-pasted preprint of "Die mißbrauchten Liebesbriefe" from *Deutsche Reichs-Zeitung*, 1865. Zentralbibliothek Zürich, Ms. GK 10.

his office could complete the task).[60] Keller responded saying he could do the gluing himself, though he then largely reserved his minimalist changes to the modest space of the margins, thereby reaffirming the authority of the previously printed text over and against the author's authority to make changes. Figure 6 displays one of the two instances in which Keller employed paper scraps with a brief penciled emendation to the print. As when preparing the book edition of the *Züricher Novellen*, the mechanically printed paper copy, after being subjected to procedures of cut and paste, becomes the new authoritative typescript of "Die mißbrauchten Liebesbriefe."

Most apposite to "Die mißbrauchten Liebesbriefe," however, is the fact that if it were not for Vieweg publishing the novella in the *Deutsche Reichs-Zeitung*, the text would never have become part

---

60. When offering to perform the gluing, Weibert interestingly attributes the print to Vieweg, perhaps subtly alluding to the shared responsibility for making, if not authoring, the text: "In such a case, I would like to suggest to you to have a larger white paper margin glued to Vieweg's print so that your revisions can be done before the typesetting. Please let me know if you agree so that I can arrange for the gluing immediately." Ferdinand Weibert to Keller, May 9, 1873, in *HKKA*, 21:538.

of *Die Leute von Seldwyla* or Keller's oeuvre. Sloppy paper management had similarly caused "Der Schmied seines Glückes," yet another story about coauthorship, also intended for the second volume of *Die Leute von Seldwyla*, to have been lost among Vieweg's papers in the intervening years, yet in this instance Keller could complete a copy himself (on the basis of a further copy he had loaned Adolf Exner[61]) and so ensured its publication in 1873 by acting as the copyist of his own text. In a letter about copying "Der Schmied seines Glückes," Keller foregrounds the materials of writing rather than the content, as does the account of copying I have described in "Die mißbrauchten Liebesbriefe": "But a little ink, paper, and effort soon remedied the damage."[62] Thus the history of the second volume of *Die Leute von Seldwyla* highlights the importance of good office-management skills, specifically of archival

---

61. After borrowing himself the copy of the manuscript of "Der Schmied seines Glückes" he had lent Exner in order to prepare a manuscript for Vieweg, Keller returned the manuscript along with a letter that emphasized the precarious materiality of the novella's paper vehicle and how it had barely escaped being incinerated, trashed, or simply lost:

Using the leisure of Ascension Day, I want with this letter to return the "Schmied" to you, which you trustingly gave me once again, for which I thank you. However, after I copied it myself and combed out all kinds of dust and the bodies of old lice, there was little reason not to throw it in the wastepaper basket. There are now three versions of this excellent work, and if you or Vieweg do not accidentally light your pipes with your little codex, then the humanists of the fourth millennium will one day rack their brains, unaware that I was my own interpolator.

Die Muße des Himmelfahrtstages benutzend will ich Ihnen hiemit den "Schmied" wieder einpacken, den Sie mir vertrauenssselig noch einmal überlassen haben, wofür ich danke; es fehlte indessen wenig, daß ich ihn, nachdem ich ihn selbst abgeschrieben u ihm dabei allerlei Staub und alte Läusebälge ausgekämmt habe, nicht in den Papierkorb geworfen. Es existieren nun drei Fassungen dieses vortrefflichen Werkes und wenn Sie oder Vieweg mit ihrem Codexlein nicht unversehens einmal die Pfeife anzünden, so werden sich die Humanisten des 4t. Jahrtausends einst die Köpfe zerbläuen, nicht ahnend, daß ich mein eigener Interpolator war.

Keller to Adolf Exner, May 22, 1873, in *HKKA*, 21:540. The thought that future philologists might be muddled by the collapse of any distinction between author and copyist leaves Keller amused.

62. "Ein bischen Tinte, Papier u Mühe hat aber dem Schaden bald abgeholfen." Keller to Ferdinand Weibert, July 4, 1873, in *HKKA*, 21:541.

practices and copying, in making literature. These are the very practices that come to the fore when "Die mißbrauchten Liebesbriefe" shifts our attention from the content of literature to the practices and purpose of writing.

Gritli's Bureau

While the novella's critique has typically been read as directed first and foremost at the epistolary novel and the system of literature to which it belongs—a system "in which books were understood as intimate letters from [male] authors to [female] readers"[63]—the text should also be understood as exploring literary authorship in relation to administrative writing tasks. I propose to read the exchange of love letters as a matter of "bureaucratic effects" that draws attention to anxieties concerning literary authorship: "What kind of narratives and discourses and what social and cultural anxieties surface when one regards texts as bureaucratic effects, as subjects of paperwork?"[64] Administrative tasks are first introduced in the novella when copying is identified with the making of literature in the satirical first half, but they become even more poignant in the por-

---

63. Bernhard Siegert, *Relays: Literature as an Epoch of the Postal System*, trans. Kevin Repp (Stanford, CA: Stanford University Press, 1999), 16. Similarly, Manuela Günter argues that the novella portrays the media conditions of literary communication and its gendered structure, which consists of a male author and a female reader, who herself remains confined to oral media. See Manuela Günter, *Im Vorhof der Kunst: Mediengeschichten der Literatur im 19. Jahrhundert* (Bielefeld: Transcript, 2008), 125–35.

64. I here follow Ilinca Iurascu's reading of the copious paper objects in Goethe's *Wilhelm Meisters Wanderjahre* as ruminations on paperwork. "In their turn, such paper objects and the concrete materiality they evoke entail a whole range of operations—from formatting and filing to cutting, recycling, and discarding—that extend beyond the acts of writing and reading proper and that, implicitly, demand the reassessment and reframing of those very acts in a broader context. What happens, therefore, when one considers paper materiality as a domain that challenges the realm of the literary? What (other) objects and operations become visible in that process?" Ilinca Iurascu, "Paper Matters: *Vielschreiberei* and Bookkeeping in August von Kotzebue's 'Das Buch Papier,'" *Seminar: A Journal of Germanic Studies* 53, no. 4 (2017): 351.

trayal of the heroine, Gritli, as representing the exemplary conduct of a bureaucrat. Rather than submit to the letter-writing arrangement Viggi seeks to impose on her in pursuit of his literary aspirations, Gritli instead establishes an office in which she acts as the copyist, the office manager or secretary, and the archivist, three fundamental tasks of a modern bureau.[65] Her office exhibits each of the basic defining features of a bureaucratic office as famously identified by Max Weber: "The management of the modern office is based upon written documents (the 'files'), which are preserved in their original or draft form, and upon a staff of subaltern officials and scribes of all sorts. The body of officials working in an agency along with the respective apparatus of material implements and the files makes up a *bureau*."[66] The handling of the files, Weber further explains, is determined by established rules, for whose execution the bureaucrat is responsible: "The management of the office follows *general rules*, which are more or less stable, more or less exhaustive, and which can be learned."[67]

Allow me to recall the basic contours of the extraordinarily efficient, frictionless, and prolific office Gritli designs. When Viggi departs on his journey, he intends to use his absence to exchange letters with his wife that will become an epistolary novel. Gritli, both unable and unwilling to participate in this theatrical show of feigned emotion demanded by her husband, designs a system of exchange that frees her from having to compose love letters. To circumvent the norms of effusive expression, she forwards the amorous letters from her husband in her name to her neighbor, a schoolteacher, who responds with letters addressed to her that she then forwards to her husband again in her name. Viggi and the neighbor, Wilhelm, each believe themselves to be in an amorous exchange of letters with Gritli, while in fact she merely acts as the medium of exchange.

---

65. Honold conversely argues that Gritli acts as the author. By enacting language games in her switch of pronouns, she transforms the letters into literature. See Honold, *Die Tugenden und die Laster*, 264.

66. Max Weber, "Bureaucracy," in *Economy and Society: An Outline of Interpretive Sociology*, ed. Guenther Roth and Claus Wittich (Berkeley: University of California Press, 1978), 957.

67. Weber, "Bureaucracy," 958.

From her literal bureau (i.e., her desk), she alternatively copies (the German term is *abschreiben*) the letters she receives from her husband, readdressing them to Wilhelm, and from Wilhelm, readdressing them to her husband, in each case revising the gender of the pronouns so that the recipient believes the letter has been written by her and is addressed to him, seals the pages, and ensures that they arrive at their intended destination: "So she went and copied out her husband's letter, changing the words as though a woman were writing to a man. Then she folded the paper neatly and sealed it, but without putting any address on it."[68] Throughout the process, Gritli is careful not to add her own voice; instead, in copying the letters, she displaces them one step further removed from the orality that the genre of the letter is intended to invoke and substitute for. To this extent, the editing she performs is commensurate with the responsibilities of either a medieval copyist or a modern secretary, each of which is conventionally charged with producing the final copy of a text by correcting and improving on an earlier draft. Copying is, to repeat the point, not mere fidelity to the original but the drafting of a finalized text.

A key responsibility of Gritli's bureau is to manage and facilitate the circulation of papers on their way to becoming archived files. She thereby creates a collaborative network much like a modern office in which contact is always mediated through an administrative position and thereby retains a degree of anonymity.[69] At the height of circulation, she copies two letters a day, each consisting of four pages (and supplies the needed paper to Wilhelm, a crucial responsibility of modern-day secretarial labor), a quantity of paperwork that transforms her from a housewife into an extraordinarily diligent copyist

---

68. "Sie ging also hin und schrieb den Brief ihres Mannes ab und zwar dergestalt, daß sie einige Worte veränderte, oder hinzusetzte, als ob eine Frau an einem Mann schreiben würde. Dann faltete sie das Papier zierlich zusammen und versiegelte es, ohne aber eine Adresse darauf zu setzen." Keller, "Love Letters," 32; Keller, "Liebesbriefe," in *HKKA*, 5:117.

69. On the systematic contours of the modern office and the role of administrative positions in its management, see Erin McGuirl, "Office Practices," in *Information: A Historical Companion*, ed. Ann Blair et al. (Princeton, NJ: Princeton University Press, 2021), 647–58.

who bridges the fading tradition of the male chancery clerk and the newly emergent and soon dominant figure of the female stenograph and secretary: "Therefore letter after letter was written so that the quills flew. Gritli grew pale and ailing, because she had to write like a court clerk."[70] Because of her prolific writing, her body suffers the fate of the bureaucrat's body: It becomes increasingly like her writing materials as she pales to the color of paper, which is described throughout the novella in gray tones.[71] The gray contrasts with different healthy, homely greens, such as Gritli's green spinning ribbon when she is first introduced or the green peas she happily shells instead of reading. When copying instead of pursuing these household tasks, she is additionally stained with ink: "Gritli now had to copy out four long letters every day, so that her fine rosy fingers were almost always ink-stained."[72] However, in contrast to Dr. Mewes's stained bedsheets, which are a symptom of his and his texts' moral depravity, Gritli's blotched fingers are indicative of her upright character, namely, of her dedication to the responsibilities of her office.

As a copyist and archivist, Gritli is not actually in the business of producing letters but is instead concerned with making documents that can be archived and later come to fulfill their documentary function. The format of the document, as Gitelman emphasizes in *Paper Knowledge*, cannot be defined by its content. Instead, documents

---

70. "Daher wurde aufs neue geschrieben und geschrieben, daß die Federn flogen. Gritli wurde bleich und angegriffen, denn sie mußte schreiben wie ein Kanzlist." Keller, "Love Letters," 40; Keller, "Liebesbriefe," in *HKKA*, 5:126. Insofar as Gritli is managing a letter-writing practice, it bears keeping in mind that she is operative at the very site where, in the late nineteenth century, rhetorical flair gives way to a more bare-bones transmission of information. As John Guillory's history of the memo reminds us, nineteenth-century letter-writing practices displayed increasingly wordy rhetorical ornament as the demands of internal business communications increased, giving rise to the document form of the memo. See John Guillory, "The Memo and Modernity," *Critical Inquiry* 31, no. 1 (Autumn 2004): 108–32, in particular 115–16. In this vein, Keller's novella could be read as advocating against the misuse of "literary" language and in favor of the plainspoken language of administration.

71. Keller, "Love Letters," 16, 24, 32; Keller, "Liebesbriefe," in *HKKA*, 5:100, 107, 110.

72. "Gritli hatte nun alle Tage vier lange Briefe abzuschreiben, weshalb ihre feinen rosigen Finger fast immer mit Dinte befleckt waren." Keller, "Love Letters," 39; Keller, "Liebesbriefe," in *HKKA*, 5:124.

become such by virtue of the processes in which they are involved: through the formalized processes of reproduction, authorization, and storage, and more generally by virtue of the "horizon of accountability" we attribute to them.[73] In other words, documents are defined by documenting: They possess an evidentiary authority established by procedures regulating their making, circulation, and storage, the very rules for handling files that Weber identifies as constitutive of bureaucracy. For this reason, a discussion of the format of the document asks us to turn our attention away from questions of content, including genre, and toward the process and procedures of production. The letters Gritli drafts become documents because of the regular way she handles them, in particular, through the routine processes of copying and then also archiving; her excellent office-management skills are evident not only in her careful, prolific copying but also in her handling of the paper artifacts. It is a crucial and unappreciated aspect of "Die mißbrauchten Liebesbriefe" that Gritli does not destroy the letters she receives and copies but instead archives them in her desk (a process that Wilhelm and Viggi mimic, as each collects the letters he receives as well), creating a set of files that documents the letter exchanges she manages and her own practice of copying.[74] If it seems unlikely to conceive of Gritli as an archivist, given that the position was, long into the twentieth century, almost entirely reserved for men, it should help to recall that throughout the nineteenth century, with the help of their private desks, women came to play an increasingly important role as archivists of family history.[75] Similarly,

---

73. Gitelman, *Paper Knowledge*, 2.

74. Numerous scholars have mistakenly stated that Gritli destroys the letters she copies, transforming them into paper waste. For example, Siegert writes that "it is only by processing their original handwriting into waste that the two men receive delivery of their ephemeral existence from circulation (the one as author, the other as lover)." Siegert, *Relays*, 132. One should not forget that Viggi's original intention is to create a collection of these letters, in his words, "an imposing collection" (eine ansehnliche Sammlung), for which purpose Gritli would have to preserve the originals she receives from Viggi. Keller, "Love Letters," 38; Keller, "Liebesbriefe," in *HKKA*, 5:123.

75. For a discussion of such private archival activity, see Markus Friedrich, "Archivists," in Blair et al., *Information*, 312–17; and Elisabeth Shepard, "Hidden Voices in the Archives: Pioneering Women Archivists in Early 20th Century England," in *Engaging with Archives and Records: Histories and Theories*, ed. Fiorella Foscarini et al. (London: Facet, 2017), 83–104.

Gritli's archive takes shape within a domestic space yet becomes public at a crucial turning point in the story, a moment when the documentary function of the archived files is made explicit.

The growing girth of the archive is emphasized throughout the novella. It is a collective documentation of this peculiar communal writing project and bespeaks the efficiency of the office:

> So the exchange went feverishly ahead and an enormous pile of love letters accumulated in three places. Viggi carefully preserved the supposed letters from his wife; Gritli kept the originals from both parties; and Wilhelm stored Gritli's fair copies in a thick wallet over his heart, while he gave no further thought to his own productions.
>
> So ging denn der Verkehr wie besessen, und an drei Orten häufte sich ein Stoß gewaltiger Liebesbriefe an. Viggi sammelte die vermeintlichen Briefe seiner Frau sorgfältig auf, Gritli verwahrte die Originale von beiden Seiten und Wilhelm bewahrte Gritlis feine Abschriften in einer dicken Brieftasche auf seiner Brust, während er sich um seine eigenen Erzeugnisse nicht mehr kümmerte.[76]

In the fateful moment when Viggi returns home to Seldwyla through the forest and finds Wilhelm's pouch of letters, which Wilhelm forgets when he is suddenly awoken by Viggi's singing, the pouch is first described by its fat girth—"a thick packet" (eine dicke Brieftasche)— and what's more, identified as the archive it is. Viggi exclaims, "And what are these archives he was carrying around with him?"[77] Upon returning home carrying both Wilhelm's pouch of letters and the letters he has received from Gritli, Viggi breaches Gritli's desk where the originals are stored. Viggi thereby inadvertently brings together the complete record of this epistolary event: "Then he pulled the letters out of his traveling bag, looked at them again and threw them too on the table. There was a pretty big pile."[78] This is the first moment in which the texts serve as documents of evidentiary

---

76. Keller, "Love Letters," 39; Keller, "Liebesbriefe," in *HKKA*, 5:125.

77. "Was Kuckucks hat er hier für ein Archiv bei sich gehabt?" Keller, "Love Letters," 42; Keller, "Liebesbriefe," *HKKA*, 5:127.

78. "Dann zog er auch die Briefe aus seiner Reisetasche hervor, beschaute sie auch nochmals und warf sie ebenfalls auf den Tisch; es gab einen ganz artigen Haufen." Keller, "Love Letters," 43; Keller, "Liebesbriefe," in *HKKA*, 5:129.

value; later in the novella, the files will act as a record both vis-à-vis Kätter when Viggi "[tells] her the story of the letters and [lays] the whole pile before her" and the court (and community) that will arbitrate over Viggi and Gritli's divorce proceedings.[79]

In her discussion of documents, Gitelman emphasizes that beyond their evidentiary "know-show" function, they are also identifiable as instruments of power, playing a crucial part in matters of control.[80] In Keller's novella, the epistemic value of the letters also depends on who controls the archive, control that is achieved through the exercise of violence. To gain access to Gritli's archive, Viggi first imprisons his wife in the cellar, where she is gathering apples, and then breaks into her desk, the very desk that acts as the centerpiece of Gritli's management process and as the primary archival technology.[81] However, the bureau is also, as becomes apparent at the moment it is violated, a metonymic representation of Gritli's body, just as it is metonymical for the bureaucrat and the bureaucratic office more generally.[82] Gritli's desk is incapable of withstanding her husband's abuse of power and, like Gritli at the later divorce proceedings, makes no attempt to conceal its secrets. Her office is not only efficient but also transparent: "Then he went up to the living room where her little writing desk stood, a fragile piece of decorative furniture that had once been given to her on her birthday and was not made to harbor dangerous secrets. The drawers opened by themselves when handled correctly and he had no need to use the keys."[83] The accessibility and completeness of its

---

79. "Als er ihr die Geschichte mit den Briefen erzählte und den ganzen Haufen vorwies." Keller, "Love Letters," 51; Keller, "Liebesbriefe," in *HKKA*, 5:137.
80. Gitelman, *Paper Knowledge*, 5.
81. On bureaus, or desks, as an archival technology, see Friedrich Kittler, "Die Herrschaft der Schreibtische," in *Work and Culture: Büro; Inszenierung von Arbeit*, ed. Herbert Lachmayer and Eleonora Louis (Klagenfurt: Ritter, 1998), 39–42.
82. On this metonymy as well as the etymology of the word *bureaucracy*, see Kafka, *The Demon of Writing*, 77.
83. "Darauf ging er in die Wohnstube hinauf, wo ihr Schreibtischchen stand, ein zerbrechliches kleines Ziermöbel, ihr einst zum Namenstage geschenkt und nicht geeignet gefährliche Geheimnisse zu beherbergen. Daher brauchte er auch den Schlüsselbund nicht und die Behältnisse öffneten sich von selbst, wie man sie nur recht berührte." Keller, "Love Letters," 43; Keller, "Liebesbriefe," in *HKKA*, 5:128–29.

records speak of Gritli's good conduct as a truly exemplary copyist, office manager, and archivist. In permitting her divorce from Viggi, the town of Seldwyla acknowledges the same.

That "Die mißbrauchten Liebesbriefe" has yet to be read as a reflection on administrative writing procedures stems overwhelmingly from a perpetuated misreading in which Gritli, although compared in passing to both a medieval copyist and a modern-day secretary, is regarded and evaluated as a private letter writer.[84] This misreading quite obviously takes its cue from the title of the novella and from the fact that Viggi and Wilhelm do indeed write love letters, but it also stems from the perpetuation of dominant nineteenth-century gender norms that deem the composition of letters to be one of the few genres of writing appropriate to women. For example, Julia Augart argues that Viggi's crime consists in abusing the conventions of the epistolary genre insofar as he intends to misuse (*mißbrauchen*) private, intimate letters as literature intended for public consumption. The genre of the letter, as Augart explains, consists in an autobiographic text composed in an individual style that substitutes for oral communication; it represents a "psychological unburdening" prompted by the previously received letter of a confidant.[85] Viggi's insistence that Gritli write to him in the effusive style he models, that she excise any of her true concerns and thoughts (at least onto a separate page), such as those concerning domestic affairs, and that she write under a pseudonym of his choice deprives her of the opportunity for authentic communication and the expression of her individual person.[86]

---

84. Günter, for example, notes that Gritli bridges the two positions of medieval copyist and a modern-day secretary when arguing that she functions as a medium of male writing. See Günter, *Im Vorhof der Kunst*, 129.

85. Julia Augart, "'Die mißbrauchten Liebesbriefe': Zur Austauschbarkeit von Identität, Geschlecht und Gefühl im Medium Brief," in *Gottfried Keller: Die Leute von Seldwyla; Kritische Studien—Critical Essays*, ed. Hans-Joachim Hahn and Uwe Seja (Bern: Peter Lang, 2007), 196.

86. The schoolteacher provides a contrasting example to Gritli's writing practice. Although his letters do not reflect, in the first instance, anterior feelings, the process of letter writing induces the appropriate feelings in him. He models, as Günter and Honold argue, the media conditions for the making of affect. See Günter, *Im Vorhof der Kunst*, 129; and Honold, *Die Tugenden und die Laster*, 271.

While it is true that Gritli is deprived of these opportunities, such a reading overlooks how the letter-producing arrangement she designs purposefully decouples her writing practice from her interiority and feeling. Hence, her writing practice should not be evaluated along the standards of authentic, effusive epistolary communication, nor should it be regarded as modeling a literary ideal of a male author and a female reader—gender codes of a literary system she very much undermines. If anything, both the original arrangement Viggi concocts and Gritli's writing practice illustrate not so much a literary ideal in the age of Goethe but instead the reality that male authorship historically relied on forms of anonymous labor by amanuenses, labor sometimes performed, as in this arrangement, by the author's wife.[87] Bringing these anonymous forms of labor into view in a shift away from the supposedly creative writing of the male author is yet another way of undermining the antithesis between administrative and literary forms of writing.

In refusing to comply with the gender norms the literary system assigns to her, either as a feminine reader of texts authored by a male writer or in composing letters herself, Gritli decisively positions herself outside the normative gender dichotomy of the nineteenth-century literary system (i.e., male authors, female consumers). Her character instead presents a bureaucratic ethos removed from binary sexual differentiation, a further instance of Keller's myriad androgynous characters. In her office, Gritli—like Heinrich and the Landvogt in "Der Landvogt von Greifensee," which is discussed in chapter 6—channels her capacity for reproduction away from biological procreation and into the reproduction of texts, thereby becoming sublimely generative. If "Die mißbrauchten Liebesbriefe" is, as the relevant scholarship asserts, inspired by Keller's dislike of the successful Berlin couple Adolf Stahr and Fanny Lewald—who were famous for coauthoring sen-

---

87. On wives as amanuenses for scholars, see Ann M. Blair, *Too Much to Know: Managing Scholarly Information Before the Modern Age* (New Haven, CT: Yale University Press, 2010), 104–5. On collaborative forms of authorship in which women served as scribes or provided secretarial labor, see also John B. Lyon and Laura Deiulio, eds., *Gender, Collaboration, and Authorship in German Culture: Literary Joint Ventures, 1750–1850* (New York: Bloomsbury Academic, 2019).

timental epistolary novels and whom Keller lampooned as "the four-legged, hermaphroditic ink animal" (das vierbeinige zweigeschlechtige Tintentier)[88]—then Gritli is their positive counterimage, a laudable exception to sexual differentiation that chooses reproductive paperwork over biological reproduction or literary authorship. Needless to say, when Gritli marries the schoolteacher at the end of the novella, she abandons her earlier androgynous perfection available only when her first and future husbands were absent, and returns in marriage to the confines of a heterosexual arrangement.

Letters and Literature

To summarize my reading of "Die mißbrauchten Liebesbriefe" thus far: The novella begins with a satirical critique of writing literature starring Viggi and his literary circle. The satire identifies their literature as reliant on practices of copying and mixing as made by possible by a media culture saturated by low-cost objects. Second, in the story of Viggi's epistolary novel, Gritli models a bureaucratic ethos in her handling of documents. The novella's opening satire and the portrayal of Gritli's office establish a contrast between perverted, appetite-driven literary endeavors and routinized administrative writing procedures, while at the same time emphasizing specific media practices they share. To this end, the effusive, tearful, and effectively grotesque outpourings of feeling performed by Wilhelm (real feeling), Viggi (feigned feeling), and Kätter Ambach in the epistolary genre and their intended publication as a work of literature are contrasted throughout the novella with the manner in which Gritli, the novella's heroine, performs administrative writing tasks. To drive this contrast home, the novella introduces the character of the *Stadtschreiber* (municipal clerk) of Seldwyla, who possesses so little sympathy for Viggi's literary project that when asked what he thinks of "Kurt vom Walde" (Viggi's pseudonym), he replies,

---

88. Keller to Lina Duncker, March 6, 1856, in *Gesammelte Briefe*, 2:154.

"What kind of ninny is that?"[89] Furthermore, at the beginning of the story, Gritli and Viggi are praised for their excellent bookkeeping, another insistence of administrative writing practices. Their bookkeeping skills are situated in a budding trend among the inhabitants of Seldwyla to make better use of paper tools to manage their monetary affairs, as recounted in the introduction to the second volume of *Die Leute von Seldwyla*: "Instead of the old thick wallets with crumpled IOUs and promissory notes, they now carry elegant little notebooks in which they briefly note orders of shares, bonds, cotton, or silk."[90] The people of Seldwyla have given up the use of paper scraps, more like waste than records, and adopted the use of a notebook for bookkeeping, a shift in cultural technologies that evidences their movement away from the carefree era of the first volume of the Seldwyla novellas to one of increasing earnestness and economic interest.

As the plot of the novella escalates, Viggi and Gritli, who are originally lauded for their skillfulness in business and household recordkeeping and are seemingly exemplary for Seldwyla's turn toward an earnest life, are increasingly compelled to choose between administrative writing and Viggi's literary endeavors. Similarly, because Wilhelm is a schoolteacher, another bureaucratic functionary, he must presumably also choose between school papers and the love letters, that is, between his task as a bureaucrat and effusive writing. As Gritli later explains to the court, she was made to neglect managing the household to participate in her husband's epistolary novel, in which she had to "express her womanly feelings in an affected and unnatural language and in letters intended for the public and, instead of pursuing her domestic life, to spend her time on a useless activity that was alien and repugnant to her."[91] The

---

89. "Was ist das für ein Kalb?" Keller, "Love Letters," 23; Keller, "Liebesbriefe," in *HKKA*, 5:107.

90. "Statt der ehemaligen dicken Brieftasche mit zerknitterten Schuldscheinen und Bagatellwechseln führen sie nun elegante kleine Notizbücher, in welchen die Aufträge in Aktien, Obligationen, Baumwolle oder Seide kurz notiert werden." Keller, *Die Leute von Seldwyla*, in *HKKA*, 5:8–9.

91. "Zuletzt aber habe er [...] von ihr verlangt, [...] ihre Frauengefühle in einer geschraubten und unnatürlichen Sprache und in langen Briefen für die Oef-

difference between these two practices of writing—literature and bookkeeping—is epitomized in the relationship between the main or "proper" part of Gritli's letters and an addendum on a "separate sheet" in her exchange with Viggi. Viggi insists that "business and domestic matters"[92]—the earliest example concerns tricking the neighbors into settling a debt—be relegated from the love letters to an extra page, a method that regrettably increases postage costs but keeps, Viggi hopes, these two types of affairs separate. The fact that the household affairs are relegated to an addendum, rather than constituting the center of their exchange, signifies Viggi's mistaken priorities and anticipates the mismanagement of his household that will culminate in the loss of his economically valuable wife. The difference between these two sheets, letters and addenda, embodies what I have been arguing constitutes the operative contrast within the novella between literary and bureaucratic writing practices. At stake in the story of the love letters is nothing less than the question of the proper purposes and functions of writing or, conversely, how those purposes can be perverted or abused (*mißbraucht*). If writing was invented for the purpose of administrative recordkeeping, then does literature represent its perfection or its perversion?[93] "Die mißbrauchten Liebesbriefe" gives an unambiguous answer to this question.

From the perspective of the nineteenth century, questions about the purpose of writing crystallize in debates concerning the value and objectives of female literacy. A basic primary education promised that future wives and mothers would acquire the rudimentary literacy needed to maintain the records of household expenses and,

---

fentlichkeit aufzuschreiben, und statt ihrem häuslichen Leben nachzugehen, die schöne Zeit mit einer ihr fremden und widerwärtigen, nutzlosen Thätigkeit zu verbringen." Keller, "Love Letters," 55; Keller, "Liebesbriefe," in *HKKA*, 5:141.

92. "NB. Wir wollen die geschäftlichen und häuslichen Angelegenheiten auf solche Extrazettel setzen." Keller, "Love Letters," 30; Keller, "Liebesbriefe," in *HKKA*, 5:115.

93. On the invention of writing for bureaucratic purposes, see Hans J. Nissen, Peter Damerow, and Robert K. Englund, *Frühe Schrift und Techniken der Wirtschaftsverwaltung im alten Vorderen Orient: Informationsspeicherung und -verarbeitung vor 5000 Jahren* (Bad Salzdetfurth: Franzbecker, 1990).

if needed, also those of the family business.[94] On the other hand, the threat posed by these writings skills—as repeatedly voiced by skeptics of primary education for girls—was nothing other than that they would be employed for the purpose of writing love letters: The "misuse" of writing manifests itself in the genre of the love letter.[95] Advocates of female literacy were accordingly compelled to direct their counterarguments at precisely the same topos and consequently retorted that a woman who relies on a male scribe for writing her love letters (just as Gritli relies on the schoolteacher, recalling the historical practices of illiterate women) risks having her trust and honor abused; better she can read and write and so maintain the privacy of that communication.[96] As Alfred Messerli summarizes in his thorough account of rising female literacy in Switzerland between the eighteenth and nineteenth centuries, "In Graubünden, Heinrich Ludwig Lehmann (1758–1805) wrote in 1790 that only noble-minded daughters would learn to read or write 'because they could *misuse* [*mißbrauchen*] it for love letters!!!' An 1808 class-visitation report on writing in the school in Anwil (in the canton of Baselland) makes the same argument. The girls had not been allowed to learn to write for a long time because their parents claimed that they would then only write love letters, 'but now they are beginning.'"[97] Messerli additionally cites a translation of a late sixteenth-century text by the Franciscan Juan de la Cerda, demonstrating the long history of this anxiety concerning female misuse of writing in the composition of love letters: "Even if some women employ the art of writing usefully and well, it is *misused* [*mißbraucht*] by most to such an extent that it would

---

94. "Only a wife who knows how to write can help her husband in his profession." Alfred Messerli, *Lesen und Schreiben, 1700 bis 1900: Untersuchung zur Durchsetzung der Literalität in der Schweiz* (Tübingen: Max Niemeyer, 2002), 54.

95. See Messerli, *Lesen und Schreiben*, 57.

96. "In the way that schoolteachers were often asked to write letters, especially love letters, as many a lusty maidservant could confirm" (wie man öfter schriftliche Arbeiten und namentlich auch Liebesbriefe durch Schullehrer anfertigen lasse; sie berufe sich hierin auf manch wackeres Dienstmädchen). Keller, "Love Letters," 56; Keller, "Liebesbriefe," in *HKKA*, 5:141.

97. Messerli, *Lesen und Schreiben*, 57; emphasis mine.

be better if it were generally suppressed."[98] An absence of female literacy runs the risk of a woman's trust being abused; endowing her with those skills risks their abuse.

"Die mißbrauchten Liebesbriefe" cites this discourse not only insofar as the question of misuse (*Mißbrauch*) is immediately raised in the title. From the very beginning of the novella, even before the letter writing begins, we learn that Viggi is subjecting his wife to an abusive literacy program that undermines the ideals elaborated in the discussions of female literacy. Although Gritli is already skilled in household bookkeeping, Viggi begins to instruct her in a self-designed great-books program—"He quickly drew up an educational plan, got together a number of books, approached his wife firmly and instructed her without fail to read and learn what he was setting before her"[99]—with the objective of perverting her already sufficient and correctly applied writing skills to the making of love letters and literature. What's more, he insists that she will, in repurposing her writing skills, perfect her gender role. He thus admonishes her, "Be a man about it and make a big effort, or rather, be a woman for once! [. . .] Call upon your lofty femininity" (Ermanne Dich, oder vielmehr erweibe Dich einmal! [. . .] Kehre Deine höhere Weiblichkeit hervor),[100] thereby forgetting that precisely in compelling her to turn away from her domestic chores and to redirect her reproductive capacities to literature rather than procreation, he will prevent her from fulfilling a normative feminine ideal.

---

98. Juan de la Cerda, *Weiblicher Lustgarten*, trans. Aegidius Albertinus (München: Nicolaus Henricus, 1605), 11 recto; emphasis mine. See Messerli, *Lesen und Schreiben*, 57. Messerli also elucidates the danger in having a young woman rely on others for her love letters: "A story with the emphatic title 'Dear People of the Country, Let Your Daughters Learn to Write' appeared in the *Bürger- und Bauernfreund* in 1819. It implicitly takes up the motif of the misuse of writing (writing love letters) but turns it into its opposite. A girl who can *not* write is at the mercy of her scribe or 'helper,' who can abuse the trust placed in him and rob her of her honor" (59).

99. "Er machte schnell einen Erziehungsplan, legte eine Anzahl Bücher zurecht, trat fest vor die Frau hin und wies sie an, unfehlbar zu lesen und zu lernen, was er ihr vorlage." Keller, "Love Letters," 26; Keller, "Liebesbriefe," in *HKKA*, 5:111.

100. Keller, "Love Letters," 28, translation modified; Keller, "Liebesbriefe," in *HKKA*, 5:112.

Gritli responds to Viggi's pedagogical program by exemplifying practices of nonreading as techniques for keeping one's spouse at bay as described at length in the first chapter of Price's *How to Do Things with Books in Victorian Britain*.[101] When read to, she falls asleep; when given books to read, she throws them away or stomps on them: "She felt ashamed of herself in this stupid and reprehensible situation and often hurled the books in a corner or stamped on them."[102] In the happy end of the novella, in which Gritli and Wilhelm have withdrawn to an agrarian idyll, she is promised a life in which her capacity for writing is reserved to household bookkeeping and her reproductive powers are employed not in copying texts but, to their supposedly natural fulfillment, in procreation. While the writing arrangement Gritli designs, like the "hermaphroditic ink animal" Keller mocked, represents an attempt to escape sexual bifurcation, the conclusion of the novella marks a reintroduction of normative sexual differentiation. As Wilhelm's wife and the mother of his children, her writing skills are returned to their natural and proper role in household administration. Viggi's attempt to harness these writing skills for the purpose of an epistolary novel, much like the example of Dr. Mewes's copying in his soiled bed, represented a misuse of writing and a deviation from a normative sexual order as well; the misuse (*Mißbrauch*) of writing or one's wife is tantamount to a form of sexual perversion.

The novella's criticism of *Die Gartenlaube*, which resurfaces throughout the novella's plot, encapsulates the trajectory of its contrast between the natural administrative uses of writing and their perversion for the purpose of literature, a contrast coded in the difference between the healthy greens of household chores and the deadening grays of paper. Tracing the critique of *Die Gartenlaube* offers an additional way to summarize the plot's driving conflict and resolution, that is, a perspective from which to perceive

---

101. See Price, *How to Do Things with Books*, 19–41. "To listen is to submit to another's power; like Trollope's character going to sleep, the wife resorts to passive resistance." Price, *How to Do Things with Books*, 215.

102. "Sie schämte sich vor sich selber in dieser thörichten und schimpflichen Lage und schleuderte die Bücher oft in eine Ecke oder trat sie unter die Füße." Keller, "Love Letters," 27; Keller, "Liebesbriefe," in *HKKA*, 5:111.

the integrity of the novella's allegedly prolix narrative arc. The aspiring authors whose practices of copying and mixing are satirically described in the novella's first half are identified as subscribers to *Die Gartenlaube*—presumably one source of the inexpensive materials needed for their own production process.[103] To comprehend the trajectory of the novella from this perspective, it is crucial to recall the renowned frontispiece of the most successful German-language periodical: It portrays a family being read to from the periodical's pages by the paterfamilias in the eponymous "arbor" (*Gartenlaube*), itself a product of cultivating labors. In this setting, the activity of reading constitutes a passing break from the wholesome practice of gardening, as the watering can hanging to rest on the right of the image reminds us (see figure 7).[104] When Wilhelm, the schoolteacher, first makes an appearance in the novella, he is busy gardening, a task he then abandons to dedicate his time to reading and writing love letters. Gritli engages him in her office by requesting his assistance through the garden's hedge, the medium of their letter exchange, thereby distracting him from attending to his blooms.[105] In the moment she first approaches, a surprised Wilhelm drops the watering can, ostensibly freeing his hands to commence writing. While the frontispiece of *Die Gartenlaube* stages reading as a substitute for gardening, Keller's novella stages an existential choice between writing and gardening, among whose alternatives Wilhelm must choose.

---

103. "Instead he bought books, subscribed to all the lending libraries and book clubs in Berne, took the *Gartenlaube* and signed up for all the special publications, which offered continuous, well-balanced study" (vielmehr schaffte er sich Bücher an, abonnierte in allen Leihbibliotheken und Lesezirkeln der Hauptstadt, hielt sich die "Gartenlaube" und unterschrieb auf alles, was in Lieferungen erschien, da hier ein fortlaufendes, schön verteiltes Studium geboten wurde). Keller, "Love Letters," 14; Keller, "Liebesbriefe," in *HKKA*, 5:98.

104. In a later edition of the frontispiece, the watering can and the interruption of watering (cultivation) are equally prominent, as one sees a young girl pause in her task and lean in to overhear the pages being read aloud. See, for example, *Die Gartenlaube*, 1875, no. 7, 106.

105. Between their gardens stands a hawthorn hedge (*Weissdornhecke*), which Honold identifies as an established motif of amorous communication. Honold, *Die Tugenden und die Laster*, 280.

Figure 7. Masthead of the first issue of
Die Gartenlaube, 1853, no. 1, 1.

Only when a brokenhearted Wilhelm departs Seldwyla and adopts his ascetic and cultivation-loving lifestyle in an idyllic cottage set in the nearby hills does he abandon writing love letters and resume gardening. Having resolved to become an impoverished and homeless day laborer, Wilhelm happens upon a "winedresser's cottage" (Winzerhäuschen): "It was a picturesque old cottage with a weathercock and round window panes."¹⁰⁶ While he was first deceived at the site of his garden hedge by a vision of literature whose origins can be traced backed to *Die Gartenlaube*, Wilhelm finally finds happiness living in a home that is itself a *Gartenlaube*. That home and its garden become the site for reconstituting the form of life that disintegrated when he previously selected writing over gardening.¹⁰⁷ There he begins to cultivate the land that has long been lying fallow, transforming it, through his labors, into a modest paradise. Indeed, he comes preciously close to recreating the periodical *Gartenlaube* in horticultural form, having realized, in his form of life, the very idyll associated with the diminutive, architectonic structure:

> One dark night he actually went down to the town and fetched shoots from his carnations and stocks, which he planted wherever there was room. Around the little garden he planted a hedge of wild roses; he set honeysuckle to climb up the banister and pillars; and when the summer came the whole place looked almost as colorful and decorative as a page from an album.
>
> In einer dunkeln Nacht holte er sich sogar in der Stadt Schößlinge von seinen Nelken und Levkojen und setzte sie, wo sich ein Raum bot; um das Gärtchen her zog er eine Hecke von wilden Rosen, an Geländer und Säulen empor ließ er Geisblatt ranken, und als der Sommer da war, sah das Ganze aus fast so bunt und zierlich wie ein Albumblatt.¹⁰⁸

The happy end of the novella can thus be understood as the act of picking up, again, the watering can, of selecting gardening and

---

106. "Es war ein malerisches altes Häuslein mit einer Wetterfahne und runden Fensterscheiben." Keller, "Love Letters," 63; Keller, "Liebesbriefe," in *HKKA*, 5:148.

107. As Saskia Haag's insightful analysis of the *Laube* in nineteenth-century literature points out, the structure represents an alternative space in which conflicts that inhabit the house or home can be renegotiated. "This is because the arbor is produced to a certain extent in the vicinity of houses that represent a disintegration of existing spatial and thus social and aesthetic orders. It is a product of the frequently criticized 'breakdown' of the house in modernity. In nineteenth-century novels and stories, the green hut appears on the side of the now questionable house as a second house, proving to be both a symptom and a figure of compensation for it." Saskia Haag, *Auf wandelbarem Grund: Haus und Literatur im 19. Jahrhundert* (Freiburg im Breisgau: Rombach, 2012), 175.

108. Keller, "Love Letters," 66–67; Keller, "Liebesbriefe," in *HKKA*, 5:152.

cultivation, and of tending to the tasks of procreative life rather than giving one's attention to the gray pages of *Die Gartenlaube*. "Die mißbrauchten Liebesbriefe" is thus organized around the structural difference of *Gartenlaube* versus *Garten* and the practices of writing associated with each: a life squandered and a technology perverted for the purpose of writing literature or, conversely, a genuinely creative life of cultivation and procreation, where writing is reserved for bookkeeping.

4

From the Office

Doodling While Documenting

Perhaps with a nod to the pervasive cultural effemination of the bureaucrat—who must sacrifice his name and creative, productive energies in the service of the anonymous and reproductive labors of the office—Keller describes his function as the state chancellor (*Staatsschreiber*) for the canton of Zurich as "a kind of girl Friday" (eine Art Mädchen für alles).[1] The responsibilities were nearly as expansive as described in the constitution of 1831, which first created the office and stated that it would encompass "all matters relating to diplomatic and federal affairs and the military. He is also the secretary of the state council."[2] Specific duties included managing the state

---

1. Keller to Georg Brandes, July 14, 1878, in Gottfried Keller, *Gesammelte Briefe in vier Bänden*, ed. Carl Helbling, 4 vols. (Bern: Benteli, 1951–1954), 4:164.
2. "In der Regel fallen in den Geschäftskreis des ersten Staatsschreibers alle Gegenstände, welche in die diplomatischen und Eidgenössischen Verhältnisse und in das Kriegswesen einschlagen. Er ist auch Secretär des Staatsrathes." Gesetz betreffend eine Geschäftsordnung für den Regierungsrath, in *Officielle Sammlung*

chancery (*Staatskanzlei*) and its secretaries, producing the first draft of the protocols (*Protokolle*)—in the sense of minutes or transcripts—of the meetings of the government council (*Regierungsrat*), signing and thereby authorizing documents for whose issuance the chancery was responsible, including municipal citizenship certificates (*Heimatscheine*) and passports, completing the official correspondence of the chancery and the government council with other cantonal governments and the Federal Council (*Bundesrat*), recording and revising newly drafted laws, ordinances, and railroad concessions, and occasionally writing, when a member of the government council was not available for the task, the annual *Bettagsmandate* (mandates for the Day of Prayer) calling upon the canton's population to repent their failings and to give thanks.[3] As I have mentioned, the *Bettagsmandate* are the only texts produced by Keller in the official position he occupied from September 14, 1861, to July 15, 1876, that have entered his collected works and have garnered any attention from Keller scholars. The incredible number of other documents produced during that lengthy period have been omitted from his oeuvre and from scholarly consideration because they are considered products of rote rules and procedures rather than expressions of an authorial persona.

From the wide swath of documents to which one could give attention, this chapter is devoted to the protocols of the meetings of the cantonal government council, to Keller's activity, in his words, as the "protocol keeper and head of the chancery of the government of

---

der seit Annahme der Verfassung vom Jahre 1831 erlassenen Gesetze, Beschlüsse und Verordnungen des Eidgenössischen Standes Zürich, vol. 1 (Zürich: Friedrich Schultheß, 1831), 350, § 62.

3. On Keller's responsibilities as state chancellor, see Emil Ermatinger, *Gottfried Kellers Leben: Mit Benutzung von Jakob Baechtolds Biographie dargestellt*, 8th rev. ed. (Zürich: Artemis, 1950), 370–95; and Hans Wysling, *Gottfried Keller, 1819–1890* (Zürich: Artemis, 1990), 226–45. Ermatinger writes, "He [Keller] was in charge of the state chancery. At the same time, he was the secretary to the directorate of political affairs. He kept the minutes of the meetings of the government council. He had to maintain official communication with the other cantonal governments and the Federal Council, had to compile the annual reports of all the departments, register or finalize drafts of laws, railroad concession agreements, and ordinances of all kinds, and sign the vast quantity of copies, passports, municipal citizenship certificates, and so on with his signature." Ermatinger, *Gottfried Kellers Leben*, 370.

this great land."[4] At least since the early Roman Republic, protocols have served as written records of oral exchanges, a purpose that has remained largely unchanged even as the reduced costs of paper and the possibilities of mechanical reproduction have dramatically increased their use and the number of archived copies. Typically formatted as a list, a protocol provides an authoritative record of events or decisions made by a governing body. Protocols derive their epistemic authority from formalized procedures of production and from belonging to a more expansive archive in which individual records are often bound together in book form and remain available for consultation, particularly when a past resolution comes into dispute. The formalized procedures of the protocol include the presence of the protocolist, the keeper of minutes, at the transcribed oral exchange (the protocol is, in Cornelia Vismann's precise words, "a medium of presence"), the approval of the protocol by the body or institution whose decision-making it is intended to record, and the effacement of the scribe's subjectivity such that it leaves no mark on the document's language.[5] To ensure the authority of the document,

---

4. "Allow me to make an odd little correction to my address. I am not the municipal clerk of Zurich but the state chancellor of the Canton and Republic of Zurich, that is, the protocol keeper and head of the chancery of the government of this great land" (Sie erlauben mir noch eine kleine komische Correktur meiner Adresse. Ich bin nämlich nicht Stadtschreiber von Zürich, sondern der Staatsschreiber des Kantons u Republik Zürich d. h. der Protokollführer u Kanzleivorstand der Regierung dieses großen Landes). Keller to Firma Vieweg, December 13, 1872, in *HKKA*, 21:519.

5. Cornelia Vismann, *Files: Law and Media Technology*, trans. Geoffrey Winthrop-Young (Stanford, CA: Stanford University Press, 2008), 10. "The person who keeps minutes is obligated to be neutral and objective and must remove themself as a subject; their role is that of a transformer who converts orality into writing. The minute keeper does not appear as an author but as a writing authority; they do not compose a work but lend duration to the contingency of the communication that took place." Michael Niehaus and Hans-Walter Schmidt-Hannisa, "Textsorte Protokoll: Ein Aufriß," in *Das Protokoll: Kulturelle Funktionen einer Textsorte*, ed. Michael Niehaus and Hans-Walter Schmidt-Hannisa (Frankfurt am Main: Peter Lang, 2005), 16. In his analysis of nineteenth-century secretaries charged with providing transcriptions of court proceedings, Peter Becker underscores the same point, writing that the genre conventions aimed at nothing less than the "virtual desubjectification" of the secretaries. See Peter Becker, "'Recht Schreiben'—Disziplin, Sprachbeherrschung und Vernunft: Zur Kunst des Protokollierens im 18. und 19. Jahrhundert," in Niehaus and Schmidt-Hannisa, *Das Protokoll*, 74.

the protocolist must serve as a "writing machine," as the role is described in an 1846 monograph examining necessary reforms to criminal proceedings.[6] In the cantonal government of Zurich, the state chancellor was accordingly charged with creating a written record of the oral proceedings and decisions made by the government council so that they could be consulted in the future by those with authorized access. These were "blabber protocols [...], which are meant for future reference when the jackasses no longer know what they decided to do," as Keller explains in a letter to Theodor Storm.[7]

Why give attention to Keller's activity as a protocolist? To begin with, since recording the protocol was a near-daily task of the state chancellor, these documents constitute, in contrast, for example, to the *Bettagsmandate*, a significant responsibility of the officeholder and a large proportion of the produced documents. Second, because they rely on different measures of institutional authorization and on the objectivity guaranteed by the subjectivity-less activity of the writing machine, protocols present a direct challenge to conventional notions of the author function, as Lisa Gitelman observes for documents in general.[8] Niehaus makes the point more bluntly in relation to the protocol: "The protocol seems to contrast sharply with literature because the protocol is not a work, the protocolist is not an author, and protocol style is not poetic."[9] For this reason, the writing of protocols, much more so than Keller's signature authorizing documents of the chancery or, on the other end of the spec-

---

6. Heinrich Albert Zachariä, *Die Gebrechen und die Reform des deutschen Strafverfahrens* (Göttingen: Dieterische Buchhandlung, 1846), 86. On Zachariä, see Niehaus and Schmidt-Hannisa, "Textsorte Protokoll," 12.

7. "Gerade als ich in mein Amt so voll eingeschossen war, [...] gabs eine trockene aber radikale Staatsumwälzung, [...] in Folge dessen eine Reihe neuer Gesetze, so daß ich [...] zwei Jahre lang fast Tag u. Nacht Schwatzprotokolle zu schreiben hatte, die nachher zur Interpretation dienen sollen, wenn die Esel nicht mehr wissen, was sie gewollt haben." Gottfried Keller to Theodor Storm, February 26, 1879, in *Theodor Storm—Gottfried Keller: Briefwechsel; Kritische Ausgabe*, ed. Karl Ernst Laage (Berlin: Erich Schmidt, 1992), 41–42.

8. See Lisa Gitelman, *Paper Knowledge: Toward a Media History of Documents* (Durham, NC: Duke University Press, 2014), 19.

9. Michael Niehaus, "Protokollstile: Literarische Verwendungsweisen einer Textsorte," *Deutsche Vierteljahrsschrift für Literaturwissenschaft und Geistesgeschichte* 79, no. 4 (2005): 696.

trum, the stylistically memorable *Bettagsmandate*, undermines a Romantic understanding of literary authorship as an imprint or index of personality. Just as "Die mißbrauchten Liebesbriefe" turns on the difference between the outpouring of subjectivity in the epistolary genre as contrasted with the effacement of subjectivity performed in Gritli's heroic copying, the idea of Keller's canonical authorship turns on the antithesis between literature as emergent from an emotive, expressive subject and the authorless protocol produced through a subjectivity-less writing machine. To summarize the point: Appreciating Keller as the author of countless protocols most immediately puts such a conception of literary authorship under pressure and thus provides an interesting case study for broadening our understanding of it.[10]

Instead of being authored, protocols derive their veracity, reliability, and authority from the process and procedures by which they are made. That process—and this constitutes the third reason for devoting this chapter to these documents—places Keller's secretarial labor in a situation of collective and largely anonymous authorship that heavily relies, moreover, on practices of copying. Copying enables the documents to be formatted in such a way that they possess the requisite authority and become compatible with a world consisting of files. Protocols emerge, in other words, from practices that resemble those featured in Gritli's bureau in "Die mißbrauchten Liebesbriefe." Keller's participation as state chancellor in a collective and anonymized writing system, in which the act of copying was central, usurps the vision of the author's individual and creative pen. Hence, I will first describe the media and process of collective

---

10. In his account of literary authors who acted as protocolists for the literary circles they participated in—another context where recordkeeping became increasingly pervasive throughout the nineteenth century—Rolf Parr too defines the protocol as "a text without an author function." Rolf Parr, "Das Protokoll als literarische Kunstform: Zur Konvergenz von künstlerischer und juridischer Selbstvergewisserung in literarisch-kulturellen Vereinen des 19. Jahrhunderts," in Niehaus and Schmidt-Hannisa, *Das Protokoll*, 175. Yet he describes Wilhelm Raabe in detail as a counterexample, an author whose elaborate minutes of such meetings, in a seemingly exceptional handling of administrative texts, are included in his collected works. That inclusion reflects not only the wit of Raabe's recordkeeping, which is to say, some argue the texts do indeed reflect Raabe's style and self, but also the more relaxed conventions of private, rather than state, recordkeeping.

authorship involved in producing the protocols of the proceedings of the government council; then I will look more closely at Keller's note-taking practices at the beginning of this process and consider how they might complicate the conventions of the genre of the protocol and the anonymity of the labor that goes into making them. In doing so, this chapter, like the preceding one, aims to undermine the dualistic relationship between administrative and literary practices of writing and to bring them into closer proximity to one another. While chapter 3 advocated for this convergence by reading "Die mißbrauchten Liebesbriefe" as a celebration of bureaucratic writing practices in contrast to the inadequacies of a literature that prides itself on subjectivity and originality, this chapter examines in what way the traces Keller left on the ideally anonymously authored protocols relate to the tensions between these two writing practices.

The collective nature of the writing system in which Keller participated is well illustrated by both the interior architecture of the *Regierungsratssaal*, the room in which the government council convened, and the house of the state chancery. Both spaces functioned as media to facilitate producing the protocols.[11] The accountability of the process was underwritten, for one, by the furnishing of the *Regierungsratssaal* (see figure 8). The centerpiece consisted of six individual desks arranged in a half circle and a chairperson's desk (*Präsidiumspult*) for the president of the government council. It also contained an oven for heating, a large closet specifically manufactured for storing completed files of past protocols (not depicted in the photograph), and a double desk for the first and, when present, the second state chancellor. Since the authority of a protocol depends on the presence of the writing machine recording the minutes of the proceedings at the meeting itself, the seven desks of the council were arranged to surround the desk of the state chancellor. The arrangement situated the one or two state chancellors (the position of the second state chancellor was only intermittently occupied) amid the verbal exchange being conducted literally across their heads; hence, their

---

11. For an expansive understanding of the media of bureaucracy, from the file and the desk to a wide array of urban and interior designs, see Friedrich Balke, Bernhard Siegert, and Joseph Vogl, "Editorial," in *Medien der Bürokratie*, ed. Friedrich Balke, Bernhard Siegert, and Joseph Vogl (Paderborn: Wilhelm Fink, 2016), 7.

Figure 8. Photograph of the meeting room of the *Regierungsrat* in the Zurich city hall (Sitzgzimer d Riergs rats Rathaus Zürich) by Jean Gut & Cie, ca. 1878. Zentralbibliothek Zürich, GKN 459.

bodies were placed in the very middle of the exchange, which also presumably rendered them subject to the observation and oversight of the council. Indeed, it is hard to imagine how Keller could have conducted from this position the private epistolary correspondence with which he is known to have occupied himself during the sessions of the government council—another moment of overlap between private and public life, between simultaneous private letter writing and minute keeping.[12]

---

12. For example, on June 8, 1870, Keller begins a private letter to Ludmilla Assing,
   In a boring government meeting, where the debate is dragging on for hours, I have finally found the opportunity to reflect on my sins, and my conscience

Beyond the generous salary, the position of the state chancellor was lucrative by virtue of the living quarters provided in the same house as the offices of the state chancery (the so-called Steinhaus at Kirchgasse 33 housed the state chancery from 1803 to 1875). The chancery building was designed to establish a collective writing body in which the division of labor and the processes of circulation were defined and regulated by the architecture of its rooms.[13] The offices of the chancery were located on the first floor, the second floor housed the office of the state chancellor, and the third and fourth his private quarters—the rooms Keller inhabited with his sister and mother, at least until the latter's death in the same house. While there are unfortunately no existing photographs of the office

---

is struck above all by the letter I have owed you for nearly two years, which burdens me with guilt toward you. As you can tell from this letter and from the paper, I am still in office, despite the recent change in the form of government of our republican system.

In einer langweiligen Regierungssitzung, in welcher stundenlang debattiert wird, finde ich endlich die Gelegenheit, meiner Sünden zu denken, und da fällt mir vor allem meine bald zweijährige Briefschuld aufs Gewissen, die mich Ihnen gegenüber drückt. Wie Sie an diesem Eingang sowie am Papier wahrnehmen können, befinde ich mich ungeachtet der vorübergegangenen Staatsveränderung unseres Republikwesens immer noch in meinem Amte.

Keller to Ludmilla Assing, June 8, 1870, in *Gesammelte Briefe*, 2:124. Like the composition of the preface to *Die Leute von Seldwyla*, the letter is yet another instance of overlap between private and bureaucratic writing materials: Keller writes on official letterhead paper at the desk of the state chancellor during a meeting of the government council.

13. The purpose and rules governing these records were defined in the 1831 Gesetz betreffend eine Geschäftsordnung für den Regierungsrat, according to which "the protocols of the government council should contain, with references to the files, complete information and precise descriptions of the matters brought before it, including all the conclusions reached about the form of the deliberations and about the matter itself together with any reasons for the decision given by the government council." Gesetz betreffend eine Geschäftsordnung für den Regierungsrath, 353, § 70. The description references the primary epistemic values governing the document: completeness and exactness. It fulfills its purpose not so much in being either drafted or read as in being an archived document available for reference and cross-referencing. This law and the different steps involved in taking and producing the protocols for the government council are described in detail by the Staatsarchiv des Kantons Zürich, which holds all the documents related to the cantonal government. See "MM 0—MM 3 Protokoll, 1803.03.10–2015.12.22 (Fonds)," Staatsarchiv des Kantons Zürich, https://suche.staatsarchiv.djiktzh.ch/detail.aspx?ID=686917.

of the state chancellor, a retrospective drawing of Keller by the local artist Burkhard Mangold portrays him at his desk (see figure 9). The sketch, which is adorned with the word "Resignation," is unabashedly eager to reify the myth of Keller's poetic sacrifice as a bureaucrat and so decorates his desk with a flood of paper materials—a

Figure 9. Burkhard Mangold, *Der Herr Staatsschreiber*, in Walther von Arx, "Gottfried Keller," in *Schweizer eigener Kraft! Nationale Charakterbilder*, ed. Eug. Richard et al. (Neuenburg: F. Zahn, 1906), facing 590.

row of large tomes that eclipses his head from view and sheets spilling from all sides—intended to manifest his dedication and productivity and the effacement of the subject effected by office work. Only the caged Pegasus and cut flower adorning his room provide melancholic reminders of Keller's true poetic calling.

To attain their final form in which they could be archived, the protocols had to circulate among the different floors and anonymous hands of the chancery building and the *Regierungsratssaal*. To begin, Keller would record notes during the meetings of the government council in his private notebooks, which I will discuss below. In a second step, these notes and those, if present, of the second state chancellor would serve in the offices at Kirchgasse 33 as the basis for fashioning the draft protocol (*Brouillonprotokoll*); this first draft would then return for review and approval to the members of the government council. Keller's notebooks bear the markings of that process: Individual entries are checked off in the margins, presumably as they were incorporated into the next draft. With the necessary revisions by the government council and cross-references to past protocols, the draft protocol would, in a third step, become the basis of a fair copy (*Reinschrift*) completed by one or two secretaries in the chancery office on the first floor. This first fair copy would be stored in a book (bound quarterly in numbered leather volumes with lettering in gold) in the office of the chancery. (The transition from loose sheet to book format performed when binding the individual files into volumes for the purpose of archiving the documents mirrors the transition from the individual issue of a periodical to a bound annual volume, a process essential to the archival function of the nineteenth-century family and literary periodicals that I will address in chapters 5 and 6.) In addition, the first fair copy would be copied, typically by a more subordinate secretary, to produce a second fair copy, which would be archived in the closet in the *Regierungsratssaal* to make it accessible to the government council for consultation and cross-referencing in later proceedings.

The fact that only two final and equally authoritative copies were foreseen while Keller occupied the position of state chancellor substantiates the impression that the chancery under Keller's management was exceedingly conservative in its paper usage and document production. The explosive use of paper and the production of records attributed to Keller's successor in the office of state chancellor, Johann Heinrich Stüssi, in comparison, has less to do, as one might first suspect, with Stüssi's modernizing introduction of the typewriter (and telephone) in the chancery. It is rather an effect of his successful motion to the government council to issue twelve instead of two copies of each protocol so that they could be stored, for one, in multiples at the chancery. The demand for this high number of copies created such an incredible backlog in unfinished protocols that it necessitated relieving the chancery secretaries of copying and employing the mechanical means of private printing offices.[14] The shift in copying technologies from chancery secretaries to mechanized printing furthermore necessitated an evolved conceptualization of what constitutes an original: While in Keller's chancery, the two handwritten fair copies were each considered originals and equally authoritative, mechanized printing rendered one document the original, while the eleven others were copies—a change that reflects the significance of the ethos of the human copyist in making an original. A copy created by a copyist could become an original; that is, it fulfilled the same evidentiary function as the text it was based on, while a machine-made copy was simply that. Similarly, in "Die mißbrauchten Liebesbriefe," Gritli's handwritten copies of the love letters constitute copy and original at once, yet Keller seemingly views a mechanical reproduction as equally authoritative to a handwritten copy insofar as he considers the printed copy of his novella in the *Deutsche Reichs-Zeitung* as possessing greater authority than the handwritten manuscript. Keller's valuation of the printed copies (in contrast to the practices of the chancery) reflects a conception of authorship that incorporates mechanical reproduction.

---

14. Stüssi's attempt to reform the protocols to include not only the final decisions but also the proceedings of the government council also led to an explosive growth in their length, was reprimanded, and was put to an end by the same body. Biographers of Keller's time as state chancellor gleefully conclude their contrasts of Keller's conservative management of the chancery and Stüssi's modernizing measures with the observation that Stüssi died prematurely after being hit by a tram from Zurich's first tramline. See, for example, Walter Baumann, *Gottfried Keller: Leben, Werk, Zeit* (Zürich: Artemis, 1986), 138.

The final copies of the protocols, drafted in the fine script and administrative language of the chancery secretaries, bear few traces of the multiple media that went into their making (see, for example, the finalized protocol for August 18, 1865, in figure 10) and seem, when one performs the comparison, nearly unrelated to their first drafting in Keller's private notebooks. Keller and his notebooks become subsumed in a collective and anonymized production process. The "Amtstil," for one, in which they are written effectively effaces any trace of the voices in which the primary oral event took place or the "voice" of those who recorded its contents. Appropriately, the cover page of the fair copy attributes the document to a different collective than those responsible for its material production, namely, to the government council, on whose authorization it relies. The collective scribes are effaced from the document and replaced by the authorizing persona of the government council. The name of the state chancellor on the cover page stands in for the many people and regulative procedures that performed the transference from ephemeral speech to an enduring document that will now determine the facts of the past.

While the protocols and accompanying files then and now belong to the Staatsarchiv des Kantons Zürich, the nine notebooks in which Keller recorded his drafts belong to his *Nachlass* archived at the Zentralbibliothek Zürich, an allocation that designates them as private notebooks despite the fact that they constituted the first draft of governmental documents in the making. Keller's notebooks fulfilled the very purposes of the medium of a notebook: They were a paper technology for *"taking notice of something,"* then for "the *noting* and *storing of notes,*" and, furthermore, for providing antecedent evidence of having been present at that "something."[15] The notebooks, in other words, were a portable medium for training attention on proceedings, generating records of them, and storing this information. Their contents demonstrate that Keller's manner for recording the meetings was formalized in a way consistent with the format of the notebook and remained consistent throughout his

---

15. On the affordances of notebooks, see Anke te Heesen, "The Notebook: A Paper-Technology," in *Making Things Public: Atmospheres of Democracy,* ed. Bruno Latour and Peter Weibel (Cambridge: MIT Press, 2005), 584.

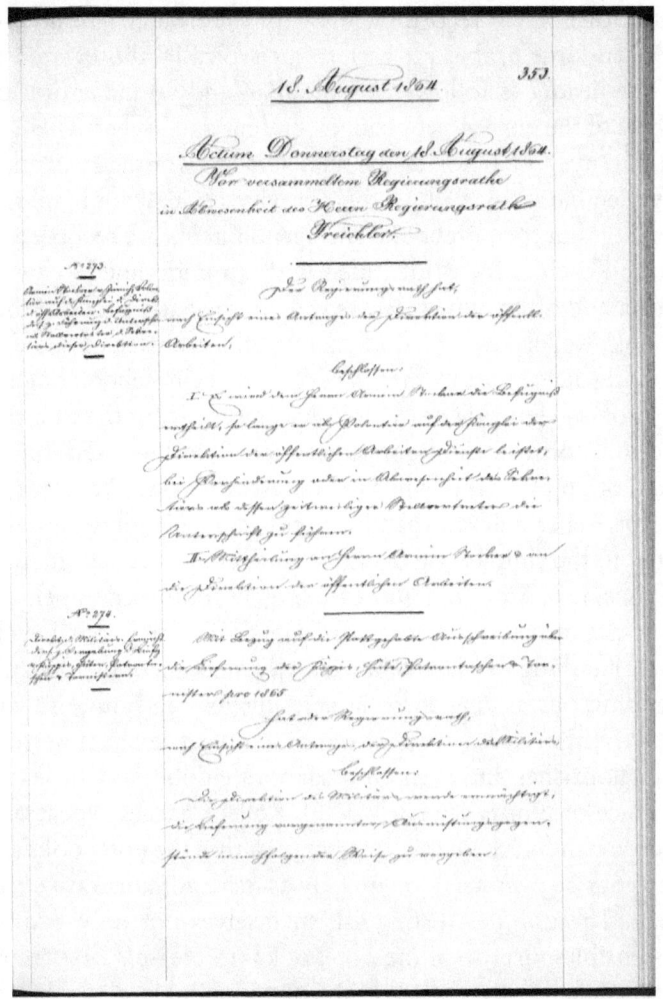

Figure 10. A finalized, official *Protokoll* of a meeting of the *Regierungsrat* of the canton of Zurich. Actum Donnerstag den 18. August 1864. Staatsarchiv des Kantons Zürich, Regierungsratsbeschlüsse, MM 2.165 RRB 1864/1447.

time in office. Each record begins with the header "Actum" occasionally in large arabesque script, but typically abbreviated to an "A." The header is followed by the date and an indication of the members of the government council present and absent. These drafts stand out, in comparison to the final versions, for their perfunctory, nearly illegible script and for their brevity, typically only filling two facing pages of the notebook. The agenda items are recorded in list form, and each entry is identified with an underlined keyword at the onset and often numerated as well. In the early pages of the first notebook, Keller attempted to manage the transfer of the agenda items to the next draft by means of folding the notebook pages: The column on the left side of the fold was reserved for the first record, the column on the right for subsequent handling and for being checked off, presumably when the notes were relayed to a secretary. However, Keller quickly abandoned this more elaborate system and resorted to the simpler use of check marks in pen to designate completed business. Thus, the notes are largely composed in pencil, and brief marks in pen or, in some cases, a blue or red pencil evidence the later handling of the notebooks in the making of the documents.

Standing out among these largely illegible and quite obviously roughly written notes are occasional, more or less elaborate calligraphic flourishes and even more elaborate doodles, whose quality and choice of motifs regularly recall Keller's earliest vocation as a landscape painter; these markings suggest that the notebooks should perhaps not be dismissed too quickly as mere administrative record-keeping. The doodles distinguish themselves not only relative to the ostensible purpose of the notebooks (to create a first record of the oral exchanges of the government council) but also when compared to Keller's manuscript collection. Although the handwriting on Keller's manuscripts is very often illegible, the manuscripts themselves are also doodle-free and composed with wide, empty margins (presumably for corrections that very rarely needed to be made). This is to say that if Keller was a frequent doodler while writing, evidence of this fact has been excised from the still extant manuscripts. To be sure, the majority of the notes for the protocols are likewise free of doodling—the habit seems to have been particularly dominant during the contentious transfer of power from the liberals to the Democrats in the late 1860s. Yet the doodles warrant our attention for the way in which they might complicate our conception of authorship, the relationship between person and text.

In light of the many pejorative views on doodling, it seems likely that Keller's doodles might be read as indicative of his state of boredom or distraction (or, equally plausibly, as a technique for maintaining attention).[16] For those eager to reify the persona of the author, these doodles might alternatively suggest that the notebooks are not so much the documentary product of a subjectivity-less writing machine but instead yet another manifestation of Keller's self and creative drives. As Polly Dickson writes in her elucidating article on arabesque "squiggles" in the work of a generation of authors preceding Keller—Laurence Sterne, E. T. A. Hoffmann, and Honoré de Balzac—the squiggle, like a signature, is considered to be a compelling record of a singular, idiosyncratic gesture. It functions as a strong reminder of authorial presence, if not also of authorial self-fashioning.[17] The evidentiary function of a doodle, squiggle, or signature, as a record of authorial presence, derives from its status vis-à-vis an economy of copying. Each doodle serves as a record of authorial presence precisely because it cannot be easily copied, because it resists forms of mechanical reproduction and instead represents a singular instance. For this reason, the doodles quite obviously had to be effaced in the making of the protocols. If one begins with this view of the evidentiary value of the squiggle or doodle, the doodles in Keller's notebooks would

---

16. For a summary of these pejorative views of doodling, see Friedrich Weltzien, "Kritzeln," in *Historisches Wörterbuch des Mediengebrauchs*, ed. Heiko Christians, Matthias Bickenbach, and Nikolaus Wegmann, vol. 1 (Köln: Böhlau, 2015), 382–92. For a brief history of the doodle, also see E. H. Gombrich, "Pleasures of Boredom: Four Centuries of Doodles," in *The Uses of Images* (London: Phaidon, 1999), 212–25, who emphasizes the doodle as bridging mastery and relaxation.

17. Dickson writes, "This shifting between modes of artistry, between drawing and writing—a shifting aptly communicated by the figure of the squiggle itself—has implications for the construction of authorial presence within the text. The redrawing of the squiggle—a form that by its very nature cannot be reproduced exactly so much as imitated, reappropriated, and adapted—traces the shape of a particular mimetic self-fashioning, after the model of Sterne." Polly Dickson, "Tracing Squiggles: Laurence Sterne, E. T. A. Hoffmann, and Honoré de Balzac," *Comparative Literature* 71, no. 2 (2020): 54.

very much undermine the image of a mere bureaucratic functionary. They have the potential to recuperate Keller's artistic hand, style, and self from a routinized, anonymous, and collective writing process that otherwise effaces his self—the potential to give expression to those artistic drives that must otherwise be repressed in the performance of official duties. One might, for example, attribute the doodles to the same "Ausdruckswillen" that Barbara Naumann identifies as motivating Heinrich's scribbling in *Der grüne Heinrich*; they would then be an expression of an artistic drive or playfulness that must otherwise be repressed in the formalized process producing the protocol.[18]

The doodles are also noteworthy because they recall a well-known thematic of Keller's work from both the *Berliner Schreibunterlage* and the monstrous doodle Heinrich produces and subsequently destroys in Munich. Yet unlike Heinrich's masterpiece, the doodles in Keller's minutes notebooks consist not only in abstract permutations of lines but also in figural drawings. Like the abstract arabesques—which develop by means of repeating, varying, and mirroring certain geometric figures (see, for example, the notebook entry from August 18, 1864, in figure 11, where a caricatured face is repeated and progressively diminished in size and complexity until the face has been reduced to a mere geometric figure)—the figural drawings display a high degree of repetition: The motifs are retained over many years of note-taking. Among the figural doodles, caricatures dominate. Keller operates with a cast of characters including a jester, a statesman, and a wanderer who could well resemble Heinrich from his novel (also reproduced in different variations in the *Studienbücher*). These caricatures are predominantly drawn in profile, a format that allows them to adorn and frame both the headings of the protocols and the list of agenda items without eclipsing them. To the enduring motifs also belong landscape sketches, which strongly echo, in style and composition (if only done in ink and pencil), Keller's

---

18. See Barbara Naumann, "Die 'kolossale Kritzelei', der 'borghesische Fechter' und andere Versuche: *Der grüne Heinrich*," in *"Der grüne Heinrich": Gottfried Kellers Lebensbuch—neu gelesen*, ed. Wolfram Groddeck (Zürich: Chronos, 2009), 173.

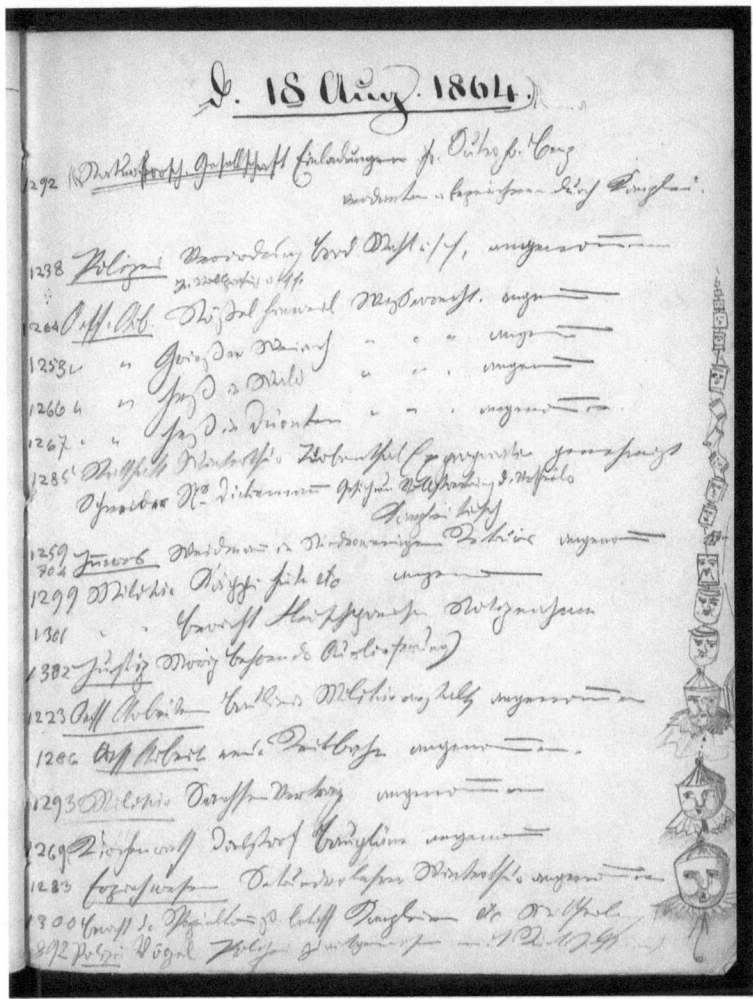

Figure 11. Gottfried Keller, Notizen über die
Verhandlungen des Regierungsrates, August 18, 1864, recto.
Zentralbibliothek Zürich, Ms. GK 54.

earlier landscapes. Many of these landscape sketches evidence considerable time and attention and are, as if to underscore that point, framed with ink lines to set them apart from the page and its scribbling in pencil. The notes from June 25, 1863 (see figure 12), for example, conclude with three landscapes, two in a

Figure 12. Gottfried Keller, Notizen über die Verhandlungen des Regierungsrates, June 25, 1863, verso. Zentralbibliothek Zürich, Ms. GK 53.

rectangular format (one of which is highly suggestive of the patriotic Schillerstein, which was dedicated in 1860) and one in an oval format. All three are framed and "pinned" to the page to suggest the illusion of being exhibited. By virtue of these frames, the small landscapes quite pointedly abandon their status as ornamental parerga to the documentary record and become the centerpiece, the ergon, of the notebook's entry.

How are these doodles to be read in relation to the process of making the protocols? Scholarly interpretations of Heinrich's doodling (*Kritzelei*) in Keller's first novel, *Der grüne Heinrich*, provide us with at least two initial interpretative possibilities.[19] While Heinrich's friend Erikson lauds Heinrich's "infinite weave of pen strokes" (unendliches Gewebe von Federstrichen) as an example of the "most delightful abstraction" (reizendsten Abstraktion),[20] from which multiple interpreters have concluded that the drawing anticipates the advent of abstract art and thus confirms Keller's antecedent modernism, identifying the dubious masterpiece as a doodle would rather suggest that the repetitive strokes are less suggestive of art freed from the constrictions of representation and more a manifestation of a drive toward formlessness plaguing artist and novel alike.[21] Such an alter-

---

19. Like the *Historisches Wörterbuch des Mediengebrauchs*, I employ the English *doodle*—the verb form of which is defined in the OED as "to draw or scrawl aimlessly"; the noun form as "an aimless scrawl made by a person while his mind is more or less otherwise applied"—as the best approximation of the German *kritzeln*, despite their strong etymological dissimilarities. See *Oxford English Dictionary*, online edition (July 2023), "doodle, n.," "doodle, v.1," https://doi.org/10.1093/OED/5627679731, https://doi.org/10.1093/OED/1103336844. The German *kritzeln*, related both to *kratzen* and *kitzeln*, has the important connotation of poor or illegible writing or drawing—according to the *Deutsches Wörterbuch*: "to write badly, laboriously, without skill"; "for writing badly, also drawing"—which is lost in the English *doodle*. See *Deutsches Wörterbuch von Jacob Grimm und Wilhelm Grimm*, online edition at Wörterbuchnetz des Trier Center for Digital Humanities (January 2023), "kritzeln," https://www.woerterbuchnetz.de/DWB. However, both terms refer to the aspect I want to highlight, namely, a form of marking that suggests a weak or absent intentionality.

20. Keller, *Der grüne Heinrich* (1st ed., 1854–1855), in *HKKA*, 11:220, 222.

21. For those who would view Heinrich's artwork as anticipating a modernist aesthetic, see Ralf Simon, "Gespenster des Realismus: Moderne-Konstellationen in den Spätwerken von Raabe, Stifter und C. F. Meyer," in *Konzepte der Moderne*, ed. Gerhart von Graevenitz (Stuttgart: J. B. Metzler, 1999), 202–33; Günter

native reading that makes no attempt to align Keller's novel with modernist aesthetics takes its cue from early nineteenth-century theories of doodling as a psychological symptom best summarized by Barbara Wittmann. *Kritzeln*, as she explains, is taken to be indicative of the "progressive regression" of the artist.[22] It is the mark-making practice of an imperiled, unstable subject whose drawing is not guided by intention or will; it is the index of a primitive, childlike, subjectivity-less person. The doodle is, to sharpen the point, a form of writing (and in this respect akin to a protocol) with no subject or author.[23] Heinrich's "pen strokes" adroitly refract these views on doodling. Keller employs precisely the same terminology to describe Heinrich's masterpiece as found in the theories of doodling Wittmann recounts. The oft-emphasized characterization of this doodle and Heinrich's early attempts at sketching as a "chaos" (Wirrsal) of "curves" (Krümmungen)[24] echoes the semantics of the earliest scientific accounts of doodles by children and childlike doodling, in which the "chaos of slightly curved lines" (Wirrwarr schwach gekrümmter Linien)[25] is interpreted as a sign of the child's as-yet-absent subjectivity and self-discipline. Read as symptomatic of the progres-

---

Hess, "Die Bilder des *Grünen Heinrich*: Gottfried Kellers poetische Malerei," in *Beschreibungskunst—Kunstbeschreibung: Ekphrasis von der Antike bis zur Gegenwart*, ed. Gottfried Boehm and Helmut Pfotenhauer (München: Wilhelm Fink, 1995), 373–95; and Andrea Meyertholen, "It's Not Easy Being Green: The Failure of Abstract Art in Gottfried Keller's *Der grüne Heinrich*," *German Studies Review* 39, no. 2 (2016): 241–58. The sheer number of contributions on this topic speaks to the popularity of the desire to regard Heinrich, and thereby Keller, as a protomodernist.

22. Barbara Wittmann, "Am Anfang: Theorien des Kritzelns im 19. Jahrhundert," in *Von selbst: Autopoietische Verfahren in der Ästhetik des 19. Jahrhunderts*, ed. Friedrich Weltzien (Berlin: Dietrich Reimer, 2006), 142.

23. Wittmann explains the destabilization of the subject effected through doodling: "But what does it mean to describe doodling as an autopoietic technique? First, it entails understanding it as an event whose subject is 'nobody,' which does not mean that it is not produced by someone. When the human body speaks 'by itself,' this 'by itself' always expresses a foreign voice—something that comes to it from the outside, that imposes itself on it, and that could not have been anticipated." Wittmann, "Am Anfang," 142.

24. Keller, *Der grüne Heinrich* (2nd ed., 1889), in *HKKA*, 2:263.

25. James Sully, *Studies of Childhood* (New York: Longmans, Green, and Co., 1895), 333; James Sully, *Untersuchungen über die Kindheit: Psychologische Abhandlungen für Lehrer und gebildete Eltern*, trans. Joseph Stimpfl (Leipzig: Ernst Wunderlich, 1897), 312. See Wittmann, "Am Anfang," 149.

sive regression of the artist, Heinrich's artwork emerges as an anticipatory metonymic representation of his own gradual deterioration, ending, at least in the first edition, in his death.[26] Thus, the first interpretative possibility for the protocol notebooks provided by *Der grüne Heinrich* reads the doodles in a psychologistic manner, namely, as the messy eruption of an unstable subject sliding into formlessness. Sabine Schneider's interpretation of Heinrich's doodling as demonstrating how the "internal dynamics of the imagination are beyond the control of reason" exemplifies this perspective.[27]

A second interpretative possibility begins with the observation that Heinrich's scribbling, like the act of *kritzeln* more generally, demonstrates an affinity to both writing and drawing. Its free-flowing signs inhabit a threshold between these two graphic systems; the compulsive, repetitive motions of scribbling upend the difference between word and image, an example of what Andrew Piper describes as "the possibility of textual and visual simultaneity," which, he explains, is "a simultaneity that nevertheless always bordered on illegibility at the moment of such synthesis."[28] The thesis that flourishes and doodling upend the difference between writing and drawing could also account for how the headings in the protocol notebooks become so densely embellished that word and image are difficult to disentangle. In the heading from October 5, 1863 (see figure 13), the enclosed spaces of the characters *A, O, c, o, 6,* and *3* are filled with expressive faces, transforming the abstract letters into figural, facial representations. The impression is reinforced by the profile on the left margin that reproduces the face of the *A*. The heading turned into a landscape from February 11, 1865 (see figure 14), provides a similar blending of script and image, though this time with a very different set of motifs:

---

26. Naumann explains the *Schreibunterlage* similarly as the pathological eruption of an unstable subject, in this case, of one succumbed to desire. "The compulsively repeated drawings on the folder reveal Keller's more or less uncensored erotic desire, recognizable in how 'Bitte Betty' gradually transforms into a *Betti* or *Bettchen* ('little bed'), which is also drawn. A direct transferal of desire into writing and image has taken place here." Naumann, "Die 'kolossale Kritzelei,'" 174.

27. Sabine Schneider, "'Poesie der Unreife': Autobiographisches Schreiben im Roman," in Groddeck, *"Der grüne Heinrich,"* 73.

28. Andrew Piper, *Dreaming in Books: The Making of the Bibliographic Imagination in the Romantic Age* (Chicago: University of Chicago Press, 2009), 189.

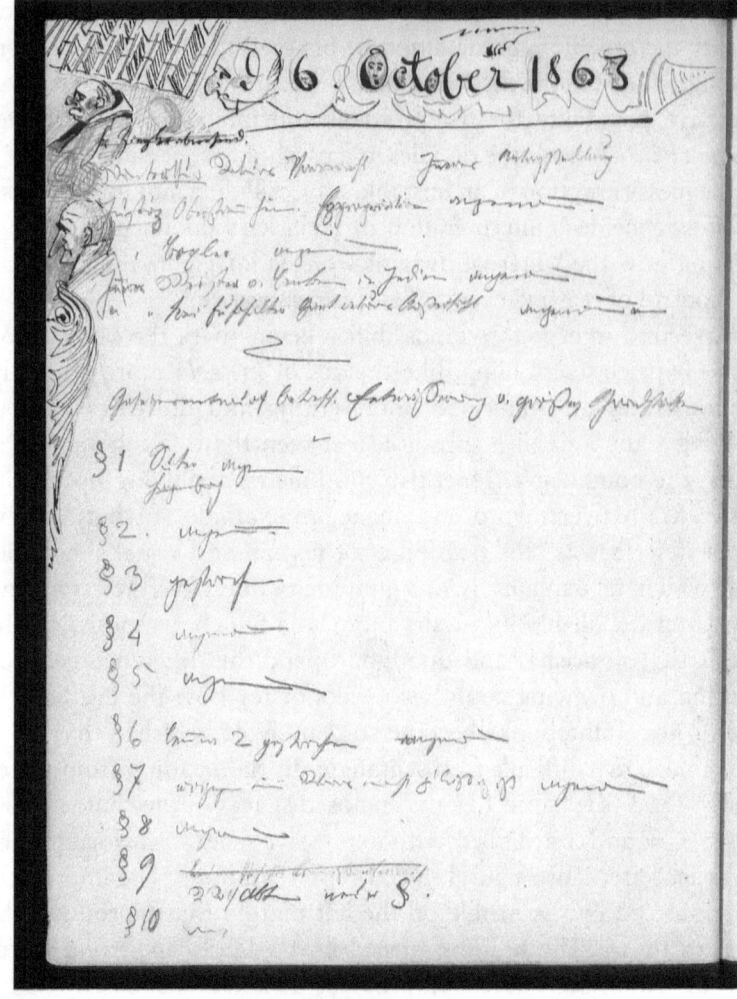

Figure 13. Gottfried Keller, Notizen über die Verhandlungen des Regierungsrates, October 6, 1863. Zentralbibliothek Zürich, Ms. GK 53.

mountains, trees, grasses, and a lake. In the case of *Der grüne Heinrich*, this threshold between text and image is taken by scholars such as W. G. Sebald and Naumann as staging a competition, indeed, a crisis between these two modes of creative expression, namely, the impossibility of recuperating images through writing,

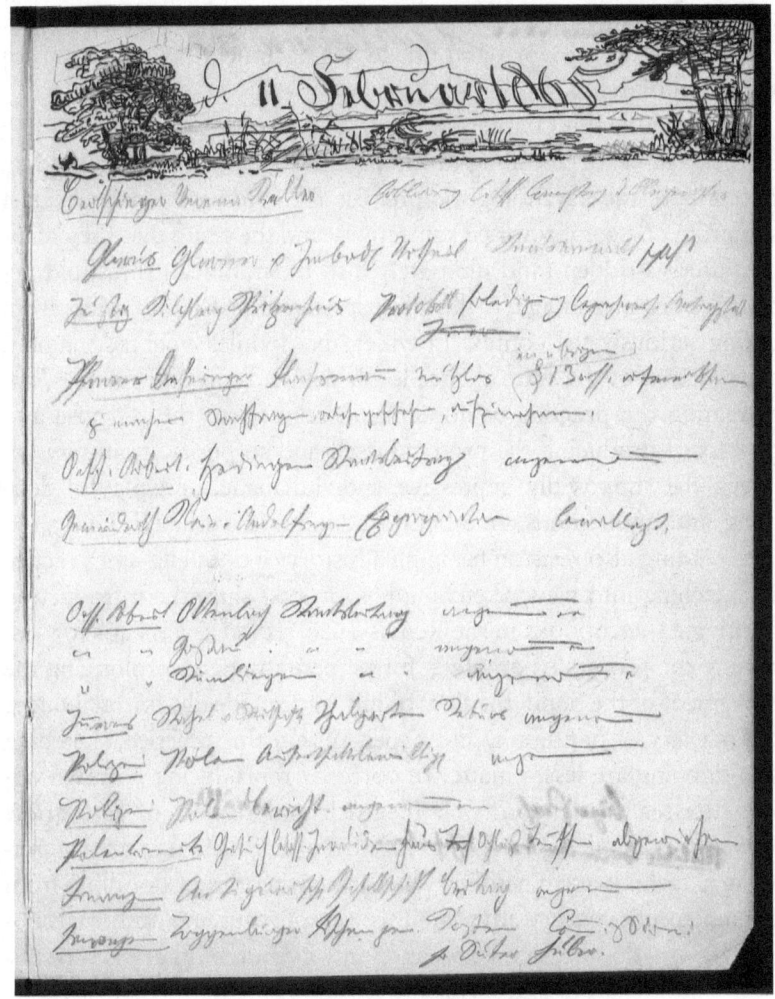

Figure 14. Gottfried Keller, Notizen über die Verhandlungen des Regierungsrates, February 11, 1865. Zentralbibliothek Zürich, Ms. GK 55.

or vice versa (a reading supported with a biographical reference to Keller's choice to abandon painting for writing).[29] The strength of

---

29. Sebald views the act of writing in Keller's novel as repressing and containing the formless threat of the doodle: "The art of writing is the attempt to contain

this interpretative possibility is evident in the degree to which the incompatibility of word and image has become a favorite topos of Keller scholarship.[30]

To conclude this chapter, I want to propose an alternative reading of the practice of doodling in the protocol notebooks. This reading rejects both the psychologistic premise for reading the doodles as a symptom of a compromised subjectivity and the claim that they manifest a crisis-ridden (and ultimately also biographical) threshold between word and image. A third interpretative possibility arises from taking seriously the context in which the doodles emerged, namely, the function of the state chancellor. It demands, in other words, appreciating the practice of doodling in relation to the purpose and process of producing the protocol itself and so posits an affinity between the supposedly expressive, individualistic, and playful doodling and anonymous, rule-bound administrative labor. This alternate reading also rests on bringing a history of doodling as a practice of sketching into view. Sketching has, at least since the introduction of private sketchbooks in the Renaissance, served as a means for sustaining the process of drawing, for perpetuating and prolonging the movement of the hand, the flow of ink, and so, ideally, for facilitating the mastery of hand, ink, and paper. Within this practice, sketching and drawing are less a matter of correctly reproducing a drawn object (the realist standard that Heinrich and readers of *Der grüne Heinrich* evaluate his early drawings by) and instead a matter of pursuing sketching as an activity. The earliest theories of doodling from the nineteenth century advocate this view: Because no authorial subject draws a doodle, that is, because only a child or otherwise "primi-

---

the teeming black scrawl which everywhere threatens to gain the upper hand, in the interest of maintaining a halfway functional personality." W. G. Sebald, "Death Draws Nigh, Time Marches On: Some Remarks on Gottfried Keller," in *A Place in the Country: On Gottfried Keller, Johann Peter Hebel, Robert Walser, and Others*, trans. Jo Catling (New York: Random House, 2013), 122–23. See also Naumann, "Die 'kolossale Kritzelei,'" 176.

30. Consider, for example, Ernst Osterkamp's argument that the ekphrastic descriptions in *Der grüne Heinrich*, particularly in the opening pages, achieve, in writing, what nineteenth-century landscape painting could no longer do: They show a world in motion and thus reconcile past, present, and a dawning modernity. See Ernst Osterkamp, "Erzählte Landschaften," in Groddeck, *"Der grüne Heinrich,"* 141–58.

tive" self draws so aimlessly, the doodle should not be regarded as an attempt at mimetically reproducing an object in an image.[31] Instead, the mimetic relationship is displaced onto the relationship between image and bodily action. The doodle *copies* the movement of the hand; it is a record of an anterior, corporeal movement. Ebenezer Cooke makes this point explicit in his account of doodling children in "Our Art Teaching and Child Nature" from 1886: "Their first attempts at drawing are muscular movements, resulting in scribbles, not without interest even to us; to them they are full of meaning [. . .]; with ideas vague, eye and hand imperfectly correlated, this is attempted in the first stage, but feebly, or on easy elliptical forms. The seen action of the hand is probably imitated; that is, the first drawings are copies, but they are copies of actions."[32]

When contextualized as taking place during the meetings of the government council, in which the state chancellor Keller bore responsibility for creating a record of the exchanges surrounding him and, consequently, in which his notes belonged to a larger undertaking of recordkeeping, Keller's doodles come into view as, if not a copy, then at least a record of those oral exchanges not in terms of their content but instead as a durational process. In doodling, as in writing the minutes, the authorial subject fades from view and the process comes to the fore.[33] While the notes serve the ostensible purpose of generating and recording the substance of the meetings for governing the canton, the doodles, in turn, constitute a record of the proceedings as a process. To employ a common aquatic metaphor for such oral exchanges: The flow of Keller's pencil in the continuous motions of doodling mimics and thereby records the flow of speech for which he and his notebook have together become the initial storage medium. That the doodles participate in the process of

---

31. See Wittmann, "Am Anfang," 142.
32. Ebenezer Cooke, "Our Art Teaching and Child Nature," in *Transactions of the Education Society, 1884–5* (London: William Rice, 1885), 82–83.
33. See Andrea Meyertholen, "From Marginalia to the Museum: The Transfiguration of the Doodle by Gottfried Keller, Hans Prinzhorn, and Jean Dubuffet," *Seminar: A Journal of Germanic Studies* 58, no. 4 (November 2022): 365. Meyertholen's article otherwise offers a conventional interpretation of Keller's interest in doodling as giving expression to a marginalized subjectivity.

recordkeeping is underscored by the fact that the doodles drawn during the sessions of the government council, including the three landscapes mentioned above, are often redrawn and edited in pen, presumably during the production of the draft protocol, when Keller would regularly use a pen to mark off agenda items that had entered the second document. In this way, the doodles become entangled in the process of making the protocols beyond their initial record and themselves form a record of the process of producing these documents. The notes serve the ostensible purpose of recording the substance of the meetings and governance; the doodles, in turn, constitute a record of the process as a process.

A recent burgeoning interest in the genre of the protocol has established several affinities between the genre and the literature of myriad authors. On first sight, it might be most tempting to draw comparisons between Keller's establishing of events (in the protocols) and fiction by describing each as a way of approximating an antecedent reality by way of abiding by specific conventions, including those of genre and of format.[34] Such a comparison might have the potential to provide an account of Keller's realism as derivative of the specific performative truth function the protocols possess. However, this chapter has pursed yet another point of convergence between administrative and literary writing practices than their realism: first, by unearthing how "Die mißbrauchten Liebesbriefe" thematizes and valorizes a bureaucratic ethos and administrative practices of writing, while literature is represented as a perversion of this cultural technique; and second, by drawing attention to writing practices shared among the supposedly antithetical forms of bureaucracy and literature, including collective, anonymous writing procedures and practices of copying, filing, and archiving as a way of producing documents from texts. The making of a protocol or a work of fiction, as the very history of the manuscript for "Die mißbrauchten Liebesbriefe" reminds us, is premised on mundane forms of paperwork, those office-management skills that Gritli spectacularly embodies and that Keller himself practiced for fifteen years.

---

34. For a comparison of administrative writing and literature on such grounds, see Johannes Türk, "Unvergleichliche Ruhe: Franz Kafkas Protokollaufnahmen," in *Gespenster des Wissens*, ed. Ute Holl, Claus Pia, and Burkhardt Wolf (Zürich: Diaphanes, 2017), 371–76.

Part III

Serial Erotics

The Periodical

5

THE MALE GAZE, SERIALIZED

Das Sinngedicht

Of the volumes that would later constitute his collected works, Keller prepublished only three in the format of a serialized periodical, the format that came to dominate the literary landscape of the nineteenth century: *Züricher Novellen* (1876–1877), *Das Sinngedicht* (1881), and *Martin Salander* (1886). Yet the shape of his oeuvre displays a broad range of serialized formats—preprints, reissues, multivolume editions, and sequels—thereby making evident that serialized formats and their logic extend far beyond periodical literature. These practices of serialization were initiated with the staggered four-volume publication of *Der grüne Heinrich*, itself rewritten and republished in second, third, and fourth editions, and concluded with Keller's collected works, which could initially be purchased as a subscription that delivered volumes as they were printed in succession. Keller's second novel draws our attention to another site of serialization, namely, the sequel. Following his discontent with his second novel, *Martin Salander*, Keller planned to write a sequel that would feature the protagonist's son, Arnold Salander. For this planned but unrealized work, seriality would have been integrated into the narrative as family genealogy.[1]

These examples make evident that the practices and frustrations of serialization extend far beyond periodical publishing, to such an extent that they destabilize the seemingly obvious difference between book and periodical formats. The plurality of editions of Keller's texts and their multivolume formats well illustrate that serialization characterized not merely nineteenth-century periodicals but also the relationship between periodicals and book formats. Book and periodical publishing were not so much competing formats as symbiotic ones, essentially dovetailing in a principle of serialization.[2] So-called preprints could be reissued in book format, while texts previously published in book format could reappear in periodicals or in further book editions. In view of a publishing history organized according to methods of serialization, the idea of the collected-works edition as unifying life and work not only imaginatively compensates for the fracture of format and self experienced when publishing the first edition of *Der grüne Heinrich*; more broadly, Keller's *Gesammelte Werke* was tasked with stabilizing a textual corpus against the fluctuations of serialized publishing, indeed, with repressing the history of varied texts and formats.

Practices of serialization are most apparent with respect to the genre that dominates Keller's oeuvre, the so-called novella cycle, of which Keller published five: *Die Leute von Seldwyla*, the *Sieben Legenden*, *Das Sinngedicht*, and the *Züricher Novellen*. In 1939, Georg Lukács suggested that Keller's partiality for the form of the novella cycle derived from his Swiss political affinities: Each of his novella

---

1. For an example of the entwinement of genealogical and serialized production structures, see Elisabeth Strowick, "'Nachkommenschaften': Stifter's Series," trans. Anthony Mahler, in *Truth in Serial Form: Serial Formats and the Form of the Series, 1850–1930*, ed. Malika Maskarinec (Berlin: Walter de Gruyter, 2023), 83–113.

2. McGillen emphasizes the same, writing that "the book and the periodical [. . .] actually marked the opposite ends of a spectrum. Periodicals gravitated to the book form when they were collected and bound together, while 'books' issued in parts shared key characteristics of the periodical." Petra S. McGillen, *The Fontane Workshop: Manufacturing Realism in the Industrial Age of Print* (New York: Bloomsbury Academic, 2019), 43n36.

cycles is akin to a federation, a loose union of largely autonomous units.[3] Even if Lukács provides an apt metaphor for describing the tenuous bonds of Keller's collections, contemporary media practices offer a more compelling account of Keller's propensity for writing novellas and novella cycles than do Keller's patriotic loyalties. A novella cycle constituted a flexible assemblage of semiautonomous entities well suited to the repetitions of serialized publishing. A loose "federation" of texts meant that their author could progressively add stories to and also extract them from the collections over time. Individual novellas or novella cycles could be preprinted in periodicals or anthologies (such as the preprint of "Die mißbrauchten Liebesbriefe" in the Deutsche Reichs-Zeitung that I discussed in chapter 3) or, alternatively, reissued, such as when "Romeo und Julia auf dem Dorfe" appeared in the Deutscher Novellenschatz (1871), securing Keller's canonical status. In the case of Die Leute von Seldwyla, Keller issued a second expanded edition of the cycle with twice as many stories seventeen years after publishing the first, another way of capitalizing on the flexible assemblage of the novella cycle. The Seldwyla setting, a second set of five novellas, and the designation "second expanded edition" (zweite vermehrte Auflage) together marked the volume as a continuation of the first cycle despite the prodigious time gap. The second expanded edition of Die Leute von Seldwyla and the unrealized novel starring Arnold Salander were modeled on their predecessors, another instance where the force of format makes itself known. The fact that Keller's literary projects were first conceived according to a projected publishing format rather than in terms of content has an unmistakable origin in serialized publishing practices. Serialized publishing, no matter whether it is manifested as periodicals, multivolume formats, preprints, reissues, or sequels, reinforces the priority of format.[4]

---

3. See Georg Lukács, "Gottfried Keller," in *German Realists in the Nineteenth Century*, trans. Jeremy Gaines and Paul Keast, ed. Rodney Livingstone (Cambridge: MIT Press, 1993), 204–5.

4. Hans-Jürgen Schrader insists on the power of the periodical's constraints, including those concerning format, when discussing the influence of the periodical market on now canonical works of literature: "On closer inspection, however, one finds that the works themselves, their genre, their structure, the theme, the motifs,

The *Züricher Novellen* constitutes a second example of such a loose assemblage of texts, and it was first published as a periodical serial: The first three novellas and the frame narrative were first serialized in the *Deutsche Rundschau* and then augmented for the book publication with two further novellas, even though they could not be accommodated within the frame narrative. Of these two additional novellas, one ("Das Fähnlein der sieben Aufrechten") had been previously published as a stand-alone text in *Berthold Auerbach's deutscher Volks-Kalender* and in the Bern newspaper *Der Bund*. The novella cycle thus offered a format superbly adapted to "serial methods" of nineteenth-century publishing broadly understood: "continuation, modification, and expansion."[5]

Keller's individual novellas acquired the autonomy conducive to prepublishing, reissuing, or being extended in sequels insofar as his novella cycles lacked the narrative closure that we commonly associate with a cyclical form. It is characteristic of Keller's novella collections that they struggle to establish a frame narrative that could formally or thematically contain the embedded stories. Consider, for example, the text that most evidently endeavors to achieve such closure: While the ending of *Das Sinngedicht* makes every attempt to force closure in the guise of a happy end artificially sealed with a kiss and the promise of matrimony, contemporary critics were quick to point out that the frame narrative was bursting at the seams and that its structures were too narrow and tenuous to contain the many novellas. Paul Heyse, for example, famously critiques the frame narrative as "not wide enough to hold everything swelling over its

---

and even details concerning word choice—everything substantial, and thus their art—are decisively shaped by this reciprocal relationship. After all, they were written in consideration of the conditions, possibilities, and latitudes given by the indispensable primary medium." Hans-Jürgen Schrader, "Autorfedern unter Preß-Autorität: Mitformende Marktfaktoren der realistischen Erzählkunst—an Beispielen Storms, Raabes und Kellers," *Jahrbuch der Raabe-Gesellschaft* 42, no. 1 (2001): 5.

5. Frank Kelleter, "Five Ways of Looking at Popular Seriality," in *Media of Serial Narrative*, ed. Frank Kelleter (Columbus: Ohio State University Press, 2017), 7. For an alternative definition of seriality in terms of repetition and variation, see Umberto Eco, "Interpreting Serials," in *The Limits of Interpretation* (Bloomington: Indiana University Press, 1990), 83–100.

edges."[6] The frame seemingly cannot contain the sprawling contents. Even more egregiously, to take another example, the frame narrative in the *Züricher Novellen* simply peters out after the third of the five novellas, making no serious gesture at containment whatsoever.[7] These insufficient or incomplete frame narratives throw into question the convention of describing these texts as novella cycles, a self-contained and closed form. In the following, I argue that at least *Das Sinngedicht* and the *Züricher Novellen*, two texts that were initially published in the *Deutsche Rundschau*, a literary periodical, and then reissued in book formats, exhibit an inherently serial rather than cyclical structure.[8] While extant scholarship has well situated each of these novella cycles in the context of the *Deutsche Rundschau* and nineteenth-century periodical culture generally, I demonstrate that the diegeses integrate serialized formatting into their narrative design, which I characterize as serial erotics.[9] *Serial erotics* desig-

---

6. Paul Heyse to Keller, June 5, 1881, in *HKKA*, 23.1:388. Keller too regularly expressed his frustrations with the genre of the novella cycle and its frame: "In some respects, one is disrupted and limited by this form; one always has to think about who is narrating and whom is being narrated to and so on" (Man ist doch in mancher Beziehung genirt und beschränkt durch diese Form; immer muß man daran denken, wer erzählt und wem erzählt wird etc.). Keller to Julius Rodenberg, September 9, 1881, in *HKKA*, 23.1:394.

7. Both the first and the second editions of *Die Leute von Seldwyla*, in comparison, make no attempt at a frame, a happy end, or any other type of closure; the novellas collected there and in the *Züricher Novellen* are related primarily by means of a shared geography, the fictional Seldwyla or the canton of Zurich.

8. Ursula Amrein and Gerhard Neumann have each made note of the serial structure of *Das Sinngedicht*. Neumann refers to "the serialization of 'love at first sight.'" Gerhard Neumann, "Der Körper des Menschen und die belebte Statue: Zu einer Grundformel in Gottfried Kellers *Sinngedicht*," in *Pygmalion: Die Geschichte des Mythos in der abendländischen Kultur*, ed. Mathias Mayer and Gerhard Neumann (Freiburg im Breisgau: Rombach, 1997), 581. Amrein similarly notes "the serial technique of repetition and variation" and the "serial arrangement." Ursula Amrein, "Gottfried Kellers 'artiger kleiner *Dekameron*': Poetik und Schreibweise des *Sinngedichts* in der Nachfolge Boccaccios," in *Boccaccio und die Folgen: Fontane, Storm, Keller, Ebner-Eschenbach und die Novellenkunst des 19. Jahrhunderts*, ed. Hugo Aust and Hubertus Fischer (Würzburg: Königshausen & Neumann, 2006), 128, 131.

9. For a discussion of Keller's texts in the context of the *Deutsche Rundschau*, see Gerhart von Graevenitz, "Wissen und Sehen: Anthropologie und Perspektivismus

nates a narrative structure adapted to serialized publishing that is also defined by a strongly gendered dynamic. Serial erotics thereby adapt narrative design to contemporary publishing practices and to the gender politics of German realism, including the perceived threat of a feminized literature, by reinforcing the authority of the male storyteller.

The following readings attend to these texts in inverse chronological order of their dates of publication. While *Das Sinngedicht* (1881) exhibits the basic dynamic of serial erotics, I read the novella "Der Landvogt von Greifensee" (1876; book edition 1877) from the *Züricher Novellen* as an allegorical interrogation of the ideals of serialized publishing, particularly as represented by the *Deutsche Rundschau*. Finally, chapter 6 examines the frame narrative of the *Züricher Novellen* to argue that Keller there develops an authorial persona that bridges the ideal of aesthetic autonomy and originality on the one hand and the realities of literature as a commercialized product of mass reproduction on the other.

Seriality

Although Keller and his critics often invoke Boccaccio's *Decameron* and the fictional practice of telling stories in the round as a model for his novella cycles, a comparison with this well-rounded set of a hundred tales ultimately explains why Keller's novella cycles *Das Sinngedicht* and *Züricher Novellen* cannot, on account of their frag-

---

in der Zeitschriftenpresse des 19. Jahrhunderts und in realistischen Texten; Zu Stifters *Bunten Steinen* und Kellers *Sinngedicht*," in *Wissen in Literatur im 19. Jahrhundert*, ed. Lutz Danneberg and Friederich Vollhardt (Tübingen: Max Niemeyer, 2002), 147–89; Daniela Gretz, "Ein literarischer 'Versuch' im Experimentierfeld Zeitschrift: Medieneffekte der *Deutschen Rundschau* auf Gottfried Kellers *Sinngedicht*," *Zeitschrift für deutsche Philologie* 134, no. 2 (2015): 191–215; Daniela Gretz, "Aufwärtsstreben als Niedergang oder Variationen des Immergleichen: Zur Ästhetik der Serialität in Gottfried Kellers *Martin Salander* in der *Deutschen Rundschau*," in *Kellers Erzählen: Strukturen—Funktionen—Reflexionen*, ed. Philipp Theisohn, 259–90; and Hans-Jürgen Schrader, "Im Schraubstock moderner Marktmechanismen: Vom Druck Kellers und Meyers in Rodenbergs *Deutscher Rundschau*," *Jahresbericht der Gottfried Keller-Gesellschaft* 62 (1993): 3–38.

ile frames, achieve the formal closure conventionally associated with the genre and, for that matter, the very concept of a cycle.[10] In *The Decameron*, storytelling in the round is famously motivated by a vital need for the storytellers to insulate themselves against the gruesome threat of the plague; seven women and three men withdraw from the city of Florence, which is beset by illness and social disintegration, to the paradisical countryside where they spend their days trading stories. Their gathering and the practice of storytelling serve to cordon themselves off from disease and anarchical disarray. Similarly, in Goethe's *Unterhaltungen deutscher Ausgewanderten*, the storytellers gather to shield themselves from the threat of the advancing French Revolutionary Army. In each case, storytelling does nothing less than reconstitute a social order in profound danger. It responds to what Andreas Gailus describes, in his brilliant reading of Goethe's novella cycle, as "systematic traumas" that threaten to undermine a social system from within.[11] As Gailus explains, for Goethe "the novella becomes a traumatic narrative concerned with the catastrophic force of newness."[12]

What is missing from Keller's novellas and novella cycles in general is any such force of newness, that is, any staging of trauma that would generate a need for closure. The novella cycles relay no challenge to the status quo, no necessity to adapt, no demand to restore the physical or political health of a community. If a crisis is staged— for example, at the beginning of *Das Sinngedicht*, the protagonist Reinhart feels his eyesight failing on account of his strenuous optical experiments—it pertains merely to an individual, is easily resolved, and is without lasting consequence (Reinhart leaves his

---

10. For an overview of Keller's relationship to *The Decameron*, see Amrein, "Gottfried Kellers 'artiger kleiner *Dekameron*.'" Referring to the same set of precedents I mentioned, Philipp Theisohn similarly argues that Keller employs the genre of the novella to mediate a crisis unresolved in *Der grüne Heinrich*, the protagonist's "erotic illiteracy." Philipp Theisohn, "Mädchenbekehrer: *Sieben Legenden* oder Gottfried Kellers Poetik des Eros," *Mitteilungen der Gottfried Keller-Gesellschaft* (2017): 16.
11. Andreas Gailus, "The Poetics of Containment: Goethe's *Conversations of German Refugees* and the Crisis of Representation," *Modern Philology* 100, no. 3 (2003): 438.
12. Gailus, "The Poetics of Containment," 442.

laboratory and, by the day's end, feels his eyesight blissfully restored).[13] And while the storytellers of *Das Sinngedicht*, in a nod to *The Decameron*, are also isolated in the Edenic setting of Lucie's garden, the surrounding countryside through which Reinhart travels before arriving there seems no less bucolic. "Der Landvogt von Greifensee," the text examined in chapter 6, lacks even a half-hearted attempt to stage a crisis, even on the moderate scale of an individual: The story is set in motion by nothing more than the whimsy of a middle-aged man reminiscing about his past. Because these novella cycles fail to initiate with any of sense of urgency, they cannot motivate an act of closure or insulation characteristic of a strict cyclical form. Instead, freed from an encompassing frame or from a logic of crisis and resolution, the novella cycle becomes a flexible genre amenable, if need be, to fitful and unreliable writing habits or to the offers and deadlines of publishers. Viewed in this way, the novella cycle unfurls, abandons its circular form, and stretches into an open-ended linear series so as to conform to the exigencies of an author plagued by procrastination and a publishing market dominated by periodical literature. Keller's novella cycles go yet one step further: The genre is chosen not merely because it adapts to those exigencies; rather, his cycles also integrate seriality into their narrative design as a way of managing exigency.

To be clear, the claim that *Das Sinngedicht* and the *Züricher Novellen* integrate a serialized format into their plots does not simply mean that these texts abide by the formatting constraints—such as word limits, conventions of typography and orthography, or mores—of periodicals as a publishing venue. Nor do I mean to recapitulate the point that periodical fiction invokes, incorporates,

---

13. Amrein, by contrast, argues that the novellas of the *Sinngedicht* respond to a pernicious, though undefined threat of modernity: "in Boccaccio the plague, in Keller pathogenic civilization." Amrein, "Gottfried Kellers 'artiger kleiner *Dekameron*,'" 126. If, however, there is such a broader threat embodied by Reinhart's diminished eyesight, then its quick resolution reveals it to be exceedingly shallow in nature. For an alternative account of the German-language realist novella as portraying an inner, psychological conflict, see Fritz Martini, "Die deutsche Novelle im 'bürgerlichen Realismus': Überlegungen zur geschichtlichen Bestimmung des Formtypus," *Wirkendes Wort: Deutsche Sprache und Literatur in Forschung und Lehre* 10 (1960): 257–78.

and contributes to the horizons of knowledge generated by periodical culture, a recent mainstay of the topical scholarship.[14] Instead, Keller's narratives participate in an epochal transition from a cyclical structuring of time to a linear, iterative, and potentially indefinite conception of time, a transition that takes place over the course of the eighteenth and nineteenth centuries and that is advanced in Karol Berger's *Bach's Cycle, Mozart's Arrow*.[15] Berger argues that the insistence on linearity and progression in European music beginning with Mozart is symptomatic of a transition from a predominantly Christian and agricultural society—which imagined itself in a cyclical, seasonal time embedded within an inaccessible divine eternity—to a secular, industrial society that casts its history as a progressive movement from past to present and into an unknown future. This indefinite, linear temporality underlies the sequential order of nineteenth-century print culture and reshapes the way in which the era narrates its fictions and its own history.

Print media—first and foremost the format of the periodical that had come to dominate literary culture and consumption—exhibit and reenforce such a serial structuring by transforming how literature was written and read. As excellent scholarship in recent years has emphasized, serialization entailed that readers consume narratives in parts rather than from beginning to end. These literary texts were read alongside an intermedia medley of images and diverse genres contained within a single periodical issue, a reading practice typically summarized as extensive reading as opposed to an intensive

---

14. Stories published in the *Deutsche Rundschau*, as Daniela Gretz has demonstrated at length with respect to German-language realism and Keller's *Das Sinngedicht* in particular, integrated new dimensions of popular knowledge that could be assumed for periodical readers. See Daniela Gretz, "Das Wissen der Literatur: Der deutsche literarische Realismus und die Zeitschriftenkultur des 19. Jahrhunderts," in *Medialer Realismus*, ed. Daniela Gretz (Freiburg im Breisgau: Rombach, 2011), 99–126; Gretz, "Ein literarischer 'Versuch'"; and Sabine Schneider, "Happy End im 'Kampf ums Dasein'? Vergessene Konstellationen von Literatur und Wissen in Kellers *Sinngedicht* und Raabes *Lar*," in *Vergessene Konstellationen literarischer Öffentlichkeit zwischen 1840 und 1885*, ed. Katja Mellmann and Jesko Reiling (Berlin: Walter de Gruyter, 2016), 321–44.

15. Karol Berger, *Bach's Cycle, Mozart's Arrow: An Essay on the Origins of Musical Modernity* (Berkeley: University of California Press, 2007).

rereading of a small corpus. Stories were open-ended yet could be comprehended in stand-alone segments, while at the same time possessing sufficient suspense that they would encourage the purchase of the following issue if not a subscription. Additionally, narratives increasingly needed to possess multiple flexible storylines so that they could be extended indefinitely, a practice at odds with the closure attributed to a more classical concept of narrative premised on a coherent beginning, middle, and end, but well suited to representing the increasingly complex social networks of urban society.[16] Serialized formats also gave unprecedented power to editors, who acted as gatekeepers by deciding where and when texts would be published, and to the public, who could express preferences by means of their purchasing power, thus seemingly demoting the singular genius author of Romanticism to one step in a brisk-paced, collaborative, and machinated production process.[17]

While chapter 6 explains how Keller responded to this perceived threat to the autonomy and originality of an author whose works had become mass-produced objects of consumption, for the moment

---

16. Catherine Delafield summarizes the perceived incompatibility of serialized formats and a closed form: "In addition, new serialized fiction was dangerously incomplete and appeared not to be shaped or sculpted. The serial within a magazine also enjoyed horizontal integration with other embedded texts and was in competition and dialogue with these other texts. Such a serial existed in a form that was not bounded and absolute. Finally, it could not be a work of art precisely because it was date-stamped and apparently ephemeral so that in spite of its collection into a whole, the serial would always betray the marks of its composition and the contingency of its original evolution." Catherine Delafield, *Serialization and the Novel in Mid-Victorian Magazines* (Surrey: Ashgate, 2015), 9. More recently, Sean Franzel has demonstrated the way in which early nineteenth-century German authors, in particular Jean Paul, embraced serial formats as a way of allowing for interruption and fragmentation and to accommodate time and history as they unfold. Jean Paul thereby comes into view as a productive counterexample to the aesthetics of closure I attribute to Keller. See Sean Franzel, *Writing Time: Studies in Serial Literature, 1780–1850* (Ithaca, NY: Cornell University Press, 2023), esp. 14–20.

17. Vance Byrd and Ervin Malakaj describe nineteenth-century literature "as a cultural field in which an auratic notion of poetic genius and aesthetic autonomy were replaced by a varied picture of professionals working collaboratively in a network." Vance Byrd and Ervin Malakaj, "Introduction: Market Strategies and German Literature in the Long Nineteenth Century," in *Market Strategies and German Literature in the Long Nineteenth Century*, ed. Vance Byrd and Ervin Malakaj (Berlin: Walter de Gruyter, 2020), 3.

I want to emphasize that the narratives of *Das Sinngedicht* and the *Züricher Novellen* are endowed with a serial order that integrates the linear, part-and-parcel structure of serialized periodicals into their plots as an erotic and gendered dynamic. The frame and embedded narratives display a basically iterative, repetitive structure, rather than being designed along a progressive trajectory or along relationships of cause and effect.[18] Seriality, in other words, relies on repetition and variation at the cost of narrative progression or development. At the same time, the serial structure of these texts, like the periodical format in which they were first printed, acts as an archival technology, generating a progressively expanding collection or archive of materials that lends itself to incorporating new discoveries and adjudicating past findings. In doing so, these two fictional texts enact an ambition of nineteenth-century periodical literature, an ambition particularly significant to the self-stylization of the *Deutsche Rundschau*: that serialized texts would give way to an expansive and enduring archive of knowledge. As archival fictions, as defined by Daniela Gretz and Nicolas Pethes, *Das Sinngedicht* and the *Züricher Novellen* aim to demonstrate that the serial restructuring of knowledge in periodical formats need not imply its fragmentation.[19]

Deutsche Rundschau

As noted, Keller's *Züricher Novellen* and *Sinngedicht* were first published in the *Deutsche Rundschau*. Understanding the periodical's ambitions provides a critical background for reading these two

---

18. My definition of a serial order draws on Eva Geulen, "Serialization in Goethe's Morphology," *Compar(a)ison: An International Journal of Comparative Literature* 2 (2008): 53–70; and Kirk Wetters, "The Law of the Series and the Crux of Causation: Paul Kammerer's Anomalies," *MLN* 134, no. 3 (April 2019): 643–60.

19. See Daniela Gretz and Nicolas Pethes, eds., *Archiv/Fiktionen: Verfahren des Archivierens in Literatur und Kultur des langen 19. Jahrhunderts* (Freiburg im Breisgau: Rombach, 2016). On the realism's archival media, see also Sean Franzel, Ilinca Iurascu, and Petra McGillen, eds., *Media Inventories* (Berlin: Walter de Gruyter, 2024).

texts, in particular the way in which "Der Landvogt von Greifensee" allegorizes serialized publishing practices. The unillustrated *Deutsche Rundschau* was printed monthly by the Verlag Gebrüder Paetel in Berlin. At its height, it boasted a circulation of ten thousand, which, while modest compared to the most popular periodicals of the era, was impressive for an elite publication of its kind. Julius Rodenberg, who became the editor of the *Deutsche Rundschau* at its founding in 1874, had already met Keller in Berlin while the latter was drafting *Der grüne Heinrich* and began to recruit him as an author in 1874 after enthusiastically reading *Die Leute von Seldwyla*. Their correspondence gives the impression that Keller's very idea to write a new novella cycle during his employment as state chancellor (*Staatsschreiber*) of the canton of Zurich was prompted by Rodenberg's ample hyperbolic flattery and incessant urging to write for the periodical: "My dear Shakespeare of the novella!" begins one letter.[20] Rodenberg's continued appeals for Keller's fidelity to the *Deutsche Rundschau* were successful, as most of the texts he wrote following his occupation as state chancellor appeared in its pages.

As a recent boom in scholarship on German-language periodical culture has amply demonstrated, family magazines, like *Die Gartenlaube* or *Daheim*, which aimed at the broadest possible readership, but also more highbrow cultural magazines, like the *Deutsche Rundschau*, regarded themselves as providing a *Bildungsprogramm* for the general public. They aimed at nothing less than the cultural and political education of good citizens. Carrying the torch of the Enlightenment in the era of mass media, periodicals operated in parallel to and more widely than the better-established institutions of schools and universities.[21] To realize this ambitious program, it was essential for periodicals to provide, for one, an overview of contemporaneous developments in science and culture. As Gerhart von Graevenitz em-

---

20. Julius Rodenberg to Keller, February 16, 1877, in *HKKA*, 22:506.

21. In contrast to an early tendency in the scholarship to regard the format and printing pace of periodicals along with their economic dependency on the market of readers as impeding the creative genius of late nineteenth-century authors, scholars have recently argued that periodicals were a field for literary experimentation. For a summary and example of this transition in views, see Gretz, "Ein literarischer 'Versuch.'"

phasizes, periodicals sought "to provide an overall *picture* of knowledge, to make possible an over*view*."²² By appealing to universalist concepts such as *nature* or *life*, family and high-culture periodicals alike intended to withstand the growing specialization and fractioning of knowledge.²³ Their pages would provide an umbrella for gathering proliferating and fragmented forms of knowledge.

Offering an overview of developments in culture, politics, history, and science was of the essence to the *Deutsche Rundschau*. The breadth of perspectives and their subservience to an all-consuming survey were already advertised in its title, *Rund-schau*. The all-encompassing vision of the *Deutsche Rundschau* is also evident in Rodenberg's early appeal to Keller "to sum up your manifestation as an author [dichterische Erscheinung] in one overall picture [Gesammtbilde]," a placeholder for the totalizing image of life and work his collected works would later secure.²⁴ The visionary breadth of the *Deutsche Rundschau* dictated the assortment and arrangement of

---

22. "*Überblick* ['overview'] [...] and *Rundschau* ['review' or 'panoramic view'] describe both the techniques and the epistemic goal of the cultivated press [Bildungspresse]: the coherence of knowledge was to be made visible through pictures and forms of visualization analogous to pictures. This also applies to a few periodicals like the *Deutsche Rundschau* that did not present any pictures but still fit, with its program of 'Rund*schau*' into the visualization context of the whole differentiated medium." Graevenitz, "Wissen und Sehen," 152.

23. In their article on the archival function of nineteenth-century journals, Gustav Frank, Madleen Podewski, and Stefan Scherer argue that:

Cultural periodicals aimed to provide as universal an overview as possible of all the fields of knowledge [...]. In this, they were still, at least in the beginning, clearly oriented on the semantics of *Bildung* (and of the nascent humanities) and increasingly integrated literature, which operated across discourses. This function explicitly determined the programmatic positions in which one repeatedly finds, up through the present, formulations that all come down to avoiding specialist discourses, partisan points of view, or a merely fashionable movement. In the German Empire and in the Weimar Republic, these orientations tended to be tied to all-embracing concepts like *life*, *being*, *mind*, *nature*, *culture*, *totality*, the *whole*, or also *modernity*.

Gustav Frank, Madleen Podewski, and Stefan Scherer, "Kultur—Zeit—Schrift: Literatur- und Kulturzeitschriften als 'kleine Archive,'" *Internationales Archiv für Sozialgeschichte der deutschen Literatur* 34, no. 2 (2010): 19.

24. Julius Rodenberg to Keller, October 22, 1875, in *Geehrter Herr—lieber Freund: Schweizer Autoren und ihre deutschen Verleger; Mit einer Umkehrung und drei Exkursionen*, ed. Rätus Luck (Basel: Stroemfeld, 1998), 130.

texts in each issue. Serialized works of literature preceded articles in science and politics and literary reviews. A reader of the first installment of the "Der Landvogt von Greifensee," for example, could turn to articles on the slave trade, Shakespeare, the American Civil War, Frédéric Chopin, and Paul Anselm von Feuerbach. The issue concluded with a "Berliner Chronik" and a "Literarische Rundschau."[25] In an editorial statement anticipating the periodical's founding, Rodenberg positions the publication as providing an overview not only of the fractious individual arts (literature, music, and the visual arts) but also of "those myriad elements of present-day education" that were otherwise dispersed among the dense market of periodicals. Rodenberg writes,

> For filling his leisure time, the German reader has illustrated magazines and other papers; he has numerous professional journals if he wants to teach himself and just as many critical guides for his orientation in the different fields of literature, theater, music, and the visual arts. He only lacks a periodical that would, by including all the myriad elements of present-day education together, enable an overview of the entire scope of all of them and address a need of the highly educated circles of our nation that has not yet been fully satisfied. The *Deutsche Rundschau* is intended to fill into this lacuna. It will offer the finest form of entertainment and concurrently follow scientific questions and political, literary, and artistic affairs with the greatest attention.[26]

Also evident in this programmatic statement addressed to a German reader—as in the red, black, and gold coloring of the covers that bind the periodical's issues into a durable book format every three months—is the *Deutsche Rundschau*'s commitment to the recently founded Prussian-led German Empire.[27] The *Deutsche Rundschau*, like *Die Gartenlaube*, was profoundly committed to cultivating a

---

25. See *Deutsche Rundschau* 11 (March 1877).
26. Julius Rodenberg, "Die Begründung der *Deutschen Rundschau*," in *Ein Rückblick* (Berlin: Gebrüder Paetel, 1899), 29–30.
27. On the *Deutsche Rundschau* as embodying a vision of the Prussian Empire after a "lesser German" solution had been agreed upon, see Günter Butzer, Manuela Günter, and Renate von Heydebrand, "Strategien zur Kanonisierung des 'Realismus' am Beispiel der *Deutschen Rundschau*," *Internationales Archiv für Sozialgeschichte der deutschen Literatur* 24, no. 1 (1999): 58–60.

national consciousness among its citizen-readers. At the same time, the title page listed alphabetically the far-flung urban booksellers around the globe, from Alexandria to Zurich, where its pages could be purchased.[28] It thereby emphasized its ambition to create a community of German readers beyond the borders of the German Empire, a transnational German-speaking diaspora whose own loyalty to the colonial empire would be strengthened by reading the periodical, thereby acknowledging that a sense of nationhood was contingent on a global, imperial consciousness. The inclusion of select Austrian and Swiss authors was integral to balancing this simultaneously nationalist and transnational mission. While including them initially underwrote Rodenberg's vision of a pan-German (*großdeutsch*) literary canon, a vision Keller very much shared, examples of Swiss literature by Keller or Conrad Ferdinand Meyer were also thought to provide the newly extant German citizen with an education in federalist political values that were necessary to balance the German overemphasis on a classical cultural education.[29] The *Züricher Novellen*, for one, takes the periodical's political purpose to heart and places the question of the good citizen's education at the center of its frame narrative. Appropriately, just as the cover of the bound *Deutsche Rundschau* marked its commitment to nation building in the red, black, and gold cover, so too did the first publication of the *Züricher Novellen* display a bright red cover (with black-and-gold lettering and embossment). The binding thus advertised the volume's commitment to the (political) education of the good German citizen in the spirit of Swiss federalism.

Along with providing an overview of a unified field of knowledge, the *Deutsche Rundschau*, like other periodicals of the era,

---

28. See, for example, the title page of the *Deutsche Rundschau* quarterly volume containing the first three installments of *Das Sinngedicht*: *Deutsche Rundschau* 26 (January–March 1881), title page.

29. "As a result of German education, Switzerland in turn became a political model for Germany—not with regard to its concrete constitution but with regard to its national consciousness, which the *Deutsche Rundschau* set out to promote in accordance with its program. [. . .] In this argumentative context, Swiss literature became a necessary component of German literature." Butzer, Günter, and Heydebrand, "Strategien zur Kanonisierung des 'Realismus,'" 64.

aspired to serve as an archive of the knowledge gathered in its pages. Graevenitz is again to the point when he writes that their pages were cast as "memoria houses" or "memory books for culture and education."[30] While each issue acted as a small-scale repository, the periodical's archival ambitions were only fully satisfied when the single issues were bound together at the quarter's end in book form and equipped with a table of contents providing an overview of its pages. After all, issues of the *Deutsche Rundschau* were not merely meant to be read and discarded but instead collected in the format of a book using the book covers provided to subscribers. As a book volume, the periodical transcended its initial ephemerality and became an encyclopedic archive of knowledge. A periodical's projection of itself as a book in the making, as Gowan Dawson explains, also helped ensure a market of readers among wealthier subscribers who did not wish to associate themselves with trivial and inexpensive periodicals.[31] Especially attuned to its function as an archive, the *Deutsche Rundschau* entirely abstained, unlike *Die Gartenlaube* or *Über Land und Meer*, from publishing news and instead placed what it hoped to be the perpetuation of the German literary canon as its lead. Claudia Stockinger emphasizes the affinity of the *Deutsche Rundschau* for the book format particularly forcefully in her history of *Die Gartenlaube* when she writes, "The *Deutsche Rundschau* [. . .] produced such a unity against or despite its periodicity. [. . .] *Die Gartenlaube* was conceived as a periodical but could become in addition a book; the *Deutsche Rundschau* was conceived as a book yet still

---

30. Gerhart von Graevenitz, "Memoria und Realismus: Erzählende Literatur in der deutschen 'Bildungspresse' des 19. Jahrhunderts," in *Memoria: Vergessen und Erinnern*, ed. Anselm Haverkamp and Renate Lachmann (München: Wilhelm Fink, 1993), 288, 283. As Frank, Podewski, and Scherer point out, this archival function differentiated the monthly periodical from more frequently published newspapers: "Instead of current affairs, they were concerned with selecting and presenting what was true and valuable with a proclivity to a nationalist, patriotic point of view." Frank, Podewski, and Scherer, "Kultur—Zeit—Schrift," 19.

31. See Gowan Dawson, "Paleontology in Parts: Richard Owen, William John Broderip, and the Serialization of Science in Early Victorian Britain," *Isis* 103, no. 4 (December 2012): 657.

remained in addition a periodical."³² Considerations for the anticipated bound-book format are especially apparent in the publishing history of *Das Sinngedicht*, whose initial publishing date was postponed no less than five times, not only because Keller could not provide the necessary manuscript but also because Rodenberg planned for the publication to span one or two periodical quarters such that the serialized parts of the text would ultimately be bound in one or two volumes.³³

That the ephemeral character of the periodical was but a mere transitory moment on the way to its final book format is perhaps best demonstrated by Keller's own handling of his copy of the *Züricher Novellen* in the *Deutsche Rundschau*. When preparing the second printing of the *Züricher Novellen* as a book edition with Weibert Verlag, Keller created his own manuscript by cutting apart the relevant issues of the *Deutsche Rundschau* and collating them into a continuous text onto which he could enter his own revisions, a procedure of copy and paste similar to his making of a typescript of "Die mißbrauchten Liebesbriefe" from the preprint in the *Deutsche Reichs-Zeitung*.³⁴ The procedure of copy and paste was premised on the realization that the format of the single-author book necessitated dismantling the holistic vision of the *Deutsche Rundschau*, for which the juxtaposition of dissimilar texts was essential. With the help of scissors and thread, Keller could transform the periodical into the template for a single-author book. A literary culture saturated with easily accessible and affordable periodical literature meant that authors like Keller, or the character Georg Nase in "Die mißbrauchten Liebesbriefe," could perpetuate their literary corpus not by crafting new texts but by using the methods of cut and paste, or needle and thread, to compile new editions from their

---

32. Claudia Stockinger, *An den Ursprüngen populärer Serialität: Das Familienblatt "Die Gartenlaube"* (Göttingen: Wallstein, 2018), 78.

33. The *Deutsche Rundschau*, published monthly, began its subscription year in October. Each volume of the bound periodical contained three issues, that is, three months. Ultimately, *Das Sinngedicht* began in the January 1881 issue so that the installments for January, February, and March would be contained in one volume.

34. Keller reports on this process in a letter to Adolf Exner dated August 12, 1877, in *HKKA*, 22:532.

own preprints. It also bears noting that while Keller revised the first edition of *Der grüne Heinrich* by making corrections in the published volumes, he wrote to Theodor Storm that the task of revision would have been much easier with a pair of scissors: "The mere use of a blue pencil and scissors would have been the easiest and most felicitous method."[35] The value Keller attributes to scissors suggests that the use of the same tool by the avant-garde has a crucial prehistory in nineteenth-century media practices.[36]

Serial Erotics in *Das Sinngedicht*

A set of historical comparisons can help bring into view the serial erotics fundamental to *Das Sinngedicht* and the *Züricher Novellen*, in which sexual desire serves as the basic premise for the serial arrangement, propelling and structuring a pattern of repetition, variation, and accumulation. To return to my first point of comparison: *The Decameron*, in which the expression of sexual desire is forbidden among the group of storytellers and consequently displaced into the highly erotic hundred tales, serves as a powerful historical example of a serial erotics; the American television series *The Bachelor*, premised on the desire of the male star, and the global boom in spin-offs it has inspired over the past two decades, bespeaks its lasting cultural allure. Situating any of Keller's novellas within such a tradition of erotic series stretching from *The Decameron* to *The Bachelor* may seem far-fetched given the overwhelming prudishness of his romantic tales. Admittedly, although *Das Sinngedicht* is composed of love stories, sexual desire is at first nearly impossible to discern, though it gradually comes into view as integral to the plot's design.[37]

---

35. "Der bloße Gebrauch von Blaustift und Scheere wäre das Einfachste und Glücklichste gewesen." Keller to Theodor Storm, June 13, 1880, in *HKKA*, 19:425.

36. On the significance of the scissors to avant-garde practices, see Juliane Vogel, "Die Schere: Karriere eines Werkzeuges in den Künsten der Moderne," *Zeitschrift für Ideengeschichte* 13, no. 3 (2019): 75–86.

37. Schrader describes how the editor of the *Deutsche Rundschau*, Julius Rodenberg, haphazardly censored published texts in the interest of the public's morality. See Schrader, "Im Schraubstock moderner Marktmechanismen," 19.

Indeed, Keller specifically conceived of the cycle *Züricher Novellen* as a break with the erotic license he took both in the scene of Judith bathing naked in *Der grüne Heinrich* and in the highly suggestive ending to the first edition of "Romeo und Julia auf dem Dorfe," both of which earned him unsparing criticism. "I am planning," he explained of the new project, "if the Lord wills, as the sanctimonious say, to write, piece by piece, a series of Zurich novellas, which should contain, in contrast to *Die Leute von Seldwyla*, more positive life."[38] In light of the fact that criticism regarding the novella primarily concerned its conclusion, the phrase "positive life" should be understood as life conforming to norms regarding sexual behavior.

Appreciating Keller's novellas as examples of a serial erotics may seem more plausible in light of Philipp Theisohn's claim that Keller's novella cycles renegotiate the failed alignment of eros and storytelling in *Der grüne Heinrich*, in which the protagonist's libidinal energies consistently reach a stalemate and can never be integrated into a history of his *Bildung*. *Das Sinngedicht* is one such experiment "at readjusting the relationship between eros and narration" (in Theisohn's reading, the *Sieben Legenden* is yet another).[39] Rather than attempt to integrate desire into a story of *Bildung* that would have to pair sexual and professional maturity, Keller's later novella cycles employ desire to perpetuate a serial structure with varying smaller narrative arcs. Like most of Keller's works, *Das Sinngedicht* originated in his early years in Berlin as a publishing project proposed to Vieweg. While still finishing *Der grüne Heinrich*, Keller suggested a collection of novellas to Vieweg—each "5–6 sheets [Bogen] long, the volume thus definitely 20–25 sheets"[40]—intended as a lighthearted, popular bestseller, a text he hoped would erase the monstrous impression he believed his novel would make on the public upon its completion: "I have also concocted some stories and novellas that

---

38. "Ich habe vor, wenn der Herr will, wie die Mucker sagen, nach u nach eine Reihe Zürchernovellen zu schreiben, welche im Gegensatz zu den Leuten von Seldwyla, mehr positives Leben enthalten sollen." Keller to Berthold Auerbach, June 25, 1860, in *HKKA*, 22:443.
39. Theisohn, "Mädchenbekehrer," 10.
40. "5–6 Bogen stark, der Band also jedenfalls 20–25 Bogen." Keller to Eduard Vieweg, November 5, 1853, in *HKKA*, 23.1:308.

[...] should erase the bad impression that my formless and monstrous novel will make on the masses."[41] Although *Das Sinngedicht* was published nearly thirty years after this first proposal to Vieweg, its mixture of romance (always in conformity with bourgeois norms), exoticism, adventure stories, confessional autobiographies, and nascent detective fiction—the full range of popular genres that came to dominate late nineteenth-century periodical storytelling—satisfied both Keller's original intention to write a lighthearted work and the norms of periodical publishing as well. It is thus no surprise that *Das Sinngedicht*—first published in the January to May issues of the *Deutsche Rundschau* in 1881 and, in the same year, as a book with Hertz Verlag—became Keller's greatest market success. That success, I would wager, is owed not only to the palette of popular genres it incorporates but also to its serial erotics.

The Male Gaze

Rather than provide an exhaustive reading of *Das Sinngedicht*, I excavate three key features of its serial erotics. Central to the serial erotics of *Das Sinngedicht* is the male protagonist responsible for initiating and perpetuating the erotic series; the series is maintained as a series by means of his indeterminate because as-yet-unsatisfied desire.[42] That logic prescribes that storytelling initiates with the ex-

---

41. "Ich habe auch einige Erzählungen und Novellen ausgeheckt, welche [...] den schlechten Eindruck verwischen sollen, den mein formloser und ungeheuilicher Roman auf den großen Haufen machen wird." Keller to Hermann Hettner, September 20, 1851, in *HKKA*, 23.1:302.

42. Scholarship on *Das Sinngedicht* has overwhelmingly focused on contextualizing the text in contemporaneous scientific discourses, particularly with respect to Darwin and Darwinism, with a nearly myopic focus on the first paragraph of the text. Such studies include Gerhard Kaiser, "Experimentieren oder Erzählen? Zwei Kulturen in Gottfried Kellers 'Sinngedicht,'" *Jahrbuch der deutschen Schillergesellschaft* 45 (2001): 278–301; Sabine Schneider, "Offene Versuchskulturen: Gottfried Kellers *Sinngedicht*," in *Labor der Phantasie: Texte zur Literatur- und Wissensgeschichte*, ed. Jutta Müller-Tamm (Berlin: Alpheus, 2015), 1–30; and Hubert Thüring, "'Kraft, oder so was': Poetik und Wissen(schaft) des Lebens in der Rahmenerzählung von Gottfried Kellers Sinngedicht," in *Lebenswissen: Poetologien des Lebendigen im langen 19. Jahrhundert*, ed. Benjamin Brückner, Judith Preiß, and Peter Schnyder

cavation of male desire. *Das Sinngedicht* appropriately begins with Reinhart reading the oft-cited epigram—"How do you want to turn a lily white into a rose red?/Kiss a white Galatea: blushing she will laugh"[43]—a text that reminds him of himself as an erotic catalyst, one capable of transforming white to red, the virginal to blushed. The recipe for turning white to red that becomes the governing principle of *Das Sinngedicht*, a kiss that first verifies a woman's chastity and then undermines it, makes evident that the text is driven by a thinly veiled fantasy of erotic transgression of the female body. The discovery of these sentences motivates Reinhart to put aside his scientific activities, to leave his dark, Faustian laboratory, and to initiate a serial kissing experiment that abides by the epigram's dictum. Reinhart's occupation as a scientist suggests that the narrative design of *Das Sinngedicht* is not only informed by the structures of serialized periodicals but also by the increasingly serialized nineteenth-century scientific experiment.[44] The serial arrangement of an experiment is here adapted to Reinhart's erotic exploits.

The serial plot begins, in other words, when the male protagonist makes himself available as an erotic catalyst; his desire and its ultimate satisfaction at the conclusion of the narrative when he kisses Lucie, making her laugh and blush, provides the minimalist plotline characterized less by progression, development, or education (i.e.,

---

(Freiburg im Breisgau: Rombach, 2016), 135–68. The erotics of the text, by contrast, have received significantly less attention, with the exception of Neumann, "Der Körper des Menschen."

43. "Wie willst du weiße Lilien zu roten Rosen machen?/Küß eine weiße Galathee: sie wird errötend lachen." Keller, *Das Sinngedicht*, in *HKKA*, 7:13.

44. On the adaptation of the serialized structure of experiments to the serialized formats for presenting and distributing scientific knowledge, including the emergence of the scientific journal, see Nick Hopwood, Simon Schaffer, and Jim Secord, "Seriality and Scientific Objects in the Nineteenth Century," *History of Science* 48, no. 3–4 (2010): 254. See also Geoffrey Cantor and Sally Shuttleworth, eds., *Science Serialized: Representations of the Sciences in Nineteenth-Century Periodicals* (Cambridge: MIT Press, 2004). Sabine Schneider, among others, notes that Reinhart's journey adopts the form of a serially conducted experiment. On her reading, Keller's text satirizes Reinhart's use of an experimental paradigm for pursuing what should be a romantic affair: "The subject of the satire is his [Reinhart's] arrogance of wanting to apply the scientific experiment to human romantic relationships." Schneider, "Offene Versuchskulturen," 24.

Bildung) than by repetition and variation. Peter Brooks's reading of the "virtually serial" structure of mid-nineteenth-century French novels, as adapted to the booming market of serialized *romans-feuilletons*, is particularly apposite to the opening scene of *Das Sinngedicht*: "Ambitious heroes of the nineteenth-century novel [. . .] may regularly be conceived as 'desiring machines' whose presence in the texts creates and sustains narrative movement through the forward march of desire, projecting the self onto the world through scenarios of desire imagined and acted upon."[45] Reinhart of *Das Sinngedicht* is designed as precisely such a "desiring machine" whose "forward march" (literalized in the journey he undertakes in the frame narrative) initiates and sustains the plot. That plot consists of a series of erotic scenarios primarily consisting of stories Reinhart himself narrates, each of which serves as an opportunity for imaginatively projecting himself into varied erotic situations. The plot only concludes when his desire comes to rest on a single object, which is to say, when it is resolved in matrimony.

In keeping with the mores of German-language realism and the programmatic ambitions of the *Deutsche Rundschau*, Reinhart's desire, responsible for initiating and sustaining the erotic series of the plot, is represented in the sublimated terms of his gaze. In the frame narrative of *Das Sinngedicht*, Reinhart leaves his laboratory to cure his eyes strained on account of his optical experiments and to conduct his kissing experiment, testing under what conditions he can bring a woman to laugh and blush simultaneously. His subsequent journey is described as an "eye treatment" (Augenkur).[46] On that journey he encounters a sequence of four women who represent the first four objects of his experimental program. Lucie, who will become the perceptual object on which Reinhart's desire comes to rest, represents the fourth woman in this initial series. Upon entering Lucie's home, Reinhart famously engages in a storytelling duel with her, in which six stories are told. Each story portrays yet another woman situated in a further set of experimental conditions: First,

---

45. Peter Brooks, *Reading for the Plot: Design and Intention in Narrative* (Cambridge, MA: Harvard University Press, 1992), 39–40.
46. Keller, *Das Sinngedicht*, in *HKKA*, 7:43.

Lucie tells the story of Salome's courtship (the third of the four women from the series of the frame narrative), then follow stories starring Regine, Hedwig, Hildeburg (Reinhart's mother), the two women (Feniza and Zambo) that Don Correa marries in the eponymous eleventh chapter,[47] the highly feminized Thibaut (a novella that occupies a very specific function in the series, as remains to be shown), and finally Lucie's own life story, for a well-rounded sum of ten. Keller's summary of *Die Leute von Seldwyla* as a set of ten "pictures of life" (Lebensbilder)[48] is equally applicable to *Das Sinngedicht*, as each "episode" portrays a female or, in one instance, feminine character. The many visual metaphors and media that nineteenth-century periodicals invoke to describe their programs become manifest in Reinhart's gaze and the series of impressions accumulated in that gaze.

The characterization of *Das Sinngedicht* as a series of "pictures of life" is especially apposite since each of the women is endowed with the quality of an image. The counterpart to the male gaze, in other words, is a series of women qua images. Appropriately, the image character of the women is made most explicit in the case of the women Reinhart encounters on his journey or portrays in his stories (as opposed to the ones in the stories narrated by Lucie or her uncle), so those who are exclusively represented from his perspective. For example, Reinhart first perceives Lucie as standing at a fountain washing roses in the style of a genre painting. The "sight of this image" (Anblick dieses Bildes) immobilizes him, mirroring the act of petrification to which his erotic gaze subjects the female protagonist.[49] Similarly, Erwin—the protagonist of "Regine," the first novella Reinhart narrates—becomes a "desiring machine," as Brooks would designate him, when he fixates on "the image of the poor maid" (das Bild der armen Magd) he encounters in the stairway, ultimately hoping to bring her home to his parents as "a picture of transfigured German national character" (ein Bild verklärten

---

47. The fact that the novella "Don Correa" features not one but two women and two marriages conforms to the two issues of the *Deutsche Rundschau* across which the novella was first printed.
48. Keller to Eduard Vieweg, April 2, 1844, in *HKKA*, 21:447.
49. Keller, *Das Sinngedicht*, in *HKKA*, 7:31.

deutschen Volkstumes).[50] Then, in the second novella Reinhart narrates, "Die arme Baronin," the male protagonist perceives the profile of the title character and is reminded of a "nun's head in an old German painting" (Nonnenkopf in einem altdeutschen Bilde);[51] in "Don Correa," the protagonist first appreciates his first and second wives as tableaus. Zambo, who will become his second wife, is explicitly described as "the beautiful sculpture" (das schöne Bildwerk).[52]

These stagings of the female characters as images, consistently portrayed from the perspective of the male protagonist's active gaze—textual instances of which could be extended nearly ad nauseam—should suffice to lay bare the dynamics of the gaze and the serial structure that emerges from it. Those dynamics endow the female characters with a timeless quality; they are both perceived in an ephemeral, singular moment (*Augenblick*) and removed from the fluctuations of time—qualities already associated with the perception of the female body in *Der grüne Heinrich* and which make them well suited to the function they serve in allegorization. On display here is an effect of the male gaze that Catriona MacLeod identifies as central to Keller's work and to German-language realism more broadly, namely, "the aestheticizing of woman, the act of conversion into a static, fetishized artwork."[53] The gaze of the male protagonist does not so much bring to life the female characters, as one might expect from a text that was initially conceived as a variation of the myth of Pygmalion, as arrest them as lifeless objects, a gesture naturally familiar from Keller's many scenes of premature burial.

From the perspective of *Der grüne Heinrich*, in which each of the predominant female characters is similarly highly aestheticized, immobilized, and made image-like, the structuring of *Das Sinngedicht* as an erotic series comes as no surprise. *Das Sinngedicht* might be understood as the elaboration of the erotic series (Anna, Judith, Agnes, Dortchen Schönfund) that Keller explored in his first novel.

---

50. Keller, *Das Sinngedicht*, in *HKKA*, 7:66, 83.
51. Keller, *Das Sinngedicht*, in *HKKA*, 7:139.
52. Keller, *Das Sinngedicht*, in *HKKA*, 7:248.
53. Catriona MacLeod, *Embodying Ambiguity: Androgyny and Aesthetics from Winckelmann to Keller* (Detroit, MI: Wayne State University Press, 1998), 199.

Or, for an even earlier example of a serial erotics in Keller's oeuvre, one might consider the cycle of poems "Von Weibern" from his volume *Neuere Gedichte*, in which each of the sixteen poems focuses on one woman who is named in the title and endowed with the character of a timeless image.[54] Elisabeth Strowick's insightful analysis of *Der grüne Heinrich* similarly points to how the male gaze becomes the driving force of a serially organized narrative. She argues that rather than exhibiting a plot of development or progression (a story of *Bildung* for example), the novel is organized as a "serialization of moments in series of 'now.'"[55] Within this arrangement, Heinrich figures neither as an active participant nor as an agent of his life story but as a passive observer of an unfolding series of timeless moments, which are revealed to be fantastic products of a perceptual apparatus instead of faithful mimetic imitations. What might be mistaken for the novel's naive mimetic realism in matter of fact reveals a serial artifice. If, in the opening scene of *Der grüne Heinrich*, Heinrich perceives the landscape around him as a series of moments unfolding in the serial ordering of writing, then Reinhart's gaze unfurls in a series of ten women, each of which is presented as an object of that gaze, that is, as an image. What these two texts, *Der grüne Heinrich* and *Das Sinngedicht*, share is that the male protagonist is identified with a gaze and, second, that this gaze serves as the intradiegetic source of the serial structure of the plot.

Woman as Image

As products of the male protagonist's desire, which initiates and sustains the series of images, each woman in *Das Sinngedicht* is little more than a fantastic erotic projection of a male ego. Each of the ten embedded narratives is a variation on the Pygmalion mythos,

---

54. On the image character of the women in *Der grüne Heinrich*, see Sabine Schneider, "Ikonen der Liebe: Heinrichs Frauenbilder," in Groddeck, *"Der grüne Heinrich,"* 201–19; and my discussion of scenes of Anna as constituting a barren *Augenblick* in chapter 1.

55. Elisabeth Strowick, "Gottfried Kellers Szenographie des Wirklichen," *Sprache und Literatur* 49, no. 2 (2020): 234.

in which the female body serves as the projection surface for male desire. But in keeping with nineteenth-century mores, desire expresses itself as a project of *Bildung* imposed on the female body. The woman qua *Bild* is made into a *Bildwerk*, to be formed and disciplined according to the idealizing imaginary of the male protagonist. Moreover, in remaking these women according to his desires, the protagonist remakes himself as an "artist" or, more concretely, as a socialized male self, a dynamic that Gerhard Neumann summarizes as "bourgeois Pygmalionism," in which vivification takes place as education.[56]

The projective, fantastical nature of the *Bildungsprojekt* is well illustrated in the scene in which Reinhart first encounters Lucie. Having navigated the uncharted territory surrounding Lucie's labyrinthine garden, which is alternatively described as a "web" (Netze), "wilderness" (Wildnis), or "chaos" (Wirrsal),[57] he finds "a thin gilded wire lattice" (ein dünnes vergoldetes Drahtgitter) that leads him to a gate: "At last he had arrived behind the fine lattice fence that enclosed the garden,"[58] a representation of stability and order. Like the lattice in Stifter's literary works, which, as Juliane Vogel demonstrates, serves as an "inaccessible border" that promises to lend the reality of things an otherwise unattainable order and calm, this trellised fence represents "stability" amidst chaos.[59] In Keller's *Sinngedicht*, the golden color of the wire lattice, reminiscent of a golden thread of life leading Heinrich to his fate, and the fairy-tale quality of the garden on the other side make evident that the perspicuous order of things is tantamount to a projective fantasy, a fantasy Reinhart, unlike Stifter's protagonists, can actually entertain and then realize by passing through the gate's entrance. At the same time, in entering through the gate or grid, Reinhart does nothing

---

56. Neumann, "Der Körper des Menschen," 566.
57. Keller, *Das Sinngedicht*, in *HKKA*, 7:29.
58. "Endlich war er hinter dem leichten Gitterchen angelangt, das den Garten verschloß." Keller, *Das Sinngedicht*, in *HKKA*, 7:30.
59. Juliane Vogel, "Stifters Gitter: Poetologische Dimensionen einer Grenzfigur," in *Die Dinge und die Zeichen: Dimensionen des Realistischen in der Erzählliteratur des 19. Jahrhunderts*, ed. Sabine Schneider and Barbara Hunfeld (Würzburg: Königshausen & Neumann, 2008), 43.

other than enter Lucie's literal hortus conclusus, an act of transgression that anticipates the end of the story in which he kisses her, making her blush red and designating her as his bride-to-be.

Once in the garden, Reinhart sets eyes upon Lucie washing roses at the fountain and is unsure whether what he sees is real or ideal. In questioning whether the shimmering appearance might be the fantasy of an "aesthete" (Schöngeist), he suppresses the fact that it is precisely his own erotic fantasy that generates the fantastic image: "The more unfamiliar the sight of this image was—which with its combination of the marble fountain and the white female figure, more closely resembled the ideal invention of an idle aesthete than real life—the more anxious the captive Reinhart became, sitting on horseback like a pillar."[60] In a playful reversal of the Pygmalion myth, not only is she petrified as an image, so too is he, so much so that he is described as a "statue" (Bildsäule). Only her invitation to enter the garden gate and so begin the *Bildungsprojekt* of storytelling reanimates him. He exits the heterotopic, disorienting space of the garden and reenters both the well-ordered domestic space of Lucie's home and the arrangement of his experimental program. Once again, it is worth noting how the erotic dynamic has changed since *Der grüne Heinrich*, in which the protagonist's desire cannot be incorporated into a form of narrative development and in which the project of socialization consequently fails. As Ernst Osterkamp points out, *Der grüne Heinrich* is exemplary of how heroes of the nineteenth-century bildungsroman must try their hand at drawing as part of the task of world making that comes with socialization; Heinrich's inability to draw the world as it is is symptomatic of his failings to fashion himself in sympathy with social expectations.[61] In *Das Sinngedicht*, by contrast, neither Reinhart

---

60. "Je ungewohnter der Anblick dieses Bildes war, das mit seiner Zusammenstellung des Marmorbrunnens und der weißen Frauengestalt eher der idealen Erfindung eines müßigen Schöngeistes, als wirklichem Leben glich, um so ängstlicher wurde es dem gefangenen Reinhart zu Mut, der wie eine Bildsäule staunend zu Pferde saß." Keller, *Das Sinngedicht*, in HKKA, 7:31.

61. Osterkamp writes:
Images play a decisive role in the biographies of the heroes of every German bildungsroman. *Bildung* is not conceivable without images, *Bilder*, in a

nor any of the protagonists of the embedded novellas makes any attempt to draw, paint, or write the world. Their efforts in world making are entirely directed at "the beautiful sculpture" (das schöne Bildwerke) they perceive in the female characters and adopt as their pet pedagogical projects, much like Viggi from "Die mißbrauchten Liebesbriefe" tries to remake his wife Gritli to fulfill his literary ambitions and ideals. In Keller's later texts, *Bildung* has been reinvented as the projective fashioning not of art but of women qua images. *Das Sinngedicht* thus fully aligns the erotic and aesthetic ambitions of the male hero in large part by making the latter subservient to the former.

Because the women of *Das Sinngedicht*, in a variation of the Pygmalion myth, are little more than erotic projections of a male fantasy that arrests if not deadens its objects, they exhibit the character of a fetish in both senses of the word. As Neumann emphasizes, the female characters are themselves object-like and only animated through male desire expressed as pedagogy. Second, each represents only a fragment, the fetishistic part of an unattainable whole.[62] Yet while each individual novella may demonstrate the impossibility of re-creating the mythic whole of Pygmalion's Galatea, the sum of the ten stories has a rather different effect. If we take their image character seriously, the text might be understood to generate a portrait gallery or image archive. The novella cycle effectively becomes a museal or archival technology for the projection and preservation of these serially organized ten portraits. Even if each individual woman, as the fantastic projection of the male gaze, necessarily represents a fetish or fragment, the series of stories compensates for

---

threefold sense: as a learning about Western painting in a process of aesthetic education, as a modeling of one's own biography based on images, and finally as the practicing of one's own perception of the world and of shaping a world artistically in the medium of drawing. That is why they all have to learn how to draw at some point, the sons and grandsons of Wilhelm Meister in the German bildungsroman, for drawing in some sense forms the transformative medium in which passive aesthetic learning about the world is translated into active aesthetic engagement with the world.

Ernst Osterkamp, "Erzählte Landschaften," in Groddeck, *"Der grüne Heinrich,"* 141.

62. Neumann, "Der Körper des Menschen," 565.

their part-and-parcel character in the accumulated set of ten. Gathered in the all-encompassing gaze of the male protagonist, the additive structure of the series achieves the programmatic ambitions of the *Deutsche Rundschau*: a holistic archive, a totality held together not with reference to the concepts of life, nature, or culture but in the petrifying gaze of the male protagonist.[63]

Not only the fantasy of accumulation but also the gendered constellation of *Das Sinngedicht* should be understood as replicating the programmatic ambitions of the *Deutsche Rundschau* and of nineteenth-century periodical culture at large. If the imaginative construction of the gaze—consisting of a male artist that constructs and beholds a feminized art object—is situated within the publishing venue of the *Deutsche Rundschau*, then it becomes evident in what way Keller's *Sinngedicht* models the gender politics of German realism. If the ambition of mixed-media periodical culture was specifically to create a shared cultural imaginary that would draw on the visual resources distributed in mass media,[64] then *Das Sinngedicht* constructs that community as organized around a male gaze; it is a literature made by men for men. In other words, *Das Sinngedicht* demonstrates one way in which German realism responds to the anxiety of a feminized literature that I sketched in the introduction. In the story of Reinhart's encounter with Lucie, the mythos of Pygmalion is adapted to combat a potentially feminized periodical culture and the cultural imaginary it engenders. Not least for that reason, *Das Sinngedicht* represents Keller's most conservative, moralistic, and reactionary text, one that is impossible to reconcile with the more fluid gender concepts imagined in *Der grüne Heinrich* and "Die mißbrauchten Liebesbriefe."

---

63. *Das Sinngedicht* thereby rehearses a gesture MacLeod excavates in Adalbert Stifter's *Der Nachsommer*. "The conversion of woman to artwork is explicable as a method of restoring lost totality in a world perceived as hopelessly fragmented." MacLeod, *Embodying Ambiguity*, 200. The rendering of the female characters as images in *Das Sinngedicht* simultaneously demonstrates their necessarily fragmented nature, while their accumulation within the series constitutes the attempt to restore them to a totality.

64. See Gerhart von Graevenitz, *Theodor Fontane: Ängstliche Moderne* (Konstanz: Konstanz University Press, 2014), 349.

Within this broader program of *Das Sinngedicht*, the ninth novella, "Die Berlocken," possesses a specific standing in the series of ten stories, not least because it projects the portrait of a highly feminized man rather than that of a woman.[65] "Die Berlocken," narrated by Lucie, recounts the story of the effeminate Thibaut, who receives, as a gift from Marie Antoinette, a pocket watch engraved and enameled on the back and in the inside of the lid with miniatures: on the back a small harbor set against the spreading rays of the sun and on the inside a tiny Amphitryon riding the ocean's wave.[66] In the tradition of the miniature, these two pictures "serve

---

65. Lucie introduces him as follows, rendering him childlike and effeminate:
Despite his military position, he was, as mentioned, still half-childish, and when he was not on duty, he would always stay with old aunts, cousins, and other suitable matrons, rummaging through their bandboxes, fashion wardrobes, and painted coffrets and letting them tell him stories while he feasted on their cream tarts, blancmanges, and sugar buns.

Trotz seiner kriegerischen Stellung war er, wie gesagt, noch halb kindisch und hielt sich, wenn er nicht Dienst hatte, immer bei alten Tanten, Basen und andern würdigen Matronen auf, deren Putzschachteln, Galanterieschränke und bemalte Coffrets er durchschnüffelte und von denen er sich Geschichten erzählen ließ, während er ihre Crêmetörtchen, Blancmangers und Zuckerbrötchen schmauste.
Keller, *Das Sinngedicht*, in *HKKA*, 7:275.

66. The passage reads:
On the back in a wreath of rocaille was engraved a small harbor and the sun rising in the background, spreading its rays very finely and evenly in all directions. The inside of the cover, however, was enameled with a colorful painting; a tiny Amphitryon rode in his chariot pulled by water horses on the green waves surrounded by a rose-colored veil, and in the blue sky stood a little white cloud.

Es war auf der Rückseite in einem Kranze von Rocaille ein kleiner Seehafen graviert, in dessen Hintergrunde die Sonne aufging und ihre Strahlenlinien sehr fein und gleichmäßig nach allen Seiten ausbreitete. Das Innere der Schale aber zeigte sich gar mit einer bunten Malerei emailliert; ein winziges Amphitritchen fuhr in seinem Wagen, von Wasserpferden gezogen, auf den grünen Wellen einher, von einem rosenfarbigen Schleier umwallt, und auf dem blauen Himmel stand ein weißes Wölkchen.
Keller, *Das Sinngedicht*, in *HKKA*, 7:276.

as fetishistic objects for (impossible) wholeness,"[67] and within the novella, they contrast with the open-ended form of the series the narrative unfolds. The original gifted watch comes with neither a chain nor a pendant, which Thibaut then acquires over the course of the narrative. To acquire these trophy-like appendages, Thibaut first deceives three women to obtain their pendant hearts made from coral, crystal, and opal, three stones that plainly stand in for the three women whom Thibaut has defrauded not only of their property but also of at least their hearts if not their virginity. The text makes no mystery of the play of substitution: "And he went to bed with the breloques and got up with them."[68] This original series of three fetish objects that Thibaut attaches to the chain along with his watch, and which are described in detail, is continued by means of a less-well-defined agglomeration of pendants that are described in passing as the fruits of his conquests.[69] Like *Das Sinngedicht*, the necklace is ultimately a serialized inventory of erotic exploits. Thibaut's final attempt to lure yet another woman with that very chain, an exoticized and eroticized "Indian girl" (indianische[s] Mädchen) he encounters in North America, spectacularly fails.[70] She successfully defrauds him of his necklace of pendants and marries a highly masculinized warrior. Lucie's story quite evidently satirizes Reinhart's experimental endeavor to kiss a series of women until he finds one who both laughs and blushes (Lucie herself, as she well knows, being the fourth woman in Reinhart's series). The embedded novella thus satirizes the basic dynamics

---

67. Catriona MacLeod, "Sweetmeats for the Eye: Porcelain Miniatures in Classical Weimar," in *The Enlightened Eye: Goethe and Visual Culture*, ed. Evelyn K. Moore and Patricia Anne Simpson (Amsterdam: Rodopi, 2007), 42.

68. "Und er ging mit den Berlocken zu Bett und stand mit denselben auf." Keller, *Das Sinngedicht*, in HKKA, 7:284.

69. The chain of pendants is ultimately described as saturated: "All the same, his pendant watch clinked and flashed [...]. In the end, he almost became bored with his fame, especially since there was no more room on his vest for new tokens of victory" (Gleichviel, sein Uhrgehänge klirrte und blitzte [...]. Zuletzt wurde ihm sein Ruhm fast langweilig, besonders da kein Plätzchen mehr für neue Siegeszeichen auf seine Weste vorhanden war). Keller, *Das Sinngedicht*, in HKKA, 7:284.

70. Keller, *Das Sinngedicht*, in HKKA, 7:285.

of the erotics of the frame narrative: A male protagonist "collects" a series of fetishized women in pendant form. It also recapitulates the serial order of the frame narrative of *Das Sinngedicht* in miniature and, in the image of the chain studded with pendants, lays bare the iterative and additive structure of the series of stories, whose open-ended form contrasts with tiny images depicted on the pocket watch, themselves (and the watch itself) models for the closure, containment, and wholeness associated with cyclical time.

In reproducing the structure of the frame narrative within the embedded novella (one notably saturated with images of miniatures and miniature images), the novella "Die Berlocken" enacts a principle of recursion also central to the novella "Der Landvogt von Greifensee." Recursively embedding the serial structure in miniature within the novella cycle serves to reinforce the structure of a frame narrative that may seem insufficiently strong to contain the series of ten portraits. In Keller's novella cycles, recursion strengthens the serial logic of the frame and additionally enables the high degree of self-reflexivity that scholars have more generally noted as a defining quality of nineteenth-century serialized literature.[71] In the case of "Der Landvogt von Greifensee," a recursive structure sets the stage for the allegorical enactment of a serialized format that overcomes the threat of fragmentation.

---

71. See Kelleter, "Five Ways of Looking," 18.

6

Allegorical Closure

Series and Cycle in the Züricher Novellen

In this chapter, the scale of argumentation shifts from the entirety of a novella cycle as exhibiting a serial structure, as in the case of *Das Sinngedicht*, to a single novella, "Der Landvogt von Greifensee," a further instance of Keller's serial erotics and one, like "Die Berlocken," specifically designed to reflect on serial arrangements. Also like "Die Berlocken," "Der Landvogt von Greifensee" allegorizes the novella cycle in which it is framed, namely, the *Züricher Novellen*, and thereby reveals how serialized formats do not merely represent a hindrance to literary form, a selling-out to the commercialization of literature, and an evacuation of original authorship, as it were. Instead, the novella refuses the open-endedness and ephemerality of the serial and imagines a form of closure that develops from, but also suspends, serialization. In short, the story's allegory enacts the closure of a serial form.

Here too the serial structure is premised on the erotic desire and desirability of the unmarried protagonist, desirability that primarily derives from his political and economic standing. In the novella, the eponymous character, the forty-two-year-old Landvogt von Greifensee, reflects on his past life and the five women he has courted, all five of whom turned him down. In the first half, he narrates the five courtships as a series of stories; in the second, he invites all five women to a flowery banquet at his estate where he will supposedly (but ultimately does not) select a wife. The novella concludes by recording his death as a bachelor at the age of seventy-seven many years after the banquet. Two features—regarding who narrates and what happens—help bring the structure of the novella and the way in which it models a novella cycle into view. To begin with, from a novella cycle we typically expect a gathering of storytellers who speak in turns. Johann Wolfgang Goethe's *Unterhaltungen deutscher Ausgewanderten* (1795), E. T. A. Hoffmann's *Die Serapionsbrüder* (1819), or Keller's *Das Sinngedicht* represent three models of such gatherings of storytellers. In "Der Landvogt von Greifensee," by contrast, the Landvogt retains an absolute monopoly on speech and storytelling. In the first half of the text, he recounts all five tales of his past courtships to his housekeeper, Marianne. Later, when the five women come to visit his castle, they are repeatedly admonished to stay silent: "Be calm" (Ruhig), he commands them.[1] The women in the novella are unanimously relegated to the position of passive listeners. The setting likewise echoes the famous frontispiece of *Die Gartenlaube*, in which the family patriarch reads aloud to a passive audience of his descendants (see figure 7); the unmarried Landvogt occupies the position of the paterfamilias, and since he does not possess a family, the women he courted compose his audience. By endowing the male protagonist with exclusive control over speech, the novella forcefully resists, even more so than *Das Sinngedicht*, both a late nineteenth-century boom in female authorship and the collective nature of periodical publishing in which editors, critics, and lay readers have a say in the progression of se-

---

1. Gottfried Keller, "The Governor of Greifensee," in *Perspectives on People: Five Stories by Gottfried Keller*, trans. Lawrence M. Washington (Sherman Oaks, CA: Banner Books, 1977), 159; Keller, "Der Landvogt von Greifensee," in *Züricher Novellen*, in *HKKA*, 6:240.

rials as well. Keller's novella relegates women to the position of mute recipients and so resists coding periodical literature as feminized writing.[2]

The second dramatic difference concerns what happens. As noted, the novella recalls five courtships, each of which failed to end in the anticipated marriage. Keller's contemporary Wilhelm Petersen spoke for many when he complained about the lack of a conventional happy ending. "The masses in northern Germany demand," he writes, "that they 'tie the knot' in the end, and although a principled opponent of marriage, I cannot help but share this vulgar taste to a certain degree."[3] The suspense and main narrative event we would expect from a tale of courtship are not simply missing; they are missing five times over and from the very beginning. What's more, the entire novella is constructed as an act of remembrance such that readers know from the very beginning that each of the courtships will fail and that the Landvogt will end the story as he begins it, namely, as a bachelor. The Landvogt's erotic availability—the central premise of the series of five stories—is instead only put to rest at the conclusion of the novella when he dies. "Der Landvogt von Greifensee" is then a story of an elderly man looking back at what has, in matter of fact, *not* happened. If the story does contain an event—the Landvogt's *not* marrying—it too has been dispersed over a series of episodes so as to ensure that there is no climactic moment of disappointment. This is a story about the noneventfulness of the past and consequently hardly seems to satisfy the expectations of newness we associate with the genre of the novella.[4]

Among early readers of "Der Landvogt von Greifensee," Theodor Fontane was particularly sensitive to the absence of eventfulness.

---

2. On the alleged femininity and thus triviality of periodical literature in contrast to the male-authored book, see Manuela Günter, "'Ermanne dich, oder vielmehr erweibe dich einmal!': Gender Trouble in der Literatur nach der Kunstperiode," *Internationales Archiv für Sozialgeschichte der deutschen Literatur* 30, no. 2 (2006): 38–61.

3. Wilhelm Petersen to Keller, June 17, 1877, in *HKKA*, 22:521.

4. For a summary history of the genre of the novella, including the "Novelle als Neuigkeit" and its growing significance in nineteenth-century entertainment culture, see Hannelore Schlaffer, *Poetik der Novelle* (Stuttgart: J. B. Metzler, 1993), 5.

His remarks provide a telling, if scathing, summary as well as a warning about the pitfalls of serial story arrangements for authors and readers alike. While scholarship today continues to thematize serial publications with regard to their supposedly action-packed (if simplistic) plots that rely on suspenseful cliffhangers to draw readers from one installment to the next, Fontane's reading is a valuable reminder that the repetitions of a series or serial could also just as well inspire little more than boredom or a headache. Fontane, one should note, read the original serialized publication of "Der Landvogt von Greifensee" in the *Deutsche Rundschau* and wrote from the cultural metropole of Berlin, where he was, by all accounts, happily married. From this position, the review imagines the unhappily unmarried Keller living with his sister in the cultural backwaters of provincial Zurich:

> The Landvogt, a charming character (but still a bit shady), was five times a suitor, also five times engaged, and still did not acquire a wife. The novella first tells his five love stories and then how as a middle-aged man he finally invites his five sweethearts, most of whom are long since married, to his castle. Each of the female figures is exquisitely characterized, and each love story is delightful, yet tires in the end and feels a familiar mill wheel in one's head. As well as the figures are distinguished, they still ultimately become muddled together, and in the end one is happy that the cruel game comes to a close. [. . .] Yet all in all, I have the impression as if he [Keller] has entered the "second epoch" when "art" must compensate for what has already been lost in actual "borax." This state of exhaustion is more likely to occur in small towns, where intellectual stimulus is lower, than in places where authors see and experience a lot.[5]

While Keller had originally imagined a story of six or seven women, the ultimate five was already too much for Fontane, for whom the basic structure of "Der Landvogt von Greifensee" is one of wearying repetition.[6] In attempting to entertain too much, it entertains too

---

5. Theodor Fontane, "*Züricher Novellen*," in *Aufsätze, Kritiken, Erinnerungen*, vol. 1, *Aufsätze und Aufzeichnungen*, ed. Jürgen Kolbe, unnumbered vol. of *Sämtliche Werke*, ed. Walter Keitel (München: Carl Hanser, 1969), 497.

6. "He lives in Greifensee Castle on the other side of the Zürichberg and invites six or seven pretty women on a Sunday to entertain himself and also for the pleasure of recalling memories after all the past love affairs" (Der haus't auf dem

little—a failure Fontane attributes to the cultural paucity of the Swiss author's experience and the ensuing decline of his creative talents. The fictional characters of the novella nearly share Fontane's assessment. The Landvogt's housekeeper, Marianne, who first listens to the series of five stories and then watches the banquet's festivities, expresses relief when it comes to an end: "I would never have thought that such a strange story like the one of five refusals could come to such an edifying and pleasant ending!"[7] Like Fontane, the intradiegetic recipient of this seemingly silly plot is happiest when it concludes.

The five novellas we now refer to as the *Züricher Novellen* stem from three different production and publishing histories, meaning that the making of the novella cycle necessitated an act of compilation. While "Das Fähnlein der sieben Aufrechten" was first published in *Berthold Auerbach's deutscher Volks-Kalender* in 1860, "Hadlaub," "Der Narr auf Manegg," "Der Landvogt von Greifensee," and the frame narrative that encompasses these three novellas first appeared serialized in the *Deutsche Rundschau* between November 1876 and April 1877. The fifth novella, "Ursula," on the other hand, was written in the summer and fall of 1877 in response to Ferdinand Weibert's proposal that the first book edition of the *Züricher Novellen* include a previously unpublished text. The book edition of the *Züricher Novellen* was thus intended as a reprint yet also as a more complete rendering of the original, as a reproduction and as the better original. Consequently, the five novellas we now refer to as the *Züricher Novellen* were first published together and in their currently familiar order in two volumes in 1877 by Weibert Verlag in Stuttgart (see the first column in table 1). There they were scheduled and appeared, surprisingly given Keller's proclivity for missing deadlines, in time for Christmas book sales—which

---

Schloß Greifensee jenseits des Zürichberges u ladet auf einen Sonntag, um sich einen Hauptspaß zu machen u auch ein Erinnerungsvergnügen, nach all' den vorübergegangenen Liebesstürmen 6 oder 7 hübsche Weibsbilder ein). Keller to Adolf Exner, August 27, 1875, in *HKKA*, 22:471.

7. "Ich hätte nie gedacht, daß eine so lächerliche Geschichte, wie fünf Körbe sind, ein so erbauliches und zierliches Ende nehmen könnte!" Keller, "Governor," 163; Keller, "Landvogt," in *HKKA*, 6:246.

Table 1. Five-part structures of the *Züricher Novellen* and the "Der Landvogt von Greifensee."

The five *Züricher Novellen* in Weibert Verlag's first book edition (1877)	The five installments of the *Züricher Novellen* in the *Deutsche Rundschau*	The five parts of "Der Landvogt von Greifensee" in both the periodical and book editions
Volume 1 1) "Hadlaub" 2) "Der Narr auf Manegg" 3) "Der Landvogt von Greifensee" Volume 2 4) "Fähnlein der Sieben" 5) "Ursula"	1) November 1876 "Hadlaub (Anfang)" 2) December 1876 "Hadlaub (Schluss)" 3) February 1877 "Der Narr auf Manegg" 4) March 1877 "Der Landvogt von Greifensee (Anfang)" 5) April 1877 "Der Landvogt von Greifensee (Schluss)"	1) Distelfink 2) Hanswurstel 3) Kapitän 4) Grasmücke 5) Amsel

Keller described to Theodor Storm as "the Christmas trade in publishing that breathes down my neck."[8] The first volume encompassed the three novellas contained within the frame story; the second comprised "Fähnlein der sieben Aufrechten" and "Ursula." Only in the first *Gesamtausgabe* of Keller's oeuvre, available for purchase beginning in 1889, were the five novellas of the *Züricher Novellen* printed together in a single volume (see table 1).

The first three novellas published in the *Deutsche Rundschau* possess a five-part structure insofar as they were published across five issues of the periodical. Each installment was titled *Züricher Novellen* followed by an installment number (1 through 5), the title of the specific novella, and, when a novella was split over two issues, the part number of that specific novella (see the second

---

8. "Schuld daran ist der buchhändlerische Weihnachtstrafic, der mir auf dem Nacken saß." Keller to Theodor Storm, June 25, 1878, in *HKKA*, 22:557.

column of table 1). As the publishing dates and missing installment for January 1877 make clear, Keller struggled to abide by the periodical's publishing deadlines, as would also be the case when publishing *Das Sinngedicht* and would again occur when writing *Martin Salander*; the missing installment of the *Züricher Novellen* in the January 1877 issue of the *Deutsche Rundschau* was replaced by Paul Heyse's "Die Frau Marchesa." It would be a mistake to simply blame this gap, or for that matter the unfinished quality of the novellas, on the rigorous publishing rhythm, a draconian editor, or, more broadly, on the unrelenting commercialization of literature. After all, throughout his career, Keller was notoriously quick to sign publishing contracts before putting pen to paper, having little more than a publishing format in mind and being consequently incapable of abiding by contractual timelines.

As I mentioned, "Der Landvogt von Greifensee" itself comprises five miniature novellas that recount the courtships of the five women and are situated within a frame narrative. In both the *Deutsche Rundschau* and in the later book editions, these five miniature novellas are set off from the embedded frame narrative by means of individual titles and line breaks such that they are typographically stylized as individual novellas contained in the novella's frame. The five imbedded novellas bear the titles of the Landvogt's infantilizing pet names for the five women he has courted. Three of the five are given generic names of birds.[9] They are (1) Distelfink (Goldfinch), (2) Hanswurstel (Little Clown), (3) Kapitän (Captain), and (4–5) Grasmücke (Warbler) and Amsel (Blackbird). The second installment of "Der Landvogt" in the *Deutsche Rundschau* begins with the story of Kapitän, whose name is the third title of the text: "Zurich Novellas./By/Gottfried Keller./(Conclusion.)/The Governor of Greifensee. (II.)/Captain" (Züricher Novellen./Von/Gottfried Keller./[Schluß.]/

---

9. Caroline Torra-Mattenklott specifically identifies the birds as miniaturized falcon specimens. The fact that the embedded stories, which I describe as miniature novellas, are titled with the names of miniaturized specimens, is significant as an example of Keller's smallness, as discussed in the epilogue. See Caroline Torra-Mattenklott, *Poetik der Figur: Zwischen Geometrie und Rhetorik; Modelle der Textkomposition von Lessing bis Valéry* (Paderborn: Wilhelm Fink, 2016), 228.

Der Landvogt von Greifensee. [II.]/Capitän).[10] The arrangement of the plot as a series of five and the breaks in the body of the text make it particularly well suited to being serialized, as the stories themselves contain interruptions. Indeed, the five miniature novellas could have also been adapted to a small periodical layout with a less generous allotment of space to works of literature than what the *Deutsche Rundschau* offered.

These five miniature novellas are framed by the story of how the Landvogt invites the five women to the castle and, seen more broadly, by the frame narrative of the *Züricher Novellen*. The structure of "Der Landvogt von Greifensee" can thus be schematized as follows, where F stands for frame, F_{ZN} for the frame of the *Züricher Novellen*, and F_{LG} for the frame of the "Langvogt":

$$F_{ZN}\ F_{LG}\ 1\ 2\ 3\ 4\ 5\ F_{LG}\ F_{ZN}$$

As scholars at least since Gerhard Kaiser have noticed, the five novellas framed in "Der Landvogt von Greifensee" anticipate the five novellas of the *Züricher Novellen*,[11] to which I would add that there is also a parallel to the five issues of the *Deutsche Rundschau* in which the original three novellas of the cycle appeared. Table 1 visualizes these multiple and, to an extent, recursive five-part structures. To these initial three structures of five, one can add that when the women first arrive at the Landvogt's estate, they are silent witnesses to his court of marital affairs, in which the Landvogt presides over five marital disputes and sentences the guilty parties to some form of absurd punishment. If these five micronarratives are included, the recursive structure of "Der Landvogt" becomes all the more poignant:

$$F_{ZN}\ F_{LG}\ 1\ 2\ 3\ 4\ 5\ F_{LG1\ 2\ 3\ 4\ 5}\ F_{ZN}$$

---

10. Gottfried Keller, "Züricher Novellen V (Schluß): Der Landvogt von Greifensee II," *Deutsche Rundschau* 11 (April 1877): 20.

11. See Gerhard Kaiser, *Gottfried Keller: Das gedichtete Leben* (Frankfurt am Main: Insel, 1981), 458.

In total, the structuring of the novella displays at least a fourfold series of five elements, each series recursively embedded within a larger sequence of the same. Although each individual series is finite, the recursions suggest that the number of sequences nested within one another might themselves be unending, thus bringing the open-ended quality of the series (in contrast to the formal closure of a cyclical form) into view. These multiple recursions and the series of five they rely on nonetheless set the stage for reading "Der Landvogt von Greifensee" as an interpolation into possible forms of closure in an age of serialization.

In yet a further variation of this recursive structure, four of the Landvogt's five courtships are initiated in similar acts of ordering, if not in the strict form of a series, then at least as acts of *Reihenbildung*. For example, in the first of the five miniature novellas recounting his courtships, he and Distelfink plant an orchard of fifty cherry trees. The fifty cherry trees (and the factor of five is of overt significance within the composition of the novella) are planted in rows of alternating species of red and white cherries—an echo of the very same color codes that are central to the serial order of *Das Sinngedicht*. Those rows can be visualized as R W R W R (where R stands for red and W for white). The fruit promised by the cherry trees, which are described as "young, slender little trees" (junge[] schlanke[] Bäumlein) and thus recall the idealized bodies of the women, does not, as one might expect, anticipate the fecundity of the Landvogt and Distelfink's sexual union, which never takes place and consequently bears no fruit.[12] Instead, the series adopts the coding of white as designating the purity of virginity and red as blushing or blemished, as familiar to us from *Das Sinngedicht*, to anticipate the marital status of the five women the Landvogt erotically pursues during his lifetime. The resulting series of R W R W R in effect stands for the alternating lost or retained virginal status of the five women when they arrive many years later at the Landvogt's castle. Three of them are married and thus tainted (red), and two are unmarried and in possession of their virginal status (white). In effect, the women too can be summarized with the series R W R W R. The series of

---

12. Keller, "Governor," 104; Keller, "Landvogt," in *HKKA*, 6:158.

cherry trees thus recursively maps or models the broader series of women from the novella.

The novella begins when the unmarried protagonist happens to meet the first of these five women he had previously unsuccessfully courted, giving rise to the desire to revisit all five episodes of his past. Arousing that desire, which will propel the remaining storyline, is premised on renouncing the state of renunciation he had previously resigned himself to, a doubling of renunciation that might also be interpreted as one of the novella's recursive structures: "Renunciation is never satisfactory in itself, and when there is nothing more to renounce, it ends up by renouncing itself."[13] Having renounced renunciation, he decides to interrupt his solitary bachelorhood by organizing the reunion with all five women at his estate—a gathering Catriona MacLeod glosses as a "'symposium' on the nature of love."[14] The whimsical decision is described as follows:

> He was suddenly seized by the desire to invite not only this one [Goldfinch] but also three or four other specimens of pretty creatures toward whom he once had also been similarly inclined. Thus, as he rode further, he felt a real yearning to see all his former flames together at the same time and to spend a day with them. [. . .] On his list of pet names, there was another one called Little Clown, another Warbler, one Captain, a fourth Blackbird, so that with Goldfinch there were five.
>
> Es befiel ihn plötzlich der Wunsch, nicht nur diese [Distelfink], sondern auch noch drei oder vier weitere Stück schöne Wesen bei sich zu versammeln, zu denen er einst in ähnlichen Beziehungen gestanden; genug, es erwachte, je weiter er ritt, eine eigentliche Sehnsucht in ihm, alle die guten Liebenswerten, die er einst gern gehabt, auf einmal bei einander zu sehen und einen Tag mit ihnen zu verleben. [. . .] Da gab es auf seinem Register der Kosenamen noch eine, die hieß der Hanswurstel, eine andere, die hieß die Grasmücke, eine der Kapitän, und eine vierte die Amsel, was mit dem Distelfink zusammen fünf ausmachte.[15]

---

13. "Die Entsagung kann sich nie genug thun, und wenn sie nichts mehr findet, ihm zu entsagen, so endigt sie damit, sich selbst zu entsagen." Keller, "Governor," 159; Keller, "Landvogt," in *HKKA*, 6:240.

14. Catriona MacLeod, *Embodying Ambiguity: Androgyny and Aesthetics from Winckelmann to Keller* (Detroit, MI: Wayne State University Press, 1998), 215.

15. Keller, "Governor," 97–98, translation modified; Keller, "Landvogt," in *HKKA*, 6:149.

What begins as a vague desire to gather three or four "pretty creatures" takes shape as the longing to gather all the women he has courted. The ensuing story is thus set in motion by the Landvogt's longing for beauty and the drive to collect or aggregate five objects from his past; it is a nearly museal drive to accumulate and to chronical. The course of the story thereby also reinforces the recursive form of the novella: First the Landvogt recalls the five women, then he conjures their presence by narrating the stories of the five courtships to the housekeeper, and then he invites the five to the estate. These three acts of recall reiterate and reestablish the series of five three times.

What both motivates and makes possible this aggregation of women is quite obviously the fact that he has married none of them. The series is again premised, in other words, on the erotic desire and availability of the male protagonist. Not only would marriage to any of the five have stopped the series short in its tracks, it also would have ostensibly robbed the Landvogt of any later desire to invite the five women to his castle and of the social license to do so. What sets the narrative in motion is, in other words, the freeing of an erotic potentiality that has escaped being made actual in being tethered to a single object. Unbound, that potential not only propels each further iteration of the series; it is also the condition, at the end of the Landvogt's life, for reiterating the series in its entirety in storytelling and the reason for his desire to aggregate five beautiful objects in his bachelor's home. The Landvogt's desire thereby equally motivates each of the three reiterations of the series. The Landvogt himself says as much when he reflects that it was precisely the failure of each of the individual courtships that made the series of five possible:

> For if the first of you had taken me, I would never have gone to the second one. If the second one had given me her hand, then the third would have always remained hidden from me, and so forth. I would not enjoy the good fortune of having a fivefold mirror of memory, not troubled by any breath of coarse reality.

> Denn hätte mich die erste von Euch genommen, so wäre ich nicht an die zweite geraten; hätte die zweite mir die Hand gereicht, so wäre die dritte

> mir ewig verborgen geblieben, und so weiter, und ich genösse nicht des Glückes, einen fünffachen Spiegel der Erinnerung zu besitzen, von keinem Hauche der rauhen Wirklichkeit getrübt.[16]

The last clause bears emphasis. Because he has not married any of them, they have become mere objects of his memory, images conjured, one might say, by his erotic fantasy, untouched by the vicissitudes of reality. It is for this reason that the women are primarily referred to by the Landvogt's pet names rather than by their given names—they are by no means intended to possess a self or a reality beyond the eroticized memory of the male protagonist. The fact that the women consequently belong to the domain of the imagination and not that of reality is nicely underscored by how, as the Landvogt remarks upon their arrival, none of the women seem to have aged since he last saw them. More image than person, they are just as beautiful as they were ten or twenty years ago, even though he himself has grown older. Although he stands in progressive, historical time, their serial order is a timeless one that emerges from an untethered erotic fantasy. Moreover, standing outside of time enables the women, as Moritz Baßler argues, to embody the very structure of allegory.[17] This situation of embodiment is made most explicit in the case of the second woman, who, though most often referred to by the comical pet name Hanswurstel, actually bears the name Figura; she is a personification of allegory itself. Here, like the prominent role the image of the thread of life plays in *Der grüne Heinrich*, Keller's specifically *real* allegory embeds elements clearly tagged as more traditionally allegorical in a realist setting and story.

---

16. Keller, "Governor," 158; Keller, "Landvogt," in *HKKA*, 6:239.

17. Baßler make the point that the Landvogt cannot marry because the women consist of timeless allegories that cannot be incorporated into a model of linear development such as a marriage: "As the opposite of the metonymic principle of progression, the image-like allegorical constellation freezes time." Moritz Baßler, "Den Mai gibt es nicht: Intensität und Code in Kellers Poetischem Realismus," in *Kellers Erzählen: Strukturen—Funktionen—Reflexionen*, ed. Philipp Theisohn (Berlin: Walter de Gruyter, 2022), 249. However, my claim in the coming pages that the set of five women serves as five topoi of the Landvogt's biography and as real allegories contradicts Baßler's argument that allegory and linear temporalities are incompatible.

While the women may stand outside time, they are not prevented from being subsumed within a broader temporal order: that of the Landvogt's own life. Tracking the diegetic time points attributed to the narcissistic projections of the bachelor's fantasy reveals that linear order. Careful attention to the details of the five embedded novellas reveals that the first courtship took place when the Landvogt was twenty-five, the second when he was twenty-six, the third when he was thirty-three, and the fourth and fifth at thirty-four. The Landvogt narrates the stories of the courtships and invites the women to his home at the age of forty-two, and he dies at the age of seventy-seven. In effect, each woman marks a different station, one might say a topos, of the Landvogt's biography. Because these five Dornröschen-like women are timeless and because the erotic fantasy of the bachelor is free to recall them, their five stories together reconstruct the totality of the Landvogt's life. What might have been a romantic novella is instead a biography, or better, a necrology.[18] Conversely, the continuity of the Landvogt's life underwrites and naturalizes what otherwise might appear to be an arbitrary series of five. While the initial nebulous desire to collect four or five beautiful women might have prompted a disordered accumulation of unrelated women, the fact that each marks a topos in his biography ensures that they are of one kind and that their ordering is determined by an external principle, the chronology of the Landvogt's life. What the narrative exemplifies, in other words, is not an arbitrary order but the form of a series organized by discernible principles.

The serial form of the Landvogt's life is wonderfully underscored by the contrasting figure of the housekeeper, Marianne. Although Marianne primarily serves as an aural and visual spectator of the novella's events, the reader learns in passing that she joined the estate only after having lost all of her nine children: "They acquired with time nine children whom she loved to the utmost and with all the passion she possessed. But they all died, and each time it almost

---

18. On the significance of necrologies and their narrative patterns in the nineteenth century, see Gerhart von Graevenitz, "Geschichte aus dem Geist des Nekrologs: Zur Begründung der Biographie im 19. Jahrhundert," *Deutsche Vierteljahresschrift für Literaturwissenschaft und Geistesgeschichte* 54, no. 1 (1980): 105–70.

broke her heart."[19] The mention of these nine children suggests that if she were the protagonist, Marianne's life might too be narrated as a series of prematurely interrupted libidinal attachments. While the early deaths of the nine children mean that they be cannot gathered in this world, Marianne anticipates her happy reunion with her series of nine in the next world, a banquet perhaps not entirely unlike the one organized by the Landvogt.[20] In the meantime, her necrology waits to be narrated, its serial form already having been prefigured in these nine tragic losses.

As I have noted, the chief plot driving "Der Landvogt von Greifensee" is the desire to collect these five objects, these five women, in a simultaneous presence, "together at the same time." The Landvogt achieves this aggregation when he and all five women are seated together at a table in an arrangement described in careful detail. The Landvogt sits at the head of the table, Distelfink across from him, Hanswurstel to his right, and Amsel to his left. Kapitän and Grasmücke, in a curious moment of ambiguity, occupy the two remaining seats. The five women, whose courtships by the Landvogt have just been narrated in serial form, are now seated together in one place at one time. Gathered in the round, they might seem to undo the linear, forward-directed historical trajectory in which they were serially introduced and to present a structure in the round in its place. Sitting at the head of the table, the Landvogt further undoes that serial order when he gazes back and forth between the five different women, opening different possible orderings and combinations. His gaze, in other words, unbinds the women from their original serial order and creates, it first seems, the possibility of endless variation determined only by his visual pleasure: "With a warm feeling of happiness he now saw them gathered at his table, and he led the conversation on all sides with great dexterity so that he could look at all of them in turn without disturbing the good tone, going

---

19. "Sie bekamen nach und nach neun Kinder, die sie über alles liebte und mit der ganzen Leidenschaftlichkeit, die ihr eigen war; aber alle starben hinweg, was ihr jedesmal fast das Herz brach." Keller, "Governor," 99; Keller, "Landvogt," in *HKKA*, 6:151.

20. See Keller, "Governor," 163; Keller, "Landvogt," in *HKKA*, 6:247.

back and forth or jumping around as he liked."²¹ However, this playful back-and-forth of his gaze gives way to a singular geometric structure, that of a pentagram, a highly symbolic star that perhaps inadvertently suggests the Landvogt's membership in a society of Freemasons. The Landvogt himself points out their starlike seating arrangement:

> I greeted you today, my dears, with the motto "Time brings roses" and surely it was very suitable since it brought a magical pentagram of five such beautiful heads before my eyes in which the magical line moves secretly from one head to another, crossing itself and returning to itself at each point, thus deflecting all harm from me.
>
> Ich habe Euch, Verehrte, heute mit dem Sprichworte: Zeit bringt Rosen! begrüßt, und sicherlich war es wohl angebracht, da sie mir ein magisches Pentagramma von fünf so schönen Häuptern vor das Auge gezeichnet hat, in welchem die zauberkräftige Linie geheimnisvoll von einem Haupte zum anderen zieht, sich kreuzt und auf jedem Punkt in sich selbst zurückkehrt, alles Unheil von mir abwendend!²²

If the five lines of the pentagram are drawn in the order of the series of courtships stories (Distelfink → Hanswurstel → Kapitän → Grasmücke → Amsel → Distelfink), it becomes clear where Grasmücke and Kapitän must be seated: Grasmücke sits to the right, Kapitän to the left of the Landvogt (see figure 15). Alternatively, if instead of drawing the lines in the order given by the series, the pentagram is regarded as a closed, completed form, then none of the individual lines can be isolated or given temporal priority. As a closed shape, the pentagram both contains but also suspends the order of the series; it endows the series with a celestial form.

In order for the seated women to serve as a "fivefold mirror of memory," as the Landvogt describes it, he must project himself from

---

21. "Mit einem warmen Glücksgefühle sah er sie so an einem Tische versammelt und unterhielt das Gespräch nach allen Seiten mit großer Beflissenheit, damit er ohne Verletzung des guten Tones alle der Reihe nach ansehen konnte, vor- und rückwärts gezählt und überspringend, wie es ihn gelüstete." Keller, "Governor," 156; Keller, "Landvogt," in *HKKA*, 6:236.

22. Keller, "Governor," 158; Keller, "Landvogt," in *HKKA*, 6:239.

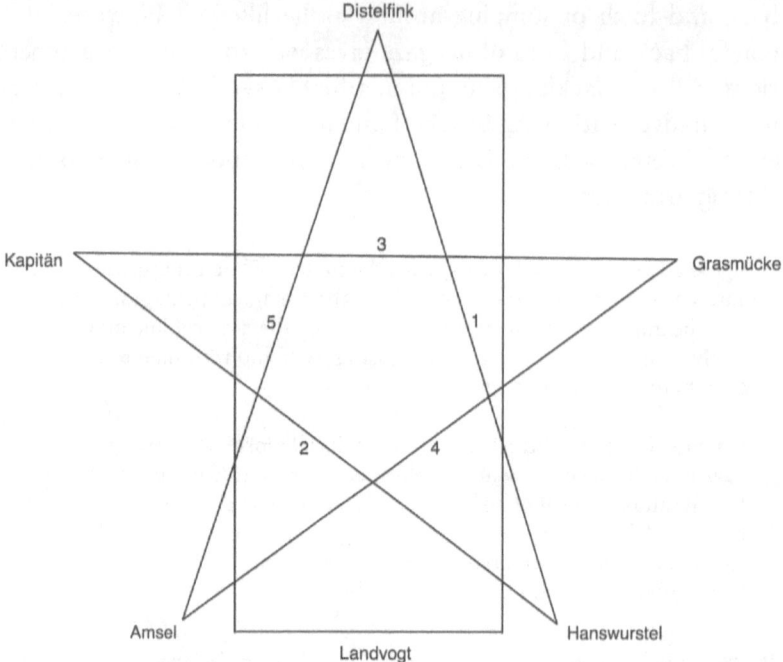

Figure 15. The seating arrangement at the Landvogt's banquet.

his side of the table into its center, as only from there can he see himself reflected in each of the five points. In other words, the Landvogt must imaginatively draw the star and then occupy its center. The Landvogt's placement of himself in the center to see his five reflections, along with the iconographic use of the pentagram since at least Leonardo da Vinci's popular *Vitruvian Man*, suggests that the pentagram consisting of the five women is a form by means of which he comes to recognize his own perfection.[23] Just as the women serve as narrative topoi for telling the Landvogt's life story, so too does their composition at the banquet table, the archive of his erotic

---

23. For a discussion of the historical iconography of the pentagram and an alternative interpretation of the Landvogt's table arrangement, see Torra-Mattenklott, *Poetik der Figur*, 220–24. Torra-Mattenklott interprets the geometric figure as a type of spell protecting the Landvogt from marriage.

exploits, create a complete image of his aggrandized selfhood. It is an image whose form retains but also transcends the previous serial order.

The image the Landvogt acquires of himself as reflected in the seating arrangement is all the more aggrandized if one not only regards the series of five as a pentagram but also takes seriously the Landvogt's opening exclamation "Time brings roses," which might first be read as a merely sentimental if not chintzy remark. In matter of fact, the roses alert us to the fact that the Landvogt is imagining the five women to conform to the simultaneously serial and cyclical order of a rosary, itself consisting of five sets of ten beads—precisely the same factors (and sum) as the cherry trees he and Distelfink planted long ago. Like in Lucie's story of Thibaut, the significance of the individual novella as an allegorical representation of the novella collection in total is again marked with the image of a pendant, though this time with one very dissimilar to the valuable, glittery chain Thibaut takes to bed. While in the rosary each decade of the first stations marks one of the mysteries in Christ's life or, when arranged as a pentagram, the five wounds of Christ's body, here each woman represents one "mystery" or "wound" in the life of the Landvogt. And as is fitting for the rosary, the five are joined by the housekeeper, Maria(nne), who stands to the side of the banquet table as an appendage or extension to the five women akin to the rosary's antiphon beads. In sum, the rosary, like the Landvogt's placement of the women around the table and the constellations he imagines them to form, consists of fifty-nine beads, a decade for each woman, and nine for Marianne—who, as noted, buried nine infants. It is then fitting that Marianne, as the diegetic recipient of the Landvogt's narrative, points back to the Landvogt himself, just as the antiphon beads of the rosary lead back to the pendant cross and Christ himself.

Arranged as a pentagram and as a rosary, the women come to represent the topoi of the Landvogt's life and become an image of the near-Christlike perfection he has attained through the trials of his courtships. Insofar as the rosary can be interpreted either as a linear string of beads or, alternatively, as a closed circuit, the comparison of the women to the rosary likewise signals the possibility that their series can be reconfigured as the closed forms of a star or pendant. It is also worth noting that as a "fivefold mirror," they also signal, as do mirrors throughout Keller's work, a programmatic reflection on his realist poetics. While the realism of the Landvogt's life story is ostensibly premised on its mirroring of an anterior history (in this case, his courting of the five women), closer inspection reveals reality to be an artfully constructed projection of a male gaze. The Landvogt's life story is not given and retold but instead created out of the arrangement of these women according to the desires of the bachelor's fantasy.

Finally, if one recalls the context of the text's first publication in the *Deutsche Rundschau*, then the unfolding of "Der Landvogt von Greifensee" from a linear series to the form of the pentagram or rosary suggests that this story is about more than the perfected form of the Landvogt's self or the artifice of poetic realism. The central transition of the novella from a potential open-ended series to a bounded form performs an allegorical reenactment of the transition from the periodical, serialized issues of the journal to the bound form of a book in which the single issues achieve a spatial and temporal simultaneity. To summarize, in "Der Landvogt von Greifensee," the five stories of the five courtships are first narrated as a series, but when the five women later arrive at the castle and are placed as a pentagram around the banquet table, they achieve spatial and temporal closure. If each of the five women is taken to embody one of the five miniature novellas in "Der Landvogt von Greifensee," which themselves stand for the five issues of the *Deutsche Rundschau* and the five novellas in the book edition of the *Züricher Novellen*, then the gathering of the five women enacts the gathering of the five novellas in one volume. The banquet, like the book format, fulfills the ambitions integral to the *Deutsche Rundschau* discussed above: to provide an overview and to archive unity within a single volume. The gathering of five women provides a comprehensive and intelligible overview of the Landvogt's erotic exploits, indeed, an overview of his life and self. Finally, just as the book, as archive, performs the task of storage or also memorialization and thus relieves its readers of that task, so too does the presence of the five women render unnecessary the Landvogt's own act of remembering and with it also serial narration. What was in the past has been made present, and in that present, it achieves a formal and symbolic closure that it could otherwise never have possessed. When gathered together and given an immutable form that supersedes the original linear, serial order, the series of the novella cycle achieves closure not despite but within the conditions of serialized publishing. To repeat the point: The narrative enacts the possibility of closure emergent from the order of a series, a closure that the open-ended serialized formats of the periodical seem to foreclose and can only supply in recourse to a bound book format.

Serial Reproduction

To conclude, I want to consider very briefly one further way the novella engages an aspect of nineteenth-century periodical literature, namely, the status of originals in the age of industrialized serial reproduction, which replaces the singular auratic object with a plurality of objects, each with an equal claim to the status of an original.[24] As a method aimed at the mass reproduction and the commodification of literature, serialization calls into question the aesthetic autonomy if not the aura of the artwork, for one because it threatens any notion

---

24. As Maria Magnin notes in her insightful reading of "Der Landvogt von Greifensee," the same question of artistic originality in the epoch of mass serialized reproduction is posed in relation to Salomon Gessner's porcelain factory that the novella's characters visit. Gessner's painted porcelain products are described as serially produced luxury commodities, yet they retain the properties of genuine—one might say, auratic—art. Magnin concludes: "Keller thus manages to demonstrate in the smallest space how the boundaries between luxury (object) and art (work) were blurred in the industrial age," an argument I would apply to Keller's vision for literature in an age of mass reproduction as well. Maria Magnin, "Landluxus für Städter in Gottfried Kellers 'Landvogt von Greifensee,'" in *Orte des Überflusses: Zur Topographie des Luxuriösen in Literatur und Kultur der Moderne*, ed. Hans-Georg von Arburg, Maria Magnin, and Raphael J. Müller (Berlin: Walter de Gruyter, 2022), 155.

of aesthetic specificity.²⁵ However, to take the so-called preprints of Keller's novellas in periodicals seriously means to call into question the long-standing status of the final edition in a collected-works edition as the authoritative text most reflective of the author's intentions and as possessing aesthetic specificity, and to embrace a plurality of texts as a feature of nineteenth-century literature.²⁶ It means, in other words, to call into question the performance of textual stability enacted by a collected-works edition. Tracking the genealogy of print editions and reading the novella "Der Landvogt von Greifensee" as reflecting on the very structure of periodical publishing undermine that status of the book publication as the authoritative text insofar as only consideration of the periodical brings the allegorical significance of the narrative structures into view; the structure and significance of the serial design of the plot only become apparent against the background of periodical publishing. Print histories thereby bring to light yet a further dimension of what Eric Downing has observed as the propensity of German realist authors for twice-told tales, a convention to which "Der Landvogt" abides. While Downing focuses on stories like Keller's *Sieben Legenden* that are borrowed from elsewhere or are at least fictionally cast as being borrowed, the multitude of editions of individual works constitutes a further case of realist repetition. Downing's observation that Keller attributes the status of original (*Urfabel*) not to the source but to the retold or recovered tale is also applicable to publication histories.²⁷ We too have come to accept that not the first publication but the "last" represents the authoritative form of a work of literature.

---

25. See Russell Berman, "Writing for the Book Industry: The Writer Under Organized Capitalism," *New German Critique* 29 (1983): 50.

26. On the origins of relying on collections rather than periodical prints in Wilhelm Dilthey's vision of the literary archive, see Vance Byrd and Sean Franzel, "Introduction: Periodical Literature in the Nineteenth Century," in "Periodical Literature in the Nineteenth Century," ed. Vance Byrd and Sean Franzel, special issue, *Colloquia Germanica* 49, no. 2–3 (2016): 105.

27. "Thus, his [Keller's] tale derives its realist quality from its retelling both of the 'actual event' and of the reality that constantly reveals itself as a repetition of an *Urfabel*. [. . .] Even as an original it seems only to manifest itself in its re-presentation." Eric Downing, *Double Exposures: Repetition and Realism in Nineteenth-Century German Fiction* (Stanford, CA: Stanford University Press, 2000), 93.

The question of how to determine the authoritative edition of a work in an age of mass reproduction, that is, which text in a chain of reproductions constitutes a textual original, is central to the *Züricher Novellen* and "Der Landvogt von Greifensee." For one, across the different frame narratives, the novella is cast as the product of four relays; four relays, four imitations, bring forth the authoritative text. First, within the novella, the Landvogt narrates the five stories to his housekeeper, Marianne. Second, in the novella, a third-person narrator relays the Landvogt's speech. The narrator claims to have done so faithfully, having only edited out Marianne's interruptions so as to make the narrative more intelligible, thereby adopting a function comparable to that of an editor responsible for coherence rather than content. The narrator explains:

> After the ice had been broken, he [the Landvogt] informed her [Marianne] from time to time, as it seemed fitting, about the five, and explained how it had all come about. In many different moods, the narrator and the listener often became confused and switched roles. Let us now tell the stories, but with everything properly divided, rounded off, and arranged so that we can understand them.

> Nachdem das Eis einmal gebrochen war, machte er sie nach und nach, wie es sich schickte, mit den fünf Gegenständen bekannt und stellte ihr dar, wie es sich damit begeben habe, wobei der Vortragende und die Zuhörerin sich in mannigfacher Laune verwirrten und kreuzten. Wir wollen die Geschichten nacherzählen, jedoch alles ordentlich einteilen, abrunden und für unser Verständnis einrichten.[28]

The narrator provides, we are to believe, a well-formatted reproduction of the Landvogt's speech, an editing job that divides the five objects or five stories in a perspicuous and intelligible order, namely, that of a series.

To these two relays are added two more staged in the frame narrative of the *Züricher Novellen*, which is set in 1820s Zurich. The story begins with a satirical portrait of the young and gloomy Herr

---

28. Keller, "Governor," 102, translation modified; Keller, "Landvogt," in *HKKA*, 6:155.

Jacques, who is profoundly worried that he has been born into an era where it is no longer possible to be original, in which personality too has become a matter of mass production. He worries "that nowadays there aren't any genuine people, not any originals anymore, but just people by the dozen and uniformly manufactured people by the thousand."[29] His fears seem realized when he attempts to write a new version of Ovid's *Metamorphoses* but gets no further than the title, which is to say, the first step in formatting his manuscript. Unhappy, Herr Jacques goes for a walk and happens to meet his godfather, who, in turn, offers to cure him of this misguided notion of originality by providing him with the historical examples of the *Züricher Novellen*, aiming to teach him that "only someone who deserves to be imitated is a good original!"[30] Jacques's godfather thereby appears to voice Keller's own doubts about artistic originality: In oft-cited lines, Keller insists on a "dialectic of cultural evolution" in which poetic material is constantly recycled and readapted, belying claims to originality and motivating realism's propensity to twice-told tales.[31] While Keller's remarks are typically read as a critique of Romantic genius, the question of originality takes on yet

---

29. "Daß es heutzutage keine ursprünglichen Menschen, keine Originale mehr gebe, sondern nur noch Dutzendleute und gleichmäßig abgedrehte Tausendspersonen." Keller, *Züricher Novellen*, in *HKKA*, 6:7.

30. "Ein gutes Original ist nur, wer Nachahmung verdient!" Keller, *Züricher Novellen*, in *HKKA*, 6:22.

31. Keller writes to Hettner:
All poetic material is part of a peculiar or rather very natural, continual cycle. [...] In one word, there isn't any individual, sovereign originality and novelty in the sense of arbitrary genius and conceited subjectivists (proof: Hebbel, who is ingenious, but precisely because he is always obsessed with the new, he invents such extremely poor plots). The only thing that is new in a good sense is what emerges from the dialectic of cultural evolution.

Das Ganze des poetischen Stoffes befindet sich in einem merkwürdigen oder vielmehr sehr natürlichen fortwährenden Kreislaufe. [...] Mit Einem Worte: es gibt keine individuelle souveraine Originalität und Neuheit im Sinne des Willkürgenies und eingebildeten Subjektivisten (Beweis Hebbel, der genial ist, aber eben weil er durchaus neusüchtig ist, so überaus schlechte Fabeln erfindet.) Neu in einem guten Sinne ist nur, was aus der Dialektik der Kulturbewegung hervorgeht.
Keller to Hermann Hettner, June 26, 1854, in *HKKA*, 21:440.

another valence and urgency in an age of commodified, serialized literature and the plurality of editions it generates.

With the goal of curing him of his desire to be an original, his godfather gives Herr Jacques a manuscript (presumably including the story of the Landvogt) and tells him to make a faithful handwritten copy. The frame narrative thus introduces the historical material employed in the *Züricher Novellen* as an explicitly therapeutic and pedagogical project—yet another respect in which it easily complies with the interests of the *Deutsche Rundschau*, which aimed to cultivate a national consciousness among a German diaspora.[32] The "writing therapy" Jacques's godfather prescribes him also represents another valuation of copying (alongside the scenes in "Hadlaub," where the protagonist copies minnesong on his way to becoming a poet and lover, and Gritli's copying in "Die mißbrauchten Liebesbriefe"), which the *Züricher Novellen* specifically laud for its pedagogical value.[33] Not only is an original something worthy of imitation, as Jacque's godfather admonishes, genius itself is only born of imitation, or at least, of copying—a prescription Keller's literature stresses repeatedly.

Within the *Züricher Novellen*, copying constitutes the third fictional relay of the text between godfather and godson. Finally, the anonymous third-person narrator of the frame narrative, whose

---

32. While Keller modeled his protagonist on the historical Landvogt von Greifensee, the novella imagines events that are absent from the historical biographies, namely, the erotic exploits overlooked in accounts of his political and military feats. For background on the historical figure, Salomon Landolt (1741–1818), Keller primarily relied on the biography by David Hess (1820). While multiple male characters, including Johann Jakob Bodmer and Salomon Geßner, have historical male counterparts, such precedents are notably absent for the novella's female characters, thereby affirming their status as projections of a male erotic fantasy. On the historical content of the novella, see Ursula Amrein, "Geschichte als Spiegelkabinett: Gottfried Kellers 'Der Landvogt von Greifensee' und das Zürich im 18. Jahrhundert," in *Alte Löcher—neue Blicke: Zürich im 18. Jahrhundert*, ed. Helmut Holzhey and Simone Zurbuchen (Zürich: Chronos, 1997), 167–77.

33. See Christian Begemann, "Roderers Bilder—Hadlaubs Abschriften: Einige Überlegungen zu Mimesis und Wirklichkeitskonstruktion im deutschsprachigen Realismus," in *Die Dinge und die Zeichen: Dimensionen des Realistischen in der Erzählliteratur des 19. Jahrhunderts*, ed. Sabine Schneider and Barbara Hunfeld (Würzburg: Königshausen & Neumann, 2008), 37.

own role in the history of the text is unclear, explains that the print edition of the novella is an exact reproduction of Herr Jacques's copy, casting the intradiegetic author as a copyist as well: The author function attributed to the fourth relay is defined through the capacity of reproduction, rather than originality. "Herr Jacques took his godfather's manuscript with him and as a matter of fact carefully and neatly made a copy of it, just as it appears not less faithfully in the following in print."[34] So between the novella and the frame, the text owes its genesis to four relays: from the Landvogt to Marianne, from Marianne to the narrator of the novella, from Herr Jacques's godfather to Herr Jacques, and from Herr Jacques to print. Each ostensibly claims to be a faithful reproduction, rather than an original. This process, let me repeat, is all for the purpose of teaching Herr Jacques that "only someone who deserves to be imitated is a good original." An original, the fictional genealogy then suggests, is something worth reproducing, or better put, an original only achieves its status as such retrospectively, through the machinations of reproduction. We are thereby confronted with an ideal of storytelling that is not only compatible with publishing practices that entail multiple editions of the same work but even embraces reproduction as a condition of originality.

Hence, at issue in the account of multiple relays and in the frame narrative in general is not merely the question of an authoritative edition but also the question of originality in an age of serialization. The frame narrative and the opening scene of "Der Landvogt von Greifensee" ultimately inscribe serial reproduction into their texts and envision an authorial body that integrates creative, productive capacities (gendered as male) and reproductive capacities (gendered as female). In doing so, the *Züricher Novellen* propose the compatibility of artistic creation with mass reproduction. In the frame narrative, Jacques's desire to become an original artist is unambiguously

---

34. "Herr Jacques nahm das Manuscript seines Herrn Paten mit und fertigte in der That mit großer Sorgfalt und Reinlichkeit eine Kopie davon an, wie sie im Nachstehenden nicht minder getreu im Druck erscheint." Keller, *Züricher Novellen*, in *HKKA*, 6:144.

attributed to his adolescence: At the cusp of sexual maturity (the text notes that he is experiencing pubescent voice changes), he becomes aware of a "Trieb" that he believes to be a drive to be original, thereby misinterpreting, as Gail Hart suggests, his adolescent libido for artistic talent.[35] The true libidinal nature of the drive is made quite evident when his godfather first intercepts him for a therapeutic walk on the Zürichberg, where they meet a cluster of adolescent girls dressed in red and white who pause to consume their sweet bread. Jacques feels pangs of hunger directed at the bread and at his first youthful infatuation with one of the girls. At the conclusion of the frame narrative, after Jacques's godfather has passed on three tales, Jacques has been cured of this misunderstanding, abandoned his artistic ambitions, and married the girl he encountered on that first walk, thereby setting the stage for the fulfillment of his sexual desire within the norms of bourgeois life, which he has wholeheartedly embraced. Jacques's education thus consists in teaching him that sexual desire should not be mistaken for artistic ambition but recognized for what it is. In the final scene of the frame narrative, the now himself moralizing Jacques visits a Roman sculptor (a contemporary Pygmalion), of whom he serves as a patron, only to find that the artist has abandoned his utterly desiccated, crumbling statue and instead redirected his creative efforts at fathering an illegitimate child. Although he is at first appalled, Jacques then sees his own wife holding the child, wishing for her own. He consequently abandons his moral outrage and becomes the child's godfather and, the text promises, the future father of his own children. Rather than striving to be an original of any sort, Jacques thus represents, at the end of the text, a reproduction of both his godfather, as he too has attained the status of godfather, and a reproduction of the artist in his guise as a progenitor of life (in the form of children) rather than of art. As an imitative instantiation of both these preceding figures, Jacques embodies both the productive childlessness of his godfather as an exemplary citizen and pedagogue and the fertility of the Roman artist. In other words, the sterility of

---

35. See Gail K. Hart, *Readers and Their Fictions in the Novels and Novellas of Gottfried Keller* (Chapel Hill: University of North Carolina Press, 1989), 90.

the original father figure is both preserved and overcome by redirecting reproductive capacities. The imitative art of Jacques's life thus bridges the difference between productive and reproductive ideals.

The opening scene of "Der Landvogt von Greifensee" introduces a similar integration of productive and reproductive ideals, and it does so in a way that specifically addresses the mass reproduction of an artwork in an age of the serialization and commodification of literature. The idea of an artwork as contingent on practices of reproduction is confirmed by the beginning of "Der Landvogt von Greifensee." It is mid-July in the year 1783, and the Landvogt is celebrating the local holiday, Kaiser Heinrichs Tag, which is dedicated to the memory of the medieval Holy Roman Emperor Heinrich II. In honor of the day, the Landvogt is reviewing a military troop of volunteers he has assembled in case the French should one day invade. He is perched on his horse on an elevated hill, observing the troops' orderly formation. Of the troops, we are told that they are all dressed in green, that most of them, according to local custom and preferences, are called Heinrich, and that all of them regard the Landvogt as a father figure. In other words, from the very beginning, the bachelor, the Landvogt von Greifensee, is the symbolic father of a literal army of young green Heinrichs standing in line, ready to defend their father's estate should it come under attack. The Landvogt, whom Kaiser appropriately identifies as a "super Heinrich,"[36] is the father figure not of just one original and authoritative green Heinrich but of a well-ordered multitude of them, just as Keller, who remains best known to this day for *Der grüne Heinrich*, is the author of not just one but of the four revised and reprinted editions of the novel issued in his lifetime.

This small army dressed in green represents Keller's vision of the work of art in the age of serial production: *Der grüne Heinrich* is a product of serial mass production, the offspring of its bachelor father, and now stands at attention in a series of Heinrichs to defend the nation. Biological procreation premised on a heterosexual union has been replaced with the bachelor's industrial-scale reproduction, out of which materializes an otherwise impossible multitude

---

36. Kaiser, *Gottfried Keller*, 461.

of green Heinrichs. Only as such, as a product of serial reproduction, does *Der grüne Heinrich* first become an original. The novella thus envisions how serial repetitions become the very condition for the achievement of the modern literary work. The Landvogt remains a bachelor not in an act of resignation but because he has made any union with a female counterpart superfluous by incorporating the capacity for (mass) reproduction into his very being. The unmarried Landvogt thus represents a hermaphroditic creature not in the sense of a sterile being but as one who has no need for another "half" because he is in possession of both the productive and reproductive capacities needed to spawn not only one but a multitude of green Heinrichs. He embodies the ideal of a fatherlike progenitor, from which a serial plurality can be born, none of whom makes a singular claim to the status of the original, each instead partaking in the life of circulation and distribution afforded by their plurality.

On a final note, it bears observing that "Hadlaub" similarly spawns a multitude of Heinrichs. In addition to Fide's father, who bears the name Bischof Heinrich von Klingenberg, the text mentions no less than ten further minor characters by the same name and notes the observance of the same Kaiser Heinrichs Tag celebrated in "Der Landvogt von Greifensee": Kaiser Heinrich VI, his son (an anticipated Heinrich VII, also dressed in green, in an obvious nod to *Der grüne Heinrich*), König Heinrich von Lüzelburg, Heinrich von Rheinsfelden, Markgraf Heinrich von Meißen, Probst Heinrich Manesse, Herzog Heinrich von Breslau, Heinrich von Ofterdingen, Heinrich von Rißach, and a character in one of the songs who is referred to as "den armen Heinrich."[37] The text effectively becomes a

---

37. For these Heinrich figures, see Keller, "Hadlaub," in *Züricher Novellen*, in *HKKA*, 6:78, 81, 99, 115, 82, 29, 42, 86, 85, 47. *Martin Salander* exhibits yet a further site of such inscription in Keller's later work. There, Marie unpacks a gold coin she received on the occasion of her baptism and now intends to cash in on so as to save her children from starvation. The coin bears the profile of and name "*Heinrich rex*," words typographically set apart in the original print. Alongside the coin she finds a note drafted by her husband that "the gold was worth ten francs; the selling price, however, might be ten times as much or even more" (der Goldwert betrage zehn Franken, der Verkaufswert könne aber auf das Zehnfache und höher steigen). Gottfried Keller, *Martin Salander*, trans. Kenneth Halwas (London: John Calder,

receptacle for the serial inscription of a single name: the dispersed generation of an omnipresent plurality of Heinrichs, who individually and collectively point back to *Der grüne Heinrich*. Both "Hadlaub" and "Der Landvogt von Greifensee" generate a multitude of green Heinrichs, retrospectively endowing the original Heinrich of *Der grüne Heinrich* with the status of a literary original: originality as a product of serialized mass reproduction.

1963), 31; Keller, *Martin Salander*, in HKKA, 8:39. The coin thus represents proliferating economic value and, with regard to its originary referent, Heinrich, cultural as well.

Epilogue

Epigonal Dwarfs

In the introduction, I observed that the format of an aesthetic object mediates in two directions: first between the media object and representation, and second between the object and a world of differently formatted media and their human users. To conclude, this book offers a view on Keller's self-positioning in the media culture of his time that broadly follows these two trajectories. The point of departure is an essay published by Emil Ermatinger in 1949 in the American journal *PLMA*. Since 1920, after publishing a biography on Keller and an edition of Keller's letters and diaries,[1] Ermatinger had occupied the professorship at the Deutsches Seminar of the Universität Zürich specifically created to manage Keller's literary estate and

---

1. Emil Ermatinger, *Gottfried Kellers Leben, Briefe und Tagebücher*, 3 vols. (Stuttgart: J. G. Cotta'sche Buchhandlung Nachfolger, 1915–1916). Ermatinger's biography and two-volume edition of Keller's letters and diaries largely reproduce Jakob Baechtold's earlier biography of Keller.

to help secure his place in the literary canon. The professorship had previously been occupied by Jakob Baechtold, the first manager of that estate, and then Adolf Frey, and it serves as a fine example of the institutional bodies needed to perform the procedures for establishing a national literature. In keeping with that responsibility, Ermatinger's essay bears the simple title "Gottfried Keller and Goethe," a combination of names that openly signals a contribution, if only by means of the power of association, to the then still precarious position of Keller's work in the history of German literature (if not the precarious global status of German-language letters tout court in 1949). The comparison promised in the article's title begins with a measuring up of heights: "With regard to their appearances, the difference between the two is larger than one can imagine. Goethe of medium height, proportionately built, a picture of male beauty, Keller almost a dwarf (he measured no more than 140 cm), with a massive head, large torso, and small limbs."[2] While the question of corporeal stature likely strikes any reader today as irrelevant and farcical, the unflattering comparison of statures establishes the procedure and tone of Ermatinger's comparative undertaking; the same comparative measurement is performed regarding all aspects of the life and work of the two authors. The comparison—consistently disparaging for Keller—culminates in the claim that Keller's cause of death was "a kind of chronic shrinkage [Schrumpfungsvorgang],"[3] a lifelong physical and mental contraction and deterioration. Symptomatic for that process was not only Keller's gradual loss in stature paired with increasing girth but also his unsuccessful late novel, *Martin Salander* (1886), whose unpoetical nature supposedly makes apparent the author's deteriorating mental faculties.

---

2. Emil Ermatinger, "Gottfried Keller und Goethe," *PLMA* 64, no. 1 (1949): 79.

3. Ermatinger, "Gottfried Keller und Goethe," 96. On his death certificate, Keller's cause of death was identified as "infirmity from old age and atrophy of the brain and spinal cord." This diagnosis received sustained attention in the juridical proceedings following Keller's death contesting his will. For a discussion of these proceedings and the debate as to whether Keller was capable of making decisions when writing his will, see Gottfried Weiss, "Der Prozeß um das Testament von Gottfried Keller," *Neue Zürcher Zeitung*, March 27, 1955.

Ermatinger ultimately identifies the difference in corporeal statures as indicative of Keller's and Goethe's differently dimensioned horizons and life.

> Goethe, incessantly productive until his last day; Keller, laboring under major creative blocks and paralyzed in his work long before the end of his life. Goethe, in the breadth and depth of his intellectual development, a sea whose shores encompass the blazing south and the dimming north, the clear west and the mysterious east; Keller, an Alpine lake with charmingly winding shores and steeply rising mountains that block the view into the wide world and also delimit the infinite sky with a sharply defined horizon.[4]

Ermatinger's pairing of the well-built and worldly Goethe alongside the small, shrinking, and narrow-minded Keller, trapped in the confines of his Alpine landscape, serves as a paradigmatic example for how the discipline of history sizes up great and mediocre men, a discourse recently mapped in detail in Michael Gamper's *Der große Mann: Geschichte eines politischen Phantasmas*.[5] Ermatinger's comparison makes evident the degree to which the Olympian Goethe— "the greatest man among the Germans," as Ermatinger praises him—had succeeded Napoleon by the late nineteenth century as the lead example of a great man, an example that Ermatinger, writing at the conclusion of World War II, might have been particularly eager to reinstate.[6]

In enshrining Goethe as the paradigmatic great man of history and measuring Keller alongside him, Ermatinger sediments a favorite biographical topos: Keller as a small, nearly dwarfish man. To begin with, Ermatinger's diagnosis of Keller's cause of death as

---

4. Ermatinger, "Gottfried Keller und Goethe," 79.
5. See Michael Gamper, *Der große Mann: Geschichte eines politischen Phantasmas* (Göttingen: Wallstein, 2016).
6. Ermatinger, "Gottfried Keller und Goethe," 80. For the transatlantic making of Goethe into a paradigmatic "great man," see Gamper, *Der große Mann*, 297–302. For the rising sentiment that after Goethe and Napoleon, an era of great men had come to a close, see Ethel Matala de Mazza, "Verkleinlichung aller Größe: Heine und Marx über Staatsmänner nach Napoleon," in *Größe: Zur Medien- und Konzeptgeschichte personaler Macht im langen 19. Jahrhundert*, ed. Michael Gamper and Ingrid Kleeberg (Zürich: Chronos, 2015), 319–33.

"chronic shrinkage" echoes Walter Benjamin's observation, on the occasion of the ongoing publication of Jonas Fränkel's edition of Keller's collected works, that "its formal law is a law of shrinkage [Schrumpfung]."[7] While Benjamin thereby means to describe Keller's "Homeric Switzerland," Ermatinger borrows the term to encompass the authorial person and his work, and to suggest that these stand in proportion to one another. Further evidence for the enduring currency of this biographical topos includes the title of Walter Muschg's 1966 essay "Der Zwerg: Umriß eines Gottfried-Keller-Porträts" (The dwarf: Outlines of a portrait of Gottfried Keller) and the first chapter of Adolf Muschg's (Walter Muschg's half brother) authoritative biography, which bears the title "Schuld I: Der kleine Mann Gottfried" (Guilt I: The small man Gottfried).[8] To be sure, the contrast Adolf Muschg draws is not with a tall, worldly Goethe but instead, as announced in the striking title of the second chapter, "Schuld II: Die große Frau Welt" (Guilt II: The great woman world), with Keller's mother and, by extension, with the economic and material realties for which she stood, realities that perpetually compromised, so Muschg claims, Keller's artistic imagination, ambitions, and ego.[9] Muschg's choice of chapter titles that establish size and gender as points of contrast confirms that a measuring up of corporeal stature is also an evaluation of relative masculinity; the dwarfish Keller, like the persona of the bureaucratic functionary he embodied for years, is consistently rendered effeminate, all the more so when compared to Goethe as a masculine ideal. With recourse to the expansive semantics of format that

---

7. Walter Benjamin, "Gottfried Keller: In Honor of a Critical Edition of His Works," trans. Rodney Livingstone, in *Selected Writings*, vol. 2.1, *1927–1930*, ed. Michael W. Jennings, Howard Eiland, and Gary Smith (Cambridge, MA: Belknap Press of Harvard University Press, 1999), 55.

8. See Walter Muschg, "Der Zwerg: Umriss eines Gottfried-Keller-Portraits," in *Homo homini homo: Festschrift für Joseph E. Drexel zum 70. Geburtstag* (München: C. H. Beck, 1966), 31–58; and Adolf Muschg, *Gottfried Keller* (München: Kindler, 1977), 13.

9. See Adolf Muschg, *Gottfried Keller*, 75, 98–99. Kaiser's highly respected *Gottfried Keller: Das gedichtete Leben* further sediments the topos and concomitant demasculinization when he speaks of the "writer gnome Keller." Gerhard Kaiser, *Gottfried Keller: Das gedichtete Leben* (Frankfurt am Main: Insel, 1981), 646.

applies not only to media but also its users, one might describe Goethe as a man of *Format*, if not *Weltformat*.¹⁰ Keller, at least in the words of Gerhard Kaiser, whose psychoanalytic readings repeatedly invoke Keller's stature, is at best a "genius only in duodecimo format."¹¹

With good reason one might think that Ermatinger's recourse to the topos of the dwarfish Keller, and its exacerbation by way of a comparison to Goethe, would threaten rather than solidify Keller's literary reputation. Being small, after all, is tantamount to being marginal, trivial, or simply lightweight: Small in size implies slight in symbolic weight. With this threat in mind, some of Keller's more faithful devotees have mounted a counterattack to these defamatory claims, attempting, on the basis of newfound documentation, to argue that Keller did, in fact, measure greater than 140 centimeters.¹² Yet to provide one final perspective on Keller's authorship, I argue that rather than embodying insult or injury to Keller's person, Ermatinger's essay and his insistence on Keller's smallness recuperate a strategy Keller himself designed to position himself in the media landscape he inhabited and to secure his future place in the canon of German literature. Just as Ermatinger's criticism of *Martin Salander* does little else than repeat Keller's own supposed criticisms of his final work of fiction, so too does his portrait of a dwarfish man recover a self-image Keller fastidiously propagated throughout his lifetime.¹³ Those who aggrandize either Keller's

---

10. Michael Niehaus, *Was ist ein Format?* (Hannover: Wehrhahn, 2018), 18–24. Niehaus attributes the first use of the term *Format* with regard to a person to a description of Thomas Mann's character Mynheer Peeperkorn, who occupies both physical and symbolic space in both the vertical and horizontal dimensions.

11. Kaiser, *Gottfried Keller*, 431.

12. Bruno Weber argues that Keller's biographers have made him out to be smaller than he actually was. Citing Keller's early passport from 1848, on which his height was listed as "5 foot 4 inches," Weber approximates Keller's height to have been 162 cm. See Bruno Weber, "Wie klein war Gottfried Keller," in "Der Gottfried-Keller-Rabe," ed. Joachim Kersten, special issue, *Der Rabe* 61 (2000): 22.

13. The author and literary historian Adolf Frey recalls Keller explaining why he was dissatisfied with his second novel: "It's not beautiful! It's not beautiful! It contains too little poetry!" (Es ist nicht schön! Es ist nicht schön! Es ist zuwenig Poesie darin!). Adolf Frey, *Erinnerungen an Gottfried Keller*, 2nd expanded ed. (Leipzig: H. Haeffel, 1893), 37–38. On Keller's dissatisfaction with his *Spätwerk*,

stature or his place in literary history misunderstand the very strategy with which Keller intended to secure his standing in the canon and its success. Keller began to develop this strategy nine decades prior to Ermatinger's essay, at the very beginning of his endeavors as a poet—an undertaking commensurate with an author who was concerned from the outset and throughout his literary career with the media formats of his legacy and their viability. Keller understood himself to be an epigone—condemned to live as one of the "backward-looking creatures," as Friedrich Nietzsche famously describes the condition[14]—and believed that the only effective strategy to secure a literary legacy would involve being measured alongside Goethe. The possibility of a legacy after Goethe resides, Keller understands, in having his life and work gauged along the standard of this classical yardstick and, more specifically, striking just the right height relative to it—sufficiently significant to warrant comparison, yet exposing a capacious difference.

Keller's strategy, in a nutshell, was one of "Selbstverkleinerung," a term I borrow from Nietzsche's condemnation of his contemporaries in *Jenseits von Gut und Böse* (1886) and *Zur Genealogie der Moral* (1887).[15] While the term has been variously translated as "self-

---

see Rolf Zuberbühler, "'Excelsior!': Idealismus und Materialismus in Kellers und Fontanes politischen Altersromanen *Martin Salander* und *Der Stechlin*," in *Gottfried Keller und Theodor Fontane: Vom Realismus zur Moderne*, ed. Ursula Amrein and Regina Dieterle (Berlin: Walter de Gruyter, 2008), 106. More recent research attributes the lack of "Poesie" to the constraints imposed by the *Deutsche Rundschau* and its editor Julius Rodenberg and less to Keller's age. See, for example, Hans-Jürgen Schrader, "Im Schraubstock moderner Marktmechanismen: Vom Druck Kellers und Meyers in Rodenbergs *Deutscher Rundschau*," *Jahresbericht der Gottfried Keller-Gesellschaft* 62 (1993): 24–25.

14. Friedrich Nietzsche, *Human, All Too Human: A Book for Free Spirits*, trans. R. J. Hollingdale (Cambridge: Cambridge University Press, 1996), 81, § 148.

15. "The Chinese have a proverb that mothers even teach children: *siao-sin*—'make your heart *small*!' This is the characteristic fundamental propensity in late civilizations: I do not doubt that an ancient Greek would recognize in us Europeans of today, too, such self-diminution [Selbstverkleinerung]; this alone would suffice for us to 'offend his taste.'—" Friedrich Nietzsche, *Beyond Good and Evil: Prelude to a Philosophy of the Future*, trans. Walter Kaufmann (New York: Vintage Books, 1966), 216, § 267. Similarly, in *Zur Geneologie der Moral*: "Has the self-belittlement [Selbstverkleinerung] of man, his *will* to self-belittlement, not progressed irresistibly

deprecation," "self-belittlement," or "self-diminution," I will gloss it in a more literal manner as "making oneself small." In attributing the generations since Copernicus with a will to making themselves small, Nietzsche laments the contemporary absence of great men—a condemnation of prevailing mediocrity and a confirmation of his era as one of epigones. The burden of epigonality for the late nineteenth century, of being born too late in a history of great men, was sufficiently vehement for Nietzsche and his generation to force the question of size and scale. Jacob Burckhardt expresses a similar sentiment in the lectures posthumously published as *Weltgeschichtliche Betrachtungen*, where he writes that the historian's perception of past greatness is conditioned on his own epoch's insignificance: "We take our starting point from our dwarfness [Knirpstum], our desultoriness and dissipation. Great is what *we* are *not*."[16] At least Keller, Nietzsche, and Burckhardt experienced the burden of being born too late as a condition of smallness.

Nietzsche's late turn against Richard Wagner in *Der Fall Wagner* (1888), published soon after his critiques of *Selbstverkleinerung*, adds a further dimension to this diagnosis. While the essay largely vilifies Wagner for his popular modern decadence, Nietzsche makes an exception for Wagner with regard to the "small." In the small, Nietzsche concedes, Wagner remains masterful: "Wagner is admirable and gracious only in the invention of what is smallest, in spinning out the details,"[17] he writes, and even repeats the point more broadly as a recommendation for an era of epigones. "What can be done well today, what can be masterly, is only what is small."[18] For all the criticism the essay remains best remembered for, Wagner still earns unqualified praise in being proclaimed as "our great *miniaturist* in

---

since Copernicus?" Friedrich Nietzsche, *On the Genealogy of Morals*, trans. Walter Kaufmann and R. J. Hollingdale (New York: Vintage Books, 1989), 155.

16. Jacob Burckhardt, *Weltgeschichtliche Betrachtungen*, in *Kritische Gesamtausgabe*, vol. 10, *Aesthetik der bildenen Kunst; Über das Studium der Geschichte*, ed. Peter Ganz (München: C. H. Beck, 2000), 497.

17. Friedrich Nietzsche, *The Case of Wagner*, in *The Birth of Tragedy and The Case of Wagner*, trans. Walter Kaufmann (New York: Vintage Books, 1967), 171.

18. Nietzsche, *The Case of Wagner*, 188.

music who crowds into the smallest space an infinity of sense and sweetness."[19] Embracing the not simply small but the very smallest or the miniature is, at least on the recommendation of *Der Fall Wagner*, the best precaution against the decadence of the moderns. While many an epigone, including most of Wagner's own work, misguidedly believes it might overcome being born too late by taking recourse to the monumental, the best approach resides in the antithesis: the very small. Keller's media strategy of *Selbstverkleinerung* likewise embraces smallness as a condition of a literary legacy in an epigonal age. Keller, like Nietzsche, understands *Selbstverkleinerung* as a manner of self-representation with respect to a bygone history of great men and the contemporary dearth of such men, and as a way of nonetheless being remembered in the future.

But what does it mean to make oneself small? What does it mean for literature to be small at all? In what way are "small," "miniature," or, conversely, "monumental" properties attributable to a literary text or a poetics? A recent boom in scholarship on small forms and small formats has provided an initial set of answers to help define the will to *Selbstverkleinerung* that is specific to Keller's oeuvre.[20] This trend in literary scholarship has consistently spotlighted a range of smaller genres, especially small or short prose (for example, the anecdote, aphorism, *Kalendergeschichte*, or parable), or media formats (the *annonce* or the tweet) that readily qualify as small on account of the dimensions of their conventional print formats or their brevity. Since Keller's oeuvre only employs such smaller genres or formats as prompts for longer texts, it may seem like a

---

19. Nietzsche, *The Case of Wagner*, 171.
20. For examples of the flourishing research field concerning small forms, see Maren Jäger, Ethel Matala de Mazza, and Joseph Vogl, eds., *Verkleinerung: Epistemologie und Literaturgeschichte kleiner Formen* (Berlin: Walter de Gruyter, 2020); Michael Gamper and Ruth Mayer, eds., *Kurz und knapp: Zur Mediengeschichte kleiner Formen vom 17. Jahrhundert bis zur Gegenwart* (Bielefeld: Transcript, 2017); Claudia Öhlschläger, Sabiene Autsch, and Leonie Süwolto, eds., *Kulturen des Kleinen: Mikroformate in Literatur, Kunst und Medien* (Paderborn: Wilhelm Fink, 2019); and Thomas Althaus, Wolfgang Bunzel, and Dirk Göttsche, eds., *Kleine Prosa: Theorie und Geschichte eines Textfeldes im Literatursystem der Moderne* (Tübingen: Max Niemeyer, 2007).

poor candidate for an example of small forms.[21] His stories tend to prolixity, as critics of *Der grüne Heinrich*, *Züricher Novellen*, and *Martin Salander* were quick to contend, and his preferred print medium was the traditional book and by no means the fleeting, lightweight rubrics of the feuilleton, which was largely responsible for a proliferation in small forms and formats in the late nineteenth-century media market. So although Keller's strategy of making himself small was intended as a way of positioning himself in his contemporaneous media landscape and thereby references both a history of and a contemporaneous boom in small forms and formats, the smallness of his work is more subtle than the dictates of, for example, a word limit. Keller's media strategy is neither evident in the manifest measurements of his manuscripts or published texts, nor in their word counts, nor in his factual height.

Keller's strategy of *Selbstverkleinerung* thus needs to be specified against such definitions of the small as relating to either genre or empirical formats. Instead, within Keller's oeuvre, *Selbstverkleinerung* is better understood as an ethos, as a set of practices that does nothing less than integrate the subject, style, and format of his work; it is a persistent, defining feature of Keller's self-representation and his fiction as well. At its core, it imaginatively reformats literature's ambitions to an era of smallness, ensuring a harmonious fit between his literature and an era of diminished men. Furthermore, because Keller's strategy of *Selbstverkleinerung* is suitably premised on an appreciation for the small not as an absolute but instead as a relative value, making oneself small is a matter of scaling back relative to a selected standard, namely, the past greats of literary history.[22] Since smallness cannot be measured in the absolute values of paper

---

21. For an alternative view advocating the significance of small forms—in particular, the proverb—in Keller's work, see Florian Fuchs, *Civic Storytelling: The Rise of Short Forms and the Agency of Literature* (New York: Zone Books, 2023), 163–78.

22. In their introduction to the volume *Verkleinerung*, Jäger, Matala de Mazza, and Vogl emphasize smallness as an operation and name four types—reduction, selection, compression, and transposition—that typically preserve density, albeit in a smaller dimension. See Maren Jäger, Ethel Matala de Mazza, and Joseph Vogl, "Einleitung," in Jäger, Matala de Mazza, and Vogl, *Verkleinerung*, 1–12. Keller's strategy, as I argue here, is less a matter of moving, whether by means of compression or

formats or word limits, the operation of scaling back best comes into view by excavating the imaginative semantic and visual resources deployed to project modest contours. Keller's strategy of making himself small thus encapsulates the view of format I have proposed throughout this book: format not merely as a sum of empirical values and rules but also as an imaginative construct that participates in literary representation.

To these semantic and visual resources for casting his own smallness belong the imaginative descriptors Keller coins to describe his own work. While the volumes of Keller's fiction are not particularly small—the volumes of the first publication of *Der grüne Heinrich*, for example, measure 16.3×10 cm (the second edition 18×11 cm), a format sufficiently modest to meet the demand of lending libraries for easily circulated volumes, yet certainly not dimensions that warrant being classified as a specifically small pocket format—Keller, throughout his life, imaginatively scaled his work back by means of diminishing neologisms. Keller employs an abundant lexicon for imaginatively fabricated small formats, sustained by the proclivity of Swiss German dialects to diminutives.[23] He describes *Der grüne Heinrich*, regardless of its four volumes or, counted differently, 107 sheets (*Bogen*), as "a sad little novel" (einen traurigen kleinen Roman).[24] The four volumes that make up the novel and spurred a crisis of disintegration as I described in chapter 1 are themselves not volumes or *Bände* but "little volumes" (Bändchen), a term he also uses to describe his earliest

---

transposition, from larger to small forms than one of scaling back relative to an imagined yardstick.

23. On the nineteenth-century use of diminutives to describe small forms, see Juliane Vogel, "Ephemeriden der Schere: Scherenschnitt und Zeitungsausschnitt im 19. Jahrhundert," in Jäger, Matala de Mazza, and Vogl, *Verkleinerung*, 15–16.

24. Keller, "Autobiographisches," *Die Gegenwart*, December 16, 1876, and January 6, 1877, in *HKKA*, 15:411. Shortly thereafter Keller also describes his intention "to write only a modest volume" (nur einen mäßigen Band zu schreiben). Keller, "Autobiographisches," in *HKKA*, 15:412. Once again, these diminutives do not posit smallness in absolute terms but as relative volumes. As Niehaus notes, the very notion of a small format is only meaningful on the basis of a standardized set of formats whose sizes are established relative to one another. See Niehaus, *Was ist ein Format?*, 15. Likewise, Keller's diminutives are meaningful only relative to an imagined set of norms (the standard-bearer being Goethe).

volumes of poetry.²⁵ The imagined fictional texts that inhabit the diegetic world of that novel are similarly scaled down to size: Heinrich Lee writes his life story on "small parchment" (Pergamentlein); the autobiographical product is "the modest little book" (das mäßige Büchlein).²⁶ The same term, "Büchlein," is then applied to *Die Leute von Seldwyla* in the book's own introduction, where the narrator insists that the novellas are merely "small scraps" (Abfällsel), thereby diminishing the cycle in terms of size and significance to that of a waste product.²⁷ Keller explicitly desired that *Die Leute von Seldwyla* be published as a "paperback" (Taschenbuch), in the hopes of producing "a handy and dainty house book" (ein bequemes und zierliches Hausbuch) that would contrast with the, to his mind, monstrous proportions of *Der grüne Heinrich*.²⁸ And in yet another twist of words, his final novel, *Martin Salander*, is, as Keller writes to Paul Heyse, a "little novel" (Romänchen).²⁹ Finally, Keller similarly scaled back the size of his total oeuvre, referring to it as his "little work" (Werklein) or also as his "modest output" (Wenigkeit), as he writes in a late autobiographical sketch for a series of author portraits published in the magazine *Die Gegenwart*.³⁰ And as if to insistently mirror his own corporeal stature, the asserted smallness of each individual work and their sum as an oeuvre still allow expansive width; the books are, as I have noted, consistently described as being "fat" (dick).³¹ So while there is nothing small about a novel or novella cycle per se,

---

25. Keller to Eduard Vieweg, August 23, 1850, in *HKKA*, 19:185; and again to Vieweg on December 26, 1850, in *HKKA*, 19:193. Keller also consistently refers to the poetry volumes as "Bändchen." See, for example, Keller to Theodor Storm, April 11, 1881, in *Theodor Storm—Gottfried Keller: Briefwechsel; Kritische Ausgabe*, ed. Karl Ernst Laage (Berlin: Erich Schmidt, 1992), 66.
26. Keller, *Der grüne Heinrich* (2nd ed., 1889), in *HKKA*, 2:93; Keller, *Der grüne Heinrich* (1st ed., 1854–1855), in *HKKA*, 11:62.
27. Keller, *Die Leute von Seldwyla*, in *HKKA*, 4:12.
28. Keller to Eduard Vieweg, September 5, 1855, in *HKKA*, 23.1:315.
29. Keller to Paul Heyse, December 25, 1882, in *HKKA*, 24:457.
30. Keller to Friedrich Theodor Vischer, October 1, 1871, in *HKKA*, 21:516; Keller, "Autobiographisches," in *HKKA*, 15:405. Keller also employs "Wenigkeit" to describe his oeuvre in a letter to Ida Freiligrath, December 20, 1880, in *HKKA*, 21:585.
31. Keller to Jakob Baechtold, November 21, 1879, in *HKKA*, 26:289.

Keller's creative lexicon assigns his texts to a world of imaginative small formats. The proclivity of Swiss dialects to diminutives becomes a lexical resource for gestures of self-belittlement and, more crucially, a means for situating oneself in a canonical history of literature.

While the success of Keller's strategy is evident from Ermatinger's assessment of comparative statures and horizons in his 1949 essay, it can be induced more broadly from the fact that it is he and not, for example, his contemporary Conrad Ferdinand Meyer who is selected to be measured with the scale of Goethe's height. Criticism in the decades after Meyer's death expressed a growing distaste for his work, in particular for his historical fiction, on account of its monumental proportions. Georg Lukács, for example, writes of Meyer's historicism:

> Here we see in a different form a similar problem to the one we observed in Flaubert: the combination of a desire for great deeds with a personal and social inability to accomplish them in reality is projected into the past, in the hope that this social impotence may lose its modern pettiness in the ostentatious attire of the Renaissance. However, this projection into an illusory monumentality—a monumentality merely of picturesque gestures, hiding the decadent, tormented broodings of the modern bourgeois—produces in the general tone of the writing notes as false and feelings and experiences as distorted as in Flaubert.[32]

From the perspective of Keller's well-chosen strategy of *Selbstverkleinerung*, Meyer must give way to Keller because Meyer failed to appreciate the imperative of the epoch to scale back. He failed at the task of self-moderation, failed to realize that the only adequate form and format of literary representation after Goethe is a small format, one apposite to the anthropological fact of modern dimin-

---

32. Georg Lukács, *The Historical Novel*, trans. Hannah Mitchell and Stanley Mitchell (Boston: Beacon, 1963), 224. In the case of Conrad Ferdinand Meyer, it is likewise tempting to extend the disproportional, monumental sizing of his work to his own stature. Meyer, who is remembered to have measured 1.8 meters tall, would have towered over the dwarfish Keller. For a discussion of the criticisms of Meyer's monumental historicism, see Sonja Osterwalder, "Auf die Fußspitzen gestellt: C. F. Meyers größere Helden," in Gamper and Kleeberg, *Größe*, 335–44.

ished greatness. His historical novels, weighed down with heavy pathos and abundant superlatives, relating stories of the heroic giants of history, disregarded the constraints of their epigonal age. Keller, in contrast, had already imaginatively developed an effective and ultimately enduring strategy of making himself small in 1853 at the beginning of his literary career.

The Great Goethe

Elucidating my claim that Keller's strategy of *Selbstverkleinerung* is, for one, an answer to the burden of epigonality merits returning to the passage from *Der grüne Heinrich* I analyzed in chapter 1 as an especially fecund expression of Keller's poetics. In the passage, Heinrich Lee encounters the high point of German classicism—namely, Goethe—that renders all latecomers epigones in the twofold form in which the latter remains present to the nineteenth century: first as a shadowy phantasm and second in the commodified form of his ever-expanding collected-works edition. The encounter is spectacular precisely on account of the convergence of these two forms: The collected-works edition renders Goethe's ghost present to Heinrich. The fantastical scene imagines Heinrich, Keller's alter ego, not simply as copresent with the older author, but bound to him in an instructive relationship of erotic, subservient intimacy that endows the younger aspiring artist with a powerful potential source of legitimacy. Essential to the staging of this encounter, and to Keller's strategy of making himself small, is the contrast between Heinrich's smallness and Goethe's greatness, a variation of which would later motivate Ermatinger's essay. The bodily and affective proximity Heinrich attains in relation to the classical predecessor is predicated on the protagonist's corporeal smallness as a signifier of his symbolic insignificance.

The passage goes to great lengths to foreground Goethe's great dimensions. When Heinrich enters his mother's house to find the books, the sight of them awakens an early childhood memory in which a carpenter announces, "The great Goethe has died."[33]

---

33. Keller, *Der grüne Heinrich* (1st ed., 1854–1855), in *HKKA*, 12:15.

Correspondingly large is Goethe's ghost that Heinrich feels present to him when absorbed in reading the collected works on the *Lotterbettchen* (whose diminutive is naturally selected to reflect back on the young and submissive body that rests on the bed): "I felt as if the great shadow himself had crossed my threshold."[34] That magnitude is also expressed in sheer numbers; many are the eighty years of Goethe's exemplary life and equally many are the volumes of the collected-works edition that index the author's longevity. Thus, when Heinrich unties the string that binds the Goethe volumes into a single body (corpus), his small hands cannot hold together the brimming cornucopia produced by this long life.[35] The contours of the specifically pederastic relationship I attributed to this passage thereby begin to take shape with reference to the great dimensions of the older poet, alongside whom Heinrich can only appear young and effeminate. It also bears recalling that the same contrast in size is constitutive of the one other encounter with Goethe in *Der grüne Heinrich*, the theater scene in which the child Heinrich does not meet Goethe himself but instead his representative, Gretchen from *Faust*, who appears to him as a large, white, shimmering body, another ghostly manifestation of the phantasmagoric Goethe. When he then sleeps at her feet, rolled together as both the meerkat whose costume he still wears and the puppy he imagines himself to be, he assumes a diminutive form of servile subjugation. To curl at the feet of past greats is to scale oneself back into a body of proper proportions that avail nearness to a bygone era. Casting his hero as either the young, effeminate eromenos of the great poet or as a young animal sleeping at Gretchen's feet, Keller provides Heinrich with a body properly scaled to the fate and future of an epigone. Along with a world of contrived small formats, these two bodies (Heinrich and the domesticated animal) are imaginative gestalts in which Keller's strategy of *Selbstverkleinerung* becomes manifest.[36]

---

34. Keller, *Der grüne Heinrich* (1st ed., 1854–1855), in *HKKA*, 12:15.
35. Keller, *Der grüne Heinrich* (1st ed., 1854–1855), in *HKKA*, 12:15.
36. In the context of this strategy, it is worth noting that Sabine Schneider reads the novel's memory work as an "autobiographical absorption in the minutiae of individual memory." Sabine Schneider, "'Poesie der Unreife': Autobiographisches

Media Landscapes

Keller's imaginative fashioning of small bodies and small formats serves to position him not only in relation to Goethe but also within a contemporaneous media culture that was driven by greater standardization and an expanding range of scales. Two iconic picture formats of the era demarcate the breadth of those scales: on the one end, the monumental panoramas adorning new massive public infrastructure such as parliamentary buildings, railway stations, museums, and the world exhibitions; on the other end, the easily reproducible and equalizing (because the scaling was standardized no matter one's social status) pocket-size portrait photographs or cartes de visite that became a common token of personal identity and, when exchanged, of one's social network. Within the spectrum of these formats, Keller decisively positions himself at the small end of the scale through an overt critique of the panorama.[37] A programmatic moment of self-positioning thus emerges from the satirical description of an Alpine panorama in the novella "Das verlorene Lachen" (1874), a text that stands out in Keller's oeuvre for its overt criticism of Switzerland's transition to a liberal, capitalist economy. The novella describes a wallpaper landscape depicting the iconic chain of the Bernese Alps. The panorama's Alpine subject makes it a fine example of the boom in monumental picture making in the late nineteenth century, which catered to Switzerland's burgeoning self-stylization as a tourist destination and was employed to adorn the infrastructure needed for that developing industry, including train stations, museums, and university or government offices.[38] In that

---

Schreiben im Roman," in *"Der grüne Heinrich"*: *Gottfried Kellers Lebensbuch—neu gelesen*, ed. Wolfram Groddeck (Zürich: Chronos, 2009), 67.

37. For an account of the rising presence and cultural significance of the panorama, see Vance Byrd, *A Pedagogy of Observation: Nineteenth-Century Panoramas, German Literature, and Reading Culture* (Lewisburg, PA: Bucknell University Press, 2017). On carte de visite portraiture, see Eva Ehninger, "Trying on the Drawing Room: 'Realness' and Truth in and out of Photographs," in *Truth in Serial Form: Serial Formats and the Form of the Series, 1850–1930*, ed. Malika Maskarinec (Berlin: Walter de Gruyter, 2023), 173–95.

38. On adorning new public infrastructure with panoramas in the nineteenth century and their contributions to sedimenting national identities, see Monika

context, the Alpine panorama in Keller's novella functions as a cipher for an aesthetics of the monumental and sublime and, furthermore, for a grand, nationalist vision of Switzerland, a representative function best satisfied when the panorama adorns equally grand and ambitious public infrastructure.

The novella's description of the panorama takes issue with both its aesthetic and political functions. In "Das verlorene Lachen," the owner of a tavern has purchased and papered the Alpine panorama to the walls of his inn's dining room, unfortunately without appreciating that the dimensions of the room are smaller than those of the picture. As a result, the Alpine peaks fold onto the ceiling, effectively decapitated, and are there additionally subject to the blackening fumes and soot that rise from the candles used to light the room.

> It was a panoramic representation of the grandeur of a Swiss landscape, running around all four walls, and depicting a world of mountains with snowy peaks, alpine meadows, waterfalls, and lakes. However, the hall for which this splendid wallpaper was originally designed was half again as high as the room into which it was now transplanted, so they had enough to cover the ceiling with it too. Consequently the mighty giants among the mountains, namely the Jungfrau, the Mönch, the Eiger, and the Wetterhorn, the Schreck- and the Finsteraarhorn, were bent over half way up and bumped their snow-covered heads together in the middle of the low ceiling, where they were, however, somewhat darkened by lamp soot and smoke.

> Dieselbe stellte eine großmächtige und zusammenhängende Schweizerlandschaft vor, welche um sämtliche vier Wände herumlief und die Gebirgswelt darstellte mit Schneespitzen, Alpen, Wasserfällen und Seeen. Da aber der Saal, für welchen dieses prächtige Tapetenwerk früher bestimmt gewesen, um die Hälfte höher war, als der Raum, in welchen es jetzt verpflanzt worden, so hatte zugleich die Decke damit bekleidet werden können, also daß die gewaltigen Bergriesen, nämlich die Jungfrau, der Mönch, der Eiger und das Wetterhorn, das Schreck- und das Finsterarhorn, sich in ihrer halben Höhe umbogen und ihre schneeigen Häupter an der Mitte der niedrigen Zimmerdecke zusammenstießen, wo sie jedoch von Dunst und Lampenruß etwas verdüstert waren.[39]

Wagner, *Allegorie und Geschichte: Ausstattungsprogramme öffentlicher Gebäude des 19. Jahrhunderts in Deutschland; Von der Cornelius-Schule zur Malerei der Wilhelminischen Ära* (Tübingen: Ernst Wasmuth, 1989).

39. Gottfried Keller, "The Lost Smile," trans. Frank G. Ryder, in *Stories*, ed. Frank G. Ryder (New York: Continuum, 1982), 242; Keller, "Das verlorene Lachen,"

Most basically, the panorama description illustrates Keller's enduring sensitivity to the question of format as mediating representation: Because the panorama has been displaced from its original location but not rescaled, it is too large for the wall onto which it has been mounted, for which reason the picture cannot fulfill the imperatives of representation. Rather than represent Alpine grandeur, the image has become ludicrous. However, within the context of Keller's strategy of *Selbstverkleinerung*, this panorama is more than a denunciation of those that fail to appreciate format as a question of fit and as an indispensable consideration for aesthetic success. The satirical description is also a wholesale rejection of an aesthetics of the monumental, sublime, and thin-aired highlands that the panorama flaunts and of the political ends to which that aesthetic might be mobilized.

A second critique of an image of panoramic dimensions in the late *Martin Salander* rehearses and sharpens the first. In *Martin Salander*, a wall mural is commissioned by the up-and-coming banker Louis Wohlwend, a character responsible for repeatedly losing the protagonist's hard-earned capital (the ruinous investment practices are unambiguously indexed in the company name: Schadenmüller, a miller of damages or harm). Wohlwend has a picture of Arnold von Winkelried, the mythic soldier and defender of the early Old Swiss Confederacy, painted on the facade of his business. Passing by, Martin Salander observes the facade:

> When he, led by his good old friend, had located Schadenmüller and Company he noticed that on the house, on a shining gold background, was painted a picture of Arnold von Winkelried with the gathered spears in his arms; next to it was the inscription: "Provide for my wife and children!" That house was owned by Mr. Louis Wohlwend who had that picture painted, but, as was shown later, for which he had never paid.
>
> Als er, von dem alten guten Bekannten geführt, das Haus Schadenmüller und Comp. gefunden, hatte er bemerkt, daß an diesem Hause wirklich

---

in *Die Leute von Seldwyla*, in *HKKA*, 5:318. For a discussion of the panorama with a greater emphasis on its political context and function, see Dorothea von Mücke, "'Das gemalte nächtliche Tapetenvaterland': Realist Aesthetics and the Politics of Representation," *Figuration: Gender, Literatur, Kultur* 20, no. 1 (2019): 35–47.

Arnold von Winkelried mit den Speeren im Arm auf Goldgrund gemalt, prangte, nebst einer Inschrift: Sorget für mein Weib und meine Kinder! Das Haus gehörte dem Herrn Louis Wohlwend, der auch das Bild malen ließ, aber nicht bezahlte, wie sich später zeigte.[40]

The gold foundation for which the speculating upstart cannot pay and the contrast between the painted slogan and the crude dealings of the banker Wohlwend, which leave Martin Salander intermittently impoverished and unable to care for his wife and children, denounce Wohlwend and late nineteenth-century parvenus as having sacrificed their way of life and their morals to partake in capitalist (and colonialist) exploits. Large-scale painting becomes the embodiment of capitalist speculation and its deleterious effects on the fabric of society.

The novel's unrealized conclusion additionally ties the critique of upward mobility promised by such speculation to an Alpine aesthetic—a foil to Keller's own politics and poetics. Keller had originally planned to title the novel "Excelsior." In the final scene, Martin Salander's family was to be assembled on a mountain peak, possibly on the occasion of the Feast of Ascension, at which point they would suffer a catastrophic fate. The novel was to conclude, in other words, with the fateful reversal of the family's economic efforts and upward mobility in the downward trajectory of a dramatic Alpine accident. In a letter to Heyse, Keller summarizes the plot's direction and tragic ending: "in which everything strives upward in both a good and a bad sense and which is to end catastrophically with a real mountain ascent by many people."[41] Heyse

---

40. Gottfried Keller, *Martin Salander*, trans. Kenneth Halwas (London: John Calder, 1963), 38; Keller, *Martin Salander*, in *HKKA*, 8:48.

41. "Ich denke jetzt wieder mehr an mein Römänchen, worin Alles im guten und schlimmen Sinne aufwärts strebt und das mit einer wirklichen Bergfahrt vieler Menschen kataströphlich abschließen soll." Keller to Paul Heyse, December 25, 1882, in *HKKA*, 24:457. In his notes to the novel, Keller imagines the catastrophic and redemptive ending as follows:

Culmination point. Convergence of various symptomatic moments with the natural phenomenon of the mountain. [...] Everything comes together and approaches downfall on the burning mountain ledge, which is cut off by the torrential thunderstorm and overflowing mountain streams. But it is still possible to find enough upright and helpful men in the folds of the land, and they come to the rescue. Cathartic turn.

dissuaded Keller from both the title and the ending, recognizing, I would argue, that such a catastrophic and cathartic ending would be antithetical to Keller's poetics. Instead, in the extant end of the novel, the story peters out to an uncertain future, only assured to be free of the pathos, sublimity, and the suspense typical of a conventional Alpine excursion, all of which would have been out of place in Keller's oeuvre, which is defined by a decisive rejection of the sublime and its conventional vertiginous settings. The satirical critique of monumental picture making that takes place in "Das verlorene Lachen" and *Martin Salander*, like the decision not to have the novel end with an Alpine accident, instead reaffirm Keller as a poet of the Swiss *Mittelland*, the relatively flat plateau at the foot of the Alps where most of the Swiss population lived and still lives and the preferred setting of the village story (*Dorfgeschichte*). Although the geography of his narratives is easily overlooked, his fiction is, on closer examination, exclusively set in these low-lying areas: the valley in which Seldwyla is located or Zurich in *Der grüne Heinrich* and the *Züricher Novellen*. In pivoting away from Alpine grandeur, Keller selects the prosaic and pathos-free subject matter apposite to the small forms and small formats he envisions for his literary oeuvre. To make the point again, a catastrophic mountain scene at the conclusion of *Martin Salander* would have represented, as Heyse must have sensed, a definitive rupture with the settings and aesthetic that define Keller's oeuvre.

If mountain scenery does make an appearance in Keller's fictional worlds, for example, in the earliest childhood memories of Heinrich Lee, then it is set far off in the distance and is typically framed by a window that serves to contain and domesticate the landscape,

---

Culminationspunkt. Zusammentreffen der verschiedenen symptomatischen Momente mit dem Naturphänomen auf dem Berge. [...] Alles kommt auf dem brennenden Bergvorsprung, der von dem reißenden Gewitterregen resp. angeschwollenen Bergbächen abgeschnitten ist, zusammen und dem Untergang nahe. Rechtliche u. hülfsfähige Männer finden sich doch noch in den Landesfalten genug vor und bringen Rettung. Reinigende Wendung.
Keller, "*Martin Salander*: Paralipomena Nr. 23; Pfingstmontag," ca. March 1883, in *HKKA*, 24:383. For an informative account of Keller's unrealized design and his correspondence with Heyse, see Zuberbühler, "'Excelsior!'"

in distinct contrast to either panoramas or the stormy, heroic landscapes Keller painted in his youth.[42] The landscape description with which *Der grüne Heinrich* famously opens, to name another example, projects such mountains only in miniature. The narrator, having proposed to capture the cities that belong "to the most beautiful of all in Switzerland," travels along the country's low-lying lakes and waterways.[43] The imposing Alpine grandeur that we and any reader of nineteenth-century Swiss tourism brochures expect to make an appearance emerges on the horizon only three pages in, seemingly as an afterthought. What's more, the peaks are presented not as sublime magnitudes but in the dainty and effeminate gestalt of a flower garland: "The river flows full and fast, and when one happens to look back again, one sees in the south the long snowy-pure chain of the Alps lying like a wreath of lilies on a green carpet."[44] The landscape has been scaled back so as to be proportional to the size of their observer, the young, effeminate protagonist of the novel.[45]

Keller's small-scale poetics are encapsulated in the story that Salander's wife narrates in the first family scene of *Martin Salander* as an attempt to distract her children from their hunger. Her fairy tale imagines a population of meerkats (*Erdmännchen*), the same species of animal Heinrich plays for the performance of *Faust* in *Der grüne Heinrich*. The small stature of the meerkat is not only appropriate to the small form of the fairy tale, the intimate family setting in which the tale is narrated, and an audience of children; it is also commensurate with Keller's strategy of scaling back and making oneself small. Like in the fairy tale of meerkats, Keller's *Mittelland*

---

42. On the general significance of windows as a site where Keller articulates his principles of poetic realism, see Peter Utz, "Verengte Aussichten, neuer Glanz: Fensterblicke in Gottfried Kellers *Der grüne Heinrich*," in *Kellers Medien: Formen—Genres—Institutionen*, ed. Frauke Berndt (Berlin: Walter de Gruyter, 2022), 129–40.

43. "Zu den Schönsten vor Allen in der Schweiz." Keller, *Der grüne Heinrich* (1st ed., 1854–1855), in *HKKA*, 11:15.

44. "Voll und schnell fließt der Strom, und indem man unversehens noch ein Mal zurückschaut, erblickt man im Süden die weite schneereine Alpenkette wie einen Lilienkranz auf einem grünen Teppich liegen." Keller, *Der grüne Heinrich* (1st ed., 1854–1855), in *HKKA*, 11:16–17.

45. On the scaled-down size of the landscape, see Osterkamp, "Erzählte Landschaften," 149.

is fittingly inhabited not by mountaineering heroes and heroines but by a cast of distinctly average, if not mediocre, good-for-nothings: Heinrich Lee, who sends his mother into ruin as he squanders his youth; the happy-go-lucky inhabitants of Seldwyla; Jacques of the *Züricher Novellen*, who ultimately abandons all his artistic ambitions; or the sisters of *Martin Salander*, who seek out their own demise. As Kaiser observes, Keller's oeuvre performs the "shrinkages" of world literature's greatest heroes, Faust and Don Quixote among them.[46] Scaling, one of the operations of formatting with which I began this book, has thus been employed in this case to resize the landscape not so much in relation to a specific medium of representation but to the middling protagonist. Although Switzerland's elevation of Keller to a national poet depended on insisting on the didactic value of his stories for the nation, Keller's programmatic position against sublimity generates a crowd of antiheroic characters, persons defined by mediocrity.

One last dimension of Keller's media strategy of making himself small in an epigonal era needs to be named, namely, his comic style. This perspective borrows from scholarship on Robert Walser, whose micrograms have understandably produced some of the best accounts of literary smallness. In an article on the ethics and aesthetics of smallness in Walser, Jens Hobus makes a passing yet highly compelling suggestion that Walser's irony could be interpreted as a method of immunization against excessive pathos: "But it is not just the attitude that is ironic in Walser; it is rather the literary technique that distinguishes his texts and immunizes them against anything pathetic. A style of writing in which the ironic dominates could accordingly be interpreted as a 'small style of writing' or as an aesthetic of the small."[47] While it is not my intention to attribute to Keller the same tenor of irony characteristic of Walser, the gentle yet pervasive comic irony of Keller's style, which his contemporaries first noted and which has become a staple of the scholarship,

---

46. See Kaiser, *Gottfried Keller*, 504.
47. Jens Hobus, "'Nun wieder diese kleine Prosa, diese Abweichungen und -zweigungen': Zur Ethik und Ästhetik des Kleinen im Werk Robert Walsers," in Öhlschläger, Autsch, and Süwolto, *Kulturen des Kleinen*, 121–43.

undoubtedly serves to place the reader at a distance that very much guards against the pathos that dramatic, sublime, or catastrophic storytelling could arouse.[48] Comic irony additionally forestalls the affective investment that could aggrandize fictional characters beyond their state of antiheroic mediocrity. The humor with which Keller presents a world drained of sublimity, grandeur, and heroism—made manifest in a preference for the *Mittelland*, in the casts of dilettantish characters, and in the resplendent detail in which these fictional worlds are painted—ensures both that his miniatures never rise beyond their prosaic nature to the status of exempla and that his representations retain the requisite lightness commensurate to the small formats he imagines them to embody.

In effect, Keller's ethos of making himself small may seem like nothing more than a manner of confirming his realism. After all, one compelling way of summarizing realism and distinguishing it from its Romantic forebears is that it exchanges stories of great deeds and great men for "the ordinary, the everyday, and the small" as the stuff of poetry.[49] While accounts of smallness in realism typically reference Adalbert Stifter's programmatic preface to the *Bunte Steine*—"The wafting of the air the trickling of the water the growing of the grain"[50]—Keller's dissimilarity to Stifter also helps

---

48. Emil Kuh was the first to recognize Keller as "the foremost humorist among our writers." Emil Kuh to Keller, March 14, 1874, in Gottfried Keller, *Gesammelte Briefe in vier Bänden*, ed. Carl Helbling, 4 vols. (Bern: Benteli, 1951–1954), 3.1:176. Keller's humor has been interpreted as mediating between the otherwise irreconcilable subjective and objective perspectives of his realism. See Erika M. Swales, *The Poetics of Skepticism: Gottfried Keller and "Die Leute von Seldwyla"* (Oxford: Berg, 1994); and Wolfgang Preisendanz, *Humor als dichterische Einbildungskraft: Studien zur Erzählkunst des poetischen Realismus*, 3rd rev. ed. (München: Wihelm Fink, 1985), 143–213.

49. As Sabine Schneider observes, realism's turn to the world of things that typically lies under the threshold of perception comes with "a striking tendency to miniaturization and marginalization"; the fictional characters of realism, in turn, become the inhabitants and careful observers of these miniatures. Sabine Schneider, "Vergessene Dinge: Plunder und Trödel in der Erzählliteratur des Realismus," in *Die Dinge und die Zeichen: Dimensionen des Realistischen in der Erzählliteratur des 19. Jahrhunderts*, ed. Sabine Schneider and Barbara Hunfeld (Würzburg: Königshausen & Neumann, 2008), 157.

50. Adalbert Stifter, "Preface," in *Motley Stones*, trans. Isabel Fargo Cole (New York: New York Review Books, 2021), 3.

specify the former's realism and the role that the small and insignificant play in it. For while in Stifter's preface the small conceals both lawfulness and a more ambiguous "greatness" that the preface's narrator promises will reveal itself through careful attention, Keller's miniatures harbor no such promise.[51] Keller's quotidian characters inhabiting the green grasses of low-lying landscapes do not conceal forms of grandeur, as the constantly comic tone of Keller's narrators persistently reminds us. Keller's self-ironizing literature frees itself of didactic and moralizing promise.

Keller's chosen strategy of making himself small is the attempt to find the appropriate subjects, style, and format—that of a *Büchlein* or *Werklein*—for an era experienced as a period of diminished, shrinking greatness, an epoch of dwarfish men. Keller's literary ethos is a counterexample to the figure of Erickson from *Der grüne Heinrich*, who embodies an unhappy mismatch between corporeal size and the format of his art objects. While of overwhelming height—he is described as "a real giant" (ein wahrer Riese)—Erickson only produces miniature landscapes: "Every three months he painted a small picture in the tiniest scale, no larger than the palm of his hand, and it was finished in one day or a day and a half."[52] The paintings are so small in relation to his body that they appear ridiculous. From Keller's perspective, fat, heavy books and large forms might still have their place in the present and future of literature, but only insofar as they acknowledge their smallness in relation to the towering figures of past greatness. Within imagined small formats, inherited forms of literature have been refitted to the

---

51. Stifter, "Preface," in *Motley Stones*, 5. As Paul Fleming, who more broadly traces realism's interest in averageness and mediocrity, writes, "The emphasis on small forms is the crux of Stifter's aesthetics." Paul Fleming, *Exemplarity and Mediocrity: The Art of the Average from Bourgeois Tragedy to Realism* (Stanford, CA: Stanford University Press, 2009), 139. On scaling in Stifter's poetics, see Agnes Hoffmann, "A Poetics of Scaling: Adalbert Stifter and the Measures of Nature Around 1850," in *Before Photography: German Visual Culture in the Nineteenth Century*, ed. Kirsten Belgum, Vance Byrd, and John D. Benjamin (Berlin: Walter de Gruyter, 2021), 267–92.

52. "Alle Vierteljahr malte er ein Bildchen vom allerkleinsten Maßstabe, nicht größer, als sein Handteller, das in einem oder anderthalb Tagen fertig war." Keller, *Der grüne Heinrich* (1st ed., 1854–1855), in *HKKA*, 12:107.

perceived anthropological realities of the late nineteenth century, an era of diminishment. Keller's strategic choice of the small format is one that selects for fit among his own corporeal stature, a set of media objects, and the fictional subjects and settings he unfolds in the contours of those media: a world scaled back not necessarily to the degree of the miniature, but sufficiently small not to be mistaken for great. It is for this reason that Keller ultimately earns Ermatinger's praise precisely for having no pretense to measure up against an earlier age of German literature. Keller's achievement was "to immediately reduce the comparison with the two greats [Goethe and Schiller] to the appropriate degree."[53] Insofar as he even attempts the comparison "Gottfried Keller und Goethe," a measurement sure to reveal Keller's dwarfish standing, Ermatinger recuperates Keller's very strategy for securing himself a place in the history of literature.

---

53. Ermatinger, "Gottfried Keller und Goethe," 81.

Acknowledgments

My interest in the issues explored in these pages developed during my time at Eikones, the Center for the Study of the Theory and History of the Image at the University of Basel. This book grew in its energizing and generous intellectual climate. My special thanks go to Ralph Ubl and Markus Klammer; their scholarship and friendship propelled the book throughout its making. I would also like to thank Johanna Függer-Vagts and Fabian Grütter, with whom I organized the workshop "Form und Format 1880–1940" in 2015, and its participants, in particular Markus Krajewski, Megan Luke, and Petra McGillen. The conversations that took place at that workshop first made clear to me what is at stake in questions of format.

Numerous colleagues and friends, including Frauke Berndt, Nicolas Detering, Sean Franzel, Patrizia McBride, Dorothea von Mücke, Gabrielle Rippl, Sabine Schneider, Rahel Villinger, Julianne Vogel, and Mario Wimmer, read and reviewed different versions of the manuscript, providing valuable criticisms. David Wellbery continues to be an unfailing source of motivation, and the following book bears innumerable traces of his insight and example. At the University of Bern, I have come to rely on the generosity and expertise of my colleague Melanie Rohner.

I would also like to acknowledge Carol Blaser, Selina Gartmann, and Simona Oliveira for their help preparing the manuscript. I am grateful to the two generous anonymous peer reviewers of the manuscript and to Cornell University Press for its support in turning the manuscript into a book. The Zentralbibliothek Zürich provided regular access to Keller's papers and the right to reproduce images from their archives. Funding from the University of Bern made it possible to publish this book open-access.

Anthony E. Mahler read, critiqued, and edited each and every draft of this book; he deserves recognition and my thanks for any measure of the book's quality. I am also daily grateful for those Maskarinecs—Gertraud, Maya, Emil, Amalia, Sibyl, Winizo, and Alex—who provide a joyful antidote to scholarly life. This book is dedicated to the memory of my father, Gregory G. Maskarinec (1951–2022), from whom I learned that the power of thought is only as great as the clarity of language.

Bibliography

Ajouri, Philip. "Chronologische Werkausgaben im 19. Jahrhundert." In Gretz and Pethes, *Archiv/Fiktionen*, 85–105.
Althaus, Thomas, Wolfgang Bunzel, and Dirk Göttsche, eds. *Kleine Prosa: Theorie und Geschichte eines Textfeldes im Literatursystem der Moderne.* Tübingen: Max Niemeyer, 2007.
Amrein, Ursula. *Augenkur und Brautschau: Zur diskursiven Logik der Geschlechterdifferenz in Gottfried Kellers "Sinngedicht."* Bern: Peter Lang, 1994.
Amrein, Ursula. "Geschichte als Spiegelkabinett: Gottfried Kellers 'Der Landvogt von Greifensee' und das Zürich im 18. Jahrhundert." In *Alte Löcher—neue Blicke: Zürich im 18. Jahrhundert*, edited by Helmut Holzhey and Simon Zurbuchen, 167–77. Zürich: Chronos, 1997.
Amrein, Ursula, ed. *Gottfried Keller-Handbuch: Leben—Werk—Wirkung.* 2nd rev. and expanded ed. Stuttgart: J. B. Metzler, 2018.
Amrein, Ursula. "Gottfried Kellers 'artiger kleiner Dekameron': Poetik und Schreibweise des *Sinngedichts* in der Nachfolge Boccaccios." In *Boccaccio und die Folgen: Fontane, Storm, Keller, Ebner-Eschenbach und die Novellenkunst des 19. Jahrhunderts*, edited by Hugo Aust and Hubertus Fischer, 119–34. Würzburg: Königshausen & Neumann, 2006.

Amrein, Ursula. "Todesfiguren: Zur Begründung des Realismus bei Gottfried Keller." In *Gottfried Keller und Theodor Fontane: Vom Realismus zur Moderne*, edited by Ursula Amrein and Regina Dieterle, 63–86. Berlin: Walter de Gruyter, 2008.

Anderson, Benedict. *Imagined Communities: Reflections on the Origin and Spread of Nationalism*. London: Verso, 1983.

Anesko, Michael. "Collected Editions and the Consolidation of Cultural Authority: The Case of Henry James." *Book History* 12 (2009): 186–208.

Apianus. "Aus unserem papiernen Zeitalter." *Die Gartenlaube*, 1874, no. 45, 730–34.

Ariès, Philippe. *The Hour of Our Death: The Classic History of Western Attitudes Toward Death over the Last One Thousand Years*. Translated by Helen Weaver. New York: Alfred A. Knopf, 1981.

Augart, Julia. "'Die mißbrauchten Liebesbriefe': Zur Austauschbarkeit von Identität, Geschlecht und Gefühl im Medium Brief." In *Gottfried Keller: Die Leute von Seldwyla: Kritische Studien—Critical Essays*, edited by Hans-Joachim Hahn and Uwe Seja, 193–212. Bern: Peter Lang, 2007.

Avenarius, Ferdinand. "Gottfried Keller als Lyriker." *Tägliche Rundschau: Feuilletonistische Beilage*, June 14, 1884, 546–47; June 15, 1884, 550–51.

Baechtold, Jakob. *Gottfried Kellers Leben: Seine Briefe und Tagebücher*. 3 vols. Berlin: Wilhelm Hertz, 1894–1897.

Balke, Friedrich, Bernhard Siegert, and Joseph Vogl. "Editorial." In *Medien der Bürokratie*, edited by Friedrich Balke, Bernhard Siegert, and Joseph Vogl, 5–12. Paderborn: Wilhelm Fink, 2016.

Banham, Rob. "The Industrialization of the Book 1800–1970." In *A Companion to the History of the Book*, edited by Simon Eliot and Jonathan Rose, 273–90. Oxford: Blackwell, 2007.

Banki, Luisa, and Kathrin Wittler. "Historische Praktiken der Lektüre in geschlechtertheoretischer Perspektive: Zur Einführung." In *Lektüre und Geschlecht im 18. Jahrhundert: Zur Situativität des Lesens zwischen Einsamkeit und Geselligkeit*, edited by Luisa Banki and Kathrin Wittler, 7–28. Göttingen: Wallstein, 2020.

Barthes, Roland. "The Death of the Author." In *Image, Music, Text*, 142–48. Translated by Stephen Heath. Glasgow: Fontana Paperbacks, 1977.

Barthes, Roland. "The Reality Effect." In *The Rustle of Language*, 141–48. Translated by Richard Howard. Berkeley: University of California Press, 1989.

Baßler, Moritz. "Den Mai gibt es nicht: Intensität und Code in Kellers Poetischem Realismus." In *Kellers Erzählen: Strukturen—Funktionen—Reflexionen*, edited by Philipp Theisohn, 245–57. Gottfried Kellers Moderne, vol. 1. Berlin: Walter de Gruyter, 2022.

Baumann, Walter. *Gottfried Keller: Leben, Werk, Zeit*. Zürich: Artemis, 1986.

Baumgartner, Alexander, SJ. *Göthe's Lehr- und Wanderjahre in Weimar und Italien*. Freiburg im Breisgau: Herder'sche Verlagshandlung, 1882.

Becker, Peter. "'Recht Schreiben'—Disziplin, Sprachbeherrschung und Vernunft: Zur Kunst des Protokollierens im 18. und 19. Jahrhundert." In Niehaus and Schmidt-Hannisa, *Das Protokoll*, 49–76.
Begemann, Christian. "Realismus und Phantastik." In *Die Wirklichkeit des Realismus*, edited by Veronika Thanner, Joseph Vogl, and Dorothea Walzer, 97–113. München: Wilhelm Fink, 2018.
Begemann, Christian. "Roderers Bilder—Hadlaubs Abschriften: Einige Überlegungen zu Mimesis und Wirklichkeitskonstruktion im deutschsprachigen Realismus." In Schneider and Hunfeld, *Die Dinge und die Zeichen*, 25–41.
Begemann, Christian. *Die Welt der Zeichen: Stifter-Lektüren*. Stuttgart: J. B. Metzler, 1995.
Begemann, Christian, and David E. Wellbery, eds. *Kunst—Zeugung—Geburt: Theorien und Metaphern ästhetischer Produktion in der Neuzeit*. Freiburg im Breisgau: Rombach, 2002.
Behrs, Jan. *Der Dichter und sein Denker: Wechselwirkungen zwischen Literatur und Literaturwissenschaft in Realismus und Expressionismus*. Stuttgart: S. Hirzel, 2013.
Behrs, Jan. "Manuskripte brennen (nicht): Nachlassbewusstsein bei Gottfried Keller." In *Nachlassbewusstsein: Literatur, Archiv, Philologie, 1750–2000*, edited by Kai Sina and Carlos Spoerhase, 294–312. Göttingen: Wallstein, 2017.
Belgum, Kirsten. *Popularizing the Nation: Audience, Representation, and the Production of Identity in "Die Gartenlaube," 1853–1900*. Lincoln: University of Nebraska Press, 1998.
Benjamin, Walter. *Selected Writings*. 4 vols. Cambridge, MA: Belknap Press of Harvard University Press, 1996–2003.
Bergengruen, Maximilian. "*Vita longa*: Transformationen einer theosophischen Denkfigur; Jean Pauls *Siebenkäs* und Novalis' *Europa*-Rede." In *Romantische Religiosität*, edited by Alexander von Bormann, 133–48. Würzburg: Königshausen & Neumann, 2005.
Berger, Karol. *Bach's Cycle, Mozart's Arrow: An Essay on the Origins of Musical Modernity*. Berkeley: University of California Press, 2007.
Berman, Russell. "Writing for the Book Industry: The Writer Under Organized Capitalism." *New German Critique* 29 (1983): 39–56.
Berndt, Frauke. *Anamnesis: Studien zur Topik der Erinnerung in der erzählenden Literatur zwischen 1800 und 1900 (Moritz—Keller—Raabe)*. Tübingen: Max Niemeyer, 2012.
Berndt, Frauke. "Grass: Gottfried Keller's Structural Realism." In "German Realisms Around 1850," edited by Frauke Berndt and Dorothea von Mücke. Special issue, *Colloquia Germanica* 53, no. 4 (2021): 421–48.
Berndt, Frauke. "'Das Meretlein': Zur Ikonographie der Novelle in Gottfried Kellers *Der grüne Heinrich*." In *Historismus und Moderne*, edited by Harald Tausch, 161–80. Würzburg: Ergon, 1996.
Berndt, Frauke, and Philipp Theisohn, eds. *Gottfried Kellers Moderne*. 4+ vols. Berlin: Walter de Gruyter, 2022–.

Blair, Ann M. *Too Much to Know: Managing Scholarly Information Before the Modern Age.* New Haven, CT: Yale University Press, 2010.
Bondeson, Jan. *Buried Alive: The Terrifying Story of Our Most Primitive Fear.* New York: W. W. Norton, 2001.
Bosse, Heinrich. *Autorschaft ist Werkherrschaft: Über die Entstehung des Urheberrechts aus dem Geist der Goethezeit.* Paderborn: Wilhelm Fink, 2014.
Breithaupt, Fritz. "Homo Oeconomicus." In *1848 oder das Versprechen der Moderne,* edited by Jürgen Fohrmann and Helmut J. Schneider, 85–112. Würzburg: Königshausen & Neumann, 2003.
Brenner, Anne. *Leseräume: Untersuchungen zu Lektüreverfahren und -funktionen in Gottfried Kellers Roman "Der grüne Heinrich."* Würzburg: Königshausen & Neumann, 2000.
Brooks, Peter. *Reading for the Plot: Design and Intention in Narrative.* Cambridge, MA: Harvard University Press, 1992.
Burckhardt, Jacob. *Werke: Kritische Gesamtausgabe.* Edited by Andreas Cesana, Hans Berner, Susanne Müller, and Elisabeth Oeggerli. 29 vols. München: C. H. Beck; Basel: Schwabe, 2000–.
Butzer, Günter, Manuela Günter, and Renate von Heydebrand. "Strategien zur Kanonisierung des 'Realismus' am Beispiel der *Deutschen Rundschau.*" *Internationales Archiv für Sozialgeschichte der deutschen Literatur* 24 (1999): 55–81.
Byrd, Vance. *A Pedagogy of Observation: Nineteenth-Century Panoramas, German Literature, and Reading Culture.* Lewisburg, PA: Bucknell University Press, 2017.
Byrd, Vance, and Ervin Malakaj. "Introduction: Market Strategies and German Literature in the Long Nineteenth Century." In *Market Strategies and German Literature in the Long Nineteenth Century,* edited by Vance Byrd and Ervin Malakaj, 1–22. Berlin: Walter de Gruyter, 2020.
Byrd, Vance, and Sean Franzel. "Introduction: Periodical Literature in the Nineteenth Century." In "Periodical Literature in the Nineteenth Century," edited by Vance Byrd and Sean Franzel. Special issue, *Colloquia Germanica* 49, no. 2–3 (2016): 105–18.
Cahn, Michael. "*Opera omnia*: The Production of Cultural Authority." In *History of Science, History of Text,* edited by Karine Chemla, 81–94. Dordrecht: Springer, 2004.
Campe, Rüdiger. "Form and Life in the Theory of the Novel." *Constellations* 18, no. 1 (2011): 53–66.
Cantor, Geoffrey, and Sally Shuttleworth, eds. *Science Serialized: Representations of the Sciences in Nineteenth-Century Periodicals.* Cambridge: MIT Press, 2004.
Casper, Scott E., Jeffrey D. Groves, Stephen W. Nissenbaum, and Michael Winship, eds. *The Industrial Book, 1840–1880.* Vol. 3 of *A History of the Book in America.* Chapel Hill: University of North Carolina Press, 2007.
Christians, Heiko, Matthias Bickenbach, and Nikolaus Wegmann, eds. *Historisches Wörterbuch des Mediengebrauchs.* Vol. 1. Köln: Böhlau, 2015.

Cooke, Ebenezer. "Our Art Teaching and Child Nature." In *Transactions of the Education Society, 1884–5*, 65–92. London: William Rice, 1885.

Corngold, Stanley. "Kafka and the Ministry of Writing." In *The Office Writings*, by Franz Kafka, edited by Stanley Corngold, Jack Greenberg, and Benno Wagner, 1–18. Princeton, NJ: Princeton University Press, 2008.

Curtius, Ernst Robert. *European Literature and the Latin Middle Ages*. Translated by Willard R. Trask. Princeton, NJ: Princeton University Press, 2013.

Danneberg, Lutz, Annette Gilbert, and Carlos Spoerhase. "Zur Gegenwart des Werks." In *Das Werk: Zum Verschwinden und Fortwirken eines Grundbegriffs*, edited by Lutz Danneberg, Annette Gilbert, and Carlos Spoerhase, 3–26. Berlin: Walter de Gruyter, 2019.

Daub, Adrian. *What the Ballad Knows: The Ballad Genre, Memory Culture, and German Nationalism*. Oxford: Oxford University Press, 2022.

Dawson, Gowan. "Paleontology in Parts: Richard Owen, William John Broderip, and the Serialization of Science in Early Victorian Britain." *Isis* 103, no. 4 (December 2012): 637–67.

Delafield, Catherine. *Serialization and the Novel in Mid-Victorian Magazines*. Surrey: Ashgate, 2015.

Deutsche Rundschau 11 (March 1877).

Deutsche Rundschau 26 (January–March 1881).

Dickson, Polly. "Tracing Squiggles: Laurence Sterne, E. T. A. Hoffmann, and Honoré de Balzac." *Comparative Literature* 71, no. 2 (2020): 53–67.

Diederichs, Rainer. "Kellers Lebensbuch: Vorwort." In Groddeck, *"Der grüne Heinrich,"* 7–9.

Dilthey, Wilhelm. "Archive für Literatur." In *Gesammelte Schriften*, edited by Karlfried Gründer, vol. 15, *Zur Geistesgeschichte des 19. Jahrhunderts: Portraits und biographische Skizzen; Quellenstudien und Literaturberichte zur Theologie und Philosophie im 19. Jahrhundert*, edited by Ulrich Herrmann, 1–16. Göttingen: Vandenhoeck & Ruprecht, 1991.

Downing, Eric. *The Chain of Things: Divinatory Magic and the Practice of Reading in German Literature and Thought, 1850–1940*. Ithaca, NY: Cornell University Press, 2018.

Downing, Eric. *Double Exposures: Repetition and Realism in Nineteenth-Century German Fiction*. Stanford, CA: Stanford University Press, 2000.

Eco, Umberto. "Interpreting Serials." In *The Limits of Interpretation*, 83–100. Bloomington: Indiana University Press, 1990.

Ehninger, Eva. "Trying on the Drawing Room: 'Realness' and Truth in and out of Photographs." In Maskarinec, *Truth in Serial Form*, 173–95.

Ermatinger, Emil. "Gottfried Keller und Goethe." *PLMA* 64, no. 1 (1949): 79–97.

Ermatinger, Emil. *Gottfried Kellers Leben*. 8th rev. ed. Zürich: Artemis, 1950.

Ermatinger, Emil. *Gottfried Kellers Leben, Briefe und Tagebücher*. 3 vols. Stuttgart: J. G. Cotta'sche Buchhandlung Nachfolger, 1915–1916.

Fleischmann, Ian. "Pederasty and/as Narrative Form: André Gide's Queer Coinages." *French Forum* 45, no. 2 (2020): 155–69.

Fleming, Paul. *Exemplarity and Mediocrity: The Art of the Average from Bourgeois Tragedy to Realism*. Stanford, CA: Stanford University Press, 2009.
Fontane, Theodor. "Züricher Novellen." In *Aufsätze, Kritiken, Erinnerungen*, vol. 1, *Aufsätze und Aufzeichnungen*, edited by Jürgen Kolbe, 496–97. Unnumbered vol. of *Sämtliche Werke*, edited by Walter Keitel. München: Carl Hanser, 1969.
Foucault, Michel. *The Archaeology of Knowledge and the Discourse on Language*. Translated by A. M. Sheridan Smith. New York: Pantheon Books, 1972.
Foucault, Michel. "What Is an Author?" In *Aesthetics, Method, and Epistemology*, edited by James D. Faubion, vol. 2 of *Essential Works of Foucault, 1954–1984*, ed. Paul Rabinow, 205–22. New York: New Press, 1998.
Frank, Gustav, Madleen Podewski, and Stefan Scherer. "Kultur—Zeit—Schrift: Literatur- und Kulturzeitschriften als 'kleine Archive.'" *Internationales Archiv für Sozialgeschichte der deutschen Literatur* 34, no. 2 (2010): 1–45.
Franzel, Sean. *Writing Time: Studies in Serial Literature, 1780–1850*. Ithaca, NY: Cornell University Press, 2023.
Franzel, Sean, Ilinca Iurascu, and Petra McGillen, eds., *Media Inventories*. Berlin: Walter de Gruyter, 2024.
Frederick, Samuel. *The Redemption of Things: Collecting and Dispersal in German Realism and Modernism*. Ithaca, NY: Cornell University Press, 2021.
Frey, Adolf. *Erinnerungen an Gottfried Keller*. 2nd expanded ed. Leipzig: H. Haeffel, 1893.
Fried, Michael. *Courbet's Realism*. Chicago: University of Chicago Press, 1990.
Fried, Michael. *Menzel's Realism: Art and Embodiment in Nineteenth-Century Berlin*. New Haven, CT: Yale University Press, 2002.
Fried, Michael. *Realism, Writing, Disfiguration: On Thomas Eakins and Stephen Crane*. Chicago: University of Chicago Press, 1987.
Fried, Michael. "Shape as Form: Frank Stella's Irregular Polygons." In *Art and Objecthood: Essays and Reviews*, 77–99. Chicago: University of Chicago Press, 1998.
Friedrich, Markus. "Archivists." In *Information: A Historical Companion*, edited by Ann Blair, Paul Duguid, Anja-Siliva Goeing, and Anthony Grafton, 312–17. Princeton, NJ: Princeton University Press, 2021.
Fuchs, Florian. *Civic Storytelling: The Rise of Short Forms and the Agency of Literature*. New York: Zone Books, 2023.
Gailey, Amanda. *Proofs of Genius: Collected Editions from the American Revolution to the Digital Age*. Ann Arbor: University of Michigan Press, 2015.
Gailus, Andreas. *Forms of Life: Aesthetics and Biopolitics in German Culture*. Ithaca, NY: Cornell University Press, 2020.
Gailus, Andreas. "The Poetics of Containment: Goethe's *Conversations of German Refugees* and the Crisis of Representation." *Modern Philology* 100, no. 3 (2003): 436–74.
Gamper, Michael. *Der große Mann: Geschichte eines politischen Phantasmas*. Göttingen: Wallstein, 2016.

Gamper, Michael, and Ruth Mayer, eds. *Kurz und knapp: Zur Mediengeschichte kleiner Formen vom 17. Jahrhundert bis zur Gegenwart*. Bielefeld: Transcript, 2017.
Die Gartenlaube, 1875, no. 7, 106–24.
Gesetz betreffend eine Geschäftsordnung für den Regierungsrath. In *Officielle Sammlung der seit Annahme der Verfassung vom Jahre 1831 erlassenen Gesetze, Beschlüsse und Verordnungen des Eidgenössischen Standes Zürich*, vol. 1, 328–56. Zürich: Friedrich Schultheß, 1831.
Gessler, Luzius. *Lebendig begraben: Studien zur Lyrik des jungen Gottfried Keller*. Bern: A. Francke, 1964.
Geulen, Eva. "Serialization in Goethe's Morphology." *Compar(a)ison: An International Journal of Comparative Literature* 2 (2008): 53–70.
Geulen, Eva. "Toward a Genealogy of Gender in Walter Benjamin's Writing." *German Quarterly* 69, no. 2 (1996): 161–80.
Gitelman, Lisa. *Paper Knowledge: Toward a Media History of Documents*. Durham, NC: Duke University Press, 2014.
Giuriato, Davide. "Paper and Poetics." *Configurations* 18, no. 3 (Fall 2010): 211–29.
Goethe, Johann Wolfgang. "Anzeige von Goethe's sämmtlichen Werken." *Intelligenz-Blatt*, no. 25, 97–99. Supplement to *Morgenblatt für gebildete Stände*, no. 171, July 19, 1826.
Goethe, Johann Wolfgang. *Aus meinem Leben: Dichtung und Wahrheit*. Edited by Klaus-Detlef Müller. Vol. 14 of *Sämtliche Werke: Briefe, Tagebücher und Gespräche*, edited by Dieter Borchmeyer, Martin Ehrenzeller, Karl Eibl, et al. Frankfurt am Main: Deutscher Klassiker Verlag, 1986.
Goethe, Johann Wolfgang. *From My Life: Poetry and Truth*. Translated by Robert R. Heitner. Edited by Thomas P. Saine and Jeffrey L. Sammons. Vol. 4 of *The Collected Works*. New York: Suhrkamp, 1994.
Goethe, Johann Wolfgang. *Goethe's Werke*. 20 vols. Stuttgart: J. G. Cotta'sche Buchhandlung, 1815–1819.
Gombrich, E. H. *The Uses of Images*. London: Phaidon, 1999.
Graeber, David. *Utopia of Rules: On Technology, Stupidity, and the Secret Joys of Bureaucracy*. New York: Melville House, 2015.
Graevenitz, Gerhart von. "Geschichte aus dem Geist des Nekrologs: Zur Begründung der Biographie im 19. Jahrhundert." *Deutsche Vierteljahresschrift für Literaturwissenschaft und Geistesgeschichte* 54, no. 1 (1980): 105–70.
Graevenitz, Gerhart von. "Das Ich am Ende: Strukturen der Ich-Erzählung in Apuleius' *Goldenem Esel*; und Grimmelshausens *Simplicissimus Teutsch*." In *Das Ende: Figuren einer Denkform*, edited by Karlheinz Stierle and Rainer Warning, 123–54. Poetik und Hermeneutik, vol. 16. München: Wilhelm Fink, 1996.
Graevenitz, Gerhart von. "Memoria und Realismus: Erzählende Literatur in der deutschen 'Bildungspresse' des 19. Jahrhunderts." In *Memoria: Vergessen und Erinnern*, edited by Anselm Haverkamp and Renate Lachmann, 283–304. München: Wilhelm Fink, 1993.

Graevenitz, Gerhart von. *Theodor Fontane: Ängstliche Moderne.* Konstanz: Konstanz University Press, 2014.
Graevenitz, Gerhart von. "Wissen und Sehen: Anthropologie und Perspektivismus in der Zeitschriftenpresse des 19. Jahrhunderts und in realistischen Texten; Zu Stifters *Bunten Steinen* und Kellers *Sinngedicht*." In *Wissen in Literatur im 19. Jahrhundert*, edited by Lutz Danneberg and Friederich Vollhardt, 147–89. Tübingen: Max Niemeyer, 2002.
Graves, Robert. *The Greek Myths.* London: Penguin Books, 1992.
Gretz, Daniela. "Aufwärtsstreben als Niedergang oder Variationen des Immergleichen: Zur Ästhetik der Serialität in Gottfried Kellers *Martin Salander* in der *Deutschen Rundschau*." In *Kellers Erzählen: Strukturen—Funktionen—Reflexionen*, edited by Philipp Theisohn, 259–90. Gottfried Kellers Moderne, vol. 1. Berlin: Walter de Gruyter, 2022.
Gretz, Daniela. "Ein literarischer 'Versuch' im Experimentierfeld Zeitschrift: Medieneffekte der *Deutschen Rundschau* auf Gottfried Kellers *Sinngedicht*." *Zeitschrift für deutsche Philologie* 134, no. 2 (2015): 191–215.
Gretz, Daniela. "Das Wissen der Literatur: Der deutsche literarische Realismus und die Zeitschriftenkultur des 19. Jahrhunderts." In *Medialer Realismus*, edited by Daniela Gretz, 99–126. Freiburg im Breisgau: Rombach, 2011.
Gretz, Daniela, and Nicolas Pethes, eds. *Archiv/Fiktionen: Verfahren des Archivierens in Literatur und Kultur des langen 19. Jahrhunderts.* Freiburg im Breisgau: Rombach, 2016.
Groddeck, Wolfram. "'Eine gewisse Unförmlichkeit': Briefeschreiben und Romangeschehen." In Groddeck, *"Der grüne Heinrich,"* 33–54.
Groddeck, Wolfram, ed. *"Der grüne Heinrich": Gottfried Kellers Lebensbuch—neu gelesen.* Zürich: Chronos, 2009.
Guercio, Gabriele. *Art as Existence: The Artist's Monograph and Its Project.* Cambridge: MIT Press, 2006.
Guillory, John. "The Memo and Modernity." *Critical Inquiry* 31, no. 1 (Autumn 2004): 108–32.
Günter, Manuela. "'Ermanne dich, oder vielmehr erweibe dich einmal!': Gender Trouble in der Literatur nach der Kunstperiode." *Internationales Archiv für Sozialgeschichte der deutschen Literatur* 30, no. 2 (2006): 38–61.
Günter, Manuela. *Im Vorhof der Kunst: Mediengeschichten der Literatur im 19. Jahrhundert.* Bielefeld: Transcript, 2008.
Günter, Manuela. "Realismus in Medien: Zu Fontanes Frauenromanen." In *Medialer Realismus*, edited by Daniela Gretz, 167–90. Freiburg im Breisgau: Rombach, 2011.
Haag, Saskia. *Auf wandelbarem Grund: Haus und Literatur im 19. Jahrhundert.* Freiburg im Breisgau: Rombach, 2012.
Hagen, Waltraud. "Werkausgaben." In *Goethe Handbuch*, edited by Bernd Witte, Theo Buck, Hans-Dietrich Dahnke, Regine Otto, and Peter Schmidt, vol. 4.2, *Personen, Sachen, Begriffe L–Z*, edited by Hans-Dietrich Dahnke and Regine Otto, 1137–47. Stuttgart: J. B. Metzler, 1998.

Hart, Gail K. *Readers and Their Fictions in the Novels and Novellas of Gottfried Keller*. Chapel Hill: University of North Carolina Press, 1989.
Hart, Heinrich, and Julius Hart. "Für und gegen Zola." *Kritische Waffengänge* 2 (1882): 44–55.
Helmstetter, Rudolf. *Die Geburt des Realismus aus dem Dunst des Familienblattes: Fontane und die öffentlichkeitsgeschichtlichen Rahmenbedingungen des poetischen Realismus*. München: Wilhelm Fink, 1998.
Hess, Günter. "Die Bilder des *Grünen Heinrich*: Gottfried Kellers poetische Malerei." In *Beschreibungskunst—Kunstbeschreibung: Ekphrasis von der Antike bis zur Gegenwart*, edited by Gottfried Böhm and Helmut Pfotenhauer, 373–95. München: Wilhelm Fink, 1995.
Hettner, Hermann. "*Der grüne Heinrich*: Roman von Gottfried Keller." *National-Zeitung*, May 5, 1854.
Hobus, Jens. "'Nun wieder diese kleine Prosa, diese Abweichungen und -zweigungen': Zur Ethik und Ästhetik des Kleinen im Werk Robert Walsers." In Öhlschläger, Autsch, and Süwolto, *Kulturen des Kleinen*, 121–43. Leiden: Brill, 2019.
Hoffmann, Agnes. "A Poetics of Scaling: Adalbert Stifter and the Measures of Nature Around 1850." In *Before Photography: German Visual Culture in the Nineteenth Century*, edited by Kirsten Belgum, Vance Byrd, and John D. Benjamin, 267–92. Berlin: Walter de Gruyter, 2021.
Honold, Alexander. *Die Tugenden und die Laster: Gottfried Kellers "Die Leute von Seldwyla."* Berlin: Schwabe, 2018.
Hopwood, Nick, Simon Schaffer, and Jim Secord. "Seriality and Scientific Objects in the Nineteenth Century." *History of Science* 48, no. 3–4 (2010): 251–85.
Iurascu, Ilinca. "Paper Matters: *Vielschreiberei* and Bookkeeping in August von Kotzebue's 'Das Buch Papier.'" *Seminar: A Journal of Germanic Studies* 53, no. 4 (2017): 349–61.
Jäger, Maren, Ethel Matala de Mazza, and Joseph Vogl. "Einleitung." In Jäger, Matala de Mazza, and Vogl, *Verkleinerung*, 1–12.
Jäger, Maren, Ethel Matala de Mazza, and Joseph Vogl, eds. *Verkleinerung: Epistemologie und Literaturgeschichte kleiner Formen*. Berlin: Walter de Gruyter, 2020.
Jancovic, Marek, Axel Volmar, and Alexandra Schneider, eds. *Format Matters: Standards, Practices, and Politics in Media Cultures*. Lüneburg: Meson, 2020.
Jonson, Ben. "To the Memory of My Beloued, The Avthor Mr. William Shakespeare: And What He Hath Left Vs." In *Mr. William Shakespeares Comedies, Histories, & Tragedies*, n.p. London: Isaac Jaggard & Edward Blount, 1623.
Joyce, James. "Buried Alive." In *Poems and Shorter Writings*, 138. London: Farber & Faber, 1991.
Joyce, James. *Letters of James Joyce*. Edited by Stuart Gilbert. Vol 1. London: Faber & Faber, 1957.
Kafka, Ben. *The Demon of Writing: Powers and Failures of Paperwork*. New York: Zone Books, 2012.

Kaiser, Gerhard. "Experimentieren oder Erzählen? Zwei Kulturen in Gottfried Kellers *Sinngedicht*." *Jahrbuch der deutschen Schillergesellschaft* 45 (2001): 278–301.
Kaiser, Gerhard. *Gottfried Keller: Das gedichtete Leben*. Frankfurt am Main: Insel, 1981.
Keller, Gottfried. *Gesammelte Briefe in vier Bänden*. Edited by Carl Helbling. 4 vols. Bern: Benteli, 1951–1954.
Keller, Gottfried. "The Governor of Greifensee." In *Perspectives on People: Five Stories by Gottfried Keller*, translated by Lawrence M. Washington, 95–164. Sherman Oaks, CA: Banner Books, 1977.
Keller, Gottfried. *Green Henry*. Translated by A. M. Holt. Rev. ed. London: Alma Classics, 2023.
Keller, Gottfried. "The Lost Smile." Translated by Frank G. Ryder. In *Stories*, edited by Frank G. Ryder, 190–270. New York: Continuum, 1982.
Keller, Gottfried. *Martin Salander*. Translated by Kenneth Halwas. London: John Calder, 1963.
Keller, Gottfried. "The Misused Love Letters." Translated by Michael Bullock. In *Two Novellas: The Misused Love Letters; Regula Amrain and Her Youngest Son*, 13–94. New York: Frederick Ungar, 1974.
Keller, Gottfried. Nachlass. Zentralbibliothek Zürich.
Keller, Gottfried. [HKKA] *Sämtliche Werke: Historisch-Kritische Ausgabe*. Edited by Walter Morgenthaler. 32 vols. Basel: Stroemfeld; Zürich: Neue Zürcher Zeitung, 1996–2013.
Keller, Gottfried. *Seldwyla Folks: Three Singular Tales*. Translated by Wolf von Schierbrand. New York: Brentano's, 1919.
Keller, Gottfried. *Seven Legends*. Translated by Martin Wyness. London: Gowans & Gray, 1911.
Keller, Gottfried. "Züricher Novellen V (Schluß): Der Landvogt von Greifensee II." *Deutsche Rundschau* 11 (April 1877): 20–55.
Keller, Gottfried, and Theodor Storm. *Theodor Storm—Gottfried Keller: Briefwechsel; Kritische Ausgabe*. Edited by Karl Ernst Laage. Berlin: Erich Schmidt, 1992.
Kelleter, Frank. "Five Ways of Looking at Popular Seriality." In *Media of Serial Narrative*, edited by Frank Kelleter, 7–37. Columbus: Ohio State University Press, 2017.
Kempner, Friederike. "Das scheintote Kind." In *Die sämtlichen Gedichte der Friederike Kempner*, edited by Eiger Blühm and Lutz Mackensen, 44–45. Bremen: Carl Schünemann, 1964.
Kennedy, J. Gerald. "Poe and Magazine Writing on Premature Burial." *Studies in the American Renaissance* (1977): 165–78.
Kittler, Friedrich. "Die Herrschaft der Schreibtische." In *Work and Culture: Büro; Inszenierung von Arbeit*, edited by Herbert Lachmayer and Eleonora Louis, 39–42. Klagenfurt: Ritter, 1998.
Kohns, Oliver, and Martin Roussel. "Kopieren." In Christians, Bickenbach, and Wegmann, *Historisches Wörterbuch des Mediengebrauchs*, vol. 1, 369–81.

König, Dominik von. "Lesesucht und Lesewut." In *Buch und Leser: Vorträge des ersten Jahrestreffens des Wolfenbütteler Arbeitskreises für Geschichte des Buchwesens 13. und 14. Mai 1976*, edited by Herbert G. Göpfert, 89–113. Hamburg: E. Hauswedell, 1977.

Koschorke, Albrecht. "Das buchstabierte Panorama: Zu einer Passage in Stifters Erzählung 'Granit.'" *Vierteljahresschrift des Adalbert-Stifter-Instituts des Landes Oberösterreich* 38, no. 1/2 (1989): 3–13.

Krajewski, Markus. "DIN A: The Basis of All Thought." Translated by Anthony Mahler and Charles Marcrum II. In Maskarinec, *Truth in Serial Form*, 253–75.

Kreiling, Jean L. "A Note on James Joyce, Gottfried Keller, and Music." *James Joyce Quarterly* 25, no. 3 (Spring 1988): 349–56.

Kriesi, Hans Max. *Gottfried Keller als Politiker*. Leipzig: Huber, 1918.

Krüger-Fürhoff, Irmela Marei. "Ab/Schreiben: Handschrift zwischen Liebesdienst und Dienstbarkeit in Goethes *Wahlverwandtschaften*, Eliots *Middlemarch* und Kellers 'Die mißbrauchten Liebesbriefe.'" In *Schreiben als Ereignis: Künste und Kulturen der Schrift*, edited by Jutta Müller-Tamm, Caroline Schubert, and Klaus Ulrich Werner, 219–39. München: Wilhelm Fink, 2018.

Kühne, Ferdinand Gustav. "*Der grüne Heinrich*: Roman von G. Keller." *Europa: Chronik der gebildeten Welt*, April 27, 1854, 286–87.

La Cerda, Juan de. *Weiblicher Lustgarten*. Translated by Aegidius Albertinus. München: Nicolaus Henricus, 1605.

Lipkin, Michael. "'A Public Spectacle': Keller, Schiller, and the Civic Festival." In *Kellers Medien: Formen—Genres—Institutionen*, edited by Frauke Berndt, 289–312. Gottfried Kellers Moderne, vol. 2. Berlin: Walter de Gruyter, 2022.

Lipkin, Michael. "'To Make an Example of Myself': The Problems of an Instructive Realism in Gottfried Keller's *Der grüne Heinrich*." *German Studies Review* 44, no. 2 (2021): 255–73.

Loewenich, Caroline von. *Gottfried Keller: Frauenbild und Frauengestalten im erzählerischen Werk*. Würzburg: Königshausen & Neumann, 2000.

Luck, Rätus, ed. *Geehrter Herr—lieber Freund: Schweizer Autoren und ihre deutschen Verleger; Mit einer Umkehrung und drei Exkursionen*. Basel: Stroemfeld, 1998.

Lukács, Georg. "Gottfried Keller." In *German Realists in the Nineteenth Century*, translated by Jeremy Gaines and Paul Keast, edited by Rodney Livingstone, 157–247. Cambridge: MIT Press, 1993.

Lukács, Georg. *The Historical Novel*. Translated by Hannah Mitchell and Stanley Mitchell. Boston: Beacon, 1963.

Lukács, Georg. "Narrate or Describe? A Preliminary Discussion of Naturalism and Formalism." In *Writer and Critic, and Other Essays*, edited and translated by Arthur Kahn, 110–48. London: Merlin, 1970.

Lyon, John B., and Deiulio, Laura, eds. *Gender, Collaboration, and Authorship in German Culture: Literary Joint Ventures, 1750–1850*. New York: Bloomsbury Academic, 2019.

MacLeod, Catriona. *Embodying Ambiguity: Androgyny and Aesthetics from Winckelmann to Keller*. Detroit, MI: Wayne State University Press, 1998.

MacLeod, Catriona. "Sweetmeats for the Eye: Porcelain Miniatures in Classical Weimar." In *The Enlightened Eye: Goethe and Visual Culture*, edited by Evelyn K. Moore and Patricia Anne Simpson, 41–72. Amsterdam: Rodopi, 2007.

Magnin, Maria. "Landluxus für Städter in Gottfried Kellers 'Landvogt von Greifensee.'" In *Orte des Überflusses: Zur Topographie des Luxuriösen in Literatur und Kultur der Moderne*, edited by Hans-Georg von Arburg, Maria Magnin, and Raphael J. Müller, 137–56. Berlin: Walter de Gruyter, 2022.

Mak, Bonnie. *How the Page Matters*. Toronto: University of Toronto Press, 2012.

Martini, Fritz. "Die deutsche Novelle im 'bürgerlichen Realismus': Überlegungen zur geschichtlichen Bestimmung des Formtypus." *Wirkendes Wort: Deutsche Sprache und Literatur in Forschung und Lehre* 10 (1960): 257–78.

Martus, Steffen. *Werkpolitik: Zur Literaturgeschichte kritischer Kommunikation vom 17. bis ins 20. Jahrhundert mit Studien zu Klopstock, Tieck, Goethe und George*. Berlin: Walter de Gruyter, 2007.

Martus, Steffen. "Zwischen Dichtung und Wahrheit: Zur Werkfunktion von Lyrik im 19. Jahrhundert." In *Lyrik im 19. Jahrhundert: Gattungspoetik als Reflexionsmedium der Kultur*, edited by Steffen Martus, Stefan Scherer, and Claudia Stockinger, 61–92. Bern: Peter Lang, 2005.

Maskarinec, Malika. "Allegory and Analogy in Menzel's *The Iron Rolling Mill*." *Zeitschrift für Kunstgeschichte* 84, no. 1 (2021): 58–77.

Maskarinec, Malika, ed. *Truth in Serial Form: Serial Formats and the Form of the Series, 1850–1930*. Berlin: Walter de Gruyter, 2023.

Matala de Mazza, Ethel. "'Verkleinlichung aller Grösse': Heine und Marx über Staatsmänner nach Napoleon." In *Größe: Zur Medien- und Konzeptgeschichte personaler Macht im langen 19. Jahrhundert*, edited by Michael Gamper and Ingrid Kleeberg, 319–33. Zürich: Chronos, 2015.

Mayer, Mathias. "Midas statt Pygmalion: Die Tödlichkeit der Kunst bei Goethe, Schnitzler, Hofmannsthal und Georg Kaiser." *Deutsche Vierteljahrsschrift für Literaturwissenschaft und Geistesgeschichte* 64, no. 2 (1990): 278–310.

McGillen, Petra S. *The Fontane Workshop: Manufacturing Realism in the Industrial Age of Print*. New York: Bloomsbury Academic, 2019.

McGuirl, Erin. "Office Practices." In *Information: A Historical Companion*, edited by Ann Blair, Paul Duguid, Anja-Siliva Goeing, and Anthony Grafton, 647–58. Princeton, NJ: Princeton University Press, 2021.

Menke, Bettine. "Allegorie: 'Ostentation der Faktur' und 'Theorie': Einleitung." In *Allegorie*, edited by Ulla Haselstein, 113–35. Berlin: Walter de Gruyter, 2016.

Menninghaus, Winfried. *Artistische Schrift: Studien zur Kompositionskunst Gottfried Kellers*. Frankfurt am Main: Suhrkamp, 1982.

Messerli, Alfred. *Lesen und Schreiben, 1700 bis 1900: Untersuchung zur Durchsetzung der Literalität in der Schweiz*. Tübingen: Max Niemeyer, 2002.

Meyertholen, Andrea. "From Marginalia to the Museum: The Transfiguration of the Doodle by Gottfried Keller, Hans Prinzhorn, and Jean Dubuffet." *Seminar: A Journal of Germanic Studies* 58, no. 4 (November 2022): 361–85.

Meyertholen, Andrea. "It's Not Easy Being Green: The Failure of Abstract Art in Gottfried Keller's *Der grüne Heinrich*." *German Studies Review* 39, no. 2 (2016): 241–58.
Moretti, Franco. *The Way of the World: The Bildungsroman in European Culture*. Translated by Albert Sbragia. London: Verso, 1987.
Morgenthaler, Walter. "Die Gesammelten und die Sämtlichen Werke." *Text: Kritische Beiträge* 10 (2005): 13–26.
Morgenthaler, Walter. "Gottfried Kellers Studienbücher." In *Bilder der Handschrift: Die graphische Dimension der Literatur*, edited by Davide Giuriato and Stephan Kammer, 107–29. Frankfurt am Main: Stroemfeld, 2006.
Morgenthaler, Walter. "Grattier, Gratthier oder Steinbock? Zur Textkonstitution bei Conrad Ferdinand Meyer und Gottfried Keller." *MLN* 117, no. 3 (April 2002): 527–43.
Morgenthaler, Walter. "Die *Grünen Heinriche*: Zur Text- und Überlieferungsgeschichte eines Romans." In Groddeck, *"Der grüne Heinrich,"* 11–32.
Morgenthaler, Walter. "Überlieferung und Textkonstitution bei Gottfried Keller." *Schweizer Monatshefte* 73 (1993): 503–15.
Morgenthaler, Walter. "Wann sind Gottfried Kellers *Leute von Seldwyla* entstanden? Zu einigen Datierungsfragen der 'zweiten vermehrten Auflage.'" *Text: Kritische Beiträge* 6 (2000): 99–110.
Mücke, Dorothea von. "'Das gemalte nächtliche Tapetenvaterland': Realist Aesthetics and the Politics of Representation." *Figuration: Gender, Literatur, Kultur* 20, no. 1 (2019): 35–47.
Mücke, Dorothea von. "'A Village Romeo and Juliet' and Gottfried Keller's Realism." In "German Realisms Around 1850," edited by Frauke Berndt and Dorothea von Mücke. Special issue, *Colloquia Germanica* 53, no. 4 (2021): 449–72.
Müller, Dominik. *"Der grüne Heinrich* (1879/80): Der späte Abschluß eines Frühwerks." In *Interpretationen: Gottfried Keller; Romane und Erzählungen*, edited by Walter Morgenthaler, 36–56. Stuttgart: Philipp Reclam, 2007.
Müller, Dominik. "Schriftsteller als Staats-Schreiber? Politische Interventionsformen der Literatur in der Schweiz—von Gottfried Keller zu Guy Krneta." In *Die Wiederkehr der res publica: Zu literarischer Repräsentation einer politischen Idee im globalen Zeitalter*, edited by Dariusz Komorowski, 105–21. Göttingen: Vandenhoeck & Ruprecht, 2021.
Müller, Gernot Michael. "Moiren." In *Mythenrezeption: Die antike Mythologie in Literatur, Musik und Kunst von den Anfängen bis zur Gegenwart*, edited by Maria Moog-Grünewald, vol. 5 of *Der Neue Pauly Supplemente*, edited by Hubert Cancik, Manfed Landfester, and Helmuth Schnieder, 436–40. Stuttgart: J. B. Metzler, 2008.
Müller, Lothar. *White Magic: The Age of Paper*. Translated by Jessica Spengler. Cambridge: Polity, 2014.
Müller, Susanne. "Formatieren." In Christians, Bickenbach, and Wegmann, *Historisches Wörterbuch des Mediengebrauchs*, vol. 1, 253–67.
Müller Nielaba, Daniel. "'Besser schreiben' gelernt—Heinrich Lees Erzähler." In Groddeck, *"Der grüne Heinrich,"* 79–90.

Muschg, Adolf. *Gottfried Keller*. München: Kindler, 1977.
Muschg, Walter. "Der Zwerg: Umriss eines Gottfried-Keller-Portraits." In *Homo homini homo: Festschrift für Joseph E. Drexel zum 70. Geburtstag*, 31–58. München: C. H. Beck, 1966.
Nash, Andrew, ed. *The Culture of Collected Editions*. Basingstoke: Palgrave Macmillan, 2003.
Naumann, Barbara. "Die 'kolossale Kritzelei', der 'borghesische Fechter' und andere Versuche: Der grüne Heinrich." In Groddeck, *"Der grüne Heinrich,"* 159–200.
Neumann, Gerhard. "Der Körper des Menschen und die belebte Statue: Zu einer Grundformel in Gottfried Kellers *Sinngedicht*." In *Pygmalion: Die Geschichte des Mythos in der abendländischen Kultur*, edited by Mathias Mayer and Gerhard Neumann, 555–91. Freiburg im Breisgau: Rombach, 1997.
Niehaus, Michael. "Protokollstile: Literarische Verwendungsweisen einer Textsorte." *Deutsche Vierteljahrsschrift für Literaturwissenschaft und Geistesgeschichte* 79, no. 4 (2005): 692–707.
Niehaus, Michael. *Was ist ein Format?* Hannover: Wehrhahn, 2018.
Niehaus, Michael, and Hans-Walter Schmidt-Hannisa, eds. *Das Protokoll: Kulturelle Funktionen einer Textsorte*. Frankfurt am Main: Peter Lang, 2005.
Niehaus, Michael, and Hans-Walter Schmidt-Hannisa. "Textsorte Protokoll: Ein Aufriß." In Niehaus and Schmidt-Hannisa, *Das Protokoll*, 7–23.
Nietzsche, Friedrich. *Beyond Good and Evil: Prelude to a Philosophy of the Future*. Translated by Walter Kaufmann. New York: Vintage Books, 1966.
Nietzsche, Friedrich. *The Case of Wagner*. In *The Birth of Tragedy and The Case of Wagner*, 153–92. Translated by Walter Kaufmann. New York: Vintage Books, 1967.
Nietzsche, Friedrich. *Human, All Too Human: A Book for Free Spirits*. Translated by R. J. Hollingdale. Cambridge: Cambridge University Press, 1996.
Nietzsche, Friedrich. *On the Genealogy of Morals*. Translated by Walter Kaufmann and R. J. Hollingdale. New York: Vintage Books, 1989.
Nissen, Hans J., Peter Damerow, and Robert K. Englund. *Frühe Schrift und Techniken der Wirtschaftsverwaltung im alten Vorderen Orient: Informationsspeicherung und -verarbeitung vor 5000 Jahren*. Bad Salzdetfurth: Franzbecker, 1990.
Öhlschläger, Claudia, Sabiene Autsch, and Leonie Süwolto, eds. *Kulturen des Kleinen: Mikroformate in Literatur, Kunst und Medien*. Leiden: Brill, 2019.
Osterhammel, Jürgen. *The Transformation of the World: A Global History of the Nineteenth Century*. Translated by Patrick Camiller. Princeton, NJ: Princeton University Press, 2014.
Osterkamp, Ernst. "Erzählte Landschaften." In Groddeck, *"Der grüne Heinrich,"* 141–58.
Osterwalder, Sonja. "Auf die Fußspitzen gestellt: C. F. Meyers größere Helden." In *Größe: Zur Medien- und Konzeptgeschichte personaler Macht im langen 19. Jahrhundert*, edited by Michael Gamper and Ingrid Kleeberg, 335–44. Zürich: Chronos, 2015.

Parr, Rolf. *Autorschaft: Eine kurze Sozialgeschichte der literarischen Intelligenz in Deutschland zwischen 1860 und 1930*. Heidelberg: Synchron, 2008.

Parr, Rolf. "Das Protokoll als literarische Kunstform: Zur Konvergenz von künstlerischer und juridischer Selbstvergewisserung in literarisch-kulturellen Vereinen des 19. Jahrhunderts." In Niehaus and Schmidt-Hannisa, *Das Protokoll*, 167–86.

Patten, Robert L. *Charles Dickens and "Boz": The Birth of the Industrial-Age Author*. Cambridge: Cambridge University Press, 2012.

Piper, Andrew. *Dreaming in Books: The Making of the Bibliographic Imagination in the Romantic Age*. Chicago: University of Chicago Press, 2009.

Pfotenhauer, Helmut. "Einspruch: 'Keine Romane mehr'; Gottfried Kellers vertrackte Absage an eine Literatur, die sich an die Stelle des Lebens drängt." In *"Das wahre Leben ist die Literatur": Konzepte radikaler Autorschaft von Jean Paul bis Robert Walser*, 83–102. Würzburg: Königshausen & Neumann, 2020.

Preisendanz, Wolfgang. *Humor als dichterische Einbildungskraft: Studien zur Erzählkunst des poetischen Realismus*. 3rd rev. ed. München: Wilhelm Fink, 1985.

Price, Leah. *How to Do Things with Books in Victorian Britain*. Princeton, NJ: Princeton University Press, 2012.

Price, Leah, and Pamela Thurschwell. *Literary Secretaries/Secretarial Culture*. Aldershot: Ashgate, 2005.

Regierungsratsbeschlüsse. Staatsarchiv des Kantons Zürich.

Rodenberg, Julius. "Die Begründung der *Deutschen Rundschau*." In *Ein Rückblick*, 29–30. Berlin: Gebrüder Paetel, 1899.

Roose, Kerstin. "'Letztes Bett' und 'schwarzer Kasten.' Der Sarg als Objekt zwischen Ausstellen und Verbergen in Texten des Realismus." *Zeitschrift für Germanistik* 31, no. 3 (2021): 439–51.

Rose, Mark. "The Author as Proprietor: *Donaldson v. Becket* and the Genealogy of Modern Authorship." *Representations* 23 (Summer 1988): 51–85.

Ruge, Arnold. "Aus dem literarischen Zürich." *Literatur- und Kunstbericht*, no. 34 (1846), 131–35; no. 35 (1846), 137–40.

Rüve, Gerlind. *Scheintod: Zur kulturellen Bedeutung der Schwelle zwischen Leben und Tod um 1800*. Bielefeld: Transcript, 2008.

Schlaffer, Hannelore. *Poetik der Novelle*. Stuttgart: J. B. Metzler, 1993.

Schmidt, Julian. "*Der grüne Heinrich*, Roman von Gottfried Keller." *Die Grenzboten: Zeitschrift für Politik und Literatur* 13, no. 1 (1854): 401–5.

Schneider, Sabine. "Einleitung." In Schneider and Hunfeld, *Die Dinge und die Zeichen*, 11–24.

Schneider, Sabine. "'Ein strenger Umriß'—Prägnanz als Leitidee von Goethes Formdenken im Kontext der Weimarer Kunsttheorie." *Goethe-Jahrbuch* 128 (2011): 98–106.

Schneider, Sabine. "Happy End im 'Kampf ums Dasein'? Vergessene Konstellationen von Literatur und Wissen in Kellers *Sinngedicht* und Raabes *Lar*." In *Vergessene Konstellationen literarischer Öffentlichkeit zwischen 1840 und*

1885, edited by Katja Mellmann and Jesko Reiling, 321–44. Berlin: Walter de Gruyter, 2016.

Schneider, Sabine. "Ikonen der Liebe: Heinrichs Frauenbilder." In Groddeck, *"Der grüne Heinrich,"* 201–19.

Schneider, Sabine. "Offene Versuchskulturen: Gottfried Kellers *Sinngedicht*." In *Labor der Phantasie: Texte zur Literatur- und Wissensgeschichte*, edited by Jutta Müller-Tamm, 1–30. Berlin: Alpheus, 2015.

Schneider, Sabine. "'Poesie der Unreife': Autobiographisches Schreiben im Roman." In Groddeck, *"Der grüne Heinrich,"* 55–77.

Schneider, Sabine. "Vergessene Dinge: Plunder und Trödel in der Erzählliteratur des Realismus." In Schneider and Hunfeld, *Die Dinge und die Zeichen*, 157–74.

Schneider, Sabine, and Barbara Hunfeld, eds. *Die Dinge und die Zeichen: Dimensionen des Realistischen in der Erzählliteratur des 19. Jahrhunderts.* Würzburg: Königshausen & Neumann, 2008.

Schrader, Hans-Jürgen. "Autorfedern unter Preß-Autorität: Mitformende Marktfaktoren der realistischen Erzählkunst—an Beispielen Storms, Raabes und Kellers." *Jahrbuch der Raabe-Gesellschaft* 42, no. 1 (2001): 1–40.

Schrader, Hans-Jürgen. "Im Schraubstock moderner Marktmechanismen: Vom Druck Kellers und Meyers in Rodenbergs *Deutscher Rundschau*." *Jahresbericht der Gottfried Keller-Gesellschaft* 62 (1993): 3–38.

Schulz, Wilhelm. "Der schweizer Dichter Gottfried Keller." *Blätter für literarische Unterhaltung*, November 1–2, 1846, 1217–22.

Sebald, W. G. "Death Draws Nigh, Time Marches On: Some Remarks on Gottfried Keller." In *A Place in the Country: On Gottfried Keller, Johann Peter Hebel, Robert Walser, and Others*, translated by Jo Catling, 93–123. New York: Random House, 2013.

Sederholm, Carl H. "Bodies out of Place: Poe, Premature Burial, and the Uncanny." *Forum* 24 (Spring 2017). https://doi.org/10.2218/forum.24.1877.

Shepard, Elisabeth. "Hidden Voices in the Archives: Pioneering Women Archivists in Early 20th Century England." In *Engaging with Archives and Records: Histories and Theories*, edited by Fiorella Foscarini, Heather MacNeil, Gillian Oliver, and Bonnie Mak, 83–104. London: Facet, 2017.

Siegert, Bernhard. *Relays: Literature as an Epoch of the Postal System.* Translated by Kevin Repp. Stanford, CA: Stanford University Press, 1999.

Simon, Ralf. "Gespenster des Realismus: Moderne-Konstellationen in den Spätwerken von Raabe, Stifter und C. F. Meyer." In *Konzepte der Moderne*, edited by Gerhart von Graevenitz, 202–33. Stuttgart: J. B. Metzler, 1999.

Spoerhase, Carlos. *Das Format der Literatur: Praktiken materieller Textualität zwischen 1740 und 1830.* Göttingen: Wallstein, 2018.

Spoerhase, Carlos. "Poetic Creativity from Material Constraints: On Goethe's *West-Eastern Divan*." In *Goethes Spätwerk/On Late Goethe*, edited by David E. Wellbery and Kai Sina, 141–56. Berlin: Walter de Gruyter, 2020.

Spoerhase, Carlos. "Skalierung: Ein ästhetischer Grundbegriff der Gegenwart." In *Ästhetik der Skalierung*, edited by Carlos Spoerhase, Siegel Steffen, and Nikolaus Wegmann, 5–16. Hamburg: Felix Meiner, 2020.

Spoerhase, Carlos, Steffen Siegel, and Nikolaus Wegmann, eds. *Ästhetik der Skalierung*. Hamburg: Felix Meiner, 2020.

Sprenger, Florian. "Standards und Standarten." *Standardisierung und Naturalisierung*, edited by Martin Müller and Christoph Neubert, 21–45. Paderborn: Wilhelm Fink, 2019.

Sterne, Jonathan. *MP3: The Meaning of a Format*. Durham, NC: Duke University Press, 2012.

Stifter, Adalbert. *Motley Stones*. Translated by Isabel Fargo Cole. New York: New York Review Books, 2021.

Stifter, Adalbert. *Werke und Briefe: Historisch-kritische Gesamtausgabe*. Edited by Alfred Doppler and Wolfgang Frühwald. 11 vols. Stuttgart: W. Kohlhammer, 1978–.

Stocker, Peter. "Gottfried Kellers Arbeitsplan 'Seldwyla II': Zur genetischen Eigendynamik entstehungsgeschichtlicher Dokumente." *Text: Kritische Beiträge* 5 (1999): 63–81.

Stockinger, Claudia. *An den Ursprüngen populärer Serialität: Das Familienblatt "Die Gartenlaube."* Göttingen: Wallstein, 2018.

Stockinger, Claudia. "Paradigma Goethe? Die Lyrik des 19. Jahrhunderts und Goethe." In *Lyrik im 19. Jahrhundert: Gattungspoetik als Reflexionsmedium der Kultur*, edited by Steffen Martus, Stefan Scherer, and Claudia Stockinger, 93–125. Bern: Peter Lang, 2005.

Strowick, Elisabeth. *Gespenster des Realismus: Zur literarischen Wahrnehmung von Wirklichkeit*. Paderborn: Wilhelm Fink, 2019.

Strowick, Elisabeth. "Gottfried Kellers Szenographie des Wirklichen." *Sprache und Literatur* 49, no. 2 (2020): 215–40.

Strowick, Elisabeth. "'Nachkommenschaften': Stifter's Series." Translated by Anthony Mahler. In Maskarinec, *Truth in Serial Form*, 83–113.

Sully, James. *Untersuchungen über die Kindheit: Psychologische Abhandlungen für Lehrer und gebildete Eltern*. Translated by Joseph Stimpfl. Leipzig: Ernst Wunderlich, 1897.

Swales, Erika M. *The Poetics of Skepticism: Gottfried Keller and "Die Leute von Seldwyla."* Oxford: Berg, 1994.

Tatlock, Lynne. "Afterlife of Nineteenth-Century Popular Fiction and the German Imaginary: The Illustrated Collected Novels of E. Marlitt, W. Heimburg, and E. Werner." In *Publishing Culture and the "Reading Nation": German Book History in the Long Nineteenth Century*, edited by Lynne Tatlock, 118–53. Rochester, NY: Camden House, 2010.

Tatlock, Lynne. "Introduction: The Book Trade and the 'Reading Nation' in the Long Nineteenth Century." In *Publishing Culture and the "Reading Nation": German Book History in the Long Nineteenth Century*, edited by Lynne Tatlock, 1–21. Rochester, NY: Camden House, 2010.

Te Heesen, Anke. "The Notebook: A Paper-Technology." In *Making Things Public: Atmospheres of Democracy*, edited by Bruno Latour and Peter Weibel, 582–89. Cambridge: MIT Press, 2005.
Theisohn, Philipp. "Mädchenbekehrer: *Sieben Legenden* oder Gottfried Kellers Poetik des Eros." *Mitteilungen der Gottfried Keller-Gesellschaft* (2017): 9–28.
Thomasson, Amie L. "Die Ontologie literarischer Werke." In *Das Werk: Zum Verschwinden und Fortwirken eines Grundbegriffs*, edited by Lutz Danneberg, Annette Gilbert, and Carlos Spoerhase, 29–46. Berlin: Walter de Gruyter, 2019.
Thüring, Hubert. "'Kraft, oder so was': Poetik und Wissen(schaft) des Lebens in der Rahmenerzählung von Gottfried Kellers *Sinngedicht*." In *Lebenswissen: Poetologien des Lebendigen im langen 19. Jahrhundert*, edited by Benjamin Brückner, Judith Preiß, and Peter Schnyder, 135–68. Freiburg im Breisgau: Rombach, 2016.
Torra-Mattenklott, Caroline. *Poetik der Figur: Zwischen Geometrie und Rhetorik; Modelle der Textkomposition von Lessing bis Valéry*. Paderborn: Wilhelm Fink, 2016.
Türk, Johannes. "Unvergleichliche Ruhe: Franz Kafkas Protokollaufnahmen." In *Gespenster des Wissens*, edited by Ute Holl, Claus Pias, and Burkhardt Wolf, 371–76. Zürich: Diaphanes, 2017.
Utz, Peter. "Verengte Aussichten, neuer Glanz: Fensterblicke in Gottfried Kellers *Der grüne Heinrich*." In *Kellers Medien: Formen—Genres—Institutionen*, edited by Frauke Berndt, 129–40. Gottfried Kellers Moderne, vol. 2. Berlin: Walter de Gruyter, 2022.
Vedder, Ulrike. "Scheintod, Koma, Testament: Wissenschaftliche und literarische Fiktionen an der Grenze des Todes." In *Engineering Life: Narrationen von Menschen in Biomedizin, Kultur und Literatur*, edited by Claudia Breger, Irmela Marei Krüger-Fürhoff, and Tanja Nusser, 53–69. Berlin: Kulturverlag Kadmos, 2008.
Vedder, Ulrike. *Das Testament als literarisches Dispositiv: Kulturelle Praktiken des Erbes in der Literatur des 19. Jahrhunderts*. München: Wilhelm Fink, 2011.
Villwock, Peter. "Betty und Gottfried: Eine Geschichte in Bildern." In "Der Gottfried-Keller-Rabe," edited by Joachim Kersten. Special issue, *Der Rabe* 61 (2000): 150–62.
Vismann, Cornelia. *Files: Law and Media Technology*. Translated by Geoffrey Winthrop-Young. Stanford, CA: Stanford University Press, 2008.
Vogel, Juliane. "Ephemeriden der Schere: Scherenschnitt und Zeitungsausschnitt im 19. Jahrhundert." In Jäger, Matala de Mazza, and Vogl, *Verkleinerung*, 15–38.
Vogel, Juliane. "Die Schere: Karriere eines Werkzeuges in den Künsten der Moderne." *Zeitschrift für Ideengeschichte* 13, no. 3 (2019): 75–86.
Vogel, Juliane. "Stifters Gitter: Poetologische Dimensionen einer Grenzfigur." In Schneider and Hunfeld, *Die Dinge und die Zeichen*, 43–53.
Volmar, Axel. "Das Format als medienindustriell motivierte Form: Überlegungen zu einem medienkulturwissenschaftlichen Formatbegriff." *Zeitschrift für Medienwissenschaft* 22, no. 1 (2020): 19–30.

Wagner, Monika. *Allegorie und Geschichte: Ausstattungsprogramme öffentlicher Gebäude des 19. Jahrhunderts in Deutschland; Von der Cornelius-Schule zur Malerei der Wilhelminischen Ära*. Tübingen: Ernst Wasmuth, 1989.
Weber, Bruno. "Wie klein war Gottfried Keller." In "Der Gottfried-Keller-Rabe," edited by Joachim Kersten. Special issue, *Der Rabe* 61 (2000): 15–30.
Weber, Max. "Bureaucracy." In *Economy and Society: An Outline of Interpretive Sociology*, edited by Guenther Roth and Claus Wittich, 956–1003. Berkeley: University of California Press, 1978.
Weiss, Gottfried. "Der Prozeß um das Testament von Gottfried Keller." *Neue Zürcher Zeitung*, March 27, 1955.
Weitzman, Erica. *At the Limit of the Obscene: German Realism and the Disgrace of Matter*. Evanston, IL: Northwestern University Press, 2021.
Wellbery, David E. "Die Enden des Menschen: Anthropologie und Einbildungskraft im Bildungsroman (Wieland, Goethe, Novalis)." In *Das Ende: Figuren einer Denkform*, edited by Karlheinz Stierle and Rainer Warning, 600–639. Poetik und Hermeneutik, vol. 16. München: Wilhelm Fink, 1996.
Weltzien, Friedrich. "Kritzeln." In Christians, Bickenbach, and Wegmann, *Historisches Wörterbuch des Mediengebrauchs*, vol. 1, 382–92.
Werle, Dirk. "Nachlass, Nachwelt und Nachruhm um 1800: Am Beispiel Johann Wolfgang Goethes." In *Nachlassbewusstsein: Literatur, Archiv, Philologie, 1750–2000*, edited by Kai Sina and Carlos Spoerhase, 115–31. Göttingen: Wallstein, 2017.
Wetters, Kirk. "The Law of the Series and the Crux of Causation: Paul Kammerer's Anomalies." *MLN* 134, no. 3 (April 2019): 643–60.
Wild, Christopher. "*Apertio Libri*: Codex and Conversion." In *Literary Studies and the Pursuits of Reading*, edited by Eric Downing, Jonathan M. Hess, and Richard V. Benson, 17–39. Rochester, NY: Camden House, 2012.
Wilson, W. Daniel. "But Is It Gay? Kissing, Friendship, and 'Pre-homosexual' Discourses in Eighteenth-Century Germany." *Modern Language Review* 103, no. 3 (July 2008): 767–83.
Wilson, W. Daniel. *Goethe, Männer, Knaben: Ansichten zur "Homosexualität."* Translated by Angela Steidele. Berlin: Insel, 2012.
Wittmann, Barbara. "Am Anfang: Theorien des Kritzelns im 19. Jahrhundert." In *Von selbst: Autopoietische Verfahren in der Ästhetik des 19. Jahrhunderts*, edited by Friedrich Weltzien, 141–54. Berlin: Dietrich Reimer, 2006.
Wittmann, Reinhard. *Geschichte des deutschen Buchhandels*. München: C. H. Beck, 2011.
Woodmansee, Martha. *The Author, Art, and the Market: Rereading the History of Aesthetics*. New York: Columbia University Press, 1994.
Woodmansee, Martha. "The Genius and the Copyright: Economic and Legal Conditions of the Emergence of the 'Author.'" In "The Printed Word in the Eighteenth Century," edited by Raymond Birn. Special issue, *Eighteenth-Century Studies* 17, no. 4 (Summer 1984): 425–48.
Wysling, Hans. *Gottfried Keller, 1819–1890*. Zürich: Artemis, 1990.

Yates, JoAnne, and Craig N. Murphy. *Engineering Rules: Global Standard Setting Since 1880*. Baltimore: Johns Hopkins University Press, 2019.
Zachariä, Heinrich Albert. *Die Gebrechen und die Reform des deutschen Strafverfahrens*. Göttingen: Dieterische Buchhandlung, 1846.
Zapp, Arthur. "Schriftstellerleiden." *Die Zukunft*, November 12, 1898, 299–305.
Zons, Raimar Stefan. "Über den Ursprung des literarischen Werks aus dem Geist der Autorschaft." In *Kolloquium Kunst und Philosophie*, vol. 3, edited by Willi Oelmüller, 104–27. Paderborn: Ferdinand Schöningh, 1983.
Zuberbühler, Rolf. "'Excelsior!' Idealismus und Materialismus in Kellers und Fontanes politischen Altersromanen *Martin Salander* und *Der Stechlin*." In *Gottfried Keller und Theodor Fontane: Vom Realismus zur Moderne*, edited by Ursula Amrein and Regina Dieterle, 87–111. Berlin: Walter de Gruyter, 2008.
Zumbusch, Cornelia. "Grauer Grund: Keller, Goethe und der Glanz der Prosa." In *Die Farben der Prosa*, edited by Eva Eßlinger, Heide Volkening, and Cornelia Zumbusch, 79–98. Freiburg im Breisgau: Rombach, 2016.

Index

Note: Page numbers in italic indicate figures or tables.

abstraction, 5, 154n2, 216, 219, 221
administrative work/writing: and authorship, 34, 154, 160–63, 182–93; circulation as feature of, 184–86; critique of, 185; doodles' role in, 34, 214–26; gender and, 190–91, 201; Keller and, 34, 153–63, 154n2, 158n7, 159n11, 161n17, 201–26, 209, 211n14; Keller's fictional representations of, 34, 158–59, 162–65, 168–69, 171, 182–93, 226; literature compared to, 8, 34, 154–57, 159–63, 163n21, 169, 192–93, 206, 226; rhetorical style of, 185n70; Weber's theory of bureaucracy and, 183, 186. *See also* archiving; copying; documents; mixing; writing

Ajouri, Philip, 89n88, 92
allegory: and collected-works editions, 109–10; and format, 10–11, 26; concept of, 8–9; "Der Landvogt von Greifensee" and, 35, 234, 240, 261, 272–73, 278–88; media history and, 10–11; real allegory, 8–9, 109–10, 272; realism and, 8–10, 8n, 13, 109–10, 272–73; and serialization, 35, 234, 240, 261, 278; thematization of print culture by means of, 8
Amor, 139
Amrein, Ursula, 129n34, 233n8, 236n; *Gottfried Keller-Handbuch* (edited volume), 20n37
Anderson, Benedict, 15n27, 119

archiving: book format as means of, 23–24; collected-works editions as means of, 112; copying as component of, 170–71; and document formats, 163; gender and, 186–87; "Der Landvogt von Greifensee" and, 271, 278–79; literature and, 11, 181–82; in "Die mißbrauchten Liebesbriefe," 185–89; novella cycles as means of, 256; periodicals/serialization and, 239, 241n23, 244, 244n30, 256–57; protocols and, 203, 208n13; realism and, 13n20; *Das Sinngedicht* and, 239; *Züricher Novellen* and, 239. *See also* documents
art and art history, 2–5, 51–52
artist's monographs, 85n80
Atropos, 101–3, 110, 111
Auerbach, Berthold, 28, 179; *Berthold Auerbach's deutscher Volks-Kalender*, 232, 265
Augart, Julia, 189
Augenblick (moment), 74–79
Augustine (saint), 99
Austen, Jane, *Northanger Abbey*, 92
authorship/literary authority: administrative work/writing and, 34, 160–63, 182–93; autonomy of, 30, 234, 238, 238n17; biographical approach to, 20, 163; collected-works editions as hallmark of, 18, 87–89, 91–92, 101, 111–16, 119–21, 131–32, 148–49, 280; commercialization of literature's effect on, 234, 238; copying and, 24, 28, 171, 175, 178, 184; death (biological) of the author and, 33–34, 114–20, 135, 136n, 144–48; death (metaphorical/theoretical) of the author and, 114–15; of documents, 186, 204; doodles and, 215–16, 215n17, 220, 220n23, 224–25; format as influence on, 24; "Gedanken eines Lebendig-Begrabenen" and, 135–36, 144–48; gender and, 29–34, 190; *Der grüne Heinrich* and, 57, 63, 116;

hermaphroditic, 31, 32, 191; and the identity of the literary work, 65–66; industrialization of literature as influence on, 7, 22, 30, 279–88; Keller and, 21, 27–28, 35, 42–43, 47, 50, 59, 63n41, 65n47, 66–68, 116, 119–21, 175n48, 206, 211, 234; Keller's private bureaucratic notebooks and, 215–16; "Der Landvogt von Greifensee" and, 281–88; media culture's effect on, 29–30, 178–80; mixing and, 175; Platonic/ideal conception of, 47; professionalization of, 29–30; property as consideration in, 65–66, 65n44; protocols and, 34, 203–6, 203n5, 205n, 210–12; published texts deemed to bear, 28–29; publishers and, 66; and reproductive capacities, 31–32, 35; reproductive printing technologies and, 178–80, 211; and revisions, 28; Romantic conception of, 30, 66, 205, 238, 282; serialization's effect on, 63, 238, 238n17, 240n21, 245–46, 262–64, 279–88; and the writing process, 42–43; *Züricher Novellen* and, 234. *See also* creativity; literary legacy; originality; writing
autonomy: of authorship, 30, 234, 238, 238n17; of literature, 16, 31, 279–80
Avenarius, Ferdinand, 133

The Bachelor (television series), 246
Baechtold, Jakob, 20, 126–28, 131, 156, 161, 164n23, 289n, 290
Balzac, Honoré de, 215
Barthes, Roland, 11n15, 114–15
Baßler, Moritz, 272, 272n17
Baumgartner, Alexander, 94n
Becker, Peter, 203n5
Begemann, Christian, 12–13
Benjamin, Walter, 27, 30, 30n52, 113–14, 292
Bergengruen, Maximilian, 144n68
Berger, Karol, 237

Berman, Russell, 45
Berndt, Frauke, 124n21
Bildung (education): Goethe's, 91; *Der grüne Heinrich* and, 19, 33, 40–41, 41n8, 83, 93, 247; male projects for women's, 254–56; periodicals' goal of providing cultural/national, 240–44, 241n22, 241n23; role of images in, 255n61. *See also* bildungsroman
bildungsroman, 19, 33, 40–41, 40n3, 41n7, 41n8, 80, 104, 255, 255n61
Blanckenburg, Friedrich von, 50
Boccaccio, Giovanni, *Decameron*, 35, 234–36, 246
body: aestheticization/spiritualization/eroticization of, in "Gedanken eines Lebendig-Begrabenen," 122–25, 137–38; of the author, 86; of the reader, 86; realistic depictions of prematurely buried, 122–23, 137–38
bookbinding, 23
book formats: archival function of, 23–24; Goethe and, 85–86, 86n82; identity as an issue for, 54–57, 55n; Keller's works shaped by, 22–29; literary works shaped by, 21–22, 47, 52–53; in nineteenth-century media culture, 17–18; paradox of, 54; periodicals in relation to, 17, 230, 230n2, 244–45, 278; variety of, 51
bookshelves, 2–4, 7n8
Bosse, Heinrich, 65, 65n46
Breithaupt, Fritz, 118
Brockhaus, Heinrich, 67n
Brooks, Peter, 250, 251
Der Bund (newspaper), 232
Burckhardt, Jacob, 1, 6, 295
bureaucratic work/writing. *See* administrative work/writing
Byrd, Vance, 238n17

Cahn, Michael, 54n29, 88
Campe, Rüdiger, 40, 50–51
canon. *See* literary canon
Cerda, Juan de la, 194–95
Christmas book market, 17, 265–66

circulation: as bureaucratic function, 184–86; collected-works editions and, 88; formats' influence on, 4; mixing as response to media in, 174–76; periodicals and, 87, 119; of poetry in the nineteenth century, 143; of protocols, 210. *See also* periodicals and serialization; publishing
classical ideals of literature and art: Keller's concern with, 7, 14, 27, 44; serialization's disruption of, 238, 238n16. *See also* closure; harmony of parts and whole; unity
closure: as ideal of classical literature and art, 7, 14, 238; "Der Landvogt von Greifensee" and, 261, 269, 275, 277–79; novella cycles and, 35, 232–33, 233n7, 235–36, 260, 263, 279; and serialization, 35, 238, 238n16; *Das Sinngedicht* and, 232–33. *See also* classical ideals of literature and art
Clotho, 101, 103, 110, 111
collected-works editions: allegorization of, 109–10; archival function of, 112; authorship/literary authority associated with, 18, 87–89, 91–92, 101, 111–16, 119–21, 131–32, 148–49, 280; circulation of, 88; first German-language, 85; gender and, 87; Goethe and, 81, 84–93, 86n82, 89n88, 100–101, 108–11, 113, 116, 148, 162, 301; *Der grüne Heinrich* and, 47, 80, 84; Jonson and, 115; Keller and, 112, 120, 131–33, 148–49, 153, 229, 292; as means to literary legacy, 86–89, 114, 148–49; in nineteenth-century media culture, 8; organization and compilation of, 88, 89, 131–32, 132n45; portraits of authors in, 89, 133; Schiller and, 118; standardization employed by, 88–89; unity of artist's life and work constituted by, 85, 85n80, 88–89, 91–92, 101, 109–11, 113, 132–33; varieties of, 87

comedy, in Keller's writing, 309–11, 310n48
commercialization of literature: authorship affected by, 234, 238; formats affected by, 21, 47; fragmentation resulting from, 27, 46; narrative voice affected by, 45–46. *See also* publishing
Cooke, Ebenezer, 225
copying: and authorship/literary authority, 24, 28, 171, 175, 178, 184; as component of archiving, 170–71; and document formats, 163; as feature of administrative work/writing, 169; in "Hadlaub," 23–24, 171; Keller and, 61n37, 178–81, 178n56, 181n61; literature in relation to, 169–74, 177, 181–82; in "Die mißbrauchten Liebesbriefe," 163, 168–74, 177, 182, 184–86; the original in relation to, 163, 170–71, 171n39, 173, 173n43, 211, 283–85; of protocols, 210–11; protocols and, 205. *See also* reproductive printing technologies
copyright, 65, 67–68
Corngold, Stanley, 160, 162
Cotta editions. *See* J. G. Cotta'sche Buchhandlung
Courbet, Gustave, 9
creativity: industrialization of literature as influence on, 18; media culture's effect on, 16–17; reproductive technologies in relation to, 8; routine work compared to, 8, 34, 154; standardization as threat to, 7. *See also* authorship/literary authority; originality
Curtius, Ernst Robert, 52, 52n25, 171n39

Daheim (periodical), 240
Dawson, Gowan, 244
death: of authors, in relation to their legacy, 33–34, 114–20, 136n, 144–48; in *Der grüne Heinrich*, 72, 76, 78–79. *See also* Keller, Gottfried: death of; premature burial

Delafield, Catherine, 238n16
Deutsche Anti-Scheintod-Liga, 127
Deutsche Reichs-Zeitung (newspaper), 164–65, 178–80, 211, 231
Deutscher Novellenschatz, 231
Deutsche Rundschau (periodical), 21, 35, 232–34, 238n14, 239–46, 241n22, 243n29, 246n37, 248, 250, 257, 265–68, 278, 283
Deutsches Seminar, Universität Zürich, 289
Dickson, Polly, 215
Dilthey, Wilhelm, 92
documents: authorship/literary authority of, 186, 204; bureaucratic essence of, 185–86; evidentiary value of, 187–88; formats of, 163, 185–86; in "Die mißbrauchten Liebesbriefe," 185–89; in nineteenth-century media culture, 8; Weber's theory of bureaucracy and, 183, 186. *See also* administrative work/writing; archiving; protocols
doodles, 34, 214–26, *217*, *218*, 219n19
Dößekel, Eduard, 128–29
Downing, Eric, 8–10, 10n, 13, 19, 76n, 93, 98n105, 127n26, 173, 173n43, 280

education. *See Bildung*
Endymion, 103, *104*, 139
epigonality, 27, 35, 121, 161–62, 294–96, 301, 309
Ermatinger, Emil, 202n3, 289–94, 289n, 300, 301, 312
erotics: in *Der grüne Heinrich*, 93–98, 111, 247, 252–53, 255; in "Der Landvogt von Greifensee," 261–63, 271, 283n32; premature burial and, 123–25; reading and, 93–98, 111; serial, 35, 233–34, 246–62; in *Das Sinngedicht*, 246–60, 249n42; in *Züricher Novellen*, 246–47
Escher, Alfred, 156
Exner, Adolf, 158n7, 181, 181n61

Fates (Moirai), 101–3, 101n111, *102*, *104*
Fichte, Johann Gottlieb, 66
Flaubert, Gustave, 300; *Madame Bovary*, 92
Follen, August Adolf Ludwig, 129n34, 130n35
Fontane, Theodor, 6, 12, 16n29, 17, 18, 153, 174, 263–65
form: aesthetic/literary, 7, 14, 35, 40–47; cyclical/closed vs. serial/open, 232–33, 236, 238n16, 259–61, 269–79; format in relation to, 8, 21–22, 25–26, 50–52; of life, shaped by collected-works editions, 80, 85, 85n80, 88–89, 91–92, 101, 109–11, 113, 132–33; of the doodle, 215n17, 219n19, 220–21, 223n, 225; of life, shaped by novels, 40–42, 45–47, 50–53, 75–76; of life, unsuccessful attempts at shaping, 100–101, 107–8, 120; of the novel, 50–53; small, 35, 296–303, 307–12; Z form, 52. *See also* formlessness
format: allegorization of, 10–11, 26; authorship/literary authority shaped by, 24; circulation influenced by, 4; commercialization of literature as influence on, 21, 47; defined, and importance of, 1–6; as description of persons, 293n10; of documents, 163, 185–86; earliest uses of the word, 3, 3n3; genre in relation to, 19–20; *Der grüne Heinrich* and, 47, 50, 52–64, 79–80, 105–7; Keller and, 7–8, 19–29, 298; of Keller's private bureaucratic notebooks, 212, 214; literary works shaped by, 26, 50–53; materials' exceeding of, 5–6; in nineteenth-century media culture, 7–8, 10, 21–29; of protocols, 203; publishing concerns linked to, 60; serialization's effect on, 46, 231, 231n4, 236; small, 35, 296–303, 307–12; universal attempts at, 7n8; users' experience influenced by, 2, 5–6; of visual art works, 2–5, 51–52. *See also* book formats; periodicals
formlessness, 40–47, 52, 56, 66, 69, 74, 88, 105, 111, 219, 248
Foucault, Michel, 54–55, 55n, 114–15, 163
fragmentation: *Der grüne Heinrich* and, 46–47, 53, 56–59, 57n31, 61, 62, 64, 67, 67n; resulting from commercial publishing in nineteenth century, 27, 46–47; as threat to classical ideals of literature, 27
Frank, Gustav, 241n23, 244n30
Fränkel, Jonas, 292
Franzel, Sean, 238n16
Frederick, Samuel, 13n20
Frey, Adolf, 290, 293n13
Fried, Michael, 8–9, 8n, 50, 51–52
Frisch, Max, 157n6
Frisch-Exner, Marie von, 58

Gailus, Andreas, 41n7, 235
Gamper, Michael, 291
Ganymede, 97
gardening, 197–200
Die Gartenlaube (periodical), 15n27, 196–200, *198*, 240, 242, 244, 262
"Gedanken eines Lebendig-Begrabenen" (Keller), 121–48; aestheticization/spiritualization/eroticization of the body in, 122–25, 137–38; authorship as theme in, 135–36, 144–48; genesis of, 127–28, 128n30; poetry as subject in, 121–22, 133–34, 138–48; premature burial as subject in, 121–23, 126–48, 126n26; publication of, 126, 127, 128n30, 130–33, 136–37; reception of, 126–30, 128n31, 128n32, 129n34, 133–34, 134n48, 148
Die Gegenwart (periodical), 299
gender: administrative work/writing and, 190–91, 201; and archival work, 186–87; authorship and, 29–34, 190; binary conceptions of, 30–31, 196; feminization of literature, 32, 84, 93–94, 190, 234,

gender (*continued*)
  257, 263; German realism and, 32, 234, 257; in *Der grüne Heinrich*, 93–98, 105–7, 257, 302; hermaphrodism and, 31, 31n52; Keller and, 29n49, 30–34, 292, 292n9; in "Der Landvogt von Greifensee," 262–63; and letter writing, 189; and literacy, 193–96, 195n98; and literature, 16, 190, 257; and male desire/gaze, 248–61, 271–72, 274–78, 276; "Die mißbrauchten Liebesbriefe" and, 182n63, 257; periodicals/serialization and, 234, 257, 263; reading habits and, 84; in *Das Sinngedicht*, 257–60. *See also* women
genre, format in relation to, 19–20
Gessler, Luzius, 134, 134n48
Geulen, Eva, 30n52
Gitelman, Lisa, 163, 185, 188, 204
Giuriato, David, 18
Goethe, Johann Wolfgang: aesthetics of, 75n64, 76, 79; and collected-works editions, 81, 84–93, 86n82, 89n88, 100–101, 108–11, 113, 116, 148, 162; *Der grüne Heinrich* and, 79–101, 111, 113, 133, 301–2; influence of, on younger readers, 92–93, 93n98, 95–100; Keller compared to, 290–94, 300–302, 312; Keller influenced by, 81n, 90–91; life of, 80, 85, 90–92, 108–13, 115, 121; occupation as state bureaucrat, 162; and premature death, 124n21; status of, in German literature, 86n82, 121
Goethe, Johann Wolfgang, works: *Dichtung und Wahrheit*, 90–92, 109; *Unterhaltungen deutscher Ausgewanderten*, 235, 262; *Vollständige Ausgabe letzter Hand*, 81–82, 86, 89–92, 89n88, 111, 114, 153; *Wilhelm Meisters Wanderjahre*, 182n64
Göschen Verlag, 85

Gottfried Kellers Moderne, 19
Graevenitz, Gerhart von, 16, 240–41, 244
Greifensee, Landvogt von, 283n32
Gretz, Daniela, 17, 26, 238n14, 239
Groddeck, Wolfram, 70n55
Grün, Anastasius, 129n34
Der grüne Heinrich (Keller), 39–112; and authorship, 57, 63, 116; autobiographical component of, 20, 39–40, 39n; barrenness as theme in, 76, 79, 97, 99, 110, 111; as bildungsroman, 19, 33, 40–41; bureaucrats represented in, 158–59, 162, 171; and collected-works editions, 47, 80, 84; erotics of, 93–98, 111, 247, 252–53, 255; format of published volumes of, 298–99; format thematized in, 47, 50, 52–64, 79–80, 105–7; formlessness of, 40–46, 52, 56, 66, 69, 74, 88, 105, 111, 219, 248; and fragmentation, 46–47, 53, 56–59, 57n31, 62, 64, 67, 67n; gender in, 93–98, 105–7, 257, 302; geographical location of, 307–8; and giving form to life, 40–42, 45–47, 53, 75–76, 80, 100–112; and Goethe, 79–101, 111, 113, 133, 301–2; identity of, 57–59, 57n31, 63, 67–70, 75–76; Keller's opinion of, 40–47, 57, 67, 69, 74, 105, 149, 247–48; mediocrity/smallness in, 309, 311; and originality, 286–88; poetry in relation to, 134; preface to, 41–46, 68; premature burial/death as leitmotif in, 122–25, 144n67; protagonist's identity in, 33, 41, 45–46, 46n17, 64, 68–73, 72n, 75–76, 93–94, 99–108, 110–11, 120, 220–21, 247; reading in, 80–85, 92–101, 111, 113; realism as a theme in, 13, 19, 46n16, 118; reception of, 33, 39–41, 44–46, 53, 57–59, 63, 297; revisions of, 28, 39–40, 56–59, 62, 72, 74n; and Schiller, 77, 84, 116–19, 143–44;

scribbling/doodling in, 216, 219–22;
thread as a leitmotif in, 100–111,
102n, 120; title pages of, *48–49*;
unity as issue for, 43–45, 60, 70, 80,
112; writing and publishing process
of, 25, 42–43, 45–46, 56–57,
57n31, 59–64, 60n35, 60n36, 61n39, 70,
74–75, 112, 149, 165n26, 229, 240
Guercio, Gabriele, 85n80
Guillory, John, 185n70
Günter, Manuela, 16, 16n29, 32,
182n63, 189n84

Haag, Saskia, 199n107
handwriting, 63, 65, 69–70, 164,
178n56, 214
harmony of parts and whole, 7, 14,
31–32, 31n55, 99. *See also* classical
ideals of literature and art; unity
Hart, Gail, 285
Hauff, Wilhelm, 18
Helmstetter, Rudolf, 16, 32
hermaphrodism, 31, 31n52, 32, 191,
287
Hertz, Wilhelm, 21, 131
Hertz Verlag, 33, 56, 248
Herwegh, Georg, 129n34
Hesekiel, George, 153
Hess, David, 283n32
Hettner, Hermann, 44–45, 74, 77,
166n29, 282n31
Heyse, Paul, 132, 232–33, 267, 299,
306–7
high art-low art binary, 8, 12, 16
Hobus, Jens, 309
Hoffmann, E. T. A., 215; *Die Serapi-
onsbrüder*, 262
Honold, Alexander, 183n65
humor, 309–11, 310n48

identity: book formats and, 54–57,
55n; collected-works editions and
the author's, 87–89, 91–92, 101,
111–12, 131–32; of *Der grüne
Heinrich*, 57–59, 57n31, 63, 67–70,
75–76; of literary works, 54–57,
54n29, 55n, 61, 65–66, 68–70; of
protagonist of *Der grüne Heinrich*,
33, 41, 45–46, 46n17, 64, 68–73,
72n, 75–76
industrialization of literature:
authorship/literary authority affected
by, 7, 22, 30, 279–88; creativity
affected by, 18; ideals of literature
affected by, 18; literary works
affected by, 22. *See also* publishing;
reproductive printing technologies
Ingarden, Roman, 54n29
irony, 309–11
Iurascu, Ilinca, 182n64

Jäger, Maren, 297n22
Jean Paul, 63n41, 83, 238n16;
Siebenkäs, 144n68
J. G. Cotta'sche Buchhandlung, 81, 86,
88, 116
Jonson, Ben, 115
Joyce, James, 141, 141n61

Kafka, Ben, 167n30
Kafka, Franz, 154, 160, 162
Kaiser, Gerhard, 93, 154n2, 157,
157n6, 161–62, 268, 292n9, 309;
*Gottfried Keller: Das gedichtete
Leben*, 20
Keller, Gottfried: allegories of realism,
13; and authorship, 21, 27–28, 35,
42–43, 47, 50, 59, 63n41, 65n47,
66–68, 116, 119–21, 175n48, 206;
comic style of, 309–11, 310n48;
death of, 290–92, 290n3; finances
of, 25, 59–60, 135, 159; format's
significance in the work of, 7–8,
19–29; and gender, 29n49, 30–34,
292, 292n9; Goethe's influence on,
81n, 90–91; handwriting of, 63, 65,
69–70, 164, 178n56, 214; "lateness"
of, 27, 35, 59–61, 121, 265, 267;
literary legacy of, 33, 85, 90, 112,
132n45, 133, 133n46; media culture
at the time of, 6–7, 19, 21–33, 289,
303, 311; *Nachlass* of, 20, 57–58,
81n, 161, 212; occupation as state
bureaucrat, 34, 153–63, 154n2,

Keller (*continued*)
158n7, 159n11, 201–26, 202n3, 209, 211n, 240; and originality, 282, 282n31, 286; as painter, 39, 214, 216, 219, 223; physical appearance of, 290–94, 293n12; political affinities of, 129n34, 156, 156n4, 157n6, 158n7, 230–31; realism in the works of, 9, 12, 13, 19, 126n26, 226, 278, 310; reception of, 128–30, 133–34, 156, 297; residence of, 208; scholarship on, 18–21; signatures of, 160–61; and Switzerland/Swiss national culture, 20, 119, 156–57, 156n5, 157n6, 162, 163, 230–31, 243, 307, 309

Keller, Gottfried, works: administrative writings, 160–63, 161n17, 202; "Aus dem Leben," 52n25; "Aus ihrem Leben: Dichtung und Wahrheit," 133; "Ballade vom dürren König," 136; *Berliner Schreibunterlage*, 161, 216; *Bettagsmandate* (official documents), 161n17, 202, 204–5; biographical approach to, 20, 20n37, 163; "Dietegen," 122, 125–26; "Eugenia," 9, 10n, 13; "Gedanken eines Lebendig-Begrabenen" (*see* "Gedanken eines Lebendig-Begrabenen" (Keller)); *Gedichte*, 126, 129n34, 130; *Gesammelte Gedichte*, 128n30, 131–35, 137–39, 147, 148; *Gesammelte Werke*, 131–34, 132n45, 136, 153, 230 (*see also* collected-works editions: Keller and); *Gesamtausgabe*, 266; *Der grüne Heinrich* (see *Der grüne Heinrich* (Keller)); "Hadlaub," 23–24, 26, 171, 265, 287–88; "Lebendig begraben," 141n61; *Die Leute von Seldwyla*, 24, 25, 29, 34, 60, 61, 62, 122, 134, 154–55, *155*, 162, 164–66, 165n26, 177–81, 230, 231, 233n7, 240, 247, 251, 299; *Martin Salander*, 25–26, 25n, 229, 267, 287n, 290, 293, 297, 299, 305–9; "Die mißbrauchten Liebesbriefe" (*see* "Die mißbrauchten Liebesbriefe" (Keller)"); *Neuere Gedichte*, 121, 136, 252; "Poetentod," 133, 146–47; private bureaucratic notebooks of, 210, 212–26, *217*, *218*, 222, 223; "Reformation," 147–48; "Romeo und Julia auf dem Dorfe," 28–29, 122, 231, 247; "Der Schmied seines Glückes," 24, 181, 181n61; *Sieben Legenden*, 9–10, 24, 31, 173, 173n43, 230, 247, 280; "Siebenundzwanzig Liebeslieder," 130, 133; *Das Sinngedicht* (see *Das Sinngedicht* (Keller)); "Sonnetten," 133; *Studienbücher*, 133n46, 216; "Tannen-Gedichte," 134, 136; "Das verlorene Lachen," 162, 303–5; "Vermischte Gedichte," 133, 146; "Von Weibern," 252; "Winternacht," 121, 124; *Züricher Novellen* (see *Züricher Novellen* (Keller)). *See also* collected-works editions: Keller and; publishing

Keller, Regula, 58
Kempner, Friederike, 127
Kohns, Oliver, 170–71, 171n39
Koschorke, Albrecht, 12
Krajewski, Markus, 7
Kriesi, Hans Max, 160–61
Kuh, Emil, 63–64, 154, 310n48
Kühne, Ferdinand Gustav, 44
Kurz, Heinrich, 130

Lachesis, 101, 103
Landolt, Salomon, 283n32
"Der Landvogt von Greifensee" (Keller): as allegory of serialization, 35, 234, 240, 261, 272–73; archiving in, 271, 278–79; authorship/literary authority as a theme in, 281–88; closure in, 261, 269, 275, 277–79; erotics of, 261–63, 271, 283n32; frame narrative of, 267–68; gender in, 262–63; and literary reproduction, 190; male desire/gaze in, 261, 271–72, 274–77, 276; motivating

plot of, 236; originality and industrialized reproduction in, 279–88; pentagram as a theme in, 275–78; publishing history of, 265, 278; reception of, 263–65; recursion as principle of, 260, 268–71; serial format/structure of, 34, 234, 261, 267–88
Leemann, Rudolf, 134–35
legacy. *See* literary legacy
Lehmann, Heinrich Ludwig, 194
lending libraries, 17, 62, 298
Leonardo da Vinci, *Vitruvian Man*, 276
Lesesucht (reading addiction), 82–84
Lessing, Gotthold Ephraim, 52, 76, 79
Lewald, Fanny, 31, 190–91
libraries. *See* lending libraries
Lindau, Paul, 153
Lipkin, Michael, 73n59
literacy, and gender, 193–96, 195n98. *See also* reading
literary authority. *See* authorship/literary authority
literary canon, 16, 20, 29, 83n76, 85–86, 120, 156, 205, 231n4, 243, 244, 290, 293–94, 300
literary legacy: author's control over, 58; author's life as component of, 34, 113–14; author's reproductive capacities and, 35; collected-works editions and, 86–89, 114, 149; death and, 33–34, 114–20, 136n, 144–48; formation of, 33; Keller's, 85, 90, 112, 132n45, 133, 133n46, 146, 148, 161–63, 289–312; writing as means to, 143–48. *See also* authorship/literary authority
literature: administrative work/writing compared to, 8, 34, 154–57, 159–63, 163n21, 192–93, 206, 226; archiving and, 11, 181–82; autonomy of, 16, 31, 279–80; book format as shaper of, 21–22, 47, 52–53; copying in relation to, 169–74, 177, 181–82; feminization of, 32, 84, 93–94, 190, 234, 257, 263; format as shaper of, 26, 50–53; gendering of, 16, 190, 257; ideals of, 7–8, 18; identity of works of, 54–57, 54n29, 55n, 61, 65–66, 68–70; media culture's effect on, 16–17, 21–22; mixing in relation to, 173–77; protocols compared to, 204–5; satire of, in "Die mißbrauchten Liebesbriefe," 162, 166–77, 166n29, 191; self-reflexivity of, 173–75, 177; smallness in, 296–97; status and character of works of, 7, 8, 16–17. *See also* classical ideals of literature and art; commercialization of literature; high art-low art binary; industrialization of literature; literary canon; literary legacy; writing
Ludwig, Otto, 12
Lukács, Georg, 230–31, 300

MacLeod, Catriona, 31, 252, 257n63, 270
magazines. *See* periodicals
Magnin, Maria, 279–80
Malakaj, Ervin, 238n17
male desire/gaze, 248–61, 271–72, 274–78, 276
Mangold, Burkhard, "Gottfried Keller," 209–10, *209*
Mann, Thomas, 293n10
Mark, Alexander von der, 101
Martus, Steffen, 21–22, 82n75, 85–86, 86n82, 91n91, 92n94, 131
Matala de Mazza, Ethel, 297n22
materiality: and the artifice of realism, 13; and the exceeding of format, 5–6
Mayer, Mathias, 136n
McGillen, Petra, 17, 18, 21, 63, 63n41, 174, 230n2
media culture: allegories of, 10; authorship affected by, 29–30; effect of, on status and character of literature, 16–17, 21–22; formats in nineteenth-century, 7–8, 10, 21–29; in Keller's time, 6–8, 19, 21–33, 289, 303, 311; standardization in, 29, 303. *See also* periodicals and serialization

media history: allegorical interpretation as methodology in, 10–11; scholarship in, 14–18
Melville, Herman, *Moby-Dick*, 144
Menninghaus, Winfried, 95
Menzel, Adolph von, 13; *Puhlmanns Bücherregal*, 2–5, 3, 10, 11, 26
Messerli, Alfred, 194, 195n98
Meyer, Conrad Ferdinand, 158n7, 243, 300, 300n
Meyer, Ferdinand, 158n7
Meyertholen, Andrea, 225n33
Midas, 136n
"Die mißbrauchten Liebesbriefe" (Keller), 162–200; archiving as a theme in, 185–89; bureaucrats and administrative writing represented in, 34, 162–65, 168–69, 171, 182–93, 226; copying as a theme in, 163, 168–74, 177, 182, 184–86; cut-and-pasted preprint of, *180*; dating of, 164–65, 164n23; documents as a theme in, 185–89; gender in, 182n63, 257; as literary satire, 162, 166–77, 166n29, 191; and literature, 34; mixing as a theme in, 173–76; reception of, 165, 189; writing and publication of, 164–66, 177–81, 178n56, 231, 245
mixing (sampling), as means of producing literature, 168, 170, 173–77
modernism, 14, 219, 219n21
Moirai. *See* Fates
moment. See *Augenblick*
Moretti, Franco, 40n3
Morgenblatt für gebildete Stände (newspaper), 91
Morgenthaler, Walter, 57n31, 61n39, 120, 131–32, 132n45, 133n46, 164–65
Mozart, Wolfgang Amadeus, 237
Müller, Dominik, 47n, 57n31, 157n6
Müller Nielaba, Daniel, 68, 69n52, 73
Muschg, Adolf, 20, 156–57, 156n5, 292

Muschg, Walter, 20, 292

Nachlass (literary estate): fictional treatments of, 72, 120, 146–47; Goethe's, 85n81; Keller's, 20, 57–58, 81n, 161, 212
Napoleon, 291
nationalism, 15, 15n27, 242–43
naturalism, 11
Naumann, Barbara, 216, 222
Neue Zürcher Zeitung (newspaper), 26
Neumann, Gerhard, 233n8, 249n42, 254, 256
Niehaus, Michael, 19, 204, 293n10, 298n24
Nietzsche, Friedrich, 35, 294–96
Noland, Kenneth, 51
novel, genre and theories of, 40–41, 45, 50–53
novella cycles: archival function of, 256; and closure, 232–33, 233n7, 235–36, 260, 263, 279; Keller's comments on genre of, 233n6; in Keller's oeuvre, 230, 236; "Der Landvogt von Greifensee" as allegorization/modeling of, 261–62, 277–78; politics linked to, 230–31; and serialization, 35, 230–36, 240, 247, 256, 260; *Das Sinngedicht*, 35, 232–36; *Züricher Novellen*, 35, 233–36, 265

organic nature of literary works. *See* harmony of parts and whole
originality: authors' claims of, 238; copying and, 163, 170–71, 171n39, 173, 173n43, 211, 283–85; *Der grüne Heinrich* and, 286–88; Keller and, 282, 282n31, 286; property as consideration in, 65n44; reproductive printing technologies and, 163, 279–88. *See also* authorship/literary authority; creativity
Osterkamp, Ernst, 77–78, 224n30, 255, 255n61
Ostwald, Wilhelm, 7n8
Ovid, *Metamorphoses*, 282

panoramas, 303–8
paper: bureaucratic use of, 210–11; literature in relation to the materiality of, 182n64; significance of, in nineteenth-century media culture, 14–15; technologies related to, 15; thematization of, in print culture, 18; world format for, 7n8
Parr, Rolf, 205n
Paul (saint), 137
pederasty, 97, 302
periodicals and serialization: allegorization of, 35, 234, 240, 261, 278; archival function of, 239, 241n23, 244n30, 256–57; authorship and, 63, 238, 238n17, 240n21, 245–46, 262–64, 279–88; books in relation to, 17, 230, 230n2, 244–45, 278; circulation of, 87, 119; classical ideals of literature and art disrupted by, 238, 238n16; and closure, 35, 238, 238n16; erotics linked to, 35, 233–34, 246–62; format determined by, 46, 231, 231n4, 236; gender and, 234, 257, 263; Keller and, 17, 35, 229–30, 240–41; "Der Landvogt von Greifensee" as allegory of, 35, 234, 261, 267–88; mixing as a process linked to, 174–76; in nineteenth-century media culture, 8, 15–16; novella cycles and, 35, 230–36, 240, 247, 256, 260; and popular knowledge, 15, 237, 237n14, 239–44, 241n22, 241n23, 257; reading practices shaped by, 237–38, 264; scholarship on, 237, 240, 240n21, 260, 264; self-reflexivity characteristic of, 260; *Das Sinngedicht* and, 35, 229, 232–34, 233n8, 236–39, 245–60; temporality of, 237; writing practices shaped by, 238; *Züricher Novellen* and, 25, 35, 229, 232–33, 236–39, 245. *See also* circulation; preprints
Petersen, Wilhelm, 263
Pethes, Nicolas, 239

Petrarch, 99
Pfotenhauer, Helmut, 165n25, 175n48
Piper, Andrew, 53, 54, 86, 221
Podewski, Madleen, 241n23, 244n30
Poe, Edgar Allan, 121–23; "The Cask of Amontillado," 122; "The Fall of the House of Usher," 123
poetry: circulation of, in print media, 143; "Gedanken eines Lebendig-Begrabenen" as rumination on, 121–22, 133–34, 138–48; *Der grüne Heinrich* and, 134; Keller and, 126–37, 127n26, 146
premature burial, as theme in Keller's works, 33–34, 120–49, 126n26, 252
preprints: of Keller's works, 21, 28, 164–65, 172, 178–80, *180*, 231, 245–46, 280; reissue of, in book formats, 28, 230; status of published works in relation to, 172, 280. *See also* periodicals and serialization
Price, Leah, 6n6, 86, 114, 163, 163n21, 196
print culture. *See* book formats; media culture; periodicals and serialization; reproductive printing technologies
property, and authorship/literary authority, 65–66, 65n44
protocols (documents), 202–26; archiving and, 203, 208n13; authorship/authority of, 34, 203–6, 203n5, 205n, 210–12; circulation of, 210; and copying, 205; finalized and official, *213*; format of, 203; Keller and, 34, 162, 202–26, *213*; literature compared to, 204–5; process of producing, 205–14, 224–26; purposes of, 203–4, 208n13, 224–26; setting for production of, 206–8
publishing: archival aspects of, 181–82; and authorship rights, 66; bureaucratic aspects of, 34; contracts with authors, 25, 27, 29, 57, 59–60, 165, 267; format linked to concerns of, 60; *Der grüne Heinrich* and, 25,

publishing (*continued*)
42–43, 45–46, 56–57, 59–64, 60n35, 60n36, 61n39, 70, 74–75, 112, 229; Keller and, 18–19, 21, 24–25, 27, 29, 30, 47n, 61, 61n37, 65n47; *Die Leute von Seldwyla* and, 177–81; "Die mißbrauchten Liebesbriefe" and, 177–80, 178n56, 231; and serialization, 231. *See also* book formats; circulation; commercialization of literature; industrialization of literature; periodicals and serialization; writing

Pygmalion, 136, 136n, 252, 254–57, 285

Raabe, Wilhelm, 17, 18, 153, 205n

reading: dangers of, 82–83, 92; erotic character of, 93–98, 111; fate and death associated with, 103; gardening and, 197; in *Der grüne Heinrich*, 80–85, 92–101, 111, 113; immersive character of, 82–84, 92–93; nineteenth-century practices of, 171–72, 237–38; serialization's effect on, 237–38, 264. *See also* literacy

realism: allegory and, 8–10, 8n, 13, 109–10, 272–73; archival function of, 13n20; bourgeois life reflected and examined in, 11–12; characteristics of, 11–12; clutter vs. order in, 13n20; gender politics in German, 32, 234; German, 8–9, 31–32, 125, 126n26, 234, 250, 252, 257, 280; *Der grüne Heinrich* and, 13, 19, 46n16; Keller's, 9, 12, 13, 19, 126n26, 226, 278, 310; mimetic standard of, 12, 14, 31–32, 224–25; mixing as technique in, 174; naturalism in relation to, 11; as protomodernism, 14; representation/signification and, 10, 12–14, 173n43; Romanticism in relation to, 11, 19; scholarship on, 12–14; and the small/insignificant, 310–11, 310n49

Regierungsratssaal, Zurich city hall, 206–10, *207*

relics, 114

representation: of authors in collected-works editions, 87–88, 111; format as influence on, 2, 4, 6, 23, 26, 50, 52, 53; modernism and, 14; realism and, 10, 12–14, 173n43. *See also* allegory

reproduction: administrative work/writing and, 190–91; authorial capacities for, 31–32, 35; gendering of biological, 30–31, 196, 284; "Der Landvogt von Greifensee" and, 190; "Die mißbrauchten Liebesbriefe" and, 190–91; as realist goal and tactic, 12, 31. *See also* copying; reproductive printing technologies

reproductive printing technologies: authorial gendering and, 31; and authorship/literary authority, 178–80, 211; books and, 54; creativity in relation to, 8; and originality, 279–88; status and character of literature affected by, 18. *See also* copying; industrialization of literature; reproduction

revision: archival function of, 244; cut-and-paste method of, 28, 179–80, 180n, *180*, 245–46; of *Der grüne Heinrich*, 28, 39–40, 56–59, 62, 72, 74n; Keller's scarce practice of, 28; of "Die mißbrauchten Liebesbriefe," 179–80, 180n, *180*; print copies as basis for, 28–29, 179–80; of *Züricher Novellen*, 28, 245

Rodenberg, Julius, 21, 240–42, 245, 246n37

Romanticism, 11, 19, 30, 66, 205, 238, 282, 310

Roose, Kerstin, 144, 144n67

Rose, Mark, 65n44

Roussel, Martin, 170–71, 171n39

Ruge, Arnold, 129–30, 129n34

sampling. *See* mixing

sarcophagus with a scene related to the myth of Endymion and Selene and the three Morai, 103, *104*

Schadow, Johann Gottfried, *Grabmal des Grafen Alexander von der Mark*, 101, *102*, 103
Scheidegger, Luise, 161
Scheintod (suspended animation), 121, 122n19, 123–24, 149
Scherer, Stefan, 241n23, 244n30
Scherer, Wilhelm, 92
Schiller, Friedrich, 77, 84, 116–19, 121, 143–44, 148, 219, 312
Schlegel, Friedrich, 50–51
Schmidt, Julian, 44
Schneider, Sabine, 11, 46n16, 73, 221, 249n44, 302n36, 310n49
Schoeck, Othmar, 141n61; "Siebenundzwanzig Liebeslieder," 141
Schrader, Hans-Jürgen, 231n4, 246n37
Schulz, Wilhelm, 128, 128n32
science, *Das Sinngedicht* and, 248n42, 249–50, 249n44
scissors, 28, 47, 102–3, 108, 113, 245–46
Sebald, W. G., 222, 223n
Selbstverkleinerung (making oneself small), 294–97, 300–302, 305
Selene, 103, 103n114
self. *See* identity
sequels, 229–30
serialization. *See* periodicals and serialization
Shakespeare, William, 28–29, 115
Simon, Ralf, 120
Das Sinngedicht (Keller): archival function of, 239; "Die Berlocken," 258–61; erotics of, 246–60, 249n42; the Fates (Moirai) in, 101n111; frame narrative of, 234–36, 260; gender in, 257–60; male desire in, 248–60; and modernity as threat, 236n; as novella cycle, 230, 234–36, 262; popular success of, 248; publishing history of, 245, 247–48, 267; reception of, 232–33; scholarship on, 248n42; science as a theme in, 248n42, 249–50, 249n44; serial format/structure of, 25, 35, 229, 232–34, 233n8, 236–39, 245–60

sketching, 224
small forms/formats, 35, 296–303, 307–12
smallness: humor as means of conveying, 309–11; of Keller's fictional characters, 308–9; Keller's physical appearance and, 290–94, 293n12; of Keller's place in literary history, 35, 267n, 290–312; Keller's self-assessment of his works as, 298–300, 298n24; Keller's strategic use of, 35, 293–312, 297n22; in literature, 296–97; the monumental contrasted with, 303–9; Nietzsche's commentary on, 294–96; realism and, 310–11, 310n49
Spoerhase, Carlos, 22, 51
Staatsarchiv des Kantons Zürich, 212
Stahr, Adolf, 31, 190–91
standardization: collected-works editions and, 88–89; meaning and significance of, 7; in nineteenth-century media culture, 29, 303; of thought, 7
Stella, Frank, 51; *Moultonboro III*, 51–52
Sterne, Laurence, 215
Stifter, Adalbert, 12–13, 18, 254, 257n63, 310–11
Stockinger, Claudia, 244–45
Storm, Theodor, 72, 132, 204, 246, 266
Strowick, Elisabeth, 41n8, 252
Sturm und Drang (Storm and Stress) period, 166n29, 177, 177n53
Stüssi, Johann Heinrich, 211, 211n

Theisohn, Philipp, 235n10, 247
Thomasson, Amie L., 54n29
Thurschwell, Pamela, 163, 163n21
time, Keller's narratives and, 237
Torra-Mattenklott, Caroline, 46n17, 267n, 276n

Über Land und Meer (periodical), 244
Uhland, Ludwig, 129n34

unity: of artists' lives and works, 80, 85, 85n80, 88–89, 91–92, 109, 111, 115, 131–33; *Der grüne Heinrich* and, 43–45, 60, 70, 80, 112; as ideal of classical literature and art, 7, 14; of knowledge conveyed by periodicals, 240–44, 241n22, 241n23; of self, 70. *See also* classical ideals of literature and art; harmony of parts and whole

Varnhagen von Ense, Karl August, 128, 128n31
Vedder, Ulrike, 126n26
Verlag Gebrüder Paetel, 240
Vieweg, Eduard, 21, 30, 59, 63, 67, 107, 159n11, 164, 164n23, 165n26, 178–81, 178n56, 180n, 181n61, 247–48
Vieweg and Söhne, 56–57, 59–62, 60n35, 60n36, 65n47
Vismann, Cornelia, 203
Vogel, Juliane, 254
Vogl, Joseph, 297n22
Volmar, Alex, 7

Wagner, Richard, 295–96
Walser, Robert, 309
Weber, Bruno, 293n12
Weber, Max, 183, 186
Weibert, Ferdinand, 21, 172, 179, 180n, 265
Weibert Verlag, 56, 265
Weitzman, Erika, 13
Wellbery, David, 40n3
Wieland, Christoph, 85
Wilson, W. Daniel, 97
Winkelried, Arnold von, 305
Winter, C. F., 126
Wittmann, Barbara, 220, 220n23
women: as images, 251–60, 272; literacy of, 193–96, 195n98; male projects for the education of, 254–56; as object of male desire and gaze, 248–61, 271–72, 274–78, 276; periodicals associated with, 234, 257, 263; as writers and readers of literature, 32, 190, 234, 257, 263. *See also* gender

Woodmansee, Martha, 65
writing: archival aspects of, 181–82; doodling and, 221–24, 223n; excessive/immoderate character of, 167, 169–70; as form-giving activity, 42, 45, 74–75, 104–5; gardening and, 197–200; in "Gedanken eines Lebendig-Begrabenen," 143–45, 148; *Der grüne Heinrich* and, 222–24, 223n, 224n30; Keller's process and practices of, 27, 42, 45, 61n37, 64, 68–70, 74–75; as means to literary legacy, 143–48; purposes of, 193–200; self-reflexivity of, 173–75; serialization's effect on, 238. *See also* administrative work/ writing; authorship/literary authority; copying; documents; literature; mixing; publishing; revision

Zentralbibliothek Zürich, 212
Ziegler, Leonhard, 127
Zons, Raimar, 54
Zumbusch, Cornelia, 75n63
Zürcherische Freitagszeitung (newspaper), 156n4
Züricher Novellen (Keller), 23, 171; archival function of, 239; authorship/authority of, 180; education of citizens as theme of, 243; erotics of, 246–47; "Das Fähnlein der sieben Aufrechten," 232, 265, 266; format of, 29; frame narrative of, 232–36, 243, 265, 268, 281–84; geographical location of, 233n7, 307; "Hadlaub," 23–24, 26, 171, 265, 287–88; Keller's position as state chancellor and, 162; mediocrity/smallness in, 309; "Der Narr auf Manegg," 265; as novella cycle, 230, 232–36; originality as a theme in, 281–88; publishing history of, 265–67, 266; reception of, 297; revisions of, 28, 245; serial format/structure of, 25, 35, 229, 232–33, 236–39, 245; "Ursula," 265, 266